Strategic Knowledge Management Technology

Petter Gottschalk
Norwegian School of Management, Norway

IDEA GROUP PUBLISHING
Hershey • London • Melbourne • Singapore

Acquisitions Editor:	Mehdi Khosrow-Pour
Senior Managing Editor:	Jan Travers
Managing Editor:	Amanda Appicello
Development Editor:	Michele Rossi
Copy Editor:	Ingrid Widitz
Typesetter:	Jennifer Wetzel
Cover Design:	Lisa Tosheff
Printed at:	Yurchak Printing Inc.

Published in the United States of America by
Idea Group Publishing (an imprint of Idea Group Inc.)
701 E. Chocolate Avenue, Suite 200
Hershey PA 17033
Tel: 717-533-8845
Fax: 717-533-8661
E-mail: cust@idea-group.com
Web site: http://www.idea-group.com

and in the United Kingdom by
Idea Group Publishing (an imprint of Idea Group Inc.)
3 Henrietta Street
Covent Garden
London WC2E 8LU
Tel: 44 20 7240 0856
Fax: 44 20 7379 3313
Web site: http://www.eurospan.co.uk

Library of Congress Cataloging-in-Publication Data

Gottschalk, Petter, 1950-
Strategic knowledge management technology / Petter Gottschalk.
p. cm.
Includes bibliographical references (p.) and index.
ISBN 1-59140-336-7 (hardcover) -- ISBN 1-59140-337-5 (pbk.) -- ISBN 1-59140-338-3 (ebook)
1. Knowledge management. 2. Information technology--Management. I. Title.
HD30.2.G677 2005
658.4'038--dc22

2004003745

British Cataloguing in Publication Data
A Cataloguing in Publication record for this book is available from the British Library.

Strategic Knowledge Management Technology

Table of Contents

Foreword

In this timely book, Dr. Gottschalk very cogently tackles the subject of Knowledge Management, its relationship with technology, and how technology can be used to leverage business success. In doing so, he brings together his immense wealth of experience as an academic and researcher, as well as one-time chief information officer and chief executive officer of several organisations.

"Knowledge is power." So said the 16th century philosopher Sir Francis Bacon. This profound yet simple statement is even more appropriate today. As we gradually move into the "informated" world, the products and services of most organisations have become extremely complex with significant non-material component. The work of organisations is increasingly based on knowledge. Their processes are based on knowledge. They compete based on knowledge. In fact, their very survival is based on knowledge — on their realising how important knowledge is to them, and in making use of knowledge. It can be argued that the organisations that can harness the power of knowledge will be the eventual winners, while the rest will remain laggards, or even disappear.

And are the organisations ready for these challenges? Recent research on Knowledge Management carried out by KPMG Consulting has found that organisations are in fact failing to tackle Knowledge Management's real challenges. This is because they do not understand — and are not supporting — the full implications of Knowledge Management implementation. While they agree on the significance of the role of technology in Knowledge Management, a majority of them lack time to share knowledge, fail to use knowledge effectively, and have difficulty in capturing tacit knowledge. Obviously there is a need to properly understand Knowledge Management and develop its underlying technology strategy which Dr. Gottschalk has done so well in this book.

Realising that different organisations may be at different stages of advancement in their pursuit of Knowledge Management, Dr. Gottschalk first deals with a number of approaches to Knowledge Management. This is to help individuals and organisations get a good grounding on the subject. He then explores the resource based strategy for knowledge management based on the tenet that knowledge is a strategic business resource just as money and material are. He does this by defining business resource from the very basics so that the reader can develop a thorough understanding of knowledge as a strategic resource.

While maintaining that IS/IT (Information System/Information Technology) is only a facilitator in helping organisations manage knowledge this book describes the role of technology in Knowledge Management and how an organisation can develop its IS/IT strategy to align with its Knowledge Management strategy. In addition it describes the role of CIO and Chief Knowledge Officer — something that most organisations will find extremely handy.

A case study at the end of each chapter is an excellent inclusion to help the reader understand the subject matter discussed in the chapter, and relate it to real world scenarios.

In all, this book is a most comprehensive guide on Knowledge Management Technology. Together with Dr. Gottchalk's original work on the stages of growth of Knowledge Management Technology in organisations, it will be indispensable for initiates and practitioners alike.

Read on.

Dr. Vijay K. Khandelwal
Senior Lecturer
School of Computing and Information Technology
University of Western Sydney, Australia

Preface

Strategic Knowledge Management Technology is based on the premise that it is difficult, if not impossible, to manage a modern business or public organization without at least some understanding of the planning, use, control and benefits of information technology to support knowledge work in the organization. This book applies the knowledge-based view of the firm that has established itself as an important perspective in strategic management.

This book provides insights into links between information technology and knowledge management that students will find vital to their professional success. The book also helps managers and professionals gain competitive advantage from knowledge management systems. It provides self-help for practitioners.

This book is designed to cover information technology and knowledge management in strategic management at colleges and universities. The book would be suitable for courses in IT, business information systems, knowledge management, and management studies. It can be considered an introductory text for management undergraduates and postgraduates that have a multi-disciplinary background.

In a larger business faculty, the text may find its way onto the highly/strongly recommended lists for lower-level, higher volume undergraduate classes. The IT dimension is important for business and management students.

Furthermore, this book would be very suitable for the MSc in knowledge and organization at some universities where information and knowledge management are being studied. The book would be suitable, indeed essential, for the new MSc in knowledge management at some universities where strategy and culture are the focus, but the IT side is an important aspect of both.

In MBA programs, this book can successfully bridge business strategy, knowledge management and information systems strategy.

Generally, this book can be used at both the undergraduate and graduate levels. At the graduate level, more emphasis can be placed on empirical studies and research methodology.

Among practitioners, there are two groups that stand out. First, persons who are often both strategically and operationally responsible for IT in the organization, typically called *IT managers*. Second, the knowledge workers exemplified in this book: lawyers and managing partners in law firms.

This book attempts to be strong in concepts coverage. It has many examples drawn from a wide range of international sources. It gives an appreciation of advanced practice in Norway. Law firms should represent a welcome addition to more traditional company examples.

Reviewers of earlier manuscript versions have stressed that this is a much-needed text in a very important and growing area. It synthesizes strategy, technology and knowledge management. One anonymous reviewer wrote about the manuscript: "It reads well, and the links between knowledge management, strategy, IS and IT are well made. It provides a very useful addition to the literature, and is one of the few texts that takes a dispassionate view of the role of IT."

INTRODUCTION TO CHAPTERS

The knowledge-based view of the firm has established itself as an important perspective in strategic management. This perspective builds on the resource-based theory of the firm. The knowledge-based view of the firm implies that information systems are designed to support knowledge management in organizations. This book applies the knowledge-based view of the firm in strategic knowledge management technology.

This book is based on the premise that it is difficult, if not impossible, to manage a modern business or public organization without at least some understanding of the planning, use, control and benefits of information technology to support knowledge creation and sharing among knowledge workers.

This book provides insights into links between information technology and knowledge management that students will find vital to their professional success. The book also helps managers and professionals gain a competitive advantage from knowledge management systems. It provides self-help for practitioners.

The scholarly value of the book and its contribution to the literature in the information technology discipline is found in three main areas. First, the value shop is identified as the typical value configuration for knowledge firms (Chapter II). Second, the book applies a stages of growth model for knowledge management technology, in which firms develop from the person-to-tools strategy, via the person-to-person strategy and the person-to-documents strategy, to the person-to-systems strategy (Chapter IV). Finally, the case of law firms is extensively explored (Chapter IV). In addition, approaches to knowledge management are organized according to schools of knowledge management (Chapter I), knowledge management is the premise for information technology (Chapter II), and IS/IT strategy for knowledge management is developed within the framework of the Y model (Chapter V).

When you read this book, you may think it has a strange title, which seems not to be reflected in the content. This book could have been titled *Information Technology Support for Knowledge Work,* as it focuses on using IT to support knowledge creation and sharing, and applying the knowledge-based view of the firm. The book could have been titled *Information Technology and Knowledge Management*, *Knowledge Management Systems*, *Stages of Growth for Knowledge Management Systems* or *Strategic Planning for Information Technology in Knowledge Management.* The book is called *Strategic Knowledge Management Technology* to link and integrate all the terms in a triangle of strategy and strategic planning, knowledge work and knowledge management, and information systems and information technology.

When you read this book, you may further think that technology, which is after all part of the book's title, is first discussed in Chapter III. The reason for this is that the book is one of the few texts that attempt to take a dispassionate view of the role of IT. Most either seem to support IT fervently without thought or decry it. IT is a tool, and you will hopefully like the way this book emphasizes that it is the business purpose that must be the driver, not IT driving the business. Since the business perspective in this book is knowledge management, it starts with approaches to knowledge management (Chapter I) and resource-based strategy for knowledge management (Chapter III), before discussing IS/IT in knowledge management (Chapter III).

There is a strong focus on the planning view of strategy in this book, leaving these discussions rather short in relation to IT, to which the more incremental views gained grounds a decade ago. In recent years, more and more business and public organizations seem to have returned to strategic planning, but using a variety of modern methods to describe the current and desired business situation and IS/IT situation.

The attention paid to critiques of strategic planning and also knowledge management may seem scant and nonexistent. For example, Earl's (2001) taxonomy of economic school, organizational school and strategic school in knowledge management may seem uncritically applied. The reason for this is that in the core of the book, our attention is paid to views on the potential role of information technology, in which knowledge management and strategic planning only provide a necessary framework for discussion.

I hope you enjoy reading my book. Any comment you may have is appreciated. Please email me at *petter.gottschalk@bi.no*.

Petter Gottschalk
Oslo, Norway
December 2003

Chapter I

Approaches to Knowledge Management

INTRODUCTION

There is a growing recognition in the business community about the importance of knowledge as a critical resource for organizations. Traditionally, this resource has not been treated with the degree of systematic, deliberate, or explicit effort devoted to managing human, material, and financial resources. But in the coming years, the firm that leaves knowledge to its own devices may be putting itself in severe jeopardy. More and more practitioners and researchers believe that knowledge resources matter more than the conventionally tended resources (material, labor, capital) and must be managed explicitly, not left to fend for itself (Holsapple & Joshi, 2000).

Knowledge management can be defined as a method to simplify and improve the process of sharing, distributing, creating, capturing and understanding knowledge in a company. Knowledge management is description, organization, sharing and development of knowledge in a firm. Knowledge management is managing knowledge-intensive activities in a company. Knowledge management refers to identifying and leveraging the collective knowledge in a company to help the company compete. Knowledge management is a method for achieving corporate goals by collecting, creating and synthesizing and sharing information, insights, reflections, thoughts and experience. Knowledge management is a discipline focused on systematic and innovative methods, practices, and tools for managing the generation, acquisition, exchange, protection, distribution, and utilization of knowledge, intellectual capital and intangible assets (Montana, 2000).

The purpose of knowledge management is to help companies create, share and use knowledge more effectively. Effective knowledge management causes fewer errors, less work, more independence in time and space for knowledge workers, fewer questions, better decisions, less reinventing of wheels, improved customer relations, improved service and improved profitability. Knowledge management is purported to increase both innovation and responsiveness. The recent interest in organizational knowledge has prompted the issue of managing knowledge to the organization's benefit (Alavi & Leidner, 2001).

Earl (2001) developed taxonomy for knowledge management that he labeled schools of knowledge management. Each school was proposed as an ideal type. No claims were made that any one school outperforms others. Each represents a particular orientation or perspective. The schools are not mutually exclusive.

In this chapter, Earl's (2001) taxonomy is applied to classify a number of approaches to knowledge management. This classification of approaches is based on an overall match to each ideal type in terms of school of knowledge management. Three relevant schools are labeled the economic school, the organizational school and the strategic school. The economic school has a focus of income, in which the aim is to exploit knowledge assets. The organizational school has a focus of networks, in which the aim is knowledge pooling. The strategic school has a focus of competitive advantage, in which the aim is to identify, exploit and explore knowledge capabilities.

THE ECONOMIC SCHOOL

According to Earl (2001), the economic school is explicitly concerned with both protecting and exploiting a firm's knowledge or intellectual assets to produce revenue streams (or rent). It is concerned with managing knowledge as an asset, in which knowledge or intellectual assets include patents, trademarks, copyrights and know-how. Intellectual property could be another means of describing the object being managed. This school is more concerned with exploitation of knowledge and less concerned with exploration. One critical success factor in this school appears to be the development of a specialist team or function to aggressively manage knowledge property through intellectual capital accounting, intellectual capital management and creation of effective and efficient knowledge marketplaces. Otherwise it is too easily forgotten.

Intellectual Capital Accounting

According to Roslender and Fincham (2001), intellectual capital is currently the focus of significant discussion and enquiry across the management disciplines and beyond. This reflects the recognition that intellectual capital provides a crucial source of value for the contemporary business enterprise. It is a resource that requires careful management if it is to fulfill its maximum potential.

In the case of those businesses whose shares are publicly quoted, the success with which organizations manage their intellectual capital is increasingly mirrored in their market values, values that are often many times the book values of enterprises. Bridging the gap between these two values provides one motivation for seeking to account for intellectual capital.

Another motivation for seeking to account for intellectual capital is the need to manage intellectual capital successfully. Given the importance of managing intellectual capital successfully, accounting is being challenged to develop new approaches to performance measurement that capture the quality of management evident in the context of intellectual capital.

Stewart (1997) has suggested several tools for measuring intellectual capital. Value is defined by the buyer, not the seller. A company, therefore, is worth what the stock market says: price per share x total number of shares outstanding = market value; what the company as a whole is worth. One measure of intellectual capital is the difference between its market value and its book equity. The assumption is that everything left in the market value after accounting for the fixed assets must be intangible assets. If Microsoft is worth 100 billion dollars, and its book value is 10 billion dollars, then its intellectual capital is 90 billion dollars.

Three components of intellectual capital can be identified. *Human capital* is the first component, consisting of the know-how, capabilities, skills and expertise of human members of an organization. *Relational capital* is the second component, consisting of any connection that people outside the organization have with it, together with customer loyalty, market share, the level of backorders, and so forth. *Structural capital* embraces the remaining component of intellectual capital, including both systems and networks, and cultures and values, together with elements of intellectual property such as patents, copyrights, trademarks, and so forth.

To begin intellectual capital accounting necessitates an acceptance that it is possible to include within the same financial statement objective measures of value, as in the case of tangible assets for which there are historical expenditures. Intangible assets such as goodwill are already problematic in accounting. For example, in the UK, only purchased goodwill can be reported in the accounts of the business that acquires it.

If goodwill continues to prove problematic for financial accounting and reporting, intellectual capital as the new goodwill serves to multiply the difficulties involved. Intellectual capital assumes many more forms than does goodwill, and while both concepts are ultimately open-ended, several years of thinking about intellectual capital have confirmed its greater breadth and depth. One consequence of this, according to Roslender and Fincham (2001), is that we might now think in terms of degrees of intangibility, so that while brands, patents and know-how still count as intangible assets, customer data, distribution channels and employee qualification profiles are more intangible. Off the scale are such assets as employee commitment, organizational culture and corporate values, yet it is just such assets that ensure that some businesses exhibit impressive market-to-book value ratios.

The market-to-book value ratio is sometimes used to indicate the value of intellectual capital in an organization. Three decades ago, the market-to-book value ratio was close to one in most businesses. Today, this ratio has grown to four on average. Microsoft is an extreme example. The book value of the company was 11 billion dollars in 1997, while the market value was 200 billion. This gives a market-to-book value ratio of 20. Afuah and Tucci (2003) argue that this ratio is caused by intellectual capital.

Figure 1 serves as an example of a balance sheet including intellectual capital in a business organization. The market-to-book value ratio in this example is four.

A number of approaches to valuing knowledge assets exist. Reliable approaches require a common language to discuss the underlying value of an organization's knowledge assets. The knowledge-value-added methodology seems to conform to this reinforcement as one of the more robust approaches. The knowledge-value-added (KVA) methodology as described by Housel and Bell (2001) addresses a need long recognized by executives and managers by showing how to leverage and measure the knowledge resident in employees, information technology, and core processes. KVA analysis produces a return-on-knowledge (ROK) ratio to estimate the value added by given knowledge assets, regardless of where they are located.

The essence of KVA is that knowledge utilized in corporate core processes is translated into numerical form. This translation allows allocation of revenue in proportion to the value added by the knowledge as well as the cost to use that

Figure 1. Balance Including Intellectual Capital in a Business Organization (this example developed by Egil Sandvik using Invisible Balance Sheet in Sveiby's Toolkit: www.sveiby.com)

Balance Sheet

Tangible assets	25,000,000		
Human capital	20,000,000	Material values	15,000,000
Relational capital	25,000,000	Immaterial values	75,000,000
Structural capital	30,000,000	Debt	10,000,000
Assets	100,000,000	Liabilities	100,000,000

knowledge. Tracking the conversion of knowledge into value while measuring its bottom-line impacts enables managers to increase the productivity of these critical assets. Housel and Bell (2001) present the following example.

The example begins with an average person who needs to learn how to produce all the outputs of a given company. In a very real sense, then, her knowledge of the company would be the embodiment of the company's value-adding processes including selling, marketing, producing, accounting for, financing, servicing, and maintaining. It is these core processes that add value while converting inputs into outputs that generate the company's revenue.

KVA provides a methodology for allocating revenue and cost to a company's core processes based on the amount of change each produces. Significantly, the knowledge required to make these changes is a convenient way to describe the conversion process.

We define knowledge in a particular way here: It is the know-how required to produce process outputs. This kind of knowledge is proportionate to the time it takes to learn it. Learning time has been found to be a quick and convenient way to measure the amount of knowledge contained in any given process. This understanding can be put to test with the example. In a widget company, there is one person, the owner, who makes and sells widgets. This person knows all there is to know in order to make and sell widgets for $1. The owner's sales-production knowledge can be used as a surrogate for the dollar of revenue generated by the owner's application of the core process knowledge. And we can determine how long it would take the widget company owner to transfer all the necessary sales and production knowledge to a new owner. Further, we can use these learning times to allocate the dollar of revenue between the sales and production processes.

In Housel and Bell's (2001) example, it is assumed that it takes 100 hours for the new owner to learn the processes, with 70 hours spent learning how to make the widget and 30 hours learning how to sell it. This would indicate that 70 percent of the knowledge and value added was contained in the production process and 30 percent in the sales process. It would follow that $0.70 of the revenue would be allocated to production knowledge and $0.30 to sales knowledge.

All that would be left to do in this example would be to determine how much it costs to use the sales and production knowledge, and then we would have a ratio of knowledge value added to knowledge utilization cost. In other words, we can measure return on knowledge (ROK). For the sake of argument, it is assumed that the total cost to sell and produce a widget was $0.50 : $0.25 for sales and $0.25 for production. The basic approach here is to find out how much it costs to use the sales and production knowledge. In this case, the cost is directly tied to how long the new owner spends performing each process. As it turns out, in this case, the new owner spends the same amount of time to do both and, therefore, the cost to use the knowledge of each process is the same.

Based on our estimates for distribution of revenue and cost, we would generate an estimate of ROK. We would conclude that the production process is a more productive use of the knowledge asset (ROK = 0.70/0.25 = 280%) than the sales process (ROK = 0.30/0.25 = 120%).

Intellectual Capital Management

One of the key authors in the area of intellectual capital is Sveiby (2001), who has developed a knowledge-based theory of the firm to guide in strategy formulation. He distinguished between three families of intangible assets. The *external structure* family consists of relationships with customers and suppliers and the reputation (image) of the firm. Some of these relationships can be converted into legal property such as trademarks and brand names. The value of such assets is primarily influenced by how well the company solves its customers' problems, and there is always an element of uncertainty here.

The *internal structure* family consists of patents, concepts, models, and computer and administrative systems. These are created by the employees and are thus generally owned by the organization. The structure is partly independent of individuals and some of it remains even if a large number of the employees leave. The *individual competence* family consists of the competence of the professional staff, the experts, the research and development people, the factory workers, sales and marketing - in short, all those that have a direct contact with customers and whose work is within the business idea.

Competence is a term introduced here. Competence can be defined as the sum of knowledge, skills and abilities at the individual level. With this definition, we say that knowledge is part of competence, and competence is part of intellectual capital.

These three families of intangible resources have slightly different definitions when compared to the capital elements. The external structure seems similar to relational capital, the internal structure seems similar to structural capital, while the individual competence seems similar to human capital.

To appreciate why a knowledge-based theory of the firm can be useful for strategy formulation, Sveiby (2001) considers some of the features that differentiate knowledge transfers from tangible goods transfers. In contrast to tangible goods, which tend to depreciate in value when they are used, knowledge grows when used and depreciates when not used. Competence in a language or a sport requires huge investments in training to build up; managerial competence takes a long time on-the-job to learn. If one stops speaking the language it gradually dissipates.

Figure 2. Knowledge Transfer Within and Between Families of Intangible Assets (Sveiby, 2001)

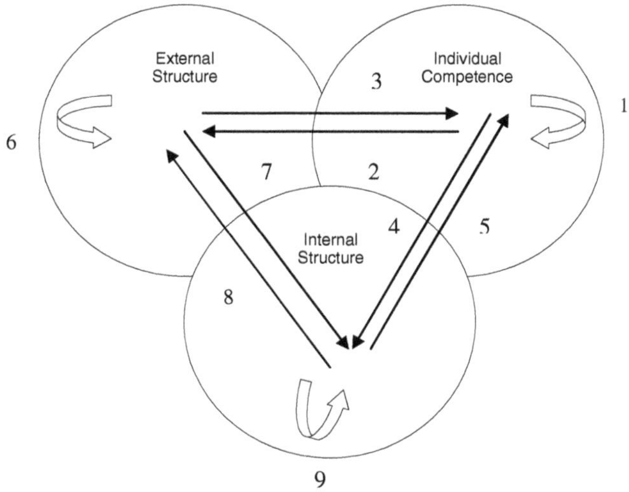

Given three families of intangible assets, it is possible to identify nine knowledge transfers. These knowledge transfers can occur within a family and between families, as illustrated in Figure 2.

Each of the nine knowledge transfers in Figure 2 can be explained as follows (Sveiby, 2001):

1. *Knowledge transfers between individuals* concern how to best enable the communication between employees within the organization. The strategic question is: How can we improve the transfer of competence between people in the organization? Activities for intellectual capital management focus on trust building, enabling team activities, induction programs, job rotation and master/apprentice scheme.
2. *Knowledge transfers from individuals to external structure* concern how the organization's employees transfer their knowledge to the outer world. The strategic question is: How can the organization's employees improve the competence of customers, suppliers and other stakeholders? Activities for intellectual capital management focus on enabling the employees to help customers learn about the products, getting rid of red tape, enabling job rotation with customers, holding product seminars and providing customer education.
3. *Knowledge transfers from external structure to individuals* occur when employees learn from customers, suppliers and community feedback through ideas, new experiences and new technical knowledge. The strate-

gic question is: How can the organization's customers, suppliers and other stakeholders improve the competence of the employees? Activities for intellectual capital management focus on creating and maintaining good personal relationships between the organization's own people and the people outside the organization.

4. *Knowledge transfers from competence to internal structure* concern the transformation of human capital into more permanent structural capital through documented work routines, intranets and data repositories. The strategic question is: How can we improve the conversion from individually held competence to systems, tools and templates? Activities for intellectual capital management focus on tools, templates, process and systems so they can be shared more easily and efficiently.
5. *Knowledge transfers from internal structure to individual competence* is the counterpart of the above. Once competence is captured in a system it needs to be made available to other individuals in such a way that they improve their capacity to act. The strategic question is: How can we improve individuals' competence by using systems, tools and templates? Activities for intellectual capital management focus on improving human-computer interface of systems, action-based learning processes, simulations and interactive e-learning environments.
6. *Knowledge transfers within the external structure* concern what customers and others tell each other about the services of an organization. The strategic question is: How can we enable the conversations among the customers, suppliers and other stakeholders so they improve their competence? Activities for intellectual capital management focus on partnering and alliances, improving the image of the organization and the brand equity of its products and services, improving the quality of the offering, and conducting product seminars and alumni programs.
7. *Knowledge transfers from external to internal structure* concern what knowledge the organization can gain from the external world and how the learning can be converted into action. The strategic question is: How can competence from the customers, suppliers and other stakeholders improve the organization's systems, tools, processes and products? Activities for intellectual capital management focus on empowering call centers to interpret customer complaints, creating alliances to generate ideas for new products and research and development alliances.
8. *Knowledge transfers from internal to external structure* is the counterpart of the above. The strategic question is: How can the organization's systems, tools and processes and products improve the competence of the customers, suppliers and other stakeholders? Activities for intellectual capital management focus on making the organization's systems, tools and

processes effective in servicing the customer, extranets, product tracking, help desks and e-business.

9. *Knowledge transfers within the internal structure* in which the internal structure is the backbone of the organization. The strategic question is: How can the organization's systems, tools, processes and products be effectively integrated? Activities for intellectual capital management focus on streamlining databases, building integrated information technology systems and improving the office layout.

Knowledge Market Framework

Within the economic school, knowledge transfers occur in knowledge markets. This is a transactional perspective, in which knowledge exchanges occur in a marketplace. In defining any market, one must be clear as to whom the buyers and sellers are, and what pricing system exists to determine what the consumer pays for a product or service. Knowledge markets exist within every organization. These markets include not only knowledge that has been codified or synthesized (realized) into a company's processes, structure, technology or strategy, but also include all dynamic exchanges of knowledge between buyers and suppliers.

According to Grover and Davenport (2001), organizations can be viewed to have two categories of buyers of knowledge, local buyers and global buyers. The local buyers are people who are searching for knowledge assets to address an issue that they need to resolve. They require more than information. Expertise, experience, insight, and judgment are needed to bring to bear on the issue. They could pay for knowledge in hard currency via for example a consultant from outside the firm, or buy the knowledge from internal suppliers. The global knowledge buyer is the firm, which has a vested interest in realizing knowledge assets into valuable products and services. The global knowledge buyer, represented by organizational stakeholders whose benefits are tied to organizational level outcomes, has a strong interest in transferring local knowledge to global knowledge. Doing so reduces dependency on knowledge sellers — in case they choose to leave the firm. Knowledge sellers are people who have knowledge (usually tacit) to sell. The quality of this knowledge might be high or low depending on the credibility of the source.

Davenport and Prusak's (1998) approach to knowledge management is concerned with knowledge markets. A knowledge market can be defined as a system in which participants exchange a scarce unit for present or future value. Buyers, sellers and brokers are the roles on knowledge markets. *Knowledge buyers* or seekers are usually people trying to resolve an issue whose complexity and uncertainty require knowledge. They seek knowledge because it has distinct value to them. *Knowledge sellers* are usually people in an organization with an internal market reputation for having substantial knowledge about a process or subject. Although almost everyone is a knowledge buyer at one time or another, not everyone is necessarily a seller. Some people are skilled but unable to articulate their tacit knowledge. Others keep themselves out of the market because they believe they benefit more from hoarding their knowledge. *Knowledge brokers* make connections between buyers and sellers. Typically, managers are in the knowledge broker role by making connections. Librarians frequently act in this role as information guides to the task of making people-to-people as well as people-to-text connections.

The concept of knowledge markets recognizes the interest that individuals have in holding onto the knowledge they possess. In order to part with it, they need to receive something in exchange. Any organization is a knowledge market in which knowledge is exchanged for other things of value — money, respect, promotions, or other knowledge (Grover & Davenport, 2001).

All markets have a price system so that value exchanges can be efficiently rendered and recorded. The price system of a knowledge market includes reciprocity, repute and altruism (Davenport & Prusak, 1998).

Reciprocity implies payment in terms of knowledge. A knowledge seller will spend the time and effort needed to share knowledge effectively if the person expects the buyer to be a willing seller when he or she is in the market for knowledge. Reciprocity may be achieved less directly than by getting knowledge back from the same person. In firms structured as partnerships, such as law firms, knowledge sharing that improves profitability will return a benefit to the sharer, now and in the future. Whether or not a knowledge seller expects to be paid with equally valuable knowledge from the buyer, the knowledge seller may believe that being known for sharing knowledge readily will make others in the company more willing to share with him or her. That is a rational assumption, since his or her reputation as a seller of valuable knowledge will make others confident of his/her willingness to reciprocate when he/she is the buyer and they have knowledge to sell: The knowledge seller's knowledge credit is good.

Repute implies being known as a knowledge source. A knowledge seller usually wants others to know him or her as a knowledgeable person with valuable expertise that he/she is willing to share with others in the company. Repute many seem intangible, but it can produce tangible results. Having a reputation for knowledge sharing makes achieving reciprocity more likely: being known as a knowledge seller makes one a more effective knowledge buyer. Having a reputation as a valuable knowledge source can also lead to the tangible benefits of job security, promotion, and all the rewards and trappings of a company guru. Although a seller does not receive cash directly, the seller may receive a higher salary or bonus from sharing knowledge with others. In professional service firms such as consulting and law firms, success hinges on repute.

Altruism implies that a knowledge seller may be so passionate about his or her knowledge that he or she is happy to share it whenever he/she gets a chance.

This seems to be the case with many university professors. Many knowledge sharers are motivated in part by a love of their subject and to some degree by altruism, whether for the good of the organization or based on a natural impulse to help others.

Knowledge markets are dependent on *market signals* that indicate where knowledge actually resides in the organization and how to gain access to it. Title and position is the most common formal signal indicating who has or should have valuable knowledge. Another knowledge market signal flows through informal networks of practice that develop in organizations. Within such networks, people ask each other who knows what.

Davenport and Prusak (1998) argue that to develop effective knowledge markets, information technology has to be used wisely, marketplaces have to be built, and knowledge market value has to be created and defined:

- *Using information technology wisely.* Networks and desktop computers, with their ability to connect people and store and retrieve virtually unlimited amounts of content, can dramatically improve knowledge market efficiency. Information technology can provide an infrastructure for moving knowledge and information about knowledge as well as for building virtual knowledge marketplaces.
- *Building marketplaces.* Physical and virtual spaces dedicated to knowledge exchange, such as knowledge fairs and corporate universities, bring people together to consider subjects of mutual interest. Electronic knowledge markets such as the Internet, intranet discussion groups, and groupware discussion databases provide convenience and choice, with desktop access to a vast variety of material.
- *Creating and defining knowledge market value.* Value can be established through empirical means, such as employees being recognized, promoted, and rewarded for sharing knowledge. A number of consulting companies have made knowledge sharing one of the basic criteria of the performance-evaluation process.

Perfect knowledge markets do not exist. Rather, the extent of market efficiency is defined. Highly efficient knowledge markets have little information asymmetry, high levels of standardization, homogenous customers, large numbers of suppliers, and a well-understood currency (Grover & Davenport, 2001):

- *Information symmetry.* Knowledge by its very nature is unique. Therefore, the seller of knowledge has the most information on the front of the knowledge process; that is, what was generated and how it is codified. The buyer might have information on how the knowledge can be realized within the context of the issue being addressed. This is a natural information asymmetry. This problem is further compounded by the fact that buyers often cannot identify good sources of knowledge and rely on close (local) networks of people they know. Even more inefficiency could exist due to the fact that certain knowledge sources might choose to keep information about their knowledge private due to cultural or political reasons. This leads to very inefficient buying and selling, in which buyers have to incur tremendous costs to reduce information asymmetry.

- *Product standardization.* Again, the unique nature of knowledge makes it very difficult to compare knowledge sources. If consultant A is prescribing methodology 1 to solve problem X, and consultant B is prescribing methodology 2, how should a company make a choice, given that problem X is unique to the context of the company and methodology 1 and 2 have never been tested within the context? Additional difficulty exists due to the recursive nature of knowledge and its discontinuous interaction. It is very difficult to predict how new knowledge will interact with the information on the issue under consideration. This interaction could yield a completely different solution set that could be of much greater value than any other originally considered. It may be almost impossible to assess the value of this knowledge a priori. Therefore, knowledge uniqueness could allow sellers to generate monopolies.
- *Homogeneity of customers.* On the demand side we can see a similar problem regarding the contexts on which knowledge needs to be brought to bear. These contexts or issues are not simple to define. They cannot be addressed by provision of information (e.g., what the relationship is between our advertising expenditures and sales), but require complex knowledge processes that need to be conducted by people or people networks with specific knowledge competencies. Therefore, customers are inherently segmented into markets of unitary size, leading to differences in expectations and prices for the same knowledge assets.
- *Large number of suppliers.* A substantial amount of knowledge tends to be tacit or in the minds of employees. If this tacit knowledge is kept invisible to the broad market or is visible only to a local market, the suppliers are essentially unavailable to a potential buyer. This buyer may then obtain the knowledge from suboptimal sources (i.e., convenience sources or external consultants) and pay a premium for what the buyer considers monopolistic knowledge. There may, however, be a large number of suppliers who, if visible to the buyer, would bring the price of the knowledge down. Again, the interaction of knowledge with information makes it very difficult in many cases to accurately predict the appropriate supplier and the quality of knowledge obtained. Therefore, the buyer may not be able to assess the relevant supplier pool — rendering greater uncertainty and inefficiency.

- *Common currency.* Although sellers outside the firm, and occasionally within the firm, might charge hard currency (based on hourly rates or a retainer) for professional expertise, many knowledge transactions do not use common currency. Some arrangements are made based on a quid pro quo arrangement or an expectation of subsequent reciprocity. Other knowledge sellers could part with their knowledge for the price of ego gratification or simply out of friendship. Further, the currency could change, based upon time or context, making it very difficult to compare knowledge assets.

Grover and Davenport (2001) find that knowledge markets are typically characterized by inefficiency. An inherent source of inefficiency in this market is the difficulty in assessing the value of knowledge. As knowledge assets evolve through generation, codification, and realization, their uncertainty is reduced and their source of value is easier to see. Therefore, while knowledge in the generation stage might have tremendous potential for value, its uncertainty reduces the present value of future returns from the asset. Knowledge in the codification stage is visible to customers and somewhat easier to assess. The value of knowledge in the transfer and realization stages might be the most tangible since its value is based on visible products and services that it can create.

Although high levels of knowledge market efficiency may never be achieved, the market concept offers a useful way for organizations to think about knowledge. In theory, high market efficiency would result in greater liquidity of knowledge flows and benefits that accrue to the buyer. Therefore, Grover and Davenport (2001) suggest that knowledge management can be framed as the problem of creating an effective and efficient knowledge marketplace in the organization. Such markets work to improve the stock of both the local and global buyer while providing appropriate compensation for the sellers.

Hansen and Haas (2001) did an interesting empirical study of knowledge markets. They looked at electronic dissemination in a management consulting company. They found that the relatively recent explosion of information available in electronic forms makes *attention*, rather than information, the scarce resource in organizations.

In their study, Hansen and Haas (2001) conceived of electronic document dissemination in an organization as an internal knowledge market. They made four assumptions about such a market. First, there is a distinct set of users of electronic documents. Second, there is a distinct set of suppliers of electronic documents, such as practice groups or marketing departments. Third, both document suppliers and document users receive rewards for their participation in the internal knowledge market, and these rewards create incentives for supplying and using knowledge. Finally, there is a nontrivial matching problem between dispersed sets of users and suppliers of documents.

Hansen and Haas (2001) discuss several strategies to gain attention for specific documents. The supplier can engage in publishing strategies to attract the attention of users. Two strategic dimensions are especially relevant. The first dimension is the extent of topic concentration based on the number of topic areas to be covered in the document supply. Choosing to offer documents on many topics is similar to pursuing a generalist strategy based on a broad product line. The second dimension is the degree of document selectivity. Selective suppliers filter and edit documents to make sure that the documents they supply are of high quality and reduce the total number of documents they offer.

In the consulting company they studied, Hansen and Haas (2001) found that the most successful strategy to gain attention was high topic concentration and high document selectivity. Document suppliers that occupied a crowded segment of the firm's internal knowledge market gained less attention from employees (measured as monthly use of their database), but they were able to combat this negative competitive effect by being selective and concentrated in their document supply.

This result reveals a paradox of information supply in competitive information markets: the less information a supplier offered, the more it was used, because the supplier developed a reputation for quality and focus (Hansen & Haas, 2001).

THE ORGANIZATIONAL SCHOOL

According to Earl (2001), the organizational school describes the use of organizational structures, or networks, to share or pool knowledge. Often described as knowledge communities, the archetypal arrangement is a group of people with a common interest, or problem, or experience. These communities are designed and maintained for a business purpose, and they can be intra- or interorganizational.

In the following, a number of approaches to knowledge management belonging to the organizational school are presented. The first approach is managing common knowledge; the second approach is the socialization-externalization-combination-internalization (SECI) process.

Managing Common Knowledge

Dixon (2000) defines common knowledge as the knowledge that employees learn from doing the organization's tasks. Common knowledge is managed through knowledge transfer mechanisms. Knowledge transfer in an organization can be defined as the process by which one unit (e.g., a group, department or division) is affected by experiences. Another definition suggests that knowledge transfer at the individual level is how knowledge acquired in one situation applies to another. Both these definitions describe knowledge transfer as something that manifests itself through changes in knowledge or performance of the recipient units.

In the management and individual psychology literature, knowledge transfer has received much attention and several mechanisms for knowledge transfer have been described. These mechanisms include movement, training, communication and observation of personnel, technology transfer, replication routines, patents, scientific publication and presentation, interaction with suppliers and customers, alliances and other forms of interorganizational relationships.

By contrast, Markus (2001) has identified four different types of knowledge reuse situations. The first reuse situation is called "shared knowledge producers," in which knowledge re-users may be close to or distant from those who produced the knowledge. A second type of knowledge re-users is "shared work practitioners," people who share a practice community, including specialists who occupy the same roles in different locations, work units, or organizations, such as consultants in a practice. The third reuse situation is called "expertise-seeking novices," and involves people who differ substantially from the knowledge creators, in which novices seek access to experts and expertise. The fourth knowledge reuse situation is "secondary knowledge miners," and is perhaps the most extreme case of reuse as it involves data mining, in which analysts attempt to extract knowledge from records that were collected by others, possibly unknown to the re-user, for very different purposes.

In this book we employ Dixon's (2000) five knowledge transfer mechanisms. The criteria that Dixon used to define these knowledge transfer mechanisms are the following: who is the intended receiver, what is the nature of the task, and what is the type of knowledge to be transferred. The five transfer mechanisms for sharing knowledge in the organization are serial, explicit, tacit, strategic and expert transfers.

Serial transfer takes place when the same group of knowledge workers performs the same work one more time by applying their own knowledge. The nature of the task is frequent and non-routine, and the type of knowledge that is transferred can be both tacit and explicit. Serial transfer is a process that moves the unique knowledge that each individual has constructed into a group or public space so that the knowledge can be integrated and made sense of by the whole team. A team can be defined as a group of people with a shared commitment and who strive for synergy among members.

Explicit transfer takes place when a group of knowledge workers performs the same work another group has done before by applying knowledge from the other group. The knowledge from the other group is transferred explicitly as words and numbers and shared in the form of data, scientific formulae, specifications, manuals and the like. The nature of the task performed by the team is frequent and routine.

Tacit transfer takes place when a group of knowledge workers performs the same work as another group by applying knowledge from the other group, but in a different context. The knowledge from the other group is transferred through social activity as tacit knowledge. The nature of the task that the group is engaged in is frequent and non-routine. This is also called near transfer, not because of the geography involved but because of the similarity between the source team and the receiving team.

Strategic transfer takes place when a team has taken on a task that happens only infrequently — a one-off project — and wants to benefit from the experience of others within the same organization that have achieved a similar task. Typical of this transfer mechanism is that the senior-level managers are often involved and define what kind of knowledge is needed to solve the task. The type of knowledge that is transferred can be both tacit and explicit.

Expert transfer takes place when generic and explicit knowledge is transferred from an expert source inside or outside the organization to enable the team to solve new problems with new methods and knowledge. This knowledge transfer is applicable when the team is performing a task that is infrequent and routine, and faces an unusual technical problem beyond the scope of the team's own knowledge. Typically, the knowledge that is requested is not found in a manual or in standard documentation.

Management has to emphasize all five mechanisms for successful sharing and creation of common knowledge. For serial transfer, management has to stimulate meetings and contacts between group members, while for explicit transfer, documentation of work by the previous group needs to be stimulated. For tacit transfer, management has to stimulate contacts between the two groups, while for strategic transfer, strategic knowledge and knowledge gaps have to be identified. For expert transfer, management has to create networks in which experts can transfer their knowledge.

The author conducted an empirical study of knowledge transfer mechanisms in Norway in 2002. Knowledge transfer mechanisms in information technology projects were studied. A project can be defined as a complex effort to achieve a specific objective within a schedule and budget target, which typically cuts across organization lines, is unique, and is usually not repetitive. Information technology projects come in many shapes and sizes, for example, feasibility studies, development projects, design projects, implementation projects, upgrade projects, migration projects and support services projects. Whether the goal is to design, install or re-engineer, technology initiatives are often driven by aggressive deadlines and periods of frequent change. To get the job done, resources must be identified and allocated, and activities must be properly organized and structured in accordance with business and technical requirements. The project management approach to solving IT problems and employing opportunities involves both leaders and end-users, and it defines activities, plans and milestones, and responsibilities.

Why are some IT projects successful while others are not? It has been argued that no more than 25 percent of all IT projects are smoothly completed in the sense that they meet cost, schedule and functionality targets. Is this a result of IT projects being so hard to manage? Others suggest that it is a leadership problem. Is knowledge management of importance for IT project success? To be more specific, can we find significance of different transfer mechanisms for knowledge management in IT projects?

Every IT project is by definition unique, for example, new people, new customers, and so forth, but some processes and tasks will always be repetitive. During these processes knowledge is created that can be distributed and shared. The following research question was addressed: What knowledge management transfer mechanisms can predict the extent of IT project success? The focus of research is important because there are few studies of knowledge management in IT projects, and there is also a lack of empirical research concerned with measuring and explaining IT project success.

IT project success is a difficult concept. There is no consistent interpretation of the term project success in the project management literature. Frequently, the following five success criteria are applied to IT project success: project performance, project outcome, system implementation, benefits for the client organization, and benefits for the stakeholders.

The five success criteria are illustrated in Figure 3. Project performance and project outcome are success criteria that are internal to the project. Systems implementation and benefits for the client are success criteria that are internal to the organization. Benefits for the stakeholders are success criteria that are external to the organization.

Figure 3. Success Criteria for IT Projects

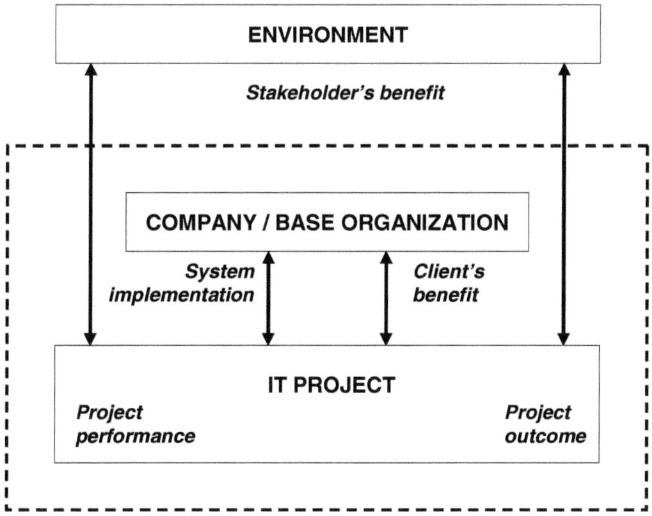

When the same project team repeats the same action in a different setting, for example, in the next project phase or in another project, a serial transfer of knowledge has been performed. The repeated work and the knowledge gained from each action occur in a serial approach. It is a process that transfers the unique knowledge contributed from each project team member into a group or public space so that this knowledge can be integrated and understood by the whole team. The next time the team acts the project work is improved because of this knowledge that the team gained. Hence, the following hypothesis was proposed in the research: Total project success is related to the extent of serial transfer (Hypothesis 1).

When a team faces a problem, which a different team has solved in another project, a more efficient solution can be achieved if the former acquires this knowledge. This kind of knowledge transfer, called explicit transfer, is applicable when a project team has learned something that the organization would like to replicate in other project teams doing similar work. In many organizations, systems or procedures have been developed to capture, appreciate, share and distribute this kind of knowledge, for example, project evaluation, databases, project experience reports, and so forth. The purpose in most of these organizations is to identify what is "best practice" to be transferred to project practice to achieve success. Hence the following hypothesis was proposed: Total project success is related to the extent of explicit knowledge transfer (Hypothesis 2).

While explicit transfer means that knowledge can be shared through various communication media (e.g., word, written specifications, manuals), this is not possible in the case of tacit transfer. Tacit transfer of knowledge usually takes place through socialization, meaning that the knowledge is shared between individuals when they work together. Other methods of tacit transfer include knowledge acquired through learning by doing, on-the-job training, learning by observation, and face-to-face meetings. It is expected that the exchange of knowledge that occurs in tacit transfer be of importance to project performance, and hence the following hypothesis was proposed: Total project success is related to the extent of tacit knowledge transfer (Hypothesis 3).

When an organization that is conducting a one-off project — a strategic task that happens only infrequently — and wants to benefit from the experience of others within the organization, the senior-level managers sometimes have to define the knowledge that is needed. Strategic transfer is a process that develops needed knowledge rather than taking advantage of existing knowledge. This knowledge is preferably shared to multiple units of the organization rather than only one team. The focus is on the users of the knowledge rather than on the source. We assume this is the situation in many strategically important IT projects and that this knowledge transfer is significant for the project outcome. Hence, the following hypothesis was proposed: Total project success is related to the extent of strategic knowledge transfer (Hypothesis 4).

Figure 4. A Research Model to Study Effects of Knowledge Transfer Mechanisms for Common Knowledge on IT Project Success

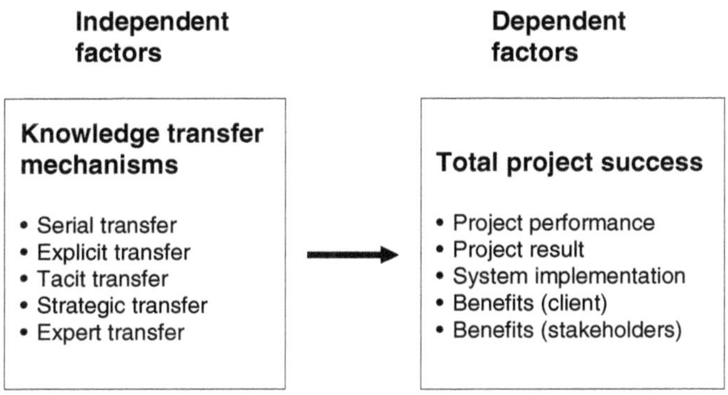

During the project period the team can face technical problems beyond the scope of the team's own knowledge. Typically, the knowledge that is requested is not found in manuals or standard documentation. In order to solve these problems, knowledge has to be obtained from experts, for example, the project office, IT department, external consultants, and the like. Since such a technical problem in the IT project can be very critical for achieving the defined requirements, expert transfer of knowledge can be of vital importance. Hence the following hypothesis was proposed: Total project success is related to the extent of expert knowledge transfer (Hypothesis 5).

In Figure 4, the research model is presented. The model consists of five independent and five dependent factors that represent the basis for the proposed hypotheses.

The study consisted of a survey conducted in Norway in 2002 to investigate knowledge transfer mechanisms (Karlsen & Gottschalk, 2003). The research instrument contained forced-answer questions with a five-point Likert scale ranging from a high of 5 to a low of 1. The respondents were asked to rate both the importance of each transfer mechanism and the success criterion as it applied to the prevailing IT project.

Hypothesis 1 predicts that total project success is related to the extent of serial transfer. The results indicate a significant correlation between the independent and dependent variable. Thus, Hypothesis 1 is supported. Consistent with expectations, total project success is related to strategic transfer as well. Thus, Hypothesis 4 is supported. It was hypothesized that total project success is positively related to the extent of expert transfer. This prediction is supported, thereby supporting Hypothesis 5.

Furthermore, the data analysis shows that the extent of serial transfer is significantly correlated to project performance and project outcome. Results show that the extent of strategic transfer is significantly correlated to system implementation, and to benefits for the client. A significant correlation between expert transfer mechanism and benefits for the stakeholders is also identified. No other correlations between the independent and dependent variables are significant. Hence, neither Hypothesis 2 nor Hypothesis 3 was supported.

This empirical study focused on the evaluation of common knowledge transfer mechanisms and their importance for IT projects success. Knowledge transfer in the organization is the process through which one unit (e.g., individual, group, department, division, etc.) is affected by the experience of another. Within the context of common knowledge transfer, Dixon (2000) has identified five mechanisms for sharing knowledge: serial transfer, explicit transfer, tacit transfer, strategic transfer and expert transfer.

The main finding in this study was that total project success is positively related to the extent of knowledge transfer. First, we hypothesized that knowledge transfer from a project team in one setting to the same team in a different setting is important for project success. The data analysis supports this assumption. Consistent with our assumption, this type of knowledge transfer mechanism is most important for project performance and project outcome. An implication of this observation is that organizations should not replace the members in the project team without careful consideration. Second, the data results indicate that strategic transfer of knowledge is positively related to project success. This demonstrates that sometimes senior-level managers have to be involved in IT projects to define the knowledge that is needed to complete the project. Third, the findings confirm our assumption that project success is related to the extent of expert transfer. While technical expertise in many organizations has become a scarce and costly commodity, this result indicates that expert transfer has become a convenient, workable and important way to share expertise that may be located anywhere in the world.

One interesting finding is that there was no significant correlation between explicit transfer and project success. Many organizations in Norway have made large investments in systems and databases for explicit knowledge transfer. Experience from projects in these organizations indicates that in most cases these systems for expert transfer are not used as intended, and consequently have no impact on project success. Further, our data indicate that there was no significant relation between tacit knowledge transfer and project success. It is our interpretation that this observation should be subjected to careful analysis since many would claim that the exchange of information on systems needs and context of usage between users, developers and stakeholders are critical to success. However, since the respondents are project managers, this result may indicate that tacit knowledge transfer among project managers is not significant to success.

Socialization-Externalization-Combination-Internalization Process

Organizations create and define problems, develop and apply knowledge to solve the problems, and then further develop new knowledge through the action of problem solving. In many organizations, developing new knowledge is even more important than keeping track of existing knowledge. The organization is not merely an information processing machine, but an entity that creates knowledge through action and interaction. It interacts with its environment, and reshapes the environment and even itself through the process of knowledge creation.

Hence, Nonaka et al. (2000) argue that the most important aspect of understanding a firm's capability concerning knowledge is the dynamic capability to continuously create new knowledge out of existing firm-specific capabilities, rather than the stock of knowledge that a firm possesses at any one point in time. With this view of an organization as an entity that creates knowledge continuously, we need to reexamine our theories of the firm, in terms of how it is organized and managed, how it interacts with its environment, and how its members interact with each other. This is the topic in a later chapter on resource-based strategy.

Knowledge creation is a continuous, self-transcending process through which one transcends the boundary of the old self into a new self by acquiring new context, a new view of the world, and new knowledge. One also transcends the boundary between self and other, as knowledge is created through the interactions among individuals or between individuals and their environment.

To understand how organizations create knowledge dynamically, Nonaka et al. (2000) proposed a model of knowledge creation, consisting of three elements: (1) *the SECI process*, the process of knowledge creation through conversion between tacit and explicit knowledge, in which SECI captures socialization, externalization, combination, and internalization (2) *ba*, the shared context for knowledge creation and the place to create knowledge, and (3) *knowledge assets*, the resources required to enable knowledge creation, such as inputs, outputs, and moderator of the knowledge creating process.

The three elements of knowledge creation have to interact with each other to form the knowledge spiral that creates knowledge. An organization creates knowledge through interactions between explicit and tacit knowledge. This interaction is called knowledge conversion. Through the conversion process, tacit and explicit knowledge expand in both quality and quantity. There are four steps in knowledge conversion: from tacit to tacit, from tacit to explicit, from explicit to explicit, and from explicit to tacit. These four steps are called socialization, externalization, combination and internalization, and they cover the SECI process (see Figure 5):

- *Socialization* is the conversion of tacit knowledge to tacit knowledge. New tacit knowledge is converted through shared experiences. New tacit knowledge is acquired through shared experience, such as spending time together or living in the same environment. Socialization takes place when new skills are acquired by spending time with others who have those skills. Socialization does also occur outside the typical workplace, when mental models and opinions are shared among persons who are present. Socialization is the sharing of tacit knowledge between individuals, usually through joint activities rather than written or verbal instructions. For example, by transferring ideas and images, apprenticeships allow newcomers to see the way others think. Knowledge is produced in a group setting not only through mere acquisition of the individuals' knowledge, but also through the sharing of common understanding. Social processes play an important role in the transition of knowledge across individuals or groups.
- *Externalization* is the conversion of tacit knowledge to explicit knowledge. Tacit knowledge is articulated into explicit knowledge. Explicit knowledge can be expressed in words and numbers and shared in the form of data, scientific formulae, specifications, manuals and the like. This kind of knowledge can be readily transmitted between individuals both formally and systematically. The successful conversion of tacit knowledge into explicit knowledge depends on the common knowledge space as well as use of means such as metaphors, analogy and mental models. Externalization involves the expression of tacit knowledge and its conversion into comprehensible forms that are easier to understand. Conventional learning methodologies require the externalization of the professor's knowledge as the initial step in the students' learning process. Externalization involves techniques that help to express ideas or images as words, concepts, visuals, or figurative language (e.g., metaphors, analogies, and narratives), and deductive/inductive reasoning or creative inference.
- *Combination* is the conversion of explicit knowledge to explicit knowledge. Explicit knowledge is converted into more complex and systematic sets of explicit knowledge. Explicit knowledge is collected from inside and outside the organization and then combined, edited and processed to form new explicit knowledge. The new knowledge is then disseminated among the members of the organization. When the financial controller collects information from all parts of the organization and puts it together to show the financial health of the organization, that report is new knowledge in the sense that it synthesizes explicit knowledge from many different sources in one context. Combination involves the conversion of explicit knowledge into more complex sets of explicit knowledge. Focusing on communication, diffusion, integration, and systemization of knowledge, combination contributes to knowledge at the group level as well as at the organizational

Figure 5. SECI Process of Knowledge Creation

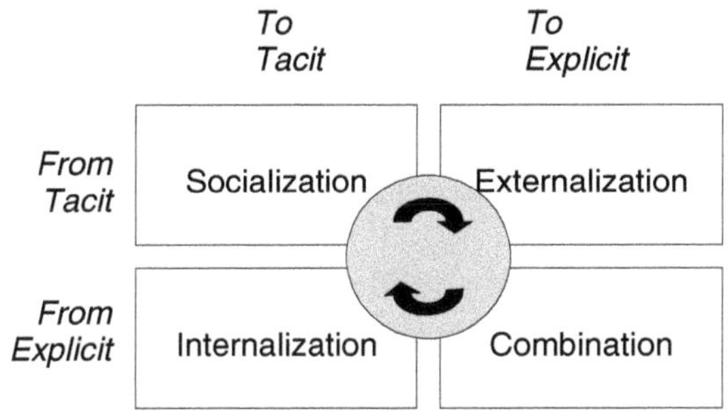

level. Innovative organizations seek to develop new concepts that are created, justified, and modeled at the organizational, and sometimes interorganizational, level. Complex organizational processes require the cooperation of various groups within the organization, and combination supports these processes by aggregating technologies and knowledge.

- *Internalization* is the conversion of explicit knowledge to tacit knowledge. Individuals convert explicit knowledge into tacit knowledge. By reading documents or manuals about their jobs and the organization, new employees can internalize this explicit knowledge in such documents to start doing their jobs. When internalization has occurred, the new knowledge becomes part of existing mental models and know-how. This tacit knowledge accumulated at the individual level can stimulate a new spiral of knowledge creation when it is shared with others through socialization. Internalization requires the individual to identify the knowledge relevant to oneself within the organization's explicit knowledge. In internalization processes, the explicit knowledge may be embodied in action and practice, so that the individual acquiring the knowledge can reexperience what others go through. Alternatively, individuals could acquire tacit knowledge in virtual situations, either vicariously by reading or listening to others' stories, or experientially through simulations or experiments. Learning by doing, on-the-job training, learning by observation, and face-to-face meetings are some of the internalization processes by which individuals acquire knowledge.

Knowledge creation is a continuous process of dynamic interactions between tacit and explicit knowledge, as illustrated in Figure 1.5. Such interactions are shaped by shifts between different modes of knowledge conversion, not just through one mode of interaction. Knowledge created through each of the four modes of knowledge conversion interacts in the spiral of knowledge creation. Nonaka et al. (2000) emphasize that it is important to note that the movement through the four modes of knowledge conversion forms a spiral, not a circle.

Becerra-Fernandez and Sabherwal (2001) conducted an empirical study of socialization, externalization, internalization and combination at NASA KSC (Kennedy Space Center). They suggested that socialization, externalization, internalization and combination processes are all associated with perceived knowledge satisfaction. Perceived knowledge satisfaction was measured through the following statements:

1. You are satisfied with the availability of knowledge for your tasks.
2. The available knowledge improves your effectiveness in performing your tasks.
3. You are satisfied with the management of knowledge you need.
4. You are satisfied with the knowledge available for the tasks in your directorate.
5. You are satisfied with knowledge sharing among individuals at your directorate.
6. The available knowledge improves the effectiveness of your directorate.
7. You are satisfied with the management of knowledge at your directorate.
8. You are satisfied with the knowledge available for various tasks across KSC.
9. You are satisfied with knowledge sharing among various directorates at KSC.
10. The available knowledge improves KSC's overall effectiveness.
11. You are satisfied with the management of knowledge at KSC.

The extent of socialization, externalization, internalization and combination was measured and compared to perceived knowledge satisfaction. It was found that only externalization and combination had significant impacts on perceived knowledge satisfaction. Thus, both of the knowledge management processes that provide explicit knowledge — that is, combination processes, which help integrate several codified areas of knowledge, and externalization processes, which help explicate tacit knowledge — contributed to knowledge satisfaction.

The first element of the Nonaka et al. (2000) model for knowledge creation is the SECI process. The second element is *ba*, which is the name given the location or context where knowledge creation takes place. Knowledge needs a context to be created. The context is defined in terms of who participates and how they participate. Knowledge needs a physical context to be created; there is no creation without a place. *Ba*, which can be translated to place, offers such a context. *Ba* does not necessarily mean a physical place. The Japanese word *ba* means a place at a specific time. *Ba* is the real cultural, social and historic context which is of importance to each knowledge worker, and which enables each knowledge worker to understand and appreciate information. *Ba* is the place where information is understood so that it becomes knowledge.

The key concept in understanding *ba* is interaction. Knowledge creation is a dynamic human process that transcends existing boundaries. Knowledge is created through the interactions among individuals or between individuals and their environments, rather than by an individual operating alone. *Ba* is the context shared by those who interact with each other, and through such interactions, those who participate in *ba* and the context itself evolve through self-transcendence to create knowledge. Participants of *ba* cannot be mere onlookers. Instead, they are committed to *ba* through action and interaction.

Ba lets participants share time and space, and yet it transcends time and space. In knowledge creation, especially in socialization and externalization, it is important for participants to share time and space. A close physical interaction is important in sharing the context and forming a common language among participants. Also, since knowledge is intangible, unbounded and dynamic and cannot be stocked, *ba* works as the platform of knowledge creation by collecting the applied knowledge of the area into a certain time and space and integrating it. However, as *ba* can be a mental or virtual place as well as a physical place, it does not have to be bound to a certain space and time.

The third and final element of the knowledge creation model is knowledge assets. Assets are firm-specific resources that are used to create value for the firm. Knowledge assets are resources required to support the knowledge-creating process. Important knowledge assets are trust, roles and routines. Trust is required to stimulate knowledge workers to share knowledge and to enter into a social knowledge creation process. Roles have to be defined so that knowledge workers are familiar with how the knowledge creation process is to take place. Routines are important to know, so that different knowledge workers in different roles handle time and place and frequencies for knowledge creation equally. Knowledge assets must be built and used internally in order to be valuable to the firm, as they cannot be acquired externally.

To understand how knowledge assets are created, acquired and exploited, Nonaka et al. (2000) proposed to categorize knowledge assets into four types: experiential knowledge assets, conceptual knowledge assets, systemic knowledge assets and routine knowledge assets. Experiential knowledge assets consist of the shared tacit knowledge that is built through shared hands-on experience amongst the members of the organization, and between the members of the organization and its customers, suppliers and affiliated firms. Skills and know-how that are acquired and accumulated by individuals through experiences at work are examples of experiential knowledge assets.

Conceptual knowledge assets consist of explicit knowledge articulated through images, symbols and language. They are the assets based on the concepts held by customers and members of the organization. Systemic knowledge assets consist of systematized and packaged explicit knowledge, such as explicitly stated technologies, product specifications, manuals, and documented and packaged information about customers and suppliers. Routine knowledge assets consist of the tacit knowledge that is routinized and embedded in the actions and practices of the organization. Know-how, organizational culture and organizational routines for carrying out the day-to-day business of the organization are examples of routine knowledge assets.

These four types of knowledge assets form the basis of the knowledge-creating process. To manage knowledge creation and exploitation effectively, a company has to map its stocks of knowledge assets. However, cataloguing the existing knowledge is not enough. As stated above, knowledge assets are dynamic, and new knowledge assets can be created from existing knowledge assets.

The three elements of the knowledge creation model — SECI, *ba* and assets — represent requirements which all have to be taken care of by management to achieve successful knowledge creation. The SECI process takes care of the interaction between tacit and explicit knowledge, while *ba* is the place for this interaction, and knowledge assets are the resources for this interaction. When moving through the SECI process in a spiral, the organization develops new knowledge. This spiral is dependent on *ba* and is stimulated by conditions of growth based on available knowledge assets.

Management is important in all three elements. Executive management is responsible for articulating corporate knowledge ambitions. Middle management is responsible for creating and sustaining *ba*. Both executive and middle management are responsible for the availability of knowledge assets. The knowledge-creating process cannot be managed in the traditional sense of management, which centers on controlling the flow of information. Managers can, however, lead the organization to actively and dynamically create knowledge by providing certain conditions.

Researchers and practitioners argue that most of the knowledge applied by individuals in organizations is tacit knowledge. Traditionally, organizations have been concerned with management of explicit knowledge, which is of less importance to the business at any point in time. However, tacit and explicit knowledge are dependent on each other to be complete sources of knowledge. When we apply the SECI process, we see that there is an interaction between explicit and tacit knowledge, which creates new knowledge. In the externalization stage, tacit knowledge is converted into explicit knowledge. The successful conversion of tacit knowledge into explicit knowledge depends on the common knowledge space as well as use of means such as metaphors, analogy and mental models. Such means help individuals express knowledge in words and numbers and share it in the form of data, scientific formulae, specifications, manuals and the like. This kind of knowledge can be readily transmitted between individuals both formally and systematically.

Nonaka et al. (2000) argue that fostering love, care, trust and commitment amongst organizational members is important, as it forms the foundation of knowledge creation. For knowledge (especially tacit knowledge) to be shared and for the self-transcending process of knowledge creation to occur, there should be strong love, caring and trust among organization members. As information creates power, an individual might be motivated to monopolize it, hiding it even from his or her colleagues. However, as knowledge needs to be shared to be created and exploited, it is important for leaders to create an atmosphere in which organization members feel safe sharing their knowledge. It is also important for leaders to cultivate commitment amongst organization members to motivate the sharing and creation of knowledge, preferably based on a corporate knowledge vision.

Nonaka et al. (2000) defined knowledge assets as firm-specific resources that are indispensable to create value for the firm; knowledge assets are inputs, outputs and moderating factors of the knowledge-creating process. For example, trust amongst organizational members is produced as an output of the knowledge-creating process, and at the same time trust moderates how *ba* functions as a platform for the knowledge-creating process. This definition of knowledge assets focuses on resources for knowledge creation.

Other researchers define knowledge assets as the knowledge itself. Knowledge assets can be all knowledge available to the organization when solving customer problems. Teece (2000) defines knowledge assets as all knowledge in the firm that gives competitive advantage to the firm, and that is impossible to buy or sell. Knowledge assets include tacit and codified experience, both technical and organizational, whether patents and copyrights protect it or not. Sustainable competitive advantage is achieved when the firm is able to create growth in knowledge assets without competitors being able to imitate the knowledge creation. Their continuous innovations, their protection of knowledge assets and their effective knowledge management characterize successful firms by using knowledge at the right time and at the right place.

Managing Knowledge Workers

Knowledge is closely linked to knowledge workers in the company. A knowledge worker can be defined as an employee who is able to find, understand and use knowledge in the organization on his or her own. A knowledge worker takes responsibility for his or her own learning. A knowledge worker is qualified to explore relevant scientific information from corporate as well as national and international sources. A knowledge worker is able to use such information in daily knowledge work to solve problems for customers. Typical knowledge workers are lawyers in a law firm, engineers in an engineering firm, medical doctors in a hospital, product developers in a manufacturing company, professors in a business school, and planning staff in a government agency.

People who are knowledgeable not only have information, but also have the ability to integrate and frame the information within the context of their experience, expertise and judgment. In doing so, they can create new information that expands the state of possibilities, and in turn allows for further interaction with experience, expertise, and judgment. Therefore, in an organizational context, all new knowledge stems from people (Grover & Davenport, 2001).

Shum (1998) makes distinctions between procedural work and knowledge work. All work is invariably a mix of the two, but increasingly, the procedural features are giving way to knowledge-based features. The distinctions are:

- *Knowledge workers are changed by the information in their environment, and they in turn seek to change others through information.* Information is to be consumed, and once "digested", is often of little further value. Information resources which may have longer-term use are often left visible and uncategorized (hence the frequent untidy piles and whiteboards), so that they can be quickly referred to. This is the antithesis of more procedural work, whose work requires a lot of filing into inflexible structures — inflexible because the scheme is often standardized across the organization, and because other staff also need to access those files.
- *Diversity and ad hoc behavior patterns are common in knowledge work.* New information is sought out, reused, and passed on in opportunistic ways, dependent on the changing context and interleaving of the worker's activities. In contrast, consistency of method and output is important in procedural work.
- *Communication networks are highly variable, with different patterns and use of media.* Teams form and disband within the space of a day. The structure and job titles on an organization chart are thus even less indicative than usual as to what someone does or with whom they work. Much of the knowledge exchanged is embedded in documents and email. Staff engaged in predominantly procedural work tend to have well-defined responsibilities and relationships, and the information flow that they maintain is more clearly defined.

According to Gartner Group (2001), knowledge work represents the ultimate free market. People manage themselves as assets, have the freedom to diversify their professional portfolios and seek sources of social and knowledge capital to stimulate and enrich them. And, unlike the case with traditional capital assets, which remain on the books for years, people involved in knowledge work can depart. Mobility becomes much more an issue of satisfaction: Knowledge work professionals will work with a company as long as the company works for them. Based on this analysis, Gartner Group (2001, p. 1) recommends the following three rules for management of knowledge workers:

Rule 1. Knowledge workers need to be energized intellectually. As knowledge work intensifies, it highlights the fundamental disconnect between enterprises' wanting to optimize their resources for efficiency and knowledge workers' wanting to optimize their experiences for effectiveness. The first way of thinking, though valid, is an artifact of the industrial era, when companies would install a piece of equipment and wring out cost efficiencies for years. The second way of thinking, newly validated, is the bulwark of information and knowledge work that paves the way toward creating value. The most effective workers are those who continuously have new opportunities to learn, assume experiences and strengthen their portfolios. Faced with the new dynamics of knowledge work, enterprises must continually ask: "Should we provide opportunities and risk that those people might leave, or should we withhold opportunities and fear that those people might stay?" The knowledge economy puts its bets on the former.

Rule 2. Shorter employment tenure will be the norm. Tenure in any one position will likely be less than three years as knowledge workers seek new ways to develop and market their experiences. Markets, technologies and requirements change so rapidly that 100 percent retention is not only futile, but potentially damaging. Enterprises must learn to manage for shorter tenure — hence for more frequent and rapid turnover — rather than to assume retention. In fact, Gartner analysis reveals that knowledge-intense enterprises should anticipate turnover of 10 percent to 15 percent, especially if they create assignments, rotations, projects and other opportunities only sporadically. (One leading networking company, growing about 40 percent annually, has staff turnover of 7.5 percent, a figure that the company's HR executive suspects may be too low for the company's fast pace of growth.) Shorter tenure demands fast integration into the workflow, tight monitoring of the workforce supply channels, job rotation, well-defined roles and responsibilities and managers who are prepared to find and offer opportunities to employees.

Rule 3. Knowledge work can be all consuming, so design workloads appropriately. According to our projections, collaborative work will increase as a percentage of people's expected output, steadily encroaching on individuals' time to work quietly on their own projects. Vacations and shorter work weeks may make work schedules more tolerable, but the actions that will best prevent burnout are the redesign of work, the redefinition of metrics for collaborative assignments, the sharing of work with appropriate support staff and the installation of appropriate software tools for meeting and working collaboratively. Balance will transform itself from something that is nice to have into something that sustains peak performance.

Knowledge workers are professionals. Professionals gain knowledge through formal education (explicit knowledge) and through learning on the job (tacit knowledge). Professionals who provide services are often required to have extensive education and training prior to entering their fields. This education and training usually provide a high level of explicit knowledge in the field of specialty (Hitt et al., 2001).

Often, there is some variation in this education and training. Students at the best universities are perceived as obtaining the highest level of explicit knowledge available. Knowledgeable external parties rank both universities and specialized programs within them. Individuals who receive their education from the best universities are assumed to have more and better knowledge and to have high intellectual potential to learn and accumulate tacit knowledge (Hitt et al., 2001).

Knowledge transfer to knowledge workers in the workplace can occur in different ways. Core capabilities may be transferred formally and explicitly. However, much knowledge, particularly knowledge with rich tacit dimensions, is transferred informally through processes of socialization and internalization. Swap et al. (2001) focused on two transfer mechanisms — mentoring and storytelling — that can leverage the knowledge of an organization, particularly its tacit knowledge, to build core capabilities among knowledge workers.

According to Swap et al. (2001), the word *mentor* can be traced back to Homer's myth of Odysseus. The king of Ithaca left his son Telemachus in the care of Mentor, who guided and taught the youth for the 10 years his father was away fighting the Trojans. A mentor, therefore, has always been considered one who draws upon a deep knowledge base to teach and guide. The recognition of mentoring as an important transfer mechanism for knowledge among knowledge workers has grown significantly in the last decade.

According to Swap et al. (2001), the word *storytelling* means the telling of an organizational story, which is defined as a detailed narrative of past management actions, employee interactions, or other intra- or extra-organizational events that are communicated informally within the organization. Such narratives will ordinarily include a plot, major characters, and outcome. A moral, or implication of the story for action, is usually implied if not explicitly stated. Normally, these stories will originate from within the organization and will therefore reflect organizational norms, values, and culture.

According to Swap et al. (2001), stories do not lend themselves equally well to transferring different kinds of knowledge. As a strategy for building core capabilities within an organization, an indiscriminate use of stories to transfer critical skills, managerial systems, and norms and values would probably be misguided. Critical skills, including deep knowledge of a content domain, would be very difficult to transfer via stories. For such concrete forms of knowledge, people rely on formal education, apprenticeships or mentoring, training programs, and self-study mastery.

Knowledge workers often belong to knowledge webs. The metaphorical symbol of a web has been used before to suggest that culture could be construed as a web of significance spun by the individuals in the organization. A *knowledge web* can be understood as symbols and metaphors related to learning and knowledge among individuals. It is a context in which knowledge is generated and disseminated (Nidumolu et al., 2001).

Knowledge workers as individuals are the source of much knowledge in the organization. Traditionally, some of this knowledge was disseminated to other individuals in their work group, some of who internalized it and used it as a component of their individual knowledge and achievement bases. Occasionally, some of the knowledge was distributed through formal feedback systems to groups elsewhere in the organization, but the use of the knowledge, if not distribution itself, was greatly hindered by functional and divisional boundaries (Jarvenpaa & Staples, 2001).

Advances in information technology have increased the potential for greater dissemination of information and knowledge beyond its creator. IT has increased both technical and social connectivity in organizations, facilitating information and knowledge sharing. What happens to knowledge workers' beliefs about ownership of knowledge?

Jarvenpaa and Staples (2001) found that a possible conflict arises because much of the organizational knowledge is controlled at the level of individual knowledge workers. Yet knowledge management argues for the management of knowledge at the level of the organization. It is assumed that, either morally or legally, the organization has the right to find, collect, store, and disseminate information that individuals have created and acquired. A common organizational norm is that an information outcome of work such as an idea, process, invention, document, or computer program that an employee creates or acquires at work or using organizational resources actually belongs to the employer rather than to the employee.

This norm goes beyond the legally enforceable employment contracts in some countries. In the late 1990s in Norway, a law was revised to state explicitly that a computer program that an employee creates at work belongs to the employer.

The norm specifies circumstances and contingencies of ownership rights of organizations that are unforeseen or too expensive to enumerate in enough details. The norm specifies that the organization is the owner of the knowledge asset (Jarvenpaa & Staples, 2001).

Jarvenpaa and Staples (2001) studied the perceptions of organization ownership of knowledge by those individuals who have created the expertise. The study found that a belief in self-ownership was positively associated with organizational ownership — suggesting a collaborative type of ownership situation for both information and expertise and for both internal (intraorganizational) and external (interorganizational) sharing situations. Organizational culture and the type of employee also influenced the beliefs of organizational ownership. For example, women were more likely to associate organizational property rights to information products or expertise that they controlled.

A central lesson emerging is that if knowledge management is going to be successful, then organizations must concentrate on people. The importance of people as creators and carriers of knowledge is forcing organizations to realize that knowledge lies less in its databases than in its people. Research shows that people most freely share experiences in informal, self-organizing networks (Ward & Peppard, 2002). Consequently, it becomes necessary for organizations to create and promote those environments. Often labeled *communities of practice*, these are groups of people informally bound together by shared expertise and passion for a joint enterprise. Communities of practice are groups of people who are informally bound to one another by exposure to a common class of problem. Communities of practice exist to build and exchange knowledge, and, in the process, develop the capabilities of members. They differ from project teams, who are composed of employees assigned by management, in that they select themselves. The glue that holds the community together is the passion, commitment and identity with the group's expertise, while for a team it is the goals and project milestones.

THE STRATEGIC SCHOOL

According to Earl (2001), the strategic school sees knowledge management as a dimension of competitive strategy. Indeed, it may be seen as the essence of a firm's strategy. Approaches to knowledge management are dependent on management perspective. Distinctions can be made between the information-based perspective, the technology-based perspective and the culture-based perspective:

- *Information-based perspective* is concerned with access to information. I have a problem, and I am looking for someone in the organization who has knowledge that can solve my problem.
- *Technology-based perspective* is concerned with applications of information technology. We have all this hardware and software in the firm: how can we use this technology to systematize, store and distribute information to knowledge workers?
- *Culture-based perspective* is concerned with knowledge sharing. We are an organization because division of labor makes us more efficient and because we can draw on each other's expertise.

All three perspectives belong in a knowledge management project to be successful. However, the main focus may vary depending on corporate situation. If reinventing the wheel all the time is the big problem, then the information-based perspective should dominate project focus. If the technology in the firm is unable to provide even basic services to knowledge users, then the technology-based perspective should dominate project focus. If knowledge workers are isolated and reluctant to share knowledge, then the culture-based perspective should dominate project focus.

Codification and Personalization Strategy

Some companies automate knowledge management, while others rely on their people to share knowledge through more traditional means. In some companies, the strategy centers on the computer. Knowledge is carefully codified and stored in databases, where it can be accessed and used easily by anyone in the company. These companies have developed elaborate ways to codify, store and reuse knowledge. Knowledge is codified using a people-to-documents approach: it is extracted from the person who developed it, made independent of that person, and reused for various purposes. Knowledge objects are developed by pulling key pieces of knowledge such as interview guides, work schedules, benchmark data, and market segmentation analysis out of documents and storing them in the electronic repository for people to use. This approach allows many people to search for and retrieve codified knowledge without having to contact the person who originally developed it. That opens up the possibility of achieving scale in knowledge reuse and thus of growing the business. Hansen et al. (1999) call this the *codification strategy* for managing knowledge.

In other companies, knowledge is closely tied to the person who developed it and is shared mainly through direct person-to-person contacts. The chief purpose of computers at such companies is to help people communicate knowledge, not to store it. These companies focus on dialogue between individuals, not knowledge objects in a database. Knowledge that has not been codified is transferred in brainstorming sessions and one-on-one conversations. Knowledge workers collectively arrive at deeper insights by going back and forth on problems they need to solve. These companies invest heavily in building networks of people. Knowledge is shared not only face-to-face, but also over the telephone, by email, and via videoconferences. Networks can be fostered in many ways: by transferring people between offices, by supporting a culture in which knowledge workers are expected to return phone calls from colleagues promptly, by creating directories of experts, and by using knowledge managers within the firm to assist project teams. These firms may also have developed electronic document systems, but the purpose of the systems is not to provide knowledge objects. Instead, knowledge workers scan documents to get up to speed in a particular area and to find out who has done work on a topic. They then approach those people directly. Hansen et al. (1999) call this the *personalization strategy* for managing knowledge.

Codification and personalization strategy can be contrasted with each other using criteria such as competitive strategy, economic model, knowledge management strategy, information technology and human resources. The competitive strategy by codification is to provide high quality, reliable, and fast information-systems implementation by reusing codified knowledge. The competitive strategy by personalization is to provide creative, analytically rigorous advice on high-level strategic problems by channeling individual expertise. The economic model for codification strategy can be labeled reuse economics, while the economic model for personalization can be labeled expert economics. Reuse economics implies investing once in a knowledge asset, and then reusing it many times. Expert economics implies charging high fees for highly customized solutions to unique problems.

Knowledge management strategy will either be people-to-documents for codification or person-to-person for personalization. People-to-documents implies developing an electronic document system that codifies, stores, disseminates, and allows reuse of knowledge. Person-to-person implies developing networks for linking people so that tacit knowledge can be shared. By codification, the company invests heavily in IT, where the goal is to connect people with reusable codified knowledge. By personalization, the company invests moderately in IT, where the goal is to facilitate conversations and exchange of tacit knowledge. By codification, the human resource approach will be concerned with training people in groups and through computer-based distance learning. By personalization, the human resource approach will be concerned with training people through one-on-one mentoring.

Hansen et al. (1999) found that companies that use knowledge effectively pursue one strategy predominantly and use the second strategy to support the first. This can be thought of as an 80-20 split: 80 percent of their knowledge sharing follows one strategy, 20 percent the other. Executives who try to excel at both strategies of codification and personalization risk failing at both.

How do companies choose the right strategy for managing knowledge? Competitive strategy must drive knowledge management strategy. Executives must be able to articulate why customers buy a company's products or services rather than those of its competitors. What value do customers expect from the company? How does knowledge that resides in the company add value for customers? Assuming the competitive strategy is clear, managers will want to consider three further questions that can help them choose a primary knowledge management strategy. The three questions developed by Hansen et al. (1999) are concerned with standardized versus customized products, mature or innovative products, and explicit versus tacit knowledge.

The first question is: Do you offer standardized or customized products? Companies that offer standardized products will fit the codification strategy, while companies that offer customized products will fit the personalization strategy. The second question is: Do you have mature or innovative products? Companies that offer mature products will fit the codification strategy, while companies that offer innovative products will fit the personalization strategy.

The final question is: Do your people rely on explicit or tacit knowledge to solve problems? Explicit knowledge is knowledge that can be codified, such as simple software code and market data. When a company's employees rely on explicit knowledge to do their work, the people-to-documents approach makes the most sense. Tacit knowledge, by contrast, is difficult to articulate in writing and is acquired through personal experience. It includes scientific expertise, operational know-how, and insights about an industry, business judgment, and technological expertise. When people use tacit knowledge most often to solve problems, the person-to-person approach works best.

Hansen et al. (1999) stress that people need incentives to participate in the knowledge sharing process. The two knowledge management strategies call for different incentive systems. In the codification model, managers need to develop a system that encourages people to write down what they know and to get those documents into the electronic repository. And real incentives — not small enticements — are required to get people to take those steps. The level and quality of employees' contributions to the document database should be part of their annual performance review. Incentives to stimulate knowledge sharing should be very different at companies that are following the personalization approach. Managers need to reward people for sharing knowledge directly with other people.

Stock, Flow and Growth Strategy

Approaches to knowledge management are dependent on knowledge focus in the organization. Distinctions can be made between expert driven business, experience-driven business and efficiency-driven business:

- *Expert-driven business* solves large, complex, risky, new and unusual problems for customers. Competitive advantage is achieved through continuous improvisation and innovation. Knowledge workers apply general high-level knowledge to understand, solve and learn. Learning from problem solving is important to be able to solve the next new and unknown problem for customers. An expert-driven business is characterized by both new problems and new methods for solution.
- *Experience-driven business* solves large and complicated problems for customers. The problems are new, but they can be solved with existing methods in a specific context every time. Competitive advantage is achieved through effective adaptation of existing problem solving methodologies and techniques. Continuous improvement in effectiveness is impor-

tant to be able to solve the next problem for customers. An experience-based business is characterized by new problems and existing methods for solution.

- *Efficiency-driven business solves* known problems. The quality of the solution is found in fast and inexpensive application to meet customer needs. Competitive advantage is achieved in the ability to make small adjustments in existing goods and services at a low price. An efficiency-driven business is characterized by known problems and known methods for solution.

Few knowledge-intensive firms are only active in one of these businesses. Most firms are active in several of these businesses. For example, medical doctors in a hospital are mainly in the experience-driven business of solving new problems with known methods. Sometimes, they are in the expert-driven business of solving new problems with new methods. Similarly, lawyers in a law firm are often in the expert-driven business, but most of the time in the experience-driven business. In some engineering firms, engineers are often in the efficiency-driven business, but most of the time in the experience-based business.

Knowledge focus will be different in expert-driven, experience-driven and efficiency-driven businesses. In the expert-driven business, learning is important, while previous knowledge becomes obsolete. In the experience-driven business, know-how concerning problem solutions is important, while knowledge of previous problems becomes obsolete. In the efficiency-based business, all knowledge concerning both problems and solutions is important in an accumulation of knowledge to improve efficiency. These differences lead us to make distinctions between the following three knowledge management strategies of stock strategy, flow strategy and growth strategy:

- *Stock strategy* is focused on collecting and storing all knowledge in information bases in the organization. Information is stored in databases and made available to knowledge workers in the organization and in knowledge networks. Knowledge workers use databases to keep updated on relevant problems, relevant methods, news and opinions. Information on problems and methods accumulate over time in databases. This strategy can also be called person-to-knowledge strategy.
- *Flow strategy* is focused on collecting and storing knowledge in information bases in the organization as long as the information is used in knowledge work processes. If certain kinds of knowledge work disappear, then information for those work processes becomes obsolete and can be deleted from databases. This is a yellow-pages strategy in which information on knowledge areas covered by individuals in the firm is registered. The link

to knowledge sources in the form of individuals is made specific in the databases, so that the person source can be identified. When a knowledge worker starts on a new project, the person will search company databases to find colleagues who already have experience in solving these kinds of problems. This strategy can also be called person-to-person strategy.

- *Growth strategy* is focused on developing new knowledge. New knowledge is developed in innovative work processes taking place when knowledge workers have to solve new problems with new methods for customers. Often, several persons are involved in the innovation, and together they have gone through a learning process. When a knowledge worker starts on a new project, the person will use the intraorganizational and interorganizational network to find information on work processes and learning environments that colleagues have used successfully in previous innovation processes.

There is a strong link between these three knowledge management strategies and the three alternatives of expert-driven, experience-driven and efficiency-driven business. In Figure 6, characteristics of the three strategies are presented. Typically, efficiency-driven businesses will apply the stock strategy, while experience-driven businesses will apply the flow strategy, and expert-driven businesses will apply the growth strategy.

Figure 6. Characteristics of Knowledge Management Strategies

Characteristics	Stock strategy	Flow strategy	Growth strategy
Knowledge focus	Efficiency-driven business	Experience-driven business	Expert-driven business
Important persons	Chief knowledge officer Chief information officer Database engineers	Chief knowledge officer Experienced knowledge workers	Management experts
Knowledge base	Databases and information systems	Information networks	Networks of experts, work processes and learning environments
Important elements	Access to databases and information systems	Access to knowledge space	Access to networks of experts and learning environments
Management task	Collecting information and making it available	Connecting persons to experienced knowledge workers	Providing access to networks
Learning	Efficiency training applying existing knowledge	Experience accumulation applying existing knowledge	Growth training developing new knowledge

BARRIERS TO KNOWLEDGE MANAGEMENT

The purpose of knowledge management is to enhance organizational performance by explicitly designing and implementing tools, processes, systems, structures, and cultures to improve the creation, sharing, and use of all kinds of knowledge that are critical for business performance. Knowledge management is typically made operational through a series of new projects, processes and activities (Long & Fahey, 2000).

A growing number of executives, consultants, and management theorists have proclaimed in recent years that knowledge now constitutes the major source of competitive advantage for organizations. This knowledge-based view argues that creating, organizing, and using knowledge assets is the essence of what firms do. Their effectiveness in these activities, relative to the competition, determines performance. Heeding this counsel, many firms have launched major programs to manage knowledge better, and it is increasingly common to see titles such as chief knowledge officer and knowledge manager in organizations. Without a doubt, knowledge management has become an important topic (Long & Fahey, 2000).

But the efforts of many companies to manage knowledge have not achieved their objectives, and there is a growing sense of disenchantment among executives about the practicality of trying to enhance organizational knowledge. Long and Fahey's (2000) research in more than 50 companies pursuing knowledge management projects revealed that organizational culture is widely held to be the major barrier to creating and leveraging knowledge assets.

Cultural Barriers

Organizational culture is increasingly recognized as a major barrier to leveraging intellectual assets. Long and Fahey (2000) identified four ways in which culture influences the behaviors central to knowledge creation, sharing and use. First, culture — and particularly subcultures — shape assumptions about which knowledge is worth managing. Second, culture defines the relationships between individual and organizational knowledge, determining who is expected to control specific knowledge, as well as who must share it and who can hoard it. Third, culture creates the context for social interaction that determines how knowledge will be used in particular situations. Fourth, culture shapes the processes by which new knowledge — with its accompanying uncertainties — is created, legitimated, and distributed in organizations. These four perspectives suggest specific actions managers can take to assess the different aspects of culture most likely to influence knowledge-related behaviors (Long & Fahey, 2000):

1. *Culture shapes assumptions about which knowledge is important.* Management has to explore how the culture's priorities are likely to support or undermine more effective creation and sharing of knowledge around a particular activity or process. For example, is being billable always more important than some other knowledge-enhancing activity, such as looking for patterns in lost customers? Is going to a skill-building training class a lower-status activity than performing daily tasks? Furthermore, management has to identify behaviors that will demonstrate that a particular set of essential knowledge-building activities is critical to the organization. Finally, management must clarify which existing norms and practices may be barriers to the new behaviors needed.
2. *Culture mediates the relationships between levels of knowledge.* Management must evaluate how the current culture facilitates or undermines the proposed redistribution of knowledge. Management must consider how attitudes towards ownership of knowledge can be changed. Management must, for example, identify what new behaviors leaders must exhibit to communicate a shift from valuing individual to collective knowledge. Management must make explicit which practices need to change to reinforce more collaborative knowledge use.
3. *Culture creates a context for social interaction.* Management must identify norms and practices that are barriers to discussing sensitive topics. Management must find and evaluate evidence that senior management is perceived as accessible and approachable. Are there elements of the culture that inhibit vertical interactions? Management must find norms and practices in the firm that encourage or discourage a high frequency of interaction and an expectation of collaborative problem solving.
4. *Culture shapes creation and adoption of new knowledge.* Management must look for important new knowledge that was ignored, discounted, or undiscovered by the organization. How did these examples prove costly to the business? What norms and practices created barriers to adopting, creating, or applying this knowledge? Management must seek out examples of new knowledge adopted or created with inputs from the external environment that led to bursts of innovation within the firm, and try to draw lessons from them.

Also, research conducted at the Cranfield School of Management in the UK has identified culture as at the top of the list of concerns among organizations regarding knowledge management. Turning a "we don't do it like that" attitude into "who knows how to do it better?" demands a sea change in working practices and relationships (Ward & Peppard, 2002). People and cultural issues dominate as both the necessary means and the key inhibitor to sharing and exploiting knowledge.

Error Barriers

Fahey and Prusak (2000) identified a set of pervasive knowledge management errors. Their focus is on fundamental errors, that is, errors that if left uncorrected inhibit genuine knowledge from being developed and leveraged. Fahey and Prusak (2000) called their set of errors the "11 deadliest sins of knowledge management":

1. Not developing a *working definition of knowledge.* Management must make distinctions between data, information and knowledge.
2. Emphasizing knowledge stock to the detriment of *knowledge flow.* The notion of flow suggests a radically different conception of knowledge. It is in constant flux and change. It is central to day-to-day doing and being.
3. Viewing knowledge as existing predominantly outside the *heads of individuals.* Knowledge cannot truly originate outside the heads of individuals.
4. Not understanding that a fundamental intermediate purpose of managing knowledge is to create a *shared context.* If knowledge exists ultimately within individuals, and it is individuals participating simultaneously in multiple group processes that make and execute key decisions, then a fundamental purpose of managing knowledge must be to build some degree of shared context. Shared context means a shared understanding of an organization's external and internal worlds and how these worlds are connected.
5. Paying little heed to the role and importance of *tacit knowledge.* A head-centered view recognizes the central role of tacit knowledge in shaping and influencing explicit knowledge.
6. Disentangling knowledge from *its uses.* Knowledge is about imbuing data and information with decision- and action-relevant meaning. This is the vital role of human intervention. Information about customers becomes knowledge when decision makers determine how to take advantage of the information. In this way, knowledge is inseparable from thinking and acting.
7. Downplaying *thinking* and reasoning. Knowledge generation and use at the level of individuals and groups is a never-ending work-in-progress. At its core, getting to different states of knowledge development requires some form of thinking and reasoning.
8. Focusing on the past and the present and not the *future.* If the intent of knowledge is to inform and influence decision-making and actions, then its focus must be on the future.
9. Failing to recognize the importance of *experimentation.* Experiments are a crucial source of the data and information necessary for the invigoration of knowledge, and in most respects, the creation of new knowledge. Experiments include trying new approaches to analysis, initiating pilot

projects, doing things on a trial-and-error basis, and allowing individuals to assume additional tasks and responsibilities.

10. Substituting technological contact for *human interface.* Although IT is a wonderful facilitator of data and information transmission and distribution, it can never substitute for the rich interactivity, communication, and learning that are inherent in dialogue.
11. Seeking to develop direct *measures of knowledge.* It seems that an increasing number of organizations seek to measure knowledge directly rather than by its outcomes, activities, and consequences.

CASE STUDY: PHOTOCURE

Radiumhospitalet is a cancer treatment hospital in Oslo. The hospital has shares worth more than half a billion Norwegian crones in PhotoCure, which is listed on the stock exchange. The drug company PhotoCure has made money on products resulting from research in the hospital. Ten medical doctors who did the research at the hospital have sued the hospital. They want one-third of the hospital's profits from PhotoCure, which is based on their research.

The drug company PhotoCure is worth 1.85 billion Norwegian crones, which is more than two hundred million U.S. dollars. The research foundation of Radiumhospitalet owns 28 percent of the stock. The value of the shares is 520 million crones. In addition, the research foundation has earlier sold shares for 37 million crones.

PhotoCure is solely based on research conducted at the hospital. That is why shares of such magnitude are owned by the hospital. Never before have hospital doctors in Norway created so large commercial values. Now the researchers want one-third of the cake, and they have sued Radiumhospitalet to get it. More than one year of negotiations between researchers and hospital has led nowhere. *"Yes, I find it disappointing that this is not solved; that the researchers did not get their money," says Arne Petter Nitter, the lawyer defending their case in court.*

As a start, the researchers want to be paid 12 million crones. Then, they want one-third of all income made by Radiumhospitalet's research foundation when selling PhotoCure shares.

Research conducted at Radiumhospitalet has led to the first drug against cancer developed in Norway. The drug is patented based on the medical doctors' research results. In the mid 1990s, all technology rights from the research were put into a new company, which was established by Radiumhospitalet. The new company was named PhotoCure, triggered by the technology to be commercialized.

The patented cancer treatment is a photodynamic treatment. Professor Johan Moan was the first to conduct research in this area in Norway. Later, a number of other researchers at Radiumhospitalet became involved in the research.

Before the technology rights were transferred to PhotoCure, the researchers themselves owned the rights. An agreement concerning profit sharing was never written between the hospital and the researchers. Instead, it was said that profits should be shared according to Radiumhospitalet's personnel policy. Nitter, the lawyer, finds that this policy gives the researchers one-third of the income from stock sale. He is also of the opinion that this is in line with the Stanford profit sharing model, which has almost become international standard in such cases.

Radiumhospitalet's CEO, Jan Vincents Johannessen, confirms that the hospital has a practice of one-third sharing when it comes to sales of patents and licensing income. The dispute now is whether this practice should also be applied to stock sale. The issue here is whether shares are the same as patents, he says, and adds that a company is more than its patents.

The problem, however, is that PhotoCure never paid for the patents; nor is the company to pay licensing fees. That is why it is unclear how the researchers are to get paid, if stock sales cannot serve as the basis for a one-third practice of profit sharing.

The researchers have been offered financial compensation, but the financial figure is not known. It is important for us to communicate that we do want the researchers to get a financial compensation, says Erlend B. Smeland, who is research executive at Radiumhospitalet. He does not think the researchers are greedy. *"This is a case of principles; what and how to share," says Smerud.*

Johannessen, Radiumhospitalet's CEO, finds it non-dramatic that the case will be tested in court. *"I am quite relaxed," he says.*

Researchers involved in the case, however, are not at all relaxed. Only one of them, Trond Warloe, is willing to talk, and he expresses bitterness. They feel that the hospital is trying to give them peanuts, in a situation where their research has created enormous commercial values in Norway.

Sources: www.photocure.no; Norwegian newspaper Aftenposten, June 14, 2001

Chapter II

Resource-Based Strategy for Knowledge Management

INTRODUCTION

Business strategy has traditionally focused on products and services to gain competitive advantage. Recent work in the area of strategic management and economic theory has begun to focus on the internal side of the equation — the firm's resources and capabilities. This new perspective is referred to as the resource-based theory of the firm.

RESOURCE-BASED THEORY OF THE FIRM

In this book we apply the knowledge-based view of the firm that has established itself as an important perspective in strategic management. This perspective builds on the resource-based theory of the firm. According to the resource-based theory of the firm, performance differences across firms can be attributed to the variance in the firms' resources and capabilities. Resources that are valuable, unique, and difficult to imitate can provide the basis for firms' competitive advantages. In turn, these competitive advantages produce positive returns. According to Hitt et al. (2001), most of the few empirical tests of the resource-based theory that have been conducted have supported positive, direct effects of resources.

The essence of the resource-based theory of the firm lies in its emphasis on the internal resources available to the firm, rather than on the external opportunities and threats dictated by industry conditions. Firms are considered to be highly heterogeneous, and the bundles of resources available to each firm are different. This is both because firms have different initial resource endowments and because managerial decisions affect resource accumulation and the direction of firm growth as well as resource utilization (Loewendahl, 2000).

The resource-based theory of the firm holds that, in order to generate sustainable competitive advantage, a resource must provide economic value and must be presently scarce, difficult to imitate, non-substitutable, and not readily obtainable in factor markets. This theory rests on two key points: first, that resources are the determinants of firm performance, and second, that resources must be rare, valuable, difficult to imitate and non-substitutable by other rare resources. When the latter occurs, a competitive advantage has been created (Priem & Butler, 2001).

Resources can simultaneously be characterized as valuable, rare, non-substitutable, and inimitable. To the extent that an organization's physical assets, infrastructure, and workforce satisfy these criteria, they qualify as resources. A firm's performance depends fundamentally on its ability to have a distinctive, sustainable competitive advantage, which derives from the possession of firm-specific resources (Priem & Butler, 2001).

The resource-based theory is a useful perspective in strategic management. Research on the competitive implications of such firm resources as knowledge, learning, culture, teamwork, and human capital was given a significant boost by resource-based theory — a theory that indicated it was these kinds of resources that were most likely to be sources of sustainable competitive advantage for firms (Barney, 2001).

Firms' resource endowments, particularly intangible resources, are difficult to change except over the long term. For example, although human resources may be mobile to some extent, capabilities may not be valuable for all firms or even for their competitors. Some capabilities are based on firm-specific knowledge, and others are valuable when integrated with additional individual capabilities and specific firm resources. Therefore, intangible resources are more likely than tangible resources to produce a competitive advantage. In particular, intangible firm-specific resources such as knowledge allow firms to add value to incoming factors of production (Hitt et al., 2001).

Resource-based theory attributes advantage in an industry to a firm's control over bundles of unique material, human, organizational and locational resources and skills that enable unique value-creating strategies. A firm's resources are said to be a source of competitive advantage to the degree that they are scarce, specialized, appropriable, valuable, rare, and difficult to imitate or substitute.

Capabilities and Resources

A fundamental idea in resource-based theory is that a firm must continually enhance its resources and capabilities to take advantage of changing conditions. Optimal growth involves a balance between the exploitation of existing resource positions and the development of new resource positions. Thus, a firm would be expected to develop new resources after its existing resource base has been fully utilized. Building new resource positions is important if the firm is to achieve sustained growth. When unused productive resources are coupled with changing managerial knowledge, unique opportunities for growth are created (Pettus, 2001).

The term resource is derived from the Latin term *resurgere*, which means "to rise" and implies an aid or expedient for reaching an end. A resource implies a potential means to achieve an end, or something that can be used to create value. The first strategy textbooks outlining a holistic perspective focused on how resources needed to be allocated or deployed to earn rents. The interest in the term was for a long time linked to the efficiency of resource allocation, but this focus has later been expanded to issues such as resource accumulation, resource stocks and resource flows (Haanaes, 1997).

Firms develop firm-specific resources and then renew these to respond to shifts in the business environment. Firms develop dynamic capabilities to adapt to changing environments. According to Pettus (2001), the term *dynamic* refers to the capacity to renew resource positions to achieve congruence with changing environmental conditions. A capability refers to the key role of strategic management in appropriately adapting, integrating, and reconfiguring internal and external organizational skills, resources, and functional capabilities to match the requirements of a changing environment.

If firms are to develop dynamic capabilities, learning is crucial. Change is costly; therefore, the ability of firms to make necessary adjustments depends upon their ability to scan the environment to evaluate markets and competitors and to quickly accomplish reconfiguration and transformation ahead of competition. However, history matters. Thus, opportunities for growth will involve dynamic capabilities closely related to existing capabilities. As such, opportunities will be most effective when they are close to previous resource use (Pettus, 2001).

According to Johnson and Scholes (2002), successful strategies are dependent on the organization having the strategic capability to perform at the level that is required for success. So the first reason why an understanding of strategic capability is important is concerned with whether an organization's strategies continue to fit the environment in which the organization is operating and the opportunities and threats that exist. Many of the issues of strategy development are concerned with changing strategic capability better to fit a changing environment. Understanding strategic capability is also important from another perspective. The organization's capability may be the leading edge of strategic developments, in the sense that new opportunities may be created by stretching and exploiting the organization's capability either in ways which competitors find difficult to match or in genuinely new directions, or both. This requires organizations to be innovative in the way they develop and exploit their capability.

In this perspective, strategic capability is about providing products or services to customers that are valued — or might be valued in the future. An understanding of what customers value is the starting point. The discussion then moves to whether an organization has the resources to provide products and services that meet these customer requirements.

By a resource is meant anything that could be thought of as a strength or weakness of a given firm. More formally, a firm's resources at a given time can be defined as those (tangible and intangible) assets that are tied to the firm over a substantial period of time. Examples of resources are brand names, in-house knowledge of technology, employment of skilled personnel, trade contracts, machinery, efficient procedures, capital, and so forth. According to the economic school, resources include human capital, structural capital, relational capital and financial capital.

Priem and Butler (2001) find it problematic that virtually anything associated with a firm can be a resource, because this notion suggests that prescriptions for dealing in certain ways with certain categories of resources might be operationally valid, whereas other categories of resources might be inherently difficult for practitioners to measure and manipulate. One example of a resource that might be difficult to measure and manipulate is tacit knowledge. Some have argued for tacit knowledge — that understanding gained from experience but that sometimes cannot be expressed to another person and is unknown to oneself — as a source of competitive advantage.

Another example is the CEO resource. Prescriptions have been made to top managers of poorly performing firms that they are the cause of the problem and should think about voluntarily exiting the firm. This is a case in which viewing a CEO as a resource would have more prescriptive implications for boards of directors than for the CEO (Priem & Butler, 2001).

Barney (2002) discusses how value, rarity, imitability, and organization can be brought together into a single framework to understand the return potential associated with exploiting any of a firm's resources and capabilities. The framework consists of the following five steps (Barney, 2002):

1. If a resource or capability controlled by a firm is *not valuable*, that resource will not enable a firm to choose or implement strategies that exploit environmental opportunities or neutralize environmental threats. Organizing to exploit this resource will increase a firm's costs or decrease its revenues. These types of resources are weaknesses. Firms will either have to fix these weaknesses or avoid using them when choosing and implementing strategies. If firms do exploit these kinds of resources and capabilities, they can expect to put themselves at a competitive disadvantage compared to firms that either do not possess these nonvaluable resources or do not use them in conceiving and implementing strategies.

Firms at a competitive disadvantage are likely to earn below-normal economic profits.

2. If a resource or capability is *valuable but not rare*, exploiting this resource in conceiving and implementing strategies will generate competitive parity and normal economic performance. Exploiting these valuable-but-not-rare resources will generally not create above-normal economic performance for a firm, but failure to exploit them can put a firm at a competitive disadvantage. In this sense, valuable-but-not-rare resources can be thought of as organizational strengths.
3. If a resource or capability is *valuable and rare but not costly to imitate*, exploiting this resource will generate a temporary competitive advantage for a firm and above-normal economic profits. A firm that exploits this kind of resource is, in an important sense, gaining a first-mover advantage, because it is the first firm that is able to exploit a particular resource. However, once competing firms observe this competitive advantage, they will be able to acquire or develop the resources needed to implement this strategy through direct duplication or substitution at no cost disadvantage compared to the first-moving firm. Over time, any competitive advantage that the first mover obtained would be competed away as other firms imitate the resources needed to compete. However, between the time a firm gains a competitive advantage by exploiting a valuable and rare but imitable resource or capability, and the time that competitive advantage is competed away through imitation, the first-moving firm can earn above-normal economic performance. Consequently, this type of resource or capability can be thought of as an organizational strength and distinctive competence.
4. If a resource is *valuable, rare, and costly to imitate*, exploiting this resource will generate a sustained competitive advantage and above-normal economic profits. In this case, competing firms face a significant cost disadvantage in imitating a successful firm's resources and capabilities, and thus cannot imitate this firm's strategies. This advantage may reflect the unique history of the successful firm, causal ambiguity about which resources to imitate, or the socially complex nature of these resources and capabilities. In any case, attempts to compete away the advantages of firms that exploit these resources will not generate above-normal or even normal performance for imitating firms. Even if these firms were able to acquire or develop the resources and capabilities in question, the very high costs of doing so would put them at a competitive disadvantage compared to the firm that already possessed the valuable, rare, and costly to imitate resources. These kinds of resources and capabilities are organizational strengths and sustainable distinctive competencies.

5. The question of organization operates as an adjustment factor in the framework. If a firm with a resource that is *valuable, rare, and costly to imitate, is disorganized*, some of its potential above-normal return could be lost. If the firm completely fails to organize itself to take advantage of this resource, it could actually lead the firm that has the potential for above-normal performance to earn normal or even below-normal performance.

Barney (2001) discusses how value and rarity of resources can be determined. *Value* is a question of conditions under which resources will and will not be valuable. Models of the competitive environment within which a firm competes can determine value. Such models fall into two large categories: (1) efforts to use structure-conduct-performance-based models to specify conditions under which different firm resources will be valuable and (2) efforts to determine the value of firm resources that apply other models derived from industrial organization models of perfect and imperfect competition.

As an example of resource value determination, Barney (2001) discusses the ability of cost leadership strategy to generate sustained competitive advantage. Several firm attributes may be associated with cost leadership, such as volume-derived economies of scale, cumulative volume-derived learning curve economies and policy choices. These firm attributes can be shown to generate economic value in at least some market settings. The logic used to demonstrate the value of these attributes is a market structure logic that is consistent with traditional microeconomics. After identifying the conditions under which cost leadership can generate economic value, it is possible to turn to the conditions under which cost leadership can be a source of competitive advantage (i.e., rare) and sustained competitive advantage (i.e., rare and costly to imitate).

The resource-based theory postulates that some resources will have a higher value for one firm than for other firms. The reasons why the value of resources may be firm-specific are multiple and include (Haanaes, 1997): the experience of working together as a team, the firm possessing superior knowledge about its resources, the bundling of the resources, and the existence of co-specialized or complementary assets.

The value of a given resource may change over time as the market conditions change, for example, in terms of technology, customer preferences or industry structure. Thus, it is often argued that firms need to maintain a dynamic, as opposed to static, evaluation of the value of different resources.

Rarity is a question of how many competing firms possess a particular valuable resource. If only one competing firm possesses a particular valuable resource, then that firm can gain a competitive advantage; that is, it can improve its efficiency and effectiveness in ways that competing firms cannot. One example of this form of testable assertion is mentioned by Barney (2001). The example is concerned with organizational culture as a source of competitive advantage. If only one competing firm possesses a valuable organizational culture (where the value of that culture is determined in ways that are exogenous to the firm), then that firm can gain a competitive advantage; that is, it can improve its efficiency and effectiveness in ways that competing firms cannot. Both these assertions are testable. If a firm uniquely possesses a valuable resource and cannot improve its efficiency and effectiveness in ways that generate competitive advantages, then these assertions are contradicted. One could test these assertions by measuring the extent to which a firm uniquely possesses valuable resources, for example, valuable organizational culture, measuring the activities that different firms engage in to improve their efficiency and effectiveness, and then seeing if there are some activities a firm with the unique culture engages in to improve its effectiveness and efficiency — activities not engaged in by other competing firms.

In general, the rarity of a resource is present as long as the number of firms that possess a particular valuable resource is less than the number of firms needed to generate perfect competition dynamics. Of course, there are difficult measurement problems associated with testing assertions of this form. Barney (2001) points out that additional research work is needed to complete the parameterization of the concept of rarity.

Efficient firms can sustain their competitive advantage only if their resources can neither be extended freely nor imitated by other firms. Hence, in order for resources to have the potential to generate rents, they must be rare. Valuable, but common, resources cannot by themselves represent sources of competitive advantage because competitors can access them. Nobody needs to pay extra for obtaining a resource that is not held in limited supply.

In addition to value and rarity, inimitability has to be determined. *Inimitability* can be determined through barriers to imitation and replication. The extent of barriers and impediments against direct and indirect imitation determine the extent of inimitability. One effective barrier to imitation is that competitors fail to understand the firm's sources of advantage. The lack of understanding can be caused by the tacitness, complexity and specificity that form bases for competitive advantage (Haanaes, 1997).

Several authors have categorized resources. A common categorization is tangibles versus intangibles. Tangibles are relatively clearly defined and easy to identify. Tangible resources include plants, technology, land, geographical location, access to raw materials, capital, equipment and legal resources. Tangible resources tend to be property-based and may also include databases, licenses, patents, registered designs and trademarks, as well as other property rights that are easily bought and sold.

Intangibles are more difficult to define and also to study empirically. Intangible resources encompass skills, knowledge, organizational capital, relationships, capabilities and human capital, as well as brands, company and product reputation, networks, competences, perceptions of quality and the ability to manage change. Intangible resources are generally less easy to transfer than tangible resources, as the value of an intangible resource is difficult to measure (Haanaes, 1997).

Resource-Based Strategy

Strategic management models traditionally have defined the firm's strategy in terms of its product/market positioning — the products it makes and the markets its serves. The resource-based approach suggests, however, that firms should position themselves strategically based on their unique, valuable, and inimitable resources and capabilities rather than the products and services derived from those capabilities. Resources and capabilities can be thought of as a platform from which the firm derives various products for various markets. Leveraging resources and capabilities across many markets and products, rather than targeting specific products for specific markets, becomes the strategic driver. While products and markets may come and go, resources and capabilities are more enduring. Therefore, a resource-based strategy provides a more long-term view than the traditional approach, and one more robust in uncertain and dynamic competitive environments. Competitive advantage based on resources and capabilities, therefore, is potentially more suitable than that based solely on product and market positioning (Zack, 1999).

According to Hitt et al. (2001), scholars argue that resources form the basis of firm strategies and are critical in the implementation of those strategies as well. Therefore, firm resources and strategy seem to interact to produce positive returns. Firms employ both tangible resources (such as buildings and financial resources) and intangible resources (like human capital and brand equity) in the development and implementation of strategy. Outside of natural resource monopolies, intangible resources are more likely to produce a competitive advantage because they are often rare and socially complex, thereby making them difficult to imitate.

According to Barney (2001), resource-based theory includes a very simple view about how resources are connected to the strategies a firm pursues. It is almost as though once a firm becomes aware of the valuable, rare, costly to imitate, and nonsubstitutionable resources it controls, the actions the firm should take to exploit these resources will be self-evident. That may be true some of the time. For example, if a firm possesses valuable, rare, costly to imitate, and nonsubstitutionable economies of scale, learning curve economies, access to low-cost factors of production, and technological resources, it seems clear that the firm should pursue a cost leadership strategy.

However, it will often be the case that the link between resources and the strategy of a firm is not so obvious. Resource-based strategy has to determine when, where and how resources may be useful. Such strategy is not obvious, since a firm's resources may be consistent with several different strategies, all with the ability to create the same level of competitive advantage. In this situation, how should a firm decide which of these several different strategies it should pursue? According to Barney (2001), this and other questions presented by Priem and Butler (2001) concerning the resource-based theory of the firm indicate that the theory is still a theory in many respects, and that more conceptual and empirical research has to be conducted to make the theory more useful to business executives who develop resource-based strategies for their firms.

Resource-based strategy is concerned with the mobilization of resources. Since perceived resources merely represent potential sources of value-creation, they need to be mobilized to create value. Conversely, for a specific resource to have value it has to increase or otherwise facilitate value-creation. The activity whereby tangible and intangible resources are recognized, combined and turned into activities with the aim of creating value is the process here called resource mobilization. The term *resource mobilization* is appropriate, as it incorporates the activity-creation based on both individual and organizational resources, as well as tangibles and intangibles. According to Haanaes (1997), alternative terms such as resource allocation, resource leveraging or resource deployment are appropriate when describing the value-creation based on tangible resources, but less so for intangibles. For example, a competence cannot be allocated, as the person controlling it has full discretion over it. Moreover, the competence can be used in different ways. An engineer can choose to work for a different organization and to work with varying levels of enthusiasm. Also, the same engineer can choose not to utilize his or her competence at all. The term resource mobilization is, thus, meant to cover the value-creation based on all types of resources, and it recognizes that all activity creation has a human aspect.

In strategic management and organization theory, the importance for the firm of reducing uncertainty and its dependence on key resources that it cannot fully control has received much attention. If a large part of the resource accumulation takes place in terms of increased competences that key professionals could easily use for the benefit of other employers, the firm needs to set priorities in terms of linking these individually controlled resources to the firm. Loewendahl (2000) suggests three alternative strategies. The simplest strategy, which may be acceptable to some firms, involves minimizing the dependence on individual professionals and their personal competence. In this sense, the firm chooses to avoid the dependence on individual tangibles. A second strategy is that of linking the professionals more tightly to the firm and reducing the probability of losing them. The third alternative strategy involves increasing the organizationally controlled competence resources without reducing the individually controlled resources. Such a strategy leads to a reduction in the relative impact of individual professionals on total performance, without reducing the absolute value of their contributions. Firms that have been able to develop a high degree of organizationally controlled resources, including relational resources that are linked to the firm rather than to individual employees, are likely to be less concerned about the exit and entry of individual professionals and more concerned about the development and maintenance of their organizational resource base.

According to Maister (1993), there is a natural, but regrettable, tendency for professional firms, in their strategy development process, to focus on new things: What new markets does the firm want to enter? What new clients does the firm want to target? What new services does the firm want to offer? This focus on new services and new markets is too often a cop-out. A new specialty (or a new office location) may or may not make sense for the firm, but it rarely does much (if anything) to affect the profitability or competitiveness of the vast bulk of the firm's existing practices.

On the other hand, an improvement in competitiveness in the firm's core businesses will have a much higher return on investment since the firm can capitalize on it by applying it to a larger volume of business. Enhancing the competitiveness of the existing practice will require changes in the behavior of employees. It implies new methods of operating, new skill development, and new accountabilities. Possible strategies for being more valuable to clients can be found in answers to the following questions (Maister, 1993):

- Can we develop an innovative approach to *hiring* so that we can be more valuable to clients by achieving a higher caliber of staff than the competition?
- Can we *train* our people better than the competition in a variety of technical and counseling skills so that they will be more valuable on the marketplace than their counterparts at other firms?
- Can we develop innovative *methodologies* for handling our matters (or engagements, transactions or projects) so that our delivery of services becomes more thorough and efficient?
- Can we develop systematic ways of helping, encouraging, and ensuring that our people are skilled at client *counseling* in addition to being top suppliers?
- Can we become better than our competition at accumulating, disseminating, and building our firm-wide expertise and experience, so that each professional becomes more valuable in the marketplace by being *empowered* with a greater breadth and depth of experience?
- Can we organize and *specialize* our people in innovative ways, so that they become particularly skilled and valuable to the market because of their focus on a particular market segment's needs?

- Can we become more valuable to our clients by being more systematic and diligent about *listening* to the market — collecting, analyzing, and absorbing the details of their business — than does our competition?
- Can we become more valuable to our clients by investing in research and *development* on issues of particular interest to them?

In resource-based strategy, there has to be consistency between resources and business. The logic behind this requirement is that the resources should create a competitive advantage in the business in which the firm competes. To meet this requirement, corporate resources can be evaluated against key success factors in each business. When doing so, it is important to keep in mind that in order to justify retaining a business, or entering a business, the resources should convey a substantial advantage. Merely having pedestrian resources that could be applied in an industry is seldom sufficient to justify entry or maintain presence in an attractive industry (Collis & Montgomery, 1997).

Moreover, managers must remember that, regardless of the advantage a particular corporate resource appears to yield, the firm must also compete on all the other resources that are required to produce and deliver the product or service in each business. One great resource does not ensure a successful competitive position, particularly if a firm is disadvantaged on other resource dimensions (Collis & Montgomery, 1997).

Activity-Based Theory of the Firm

The resource-based theory of the firm grew out of efforts to explain the growth of firms. Although its origins lay primarily in economics, researchers in strategy have developed the resource-based theory. The main attraction of the resource-based theory is that it focuses on explaining why firms are different and its effect on profitability. The main tenets of the resource-based theory are that firms differ in their resource endowments, that these differences are persistent, and that firm-level performance differentials can be explained by analyzing a firm's resource position. Differences in resources are seen to lead to non-replicable efficiency rents.

Sheehan (2002) discussed comparing and contrasting the resource-based theory with the activity-based theory, and his discussion is presented in the following.

The activity-based theory conceives the firm as a bundle of activities, while the resource-based theory conceives the firm as a bundle of resources. The resource-based theory focuses on explaining why firms create more value than others by examining differences in resource stocks. However, the resource-based theory places little or no emphasis on resource flows. The role of the production function in transforming inputs into end products (other than having the latent ability to transform) is under-conceptualized in the resource-based theory. On the other hand, the activity-based theory focuses on flows of resources in activities. It emphasizes the impact of the firm's production function on creating value, while placing little attention on differences in stocks of resources. It is implicitly assumed that all necessary inputs (resources) can be acquired from the market.

The goal of strategy formulation in the resource-based theory is to identify and increase those resources that allow a firm to gain and sustain superior rents. Firms owning strategic resources are predicted to earn superior rents, while firms possessing no or few strategic resources are thought to earn industry average rents or below average rents. The goal of strategy formulation in the activity-based theory is to identify and explore drivers that allow a firm to gain and sustain superior rents. Drivers are a central concept in the activity-based theory. To be considered drivers, firm level factors must meet three criteria: they are structural factors at the level of activities, they are more or less controllable by management, and they impact the cost and/or differentiation position of the firm. The definition of drivers is primarily based on what drivers do. Drivers are abstract, relative and relational properties of activities. For example, scale of an activity is a driver, as the size of the activity relative to competitors may represent a competitive advantage.

The analytical focus of the resource-based theory is potentially narrower than that of the activity-based theory. While the activity-based theory takes the firm's entire activity set as its unit of analysis, the resource-based theory focuses on individual resources or bundles of resources. Having a narrower focus means that the resource-based theory may not take into account the negative impact of resources, how a resource's value may change as the environment changes, or the role of non-core resources in achieving competitive advantage.

The activity-based and resource-based theories are similar as they both attempt to explain how firms attain superior positions through factors that increase firm differentiation or lower firm cost. While drivers and resources share a common goal of achieving and sustaining superior positions, the manner by which they are seen to reach a profitable position is different. With the resource-based theory it is the possession or control of strategic resources that allows a firm to gain a profitable position. On the other hand, drivers within the activity-based theory are not unique to the firm. They are generic, structural factors, which are available to all firms in the industry, in the sense that they are conceptualized as properties of the firm's activities. A firm gains a profitable position by configuring its activities using drivers. It is this position that a firm may own, but only if it is difficult for rivals to copy the firm's configuration.

The sustainability of superior positions created by configuring drivers or owning resources is based on barriers to imitation. The sustainability of competitive advantage as per the activity-based theory is through barriers to imitation at the activity level. If the firm has a competitive advantage, as long as competitors are unable to copy the way activities are performed and configured through the drivers, the firm should be able to achieve above average earnings over an extended period. The sustainability of superior profitability in the resource-based theory is through barriers to imitation of resources and immobility of resources. If resources are easily copied or substituted then the sustainability of the position is suspect.

Sheehan (2002) concludes his discussion by finding similarities between the resource-based theory and the activity-based theory. Resources in the resource-based theory are similar to drivers in the activity-based theory, as both are based on earning efficiency rents. Furthermore, capabilities in the resource-based theory are similar to activities in the activity-based theory, as both imply action.

KNOWLEDGE AS A STRATEGIC RESOURCE

The knowledge-based view of the firm argues that the products and services produced by tangible resources depend on how they are combined and applied, which is a function of the firm's know-how. This knowledge is embedded in and carried through individual employees as well as entities such as organization culture and identity, routines, policies, systems, and documents. The knowledge-based view of the firm posits that these knowledge assets may produce long-term sustainable competitive advantage for the organization because knowledge-based resources are socially complex to understand and difficult to imitate by another organization (Alavi & Leidner, 2001).

According to Alavi and Leidner (2001), it is less the knowledge existing at any given time per se than the firm's ability to effectively apply the existing knowledge to create new knowledge and to take action that forms the basis for achieving competitive advantage from knowledge-based assets. It is here that information technologies may play an important role in effectuating the knowledge-based view of the firm. Advanced information technologies (e.g., the Internet, intranets, extranets, browsers, data warehouses, data mining techniques, and software agents) can be used to systematize, enhance, and expedite large-scale intra- and inter-firm knowledge management. While having unique access to valuable resources is one way to create competitive advantage, in some cases either this may not be possible, or competitors may imitate or develop substitutes for those resources. Companies having superior knowledge, however, are able to coordinate and combine their traditional resources and capabilities in new and distinctive ways, providing more value for their customers than can their competitors. That is, by having superior intellectual resources, an organization can understand how to exploit and develop their traditional resources better than competitors, even if some or all of those traditional resources are not unique. Therefore, knowledge can be considered the most important strategic resource, and the ability to acquire, integrate, store, share, and apply it the most important capability for building and sustaining competitive advantage. The broadest value proposition, then, for engaging in knowledge management is that it can enhance the organization's fundamental ability to compete (Zack, 1999).

Alavi and Leidner (2001) suggest that the long-term sustainable competitive advantage comes from the firm's ability to effectively apply the existing knowledge to create new knowledge and to take action that forms the basis for achieving competitive advantage from knowledge-based assets. The knowledge existing at any given time per se is not sufficient to form such a basis for long-term sustainable competitive advantage.

The special capabilities of organizations for creating and transferring knowledge are being identified as a central element of organizational advantage. Knowledge is a renewable, reusable and accumulating asset of value to firms that increases in value with employee experience and organizational life. Knowledge is intangible, dynamic and without boundaries. If it is not used at a specific time in a specific place, it is of no value.

Human capital has long been argued as a critical resource in most firms. Recent research suggests that human capital attributes (including education, experience, and skills) affect firm outcomes (Hitt et al., 2001).

What is it about knowledge that makes the advantage sustainable? Knowledge — especially context-specific, tacit knowledge embedded in complex organizational routines and developed from experience — tends to be unique and difficult to imitate. Unlike many traditional resources, it is not easily purchased in the marketplace in a ready-to-use form. To acquire similar knowledge, competitors have to engage in similar experiences. However, acquiring knowledge through experience takes time, and competitors are limited in how much they can accelerate their learning merely through greater investment (Zack, 1999).

Knowledge-based competitive advantage is also sustainable because the more a firm already knows, the more it can learn. Learning opportunities for an organization that already has a knowledge advantage may be more valuable than for competitors having similar learning opportunities but starting off knowing less. Sustainability may also come from an organization already knowing something that uniquely complements newly acquired knowledge, which provides an opportunity for knowledge synergy not available to its competitors. New knowledge is integrated with existing knowledge to develop unique insights and create even more valuable knowledge. Organizations should therefore seek areas of learning and experimentation that can potentially add value to their existing knowledge via synergistic combination (Zack, 1999).

Sustainability of knowledge advantage, then, comes from knowing more about some things than competitors, combined with the time constraints faced by competitors in acquiring similar knowledge, regardless of how much they invest to catch up. This represents what economists call increasing returns. Unlike traditional physical goods that are consumed as they are used (providing decreasing returns over time), knowledge provides increasing returns as it is used. The more it is used, the more valuable it becomes, creating a self-reinforcing cycle. If an organization can identify areas where its knowledge leads the competition, and if that unique knowledge can be applied profitably in the marketplace, it can represent a powerful and sustainable competitive advantage (Zack, 1999).

Information sensing, collection, organization, communication, and use are critical to the knowledge-based organization. According to Kettinger and Grover (1995), information can be a source of power, justify ideologically based decisions, as well as symbolize adherence to norms. Knowledge, the combination of experience and information, applied to a context, has a dynamic quality and is defined by individuals in shared and coordinated interaction. The strength and characteristics of individual and group ties impact knowledge transmission. Knowledge-sharing capability can determine an organization's processes and structural form. The capability of an organization to share and leverage knowledge as a whole facilitates its ability to change.

Organizations should strive to use their learning experiences to build on or complement knowledge positions that provide a current or future competitive advantage. Systematically mapping, categorizing, and benchmarking organizational knowledge not only can help make knowledge more accessible throughout an organization, but by using a knowledge map to prioritize and focus its learning experiences, an organization can create greater leverage for its learning efforts. It can combine its learning experiences into a critical learning mass around particular strategic areas of knowledge (Zack, 1999).

The knowledge-based view of the firm stems from theorization of why firms have performance differences. According to Grover and Davenport (2001), debate on the "theory of the firm" originates from two viewpoints, one based in transaction cost economics, and the other in resource-based theory. While transaction cost economics posits that firms exist in lieu of markets due to their reduced potential for opportunism, resource-based theory asserts that long-run superior performance is associated with the possession of scarce, valuable, and inimitable firm-specific resources. The tenet is that knowledge as a focal resource creates unique advantages for governing economic activities through a logic that is very different from a market.

The knowledge-based view argues that the success of firms is not only based on the economics of the contracts it implements (property rights, incentives), but also on its heterogeneous stocks and flows of knowledge. Further work from this perspective has examined different models of organizational design and development of organizational capabilities. The latter view conceptualizes the firm as an institution for integrating knowledge and examines how the mechanisms for integration establish flexible response capabilities in hypercompetitive markets (Grover & Davenport, 2001).

While a knowledge advantage may be sustainable, building a defensible competitive knowledge position internally is a long-term effort, requiring foresight and planning as well as luck. Long lead-time explains the attraction of strategic alliances and other forms of external ventures as potentially quicker means for gaining access to knowledge. It also explains why the strategic threat from technological discontinuity tends to come from firms outside of or peripheral to an industry. New entrants often enjoy a knowledge base different than that of incumbents, one that can be applied to the products and services of the industry under attack. This has been especially evident in industries in which analog products are giving way to digital equivalents (Zack, 1999).

Knowledge has a strategic role if unique firm knowledge can successfully be applied to value-creating tasks and if it can be used to capitalize on existing business opportunities. Since competitors, in developing their own survival strategies, are likely to benchmark themselves against the industry leader to level out performance, knowledge must be difficult to imitate (Krogh et al., 2000).

Characteristics of Knowledge

Knowledge is a renewable, reusable and accumulating resource of value to the firm when applied in the production of products and services. Knowledge cannot be stored in computers; it can only be stored in the human brain. According to Fahey and Prusak (1998, p. 267), knowledge is what a knower knows; there is no knowledge without someone knowing it:

Knowledge therefore must be viewed as originating 'between the ears' of individuals. Taken literally, the need for a knower raises profound questions as to whether and how knowledge can exist outside the heads of individuals. Although knowledge can be represented in and often embedded in organizational processes, routines, and networks, and sometimes in document repositories, it cannot truly originate outside the heads of individuals. Nor is it ever complete outside of an individual.

The need for a knower in knowledge existence raises the question as to how knowledge can exist outside the heads of individuals. Although knowledge cannot originate outside the heads of individuals, it can be argued that knowledge can be represented in and often embedded in organizational processes, routines, and networks, and sometimes in document repositories. However, knowledge is never complete outside of an individual.

Knowledge is information combined with experience, context, interpretation, reflection, intuition and creativity. Information becomes knowledge once it is processed in the mind of an individual. This knowledge then becomes information again once it is articulated or communicated to others in the form of text, computer output, spoken or written words or by other means. Six characteristics of knowledge can distinguish it from information: knowledge is a human act, knowledge is the residue of thinking, knowledge is created in the present moment, knowledge belongs to communities, knowledge circulates through communities in many ways, and new knowledge is created at the boundaries of old.

Today, any discussion of knowledge quickly leads to the issue of how knowledge is defined. A pragmatic definition defines the topic as the most valuable form of content in a continuum starting at data, encompassing information, and ending at knowledge. Typically, data are classified, summarized, transferred or corrected in order to add value, and become information within a certain context. This conversion is relatively mechanical and has long been facilitated by storage, processing, and communication technologies. These technologies add place, time, and form utility to the data. In doing so, the information serves to inform or reduce uncertainty within the problem domain. Therefore, information is united with the context; that is, it only has utility within the context (Grover & Davenport, 2001).

Knowledge has the highest value, the most human contribution, the greatest relevance to decisions and actions, and the greatest dependence on a specific situation or context. It is also the most difficult of content types to manage, because it originates and is applied in the minds of human beings. People who are knowledgeable not only have information, but also have the ability to integrate and frame the information within the context of their experience, expertise, and judgment. In doing so, they can create new information that expands the state of possibilities, and in turn allows for further interaction with experience, expertise and judgment. Therefore, in an organizational context, all new knowledge stems from people. Some knowledge is incorporated in organizational artifacts like processes, structures, and technology. However, institutionalized knowledge often inhibits competition in a dynamic context, unless adaptability of people and processes (higher order learning) is built into the institutional mechanisms themselves (Grover & Davenport, 2001).

Our concern with distinctions between information and knowledge is based on real differences as well as technology implications. Real differences between information and knowledge do exist, although for most practical purposes these differences are of no interest at all. Information technology implications are concerned with the argument that computers can only manipulate electronic information, not electronic knowledge. Business systems are loaded with information, but without knowledge.

Davenport and Prusak (1998) define knowledge as a fluid mix of framed experience, values, contextual information, and expert insights that provides a framework for evaluating and incorporating new experiences and information. It originates and is applied in the minds of knowers. In organizations, it often becomes embedded not only in documents or repositories but also in organizational routines, processes, practices, and norms. Distinctions are often made between data, information, knowledge and wisdom:

- *Data* are letters and numbers without meaning. Data are independent, isolated measurements, characters, numerical characters and symbols.
- *Information* is data that are included in a context that makes sense. For example, 40 degrees can have different meanings depending on the context. There can be a medical, geographical or technical context. If a person has 40 degrees Celsius in fever, that is quite serious. If a city is located 40 degrees north, we know that it is far south of Norway. If an angle is 40 degrees, we know what it looks like. Information is data that make sense, because it can be understood correctly. People turn data into information by organizing it into some unit of analysis, for example, dollars, dates, or customers. Information is data endowed with relevance and purpose.
- *Knowledge* is information combined with experience, context, interpretation and reflection. Knowledge is a renewable resource that can be used over and over, and that accumulates in an organization through use and combination with employees' experience. Humans have knowledge; knowledge cannot exist outside the heads of individuals in the company. Information becomes knowledge when it enters the human brain. This knowledge transforms into information again when it is articulated and communicated to others. Information is an explicit representation of knowledge; it is in itself not knowledge. Knowledge can be both truths and lies, perspectives and concepts, judgments and expectations. Knowledge is used to receive information by analyzing, understanding and evaluating; by combining, prioritizing and decision making; and by planning, implementing and controlling.
- *Wisdom* is knowledge combined with learning, insights and judgmental abilities. Wisdom is more difficult to explain than knowledge, since the levels of context become even more personal, and thus the higher-level nature of wisdom renders it more obscure than knowledge. While knowledge is mainly sufficiently generalized solutions, wisdom is best thought of as sufficiently generalized approaches and values that can be applied in numerous and varied situations. Wisdom cannot be created like data and information, and it cannot be shared with others like knowledge. Because the context is so personal, it becomes almost exclusive to our own minds and

incompatible with the minds of others without extensive transaction. This transaction requires not only a base of knowledge and opportunities for experiences that help create wisdom, but also the processes of introspection, retrospection, interpretation and contemplation. We can value wisdom in others, but we can only create it ourselves (Wang et al., 2001).

These are the definitions applied in this book. Grover and Davenport (2001) calls these definitions pragmatic, as a continuum is used, starting from data, encompassing information, and ending at knowledge in this book. The most valuable form of content in the continuum is knowledge. Knowledge has the highest value, the most human contribution, the greatest relevance to decisions and actions, and the greatest dependence on a specific situation or context. It is also the most difficult of content types to manage, because it originates and is applied in the minds of human beings.

It has been argued that expert systems using artificial intelligence are able to do knowledge work. The chess-playing computer called Deep Blue by IBM is frequently cited as an example. Deep Blue can compete with the best human players because chess, though complex, is a closed system of unchanging and codifiable rules. The size of the board never varies, the rules are unambiguous, the moves of the pieces are clearly defined, and there is absolute agreement about what it means to win or lose (Davenport & Prusak, 1998). Deep Blue is no knowledge worker; the computer only performs a series of computations at extremely high speed.

While knowledge workers develop knowledge, organizations learn. Therefore, the learning organization has become a term frequently used. The learning organization is similar to knowledge development. While knowledge development is taking place at the individual level, organizational learning is taking place at the firm level. Organizational learning occurs when the firm is able to exploit individual competence in new and innovative ways. Organizational learning also occurs when the collective memory — including local language, common history and routines — expands. Organizational learning causes growth in the intellectual capital. Learning is a continuous, never-ending process of knowledge creation. A learning organization is a place in which people are constantly driven to discover what has caused the current situation, and how they can change the present.

Alavi and Leidner (2001) make the case that the hierarchy of data-information-knowledge can be of a different nature. Specifically, they claim that knowledge can be the basis for information, rather than information the basis for knowledge. Knowledge must exist before information can be formulated and before data can be measured to form information. As such, raw data do not exist — the thought or knowledge processes that led to its identification and collection have already influenced even the most elementary piece of data. It is argued that knowledge exists which, when articulated, verbalized, and structured, becomes information which, when assigned a fixed representation and standard interpretation, becomes data (Alavi & Leidner, 2001, p. 109):

Critical to this argument is the fact that knowledge does not exist outside an agent (a knower): it is indelibly shaped by one's needs as well as one's initial stock of knowledge. Knowledge is thus the result of cognitive processing triggered by the inflow of new stimuli. Consistent with this view, we posit that information is converted to knowledge once it is processed in the mind of individuals and the knowledge becomes information once it is articulated and presented in the form of text, graphics, words, or other symbolic forms. A significant implication of this view of knowledge is that for individuals to arrive at the same understanding of data or information, they must share a certain knowledge base. Another important implication of this definition of knowledge is that systems designed to support knowledge in organizations may not appear radically different from other forms of information systems, but will be geared toward enabling users to assign meaning to information and to capture some of their knowledge in information and/or data.

It is not difficult to agree with this reasoning. In fact, our hierarchy from data via information to knowledge is not so much a road or direction, as it is a way of suggesting resource value levels. Knowledge is a more valuable resource to the firm than information, and information is a more valuable resource than data. This is illustrated in Figure 1. The figure illustrates that it is less the knowledge existing at any given time per se than the firm's ability to effectively apply the existing knowledge to develop new knowledge and to take action that forms the basis for achieving long-term competitive advantage from knowledge-based assets.

According to Grover and Davenport (2001), knowledge processes lie somewhere between information and the firm's source of revenue, its products and services. This process can be generically represented in three subprocesses: knowledge generation, knowledge codification, and knowledge transfer/realization. Knowledge generation includes all processes involved in the acquisition and development of knowledge. Knowledge codification involves the conversion of knowledge into accessible and applicable formats. Knowledge transfer includes the movement of knowledge from its point of generation or codified form to the point of use.

One of the reasons that knowledge is such a difficult concept is because this process is recursive, expanding, and often discontinuous. According to Grover and Davenport (2001), many cycles of generation, codification, and transfer are concurrently occurring in businesses. These cycles feed on each other. Knowl-

Figure 1. Value Levels of Resources in the Firm

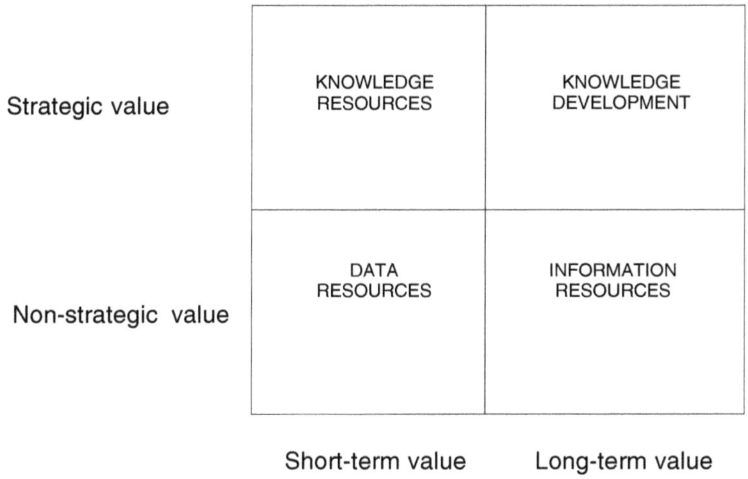

edge interacts with information to increase the state space of possibilities and provide new information, which can then facilitate generation of new knowledge. The knowledge process acts on information to create new information that allows for greater possibilities to fulfill old or possibly new organizational needs. This process is often discontinuous, in which new needs and their fulfillment mechanism could be created.

In our resource-based perspective of knowledge, data are raw numbers and facts, information is processed data, and knowledge is information combined with human thoughts. Knowledge is the result of cognitive processing triggered by the inflow of new stimuli. Information is converted to knowledge once it is processed in the mind of individuals, and the knowledge becomes information once it is articulated and presented to others. A significant implication of this view of knowledge is that for individuals to arrive at the same understanding of information, they must share the same knowledge framework.

In Figure 1, we can imagine that data are assigned meaning and become information, that information are understood and interpreted by individuals and become knowledge, and that knowledge is applied and develops into new knowledge. We can also imagine the opposite route. Knowledge develops in the minds of individuals. This knowledge development causes an increase in knowledge resources. When the new knowledge is articulated, verbalized and structured, it becomes information and causes an increase in information resources. When information is assigned a fixed representation and standard interpretation, it becomes data and causes an increase in data resources.

There are alternatives to our perspective of knowledge as a resource in the firm. Alavi and Leidner (2001) list the following alternatives: knowledge is a state of mind, knowledge is an object to be stored, knowledge is a process of applying expertise, knowledge is a condition of access to information, and knowledge is the potential to influence action.

This book applies the resource-based theory of the firm, in which the knowledge-based perspective identifies the primary role of the firm as integrating the specialist knowledge resident in individuals into goods and services. The task of management is to establish the coordination necessary for this knowledge integration. The knowledge-based perspective serves as a platform for a view of the firm as a dynamic system of knowledge production and application.

To define knowledge as a resource, there has to be a need for that knowledge. Hence, identification of knowledge needs in an organization is important. Three supplementary methods exist to identify needs for knowledge, as illustrated in Figure 2:

- *Problem Decision Analysis.* This method aims at identifying and specifying problems that knowledge workers have, solutions they can find, decisions they have to make, and what knowledge they need to solve problems and make decisions. For a lawyer, the problem can be an insurance claim by a client, the decision can be how to approach the insurance company, and the knowledge need can be outcomes of similar cases handled by the law firm.
- *Critical Success Factors.* This method aims at identifying and specifying what factors cause success. Success can be at firm level, individual level or individual case level. For a lawyer, critical success factors at the individual case level can be quality of legal advice and service level of advice delivery. Critical knowledge in this case includes legal knowledge as well as procedural knowledge.
- *Ends Means Analysis.* This method aims at identifying and specifying external demands and expectations to goods and services from the firm. For a lawyer, the client expectation might be that she or he wins the case. The end is winning the case. Knowledge needs associated with winning a case include legal, procedural and analytical knowledge of successful cases in the past. The means for winning a case might be access to resources of various kinds, such as client documents and client funds. Knowledge needs associated with means include historical records and analysis of legal client practice.

Many researchers have tried to define categories and dimensions of knowledge. A common distinction is made between explicit and tacit knowledge. *Explicit knowledge* can be expressed in words and numbers and shared in the

Figure 2. Methods to Identify Knowledge Needs

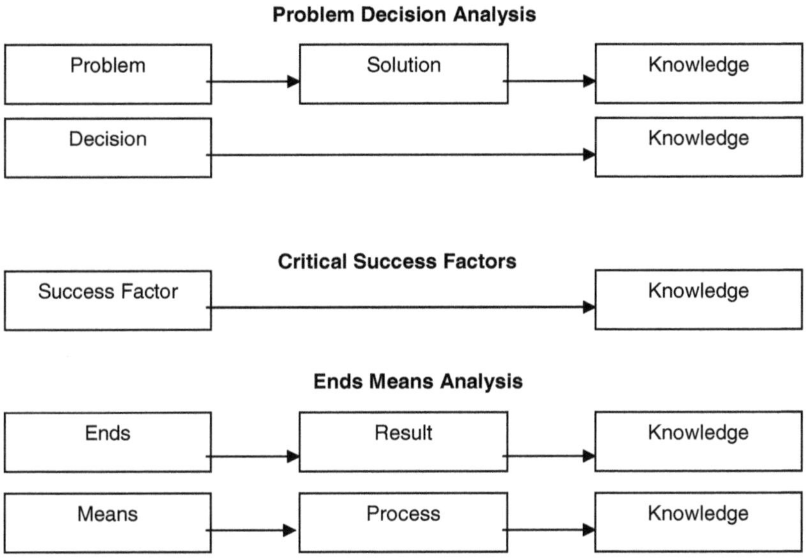

form of data, scientific formulae, specifications, manuals and the like. This kind of knowledge can be readily transmitted between individuals both formally and systematically. *Tacit knowledge* is, on the other hand, highly personal and hard to formalize, making it difficult to communicate or share with others. Subjective insights, intuitions, and hunches fall into this category of knowledge. Tacit knowledge is deeply rooted in an individual's actions and experience as well as in the ideals, values, or emotions he or she embraces. Tacit knowledge is embedded in the human brain and cannot be expressed easily, while explicit knowledge can be easily codified. Both types of knowledge are important, but Western firms have focused largely on managing explicit knowledge (Grover & Davenport, 2001).

Tacitness may be considered as a variable, with the degree of tacitness being a function of the extent to which the knowledge is or can be codified and abstracted. Knowledge may dynamically shift between tacit and explicit over time, although some knowledge always will remain tacit. Nonaka et al. (2000) have suggested that knowledge creation is a spiraling process of interactions between explicit and tacit knowledge. This spiraling process consists of socialization, externalization, combination and internalization, as we will see later in this chapter.

The concept of tacit knowledge corresponds closely to the concept of knowledge with a low level of codification. Codification is the degree to which knowledge is fully documented or expressed in writing at the time of transfer between two persons. The complexity of knowledge increases with lower levels of codification. A similar distinction which scholars frequently make is between practical, experience-based knowledge and the theoretical knowledge derived from reflection and abstraction from that experience.

A distinction is sometimes made between codification and personalization. This distinction is related to the tacit versus explicit concept. It involves an organization's approach to knowledge transfer. Companies using codification approaches rely primarily on repositories of explicit knowledge. Personalization approaches imply that the primary mode of knowledge transfer is direct interaction among people. Both are necessary in most organizations, but an increased focus on one approach or the other at any given time within a specific organization may be appropriate (Grover & Davenport, 2001).

Boland et al. (2001) studied knowledge representations and knowledge transfer. They found that interpretive knowledge representations were most successful in knowledge transfer for decision making. Interpretive representations can be both abstract and concrete, but they are always figurative rather than literal.

Explicit knowledge is sometimes called articulable knowledge (Hitt et al., 2001). Articulable knowledge can be codified and thus can be written and easily transferred. Tacit knowledge is not articulable and therefore cannot be easily transferred. Tacit knowledge is often embedded in uncodified routines and in a firm's social context. More specifically, it is partially embedded in individual skills and partially embedded in collaborative working relationships within the firm. Tacit knowledge is integral to professional skills. As a result, tacit knowledge is often unique, difficult to imitate and uncertain. It has a higher probability of creating strategic value than articulable knowledge.

Distinctions can be made between core, advanced and innovative knowledge. These knowledge categories indicate different levels of knowledge sophistication. Core knowledge is that minimum scope and level of knowledge required for daily operations, while advanced knowledge enables a firm to be competitively viable, and innovative knowledge is the knowledge that enables the firm to lead its industry and competitors:

- *Core knowledge* is the basic knowledge required to stay in business. This is the type of knowledge that can create efficiency barriers for entry of new companies, as new competitors are not up to speed in basic business processes. Since core knowledge is present at all existing competitors, the firm must have this knowledge even though it will provide the firm with no advantage that distinguishes it from its competitors. Core knowledge is that minimum scope and level of knowledge required just to play the game. Having that level of knowledge and capability will not assure the long-term competitive viability of the firm, but does present a basic industry knowledge barrier to entry. Core knowledge tends to be commonly held by members of an industry and therefore provides little advantage other than over nonmembers (Zack, 1999).

In a law firm, examples of core knowledge include knowledge of the law, knowledge of the courts, knowledge of clients and knowledge of procedures. For a student in the business school, core knowledge includes knowledge of what subjects to study this term and where the lectures take place.

According to Tiwana (2002), core knowledge is the basic level of knowledge required just to play the game. This is the type of knowledge that creates a barrier for entry of new companies. Since this level of knowledge is expected of all competitors, you must have it even though it will provide your company with no advantage that distinguishes it from its competitors. Let's take two examples: One from the consumer electronics (hard product) business and one from Internet programming (soft product). To enter the modem manufacturing market, a new company must have extensive knowledge of these aspects: a suitable circuit design, all electronic parts that go into a modem, fabricating surface mount (SMD) chip boards, how to write operating system drivers for modems, and familiarity with computer telephony standards. Similarly, a company developing Websites for, say, florists, needs server hosting capabilities, Internet programming skills, graphic design skills, clearly identified target markets, and necessary software. In either case, just about any competitors in those businesses are assumed to have this knowledge in order to compete in their respective markets; such essential knowledge therefore provides no advantage over other market players.

- *Advanced knowledge* is what makes the firm competitively visible and active. Such knowledge allows the firm to differentiate its products and services from that of a competitor through the application of superior knowledge in certain areas. Such knowledge allows the firm to compete head-on with its competitors in the same market and for the same set of customers. Advanced knowledge enables a firm to be competitively viable. The firm may have generally the same level, scope, or quality of knowledge as its competitors, although the specific knowledge content will often vary among competitors, enabling knowledge differentiation. Firms may choose to compete on knowledge head-on in the same strategic position, hoping to know more than a competitor. They instead may choose to compete for that position by differentiating their knowledge (Zack, 1999).

  In a law firm, examples of advanced knowledge include knowledge of law applications, knowledge of important court rulings and knowledge of successful procedural case handling. For a student in the business school, advanced knowledge includes knowledge of important articles and books that are compulsory literature in subjects this term.

According to Tiwana (2002), advanced knowledge is what makes your company competitively viable. Such knowledge allows your company to differentiate its product from that of a competitor, arguably, through the application of superior knowledge in certain areas. Such knowledge allows your company to compete head-on with its competitors in the same market and for the same set of customers. In the case of a company trying to compete in modem manufacturing markets, superior or user-friendly software or an additional capability in modems (such as warning online users of incoming telephone calls) represents such knowledge. In the case of a Website development firm, such knowledge might be about international flower markets and collaborative relationships in Dutch flower auctions that the company can use to improve Websites delivered to its customers.

- *Innovative knowledge* allows a firm to lead its entire industry to an extent that clearly differentiates it from competition. Such knowledge allows a firm to change the rules of the game by introducing new business practices. Such knowledge enables a firm to expand its market share by winning new customers and by increasing service levels to existing customers. Innovative knowledge is that knowledge that enables a firm to lead its industry and competitors and to significantly differentiate itself from its competitors. Innovative knowledge often enables a firm to change the rules of the game itself (Zack, 1999).

  In a law firm, examples of innovative knowledge include knowledge of standardizing repetitive legal cases, knowledge of successful settlements and knowledge of modern information technology to track and store vast amounts of information from various sources. For a student in the business school, innovative knowledge includes knowledge of important topics within subjects, links between subjects, typical exam questions and knowledge of business cases where theory can be applied.

  According to Tiwana (2002), innovative knowledge allows a company to lead its entire industry to an extent that clearly differentiates it from competition. Innovative knowledge allows a company to change the rules of the game. Patented technology is an applicable example of changing the rules. Innovative knowledge cannot always be protected by patents, as the lawsuit between Microsoft and Apple in the 1980s should serve to remind us. Apple sued Microsoft for copying the look and feel of its graphical user interface (GUI). The Supreme Court ruled that things like look and feel cannot be patented; they can only be copyrighted. Microsoft won the case, since it copied the look and feel but used entirely different code to create it in the first place.

Many more categories and dimensions of knowledge have been suggested by researchers. The problem with most of these classifications is that they do not seem to satisfy three important criteria for classification. The first requirement is that a classification should always be complete; there should be no category missing. The second requirement is that each category should be different from all other categories; there should be no overlap between categories. The final requirement is that each category should be at the same level; there should be no category including another category. Consider the following categories suggested by researchers: formal knowledge, instrumental knowledge, informal knowledge, tacit knowledge, meta-knowledge and context-independent knowledge. These categories seem to violate some of the classification rules. For example, there seems to be an overlap between informal knowledge and tacit knowledge. Maybe Long and Fahey's (2000) classification into human knowledge, social knowledge and structured knowledge satisfies our requirements:

- *Human knowledge.* This constitutes the know-what, know-how and know-why of individuals. Human knowledge is manifested in individual skills (e.g., how to interview law firm clients) or expertise (e.g., why this case is similar to a previous case). Individual knowledge usually combines explicit and tacit knowledge. This type of knowledge may be located in the body, such as knowing how to type touch on a PC or how to ride a bicycle. This type of knowledge may be cognitive; that is, largely conceptual and abstract.
- *Social knowledge.* This kind of knowledge exists only in relationships between individuals or within groups. For example, high-performing teams of tax lawyers share certain collective knowledge that is more than the sum of the individual knowledge of the team's members. Social or collective knowledge is mainly tacit knowledge, shared by team members, and develops only as a result of team members working together. Its presence is reflected by an ability to collaborate effectively.
- *Structured knowledge.* This is embedded in an organization's systems, processes, tools, routines and practices. Knowledge in this form is explicit and often rule-based. A key distinction between structured knowledge and the first two types of knowledge is that structured knowledge is assumed to exist independently of individual knowers. It is, instead, an organizational resource. However, to be complete, this knowledge has to be in the heads of individuals.

Two dimensions have been introduced to classify knowledge. The first dimension is concerned with whether an individual knows. The second dimension is concerned with whether an individual knows whether he or she knows. This is illustrated in Figure 3. I can either have the knowledge (I do know) or not have the knowledge (I don't know). I can either be aware of it (I know it) or not be aware of it (I don't know it).

Figure 3. Dimensions of Individual Knowledge

	I know it	I don't know it
I do know	I know that I know	I don't know that I know
I don't know	I know that I don't know	I don't know that I don't know

Some researchers have argued that the real tacit knowledge is found in the right upper quadrant. In this dimension, I do know, but I don't know that I know. Tacit knowledge in this sense is also called hidden knowledge or non-accessible knowledge. In this book, we do not use this extremely limited definition of tacit knowledge. We define tacit knowledge as personal and difficult, but not impossible, to communicate.

Classification of knowledge into categories and dimensions may depend on industry. For example, there are likely to be different knowledge categories in a bank compared to a law firm. At the same time, there will be certain generic knowledge categories such as market intelligence and technology understanding in most companies independently of industry. When classifying knowledge in a firm, it is important to do the analysis without the organization chart. If you classify knowledge into technology knowledge, production knowledge, marketing knowledge and financial knowledge, it may be because the firm according to the organization chart consists of a development department, production department, marketing department and financial department. It might be more useful to introduce new knowledge categories such as product knowledge, which includes knowledge of development, production, marketing and finance. By identifying cross-sectional knowledge categories and dimensions, solutions for improved knowledge flows in the organization will emerge.

A law firm is a good example. A law firm is organized according to legal disciplines. Some lawyers work in the tax department, while others work in the department for mergers and acquisitions. The types of knowledge involved in the practice of law can be categorized as administrative, declarative, procedural and analytical knowledge (Edwards & Mahling, 1997):

- *Administrative knowledge*, which includes all the nuts and bolts information about firm operations, such as hourly billing rates for lawyers, client names and matters, staff payroll data, and client invoice data.
- *Declarative knowledge*, which is knowledge of the law, the legal principles contained in statutes, court opinions and other sources of primary legal authority; law students spend most of their law school time acquiring this kind of knowledge.
- *Procedural knowledge*, which involves knowledge of the mechanisms of complying with the law's requirements in a particular situation: how documents are used to transfer an asset from Company A to Company B, or how forms must be filed to create a new corporation. Declarative knowledge is sometimes labeled know-that and know-what, while procedural knowledge is labeled know-how.
- *Analytical knowledge* that pertains to the conclusions reached about the course of action a particular client should follow in a particular situation. Analytical knowledge results, in essence, from analyzing declarative knowledge (i.e., substantive law principles) as it applies to a particular fact setting.

Classification of knowledge into categories and dimensions has important limitations. For example, the classification into explicit and tacit knowledge may create static views of knowledge. However, knowledge development and sharing are dynamic processes, and these dynamic processes cause tacit knowledge to become explicit, and explicit knowledge to become tacit over time. Tacit and explicit knowledge depend on each other, and they influence each other.

Alavari and Leidner (2001) suggest the existence of a shared knowledge space that is required in order for individual A to understand individual B's knowledge. The knowledge space is the underlying overlap in knowledge base of A and B. This overlap is typically tacit knowledge. For example, in a law firm, lawyers in the maritime law department may have a large knowledge space, so that even a very limited piece of explicit knowledge can be of great value to the lawyers. Alavi and Leidner (2001, p. 112) discuss knowledge space in the following way:

Whether tacit or explicit knowledge is the more valuable may indeed miss the point. The two are not dichotomous states of knowledge, but mutually dependent and reinforcing qualities of knowledge: tacit knowledge forms the background necessary for assigning the structure to develop and interpret explicit knowledge. The inextricable linkage of tacit and explicit knowledge suggests that only individuals with a requisite level of shared knowledge can truly exchange knowledge: if tacit knowledge is necessary to the understanding of explicit knowledge, then in order for Individual B to understand Individual A's knowledge, there must be some overlap in their underlying knowledge bases (a shared knowledge space). However, it is precisely in applying technology to increase 'weak ties' in organizations, and thereby increase the breadth of knowledge sharing, that IT holds promise. Yet, absent a shared knowledge space, the real impact of IT on knowledge exchange is questionable. This is a paradox that IT researchers have somewhat eschewed, and that organizational researchers have used to question the application of IT to knowledge management. To add to the paradox, the very essence of the knowledge management challenge is to amalgamate knowledge across groups for which IT can play a major role. What is most at issue is the amount of contextual information necessary for one person or group's knowledge to be readily understood by another.

It may be argued that the greater the shared knowledge space, the less the context needed for individuals to share knowledge within the group and, hence, the higher the value of explicit knowledge and the greater the value of IT applied to knowledge management. On the other hand, the smaller the existing shared knowledge space in a group, the greater the need for contextual information, the less relevant will be explicit knowledge, and hence the less applicable will be IT to knowledge management.

Some researchers are interested in the total knowledge within a company, while others are interested in individual knowledge. Dixon (2000) was interested in the knowledge that knowledge workers develop together in the organization. Employees gain this knowledge from doing the organization's tasks. This knowledge is called common knowledge to differentiate it from book knowledge or lists of regulations or databases of customer information. Some examples of common knowledge are what medical doctors in a hospital have learned about how to carry out certain kinds of surgery, what an organization has learned about how to introduce a new drug into the diabetes market, how to reduce cost on consulting projects, and how to control the amount of analysis in maritime law cases. These examples all include the how-to rather than the know-what of school learning. Moreover, it is know-how that is unique to a specific company. In the law firm example, procedural knowledge was classified as know-how.

The Knowledge-Strategy Link

The long learning lead-time (knowledge friction) highlights the importance of benchmarking and evaluating the strengths, weaknesses, opportunities and threats (SWOT) of an organization's current knowledge platform and position, as this knowledge provides the primary opportunity (and constraint) from which to compete and grow over the near-to-intermediate term. This must, in turn, be balanced against the organization's long-term plans for developing its knowledge platform (Zack, 1999).

The traditional SWOT framework, updated to reflect today's knowledge-intensive environment, provides a basis for describing a knowledge strategy. In essence, firms need to perform a knowledge-based SWOT analysis, mapping their knowledge resources and capabilities against their strategic opportunities and threats to better understand their points of advantage and weakness. They can use this map to strategically guide their knowledge management efforts, bolstering their knowledge advantages and reducing their knowledge weaknesses. Knowledge strategy, then, can be thought of as balancing knowledge-based resources and capabilities with the knowledge required for providing products or services in ways superior to those of competitors. Identifying which knowledge-based resources and capabilities are valuable, unique, and inimitable as well as how those resources and capabilities support the firm's product and market positions are essential elements of a knowledge strategy (Zack, 1999).

To explicate the link between strategy and knowledge, an organization must articulate its strategic intent, identify the knowledge required to execute its intended strategy, and compare that to its actual knowledge, thus revealing its strategic knowledge gaps (Zack, 1999).

Every firm competes in a particular way — operating within some industry and adopting competitive position within that industry. Competitive strategy may result from an explicit grand decision — the traditional perspective on strategy — or from an accumulation of smaller incremental decisions. It may even be revealed in hindsight, by looking back on actual behaviors and events over time. Regardless of the strategy formation process, organizations have a de facto strategy that must first be articulated (Zack, 1999).

Every strategic position is linked to some set of intellectual resources and capabilities. That is, given what the firm believes it must do to compete, there are some things it must know and know how to do. The strategic choices that companies make — regarding technologies, products, services, markets, and processes — have a profound influence on the knowledge, skills, and core competencies required to compete and excel in an industry (Zack, 1999).

On the other hand, what a firm does know and knows how to do limits the ways it can actually compete. The firm, given what it knows, must identify the best product and market opportunities for exploiting that knowledge. The firm's existing knowledge creates an opportunity and a constraint on selecting viable competitive positions, while the firm's selected competitive position creates a knowledge requirement. Success requires dynamically aligning knowledge-based requirements and capabilities (Zack, 1999).

Assessing an organization's knowledge position requires cataloging its existing intellectual resources by creating what is commonly called a knowledge map. Knowledge can be characterized in many ways. Popular taxonomies distinguish between tacit and explicit knowledge, general and situated context-specific knowledge, and individual and collective knowledge. Knowledge can also be categorized by type, including declarative (knowledge about), procedural (know-how), causal (know-why), conditional (know when), and relational (know-with). While these distinctions are useful for mapping and managing knowledge at the process level once a knowledge strategy has been formulated, our purpose requires a knowledge taxonomy oriented towards strategy and which reflects the competitive uniqueness of each organization (Zack, 1999).

Categorizing or describing what a business firm knows and must know about its industry or competitive position is not easy. Although firms within particular industries, firms maintaining similar competitive positions, or those employing similar technologies and other resources often share some common knowledge, there are no simple answers regarding what a firm must know to be competitive — if there were, then there would be no sustainable advantage (Zack, 1999).

A typical company develops an approach to describing and classifying its strategic or competitive knowledge that is in some ways unique. In fact, each firm's general awareness of and orientation to the link between knowledge and strategy tends to be somewhat unique and may, itself, represent an advantage. Regardless of how knowledge is categorized based on content, every firm's strategic knowledge can be categorized by its ability to support a competitive position. Specifically, knowledge can be classified according to whether it is core, advanced, or innovative (Zack, 1999).

Knowledge is not static and what is innovative knowledge today will ultimately become the core knowledge of tomorrow. Thus defending and growing a competitive position requires continual learning and knowledge acquisition. The ability of an organization to learn, accumulate knowledge from its experiences, and reapply that knowledge is itself a skill or competence that — beyond the core competencies directly related to delivering its product or service — may provide strategic advantage (Zack, 1999).

Although knowledge is dynamic, the strategic knowledge framework in Figure 4 does offer the ability to take a snapshot of where the firm is today vis-à-vis its desired strategic knowledge profile (to assess its external knowledge gaps). Additionally, it can be used to plot the historical path and future trajectory of the firm's knowledge. The framework may be applied by area of competency or, taking a more traditional strategic perspective, by strategic business unit, division, product line, function, or market position. Regardless of the particular way each firm categorizes its knowledge, each category can be further broken down into elements that are core, competitive, or innovative to produce a strategic knowledge map (Zack, 1999).

Having mapped the firm's competitive knowledge position, an organization can perform a gap analysis. The gap between what a firm must do to compete and what it actually is doing represents a strategic gap. Addressing this gap is the

Figure 4. Strategic Knowledge Framework

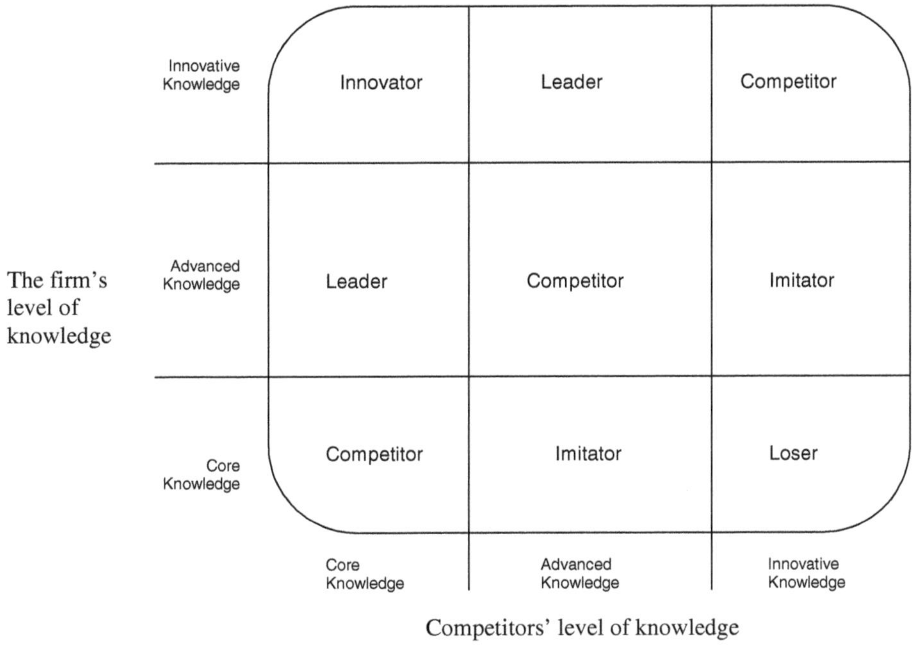

stuff of traditional strategic management. As suggested by the SWOT framework, strengths and weaknesses represent what the firm can do; opportunities and threats dictate what it must do. Strategy, then, represents how the firm balances its competitive cans and musts to develop and protect its strategic niche (Zack, 1999).

At the same time, underlying a firm's strategic gap is a potential knowledge gap. That is, given a gap between what a firm must do to compete and what it can do, there may also be a gap between what the firm must know to execute its strategy and what it does know. Based on a strategic knowledge and capabilities map, an organization can identify the extent to which its various categories of existing knowledge are in alignment with its strategic requirements. The result is a set of potential knowledge gaps. In some cases, an organization might even know more than needed to support its competitive position. Nevertheless, a knowledge strategy must address any possible misalignments. The greater the number, variety, or size of the current and future knowledge gaps, and the more volatile the knowledge base because of a dynamic or uncertain competitive environment, the more aggressive the knowledge strategy required. A firm not capable of executing its intended or required strategy must either align its strategy with its capabilities or acquire the capabilities to execute its strategy (Zack, 1999).

Figure 5. Knowledge Gap Derived From and Aligned with Strategic Business Gap

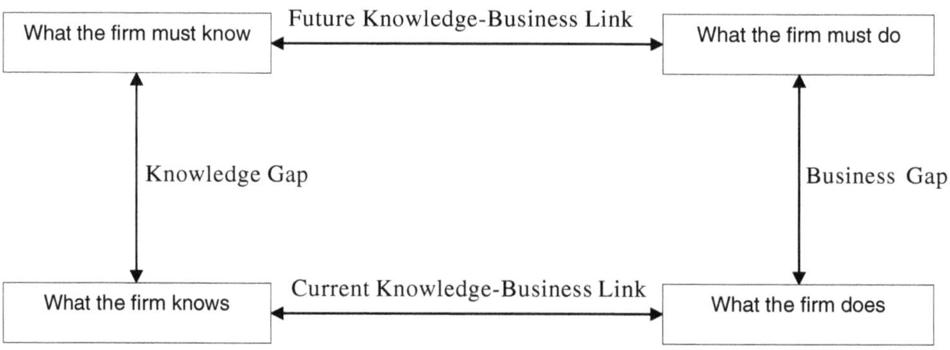

Having performed a strategic evaluation of its knowledge-based resources and capabilities, an organization can determine which knowledge should be developed or acquired. To give knowledge management a strategic focus, the firm's knowledge management initiatives should be directed toward closing this strategic knowledge gap. The important issue is that the knowledge gap is directly derived from and aligned with the strategic gap, as illustrated in Figure 5. This simultaneous alignment of strategy and knowledge is a crucial element of a firm's knowledge strategy. In many firms, knowledge management efforts are divorced from strategic planning and execution. However, having an appropriate knowledge strategy in place is essential for assuring that knowledge management efforts are being driven by and are supporting the firm's competitive strategy (Zack, 1999).

VALUE CONFIGURATIONS FOR BUSINESS ORGANIZATIONS

To comprehend the value that information technology provides to organizations, we must first understand the way a particular organization conducts business and how information systems affect the performance of various component activities within the organization. Understanding how firms differ is a central challenge for both theory and practice of management. For a long time, Porter's (1985) value chain was the only value configuration known to managers. Stabell and Fjeldstad (1998) have identified two alternative value configurations. A value shop schedules activities and applies resources in a fashion that is dimensioned and appropriate to the needs of the client's problem, while a value chain performs a fixed set of activities that enables it to produce a standard product in large numbers. Examples of value shops are professional service firms, as found in medicine, law, architecture and engineering. A value network links clients or customers who are or wish to be interdependent. Examples of value networks are telephone companies, retail banks and insurance companies.

A value configuration describes how value is created in a company for its customers. A value configuration shows how the most important business processes function to create value for customers. A value configuration represents the way a particular organization conducts business.

The Firm as a Value Chain

The best-known value configuration is the value chain. In the value chain, value is created through efficient production of goods and services based on a variety of resources. The company is perceived as a series or chain of activities. Primary activities in the value chain include inbound logistics, production, outbound logistics, marketing and sales, and service. Support activities include infrastructure, human resources, technology development and procurement. Attention is on performing these activities in the chain in efficient and effective ways. In Figure 6, examples of IS/IT are assigned to primary and support activities. This figure can be used to describe the current IS/IT situation in the organization as it illustrates the extent of coverage of IS/IT for each activity.

The knowledge intensity of systems in the different activities can be illustrated by different shading, where dark shading indicates high knowledge intensity. In this example, it is assumed that the most knowledge intensive activities are computer aided design and customer relationship management.

Figure 6. Examples of IS/IT in the Value Chain

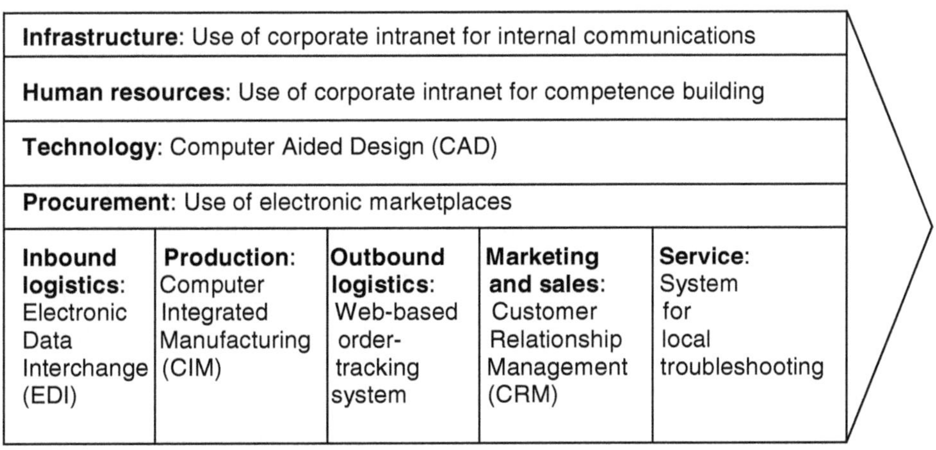

The Firm as a Value Shop

Value cannot only be created in value chains. Value can also be created in two alternative value configurations: value shop and value network (Stabell & Fjeldstad, 1998). In the value shop, activities are scheduled and resources are applied in a fashion that is dimensioned and appropriate to the needs of the client's problem, while a value chain performs a fixed set of activities that enables it to produce a standard product in large numbers. The value shop is a company that creates value by solving unique problems for customers and clients. Knowledge is the most important resource, and reputation is critical to firm success.

While typical examples of value chains are manufacturing industries such as paper and car production, typical examples of value shops are law firms and medical hospitals. Often, such companies are called professional service firms or knowledge-intensive service firms. Like the medical hospital as a way to practice medicine, the law firm provides a standard format for delivering complex legal services. Many features of its style — specialization, teamwork, continuous monitoring on behalf of clients (patients), and representation in many forums — have been emulated in other vehicles for delivering professional services (Galanter & Palay, 1991).

Knowledge-intensive service firms are typical value shops. Sheehan (2002) defines knowledge-intensive service firms as entities that sell problem-solving services, in which the solution chosen by the expert is based on real-time feedback from the client. Clients retain knowledge-intensive service firms to reduce their uncertainty. Clients hire knowledge-intensive service firms precisely because the client believes the firm knows something that the client does not and believes it is necessary to solve their problems.

While expertise plays a role in all firms, its role is distinctive in knowledge-intensive service firms. Expert, often professional, knowledge is at the core of the service provided by the type of firm.

Knowledge-intensive service firms not only sell a problem-solving service, but equally a problem-finding, problem-defining, solution-execution, and monitoring service. Problem finding is often a key for acquiring new clients. Once the client is acquired and their problem is defined, not all problems will be solved by the firm. Rather, the firm may only clarify that there is no problem (i.e., the patient does not have a heart condition) or that the problem should be referred to another specialist (i.e., the patient needs a heart specialist). If a problem is treated within the firm, then the firm needs to follow up on the implementation to ensure that the problem in fact has been solved (i.e., is the patient's heart now working properly?). This follows from the fact that there is often uncertainty in both problem diagnosis and problem resolution.

Sheehan (2002) has created a typology of knowledge-intensive service firms consisting of the following three types. First, knowledge-intensive search firms search for opportunities. The amount of value they create depends on the size of the finding or discovery, where size is measured by quality rather than quantity. Examples of search firms include petroleum and mineral exploration, drug discovery in the pharmaceutical industry, and research in the biotechnology industry. Second, knowledge-intensive diagnosis firms create value by clarifying problems. Once the problem has been identified, the suggested remedy usually follows directly. Examples of diagnosis firms include doctors, surgeons, psychotherapists, veterinarians, lawyers, auditors and tax accountants, and software support. Finally, knowledge-intensive design firms create value by conceiving new ways of constructing material or immaterial artifacts. Examples of design firms include architecture, advertising, research and development, engineering design, and strategy consulting.

Knowledge-intensive service firms create value through problem acquisition and definition, alternative generation and selection, implementation of an alternative, and follow up to see if the solution selected resolves the problem. To reflect this process, Stabell and Fjeldstad (1998) have outlined the value configuration of a value shop.

A value shop is characterized by five primary activities: problem finding and acquisition, problem-solving, choice, execution, and control and evaluation, as

Figure 7. Examples of IS/IT in the Value Shop

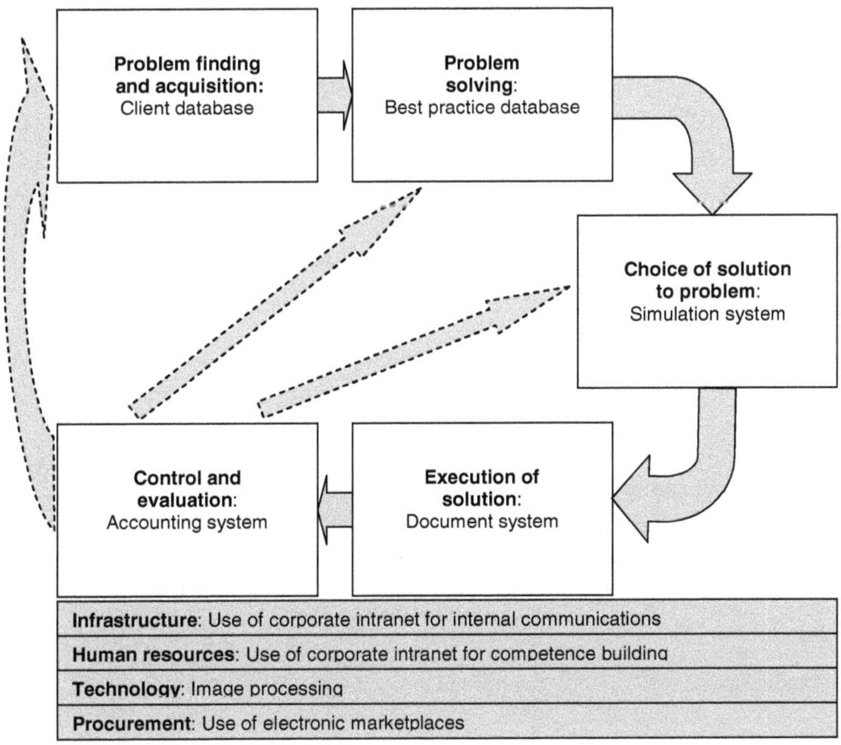

illustrated in Figure 7. Problem finding and acquisition involves working with the customer to determine the exact nature of the problem or need. It involves deciding on the overall plan of approaching the problem. Problem-solving is the actual generation of ideas and action (or treatment) plans.

Choice represents the decision of choosing between alternatives. While the least important primary activity of the value shop in terms of time and effort, it is also the most important in terms of customer value. Execution represents communicating, organizing, and implementing the decision, or performing the treatment. Control and evaluation activities involve monitoring and measurement of how well the solution solved the original problem or met the original need.

This may feed back into the first activity, problem finding and acquisition, for two reasons. First, if the proposed solution is inadequate or did not work, it feeds back into learning why it was inadequate and begins the problem-solving phase anew. Second, if the problem solution was successful, the firm might enlarge the scope of the problem-solving process to solve a bigger problem related to or dependent upon the first problem being solved (Affuah & Tucci, 2001).

Figure 7 can be used to identify current IS/IT in the organization. We let a law firm serve as an example in Figure 8. Within each of the five activities, there are many tasks in a law firm. For each task, there may be IS/IT support. For example, problem-solving may consist of the two tasks of case analysis and reference search. Lawyers will be eager to discuss the case and to search for more information on similar cases. A system for case-based reasoning may be installed, in which the current case can be compared to similar cases handled by the law firm. Also, intelligent search engines with a thesaurus may be available in the law firm to find relevant information on the Internet and in legal databases.

A law firm can be defined as a value shop. The value creation logic is problem-solving by the change from an existing to a more desired state. There are five generic categories of primary value shop activities: Problem-finding, problem-solving, choice, execution, control and evaluation.

Figure 8. Examples of IS/IT in the Value Shop

Activities	**Tasks**	**IS/IT**
Problem finding and acquisition	Register client information	Financial system
	Register case information	Case database
Problem-solving	Do case analysis	Case-based reasoning
	Do reference search	Library search engine
Choice	Evaluate alternatives	Case-based reasoning
	Make recommendation to client	Office systems
Execution	Participate at meetings	Office systems
	Revise recommendation	Office systems
Control and evaluation	Register recommendation	Case database
	Check client satisfaction	Financial system

Figure 9. Benefits in Value Shop Activities

Value Shop Activity	Score	Interpretation
Problem-finding	3.2	No benefits
Problem-solving	5.6	Some benefits
Choice	5.6	Some benefits
Execution	4.4	No benefits
Control and evaluation	5.1	Some benefits

Note: The Likert scale went from 1 to 9

Information technology facilitating interorganizational knowledge networks may be important in all five value shop activities. The study in 2001 involved a questionnaire to Eurojuris law firms on benefits from IT in the Eurojuris law firm network (Gottschalk 2001). Figure 9 lists results for all five value shop activities. The scale went from 1 (completely disagree) to 9 (completely agree). The average number on this scale is 5, so we can interpret responses in such a way that benefits are reported if the score is higher than 5. Responding Eurojuris law firms report some IT network benefits in the activities of choice, execution, and control and evaluation.

The questionnaire did also ask for benefits depending on knowledge category and knowledge level. Knowledge categories are administrative, declarative, procedural and analytical knowledge. Knowledge levels are core, advanced and innovative knowledge. From the tables in Figures 10 and 11 we see

Figure 10. Benefits for Knowledge Categories

Knowledge Category	Score	Interpretation
Administrative knowledge	3.3	No benefits
Declarative knowledge	4.9	No benefits
Procedural knowledge	3.6	No benefits
Analytical knowledge	4.0	No benefits

Note: The Likert scale went from 1 to 9

Figure 11. Benefits for Knowledge Levels

Knowledge Level	Score	Interpretation
Core knowledge	3.3	No benefits
Advanced knowledge	5.4	Some benefits
Innovative knowledge	3.8	No benefits

Note: The Likert scale went from 1 to 9

that the only case of benefits is related to advanced knowledge. If we link results from the two tables, we can assume that benefits are associated with advanced declarative knowledge, as declarative knowledge achieved the highest score among knowledge categories.

When we combine all results from this survey, we may find that benefits are associated with advanced declarative knowledge applied in the problem-solving and choice activities. If this interpretation is correct, Eurojuris law firms should in the future use IT applications that support advanced declarative knowledge in problem-solving and choice in their interorganizational knowledge network.

Knowledge-intensive service firms are typical value shops, and such firms depend on reputation for success, as reputation is a key driver of firm value creation. Reputation is a relational concept, in the sense that firms are judged by their stakeholders relative to their competitors. Reputation is what is generally said or believed about an entity by someone; it is the net perception of a firm held by stakeholders judged relative to other firms. According to Sheehan (2002), there are four conditions that must be present for reputation to work. Firstly, rents earned from maintaining a good reputation must be greater than not. Secondly, there must be a minimum of contact among stakeholders to allow for the changes in reputation to be communicated. Thirdly, there needs to be a possibility of repeat business. And lastly, there must be some uncertainty regarding the firm's type and/or behavior.

Reputation is related to the asymmetry of information, which is a typical feature of knowledge-intensive service firms. Asymmetry is present when clients believe the firm knows something that the clients do not and believe it is necessary to know to solve their problems.

Reputation can be classified as a strategic resource in knowledge-intensive firms. To be a strategic resource, it has to be valuable, rare, costly to imitate, and possible to organize. Reputation is valuable, as it increases the value received by the client. Reputation is rare, as by definition only a few firms can be considered best in the industry. Reputation is costly to imitate, as it is difficult to build a reputation in the short run. Reputation is possible to organize in the general sense of controllability, which implies that a firm can be organized to take advantage of reputation as a resource.

The Firm as a Value Network

The third and final value configuration is the value network. A value network is a company that creates value by connecting clients and customers that are, or want to be, dependent on each other. These companies distribute information, money, products and services. While activities in both value chains and value shops are done sequentially, activities in value networks occur in parallel. The number and combination of customers and access points in the network are important value drivers in the value network. More customers and more connections create higher value to customers.

Stabell and Fjeldstad (1998) suggest that managing a value network can be compared to managing a club. The mediating firm admits members that complement each other, and in some cases exclude those that do not. The firm establishes, monitors, and terminates direct or indirect relationships among members. Supplier-customer relationships may exist between the members of the club, but to the mediating firm they are all customers.

Examples of value networks include telecommunication companies, financial institutions such as banks and insurance companies, and stockbrokers. Value networks perform three activities (see Figure 12):

- Development of customer network through marketing and recruiting of new customers, to enable increased value for both existing customers and new customers.
- Development of new services and improvement in existing services.
- Development of infrastructure so that customer services can be provided more efficiently and effectively.

The current IS/IT situation in a value network will mainly be described through the infrastructure that typically will consist of information technology. In addition, many of the new services may be information systems that will be used

Figure 12. Examples of IS/IT in the Value Network

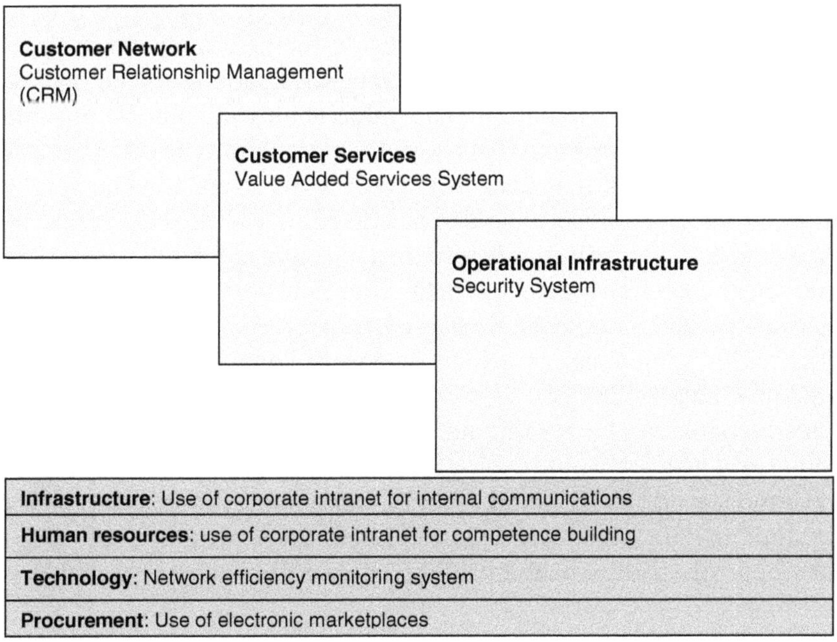

Figure 13. Characteristics of Value Configurations

Characteristics	Value Chain	Value Shop	Value Network
Value creation	Transformation of input to output	Solving clients' and customers' problems	Connecting clients and customers to each other
Work form	Sequential production	Integrated and cyclical problem-solving	Monitored and simultaneous connections
Information systems	Making production more efficient	Adding value to the knowledge work	Main value by use of IT infrastructure
Example	Paper factory	Law firm	Telecom company

by customers in their communication and business transactions with other customers. The knowledge component will mainly be found in the services of a value network, as information systems are made available to customers to exchange relevant information.

Comparison of Value Configurations

Value chain, value shop and value network are alternative value configurations that impact the use of information technology in the company, as illustrated in Figure 13. While the role of IT is to make production more efficient in a value chain, IT creates added value in the value shop, while IT in the form of infrastructure is the main value in the value network. Some companies have more than one value configuration, but most companies have one dominating configuration.

In the long term, business organizations can choose to change their value configurations. A bank, for example, can be a value shop when it focuses on converting inputs to outputs. The value resides in the output and once you have the output, you can remove the production organization. This removal does not impact on the value of the output. The value shop is a solution provider. It is somebody that solves problems. The input is a problem. The output is a solution to the problem. A bank that does this would view itself as a financial service operator, a financial advisor that also has the ability to provide the money. But what it would do is identify client problems, it would address those problems, and it would select a solution together with the client and help to implement it. It would have stringent quality controls. As part of its offering, it would probably supply the client with some cash as a loan or accept some of the client's cash for investment (Chatzkel, 2002).

Or, the bank can be a value network, which is basically the logic of the marketplace. The bank would define its role as a conduit between people that do not have money and those people that do have money. What the bank does is arrange the flow of cash between them. The bank will attract people with money to make deposits and investments. The bank will also attract people without money to make loans. As a value network, the bank will connect people with opposite financial needs. The network consists of people with different financial needs. Over time, persons in the network may change status from one in need of money to money provider and vice versa (Chatzkel, 2002).

Both as a value shop and as a value network, the business organization can be identified as a bank. But it would have completely different consequences for what it will focus on doing well, what it will focus on doing itself, versus what it would not want to do itself. This provides a kind of strategic systems logic. It asks, "Which strategic system in terms of value configuration are we going to operate in?" Choosing an appropriate value configuration is a long-term decision with long-term consequences.

CASE STUDY: NOKIA

Nokia Telecommunications has adopted a knowledge management business strategy to move the organization from a hierarchical structure to a network-based learning organization. The company believes that success in global terms will be derived from:

- Global efficiency and effectiveness.
- Learning across organizational boundaries.
- Local flexibility and responsiveness.

Ms. Kaisa Kautto-Koivula was appointed Head of Knowledge Management Development in 1996. She is responsible for establishing the basic concepts and strategies and has initiated some of the first knowledge management solutions in Nokia.

Ms. Kautto-Koivula says: "The value of knowledge management to Nokia was demonstrated by appointing me to the position of Head of Knowledge Management Development." Following her appointment, Nokia conducted a survey of knowledge management within the business to discover areas of best practice. This was followed by workshops and creating a knowledge management map to aid senior managers in understanding the benefits of pursuing a KM strategy.

Nokia's lessons learned include taking small steps and integrating them with other organizational activities and programs; not falling into the trap that knowledge management is an advanced form of information technology; and addressing the human aspects of change, work activities and reward and recognition.

Nokia has emphasized the role of knowledge management in global success. Ilkka Tuomi, the chief researcher of Nokia Research Centre, states that knowledge creation, supply, and utilization are the most essential tasks in modern business world. Out of all information, Tuomi regards tacit (implicit) information as the most important one. In order to reach a global success, Nokia was forced to manage with the explosive increase of knowledge intensity. Thus it was extremely important to coordinate all the factors that are associated with knowledge management; that means personnel, information systems, strategy, quality, and process developers.

Furthermore, Tuomi says that the theory of knowledge management provides Nokia with new ideas about future organizations and their nature of activities. This is very essential because successful new product development is based on strict prioritization of pilot projects, which are used to test future visions. In fact, Nokia does not predict the future but create knowledge that can be used to understand it when it is present.

Sources: www.mjm.co.uk, www.uwasa.fi

Chapter III

IS/IT in Knowledge Management

INTRODUCTION

As we trace the evolution of computing technologies in business, we can observe their changing level of organizational impact. The first level of impact was at the point where work got done and transactions (e.g., orders, deposits, reservations) took place. The inflexible, centralized mainframe allowed for little more than massive number crunching, commonly known as electronic *data* processing. Organizations became data heavy at the bottom and data management systems were used to keep the data in check. Later, the management *information* systems were used to aggregate data into useful information reports, often prescheduled, for the control level of the organization – people who were making sure that organizational resources like personnel, money, and physical goods were being deployed efficiently. As information technology (IT) and information systems (IS) started to facilitate data and information overflow, and corporate attention became a scarce resource, the concept of *knowledge* emerged as a particularly high-value form of information (Grover & Davenport, 2001).

Information technology can play an important role in successful knowledge management initiatives. However, the concept of coding and transmitting knowledge in organizations is not new: training and employee development programs, organizational policies, routines, procedures, reports, and manuals have served this function for many years. What is new and exciting in the knowledge management area is the potential for using modern information technology (e.g., the Internet, intranets, extranets, browsers, data warehouses, data filters, software agents, expert systems) to support knowledge creation, sharing and exchange in an organization and between organizations. Modern information technology can collect, systematize, structure, store, combine, distribute and present information of value to knowledge workers (Nahapiet & Ghoshal, 1998).

According to Davenport and Prusak (1998), more and more companies have instituted knowledge repositories, supporting such diverse types of knowledge as best practices, lessons learned, product development knowledge, customer knowledge, human resource management knowledge, and methods-based knowledge. Groupware and intranet-based technologies have become standard knowledge infrastructures. A new set of professional job titles — the knowledge manager, the chief knowledge officer (CKO), the knowledge coordinator, and the knowledge-network facilitator — affirms the widespread legitimacy that knowledge management has earned in the corporate world.

The low cost of computers and networks has created a potential infrastructure for knowledge sharing and opened up important knowledge management opportunities. The computational power as such has little relevance to knowledge work, but the communication and storage capabilities of networked computers make it an important enabler of effective knowledge work. Through email, groupware, the Internet, and intranets, computers and networks can point to people with knowledge and connect people who need to share knowledge independent of time and place.

According to Grover and Davenport (2001), most knowledge management projects in organizations involve the use of information technology. Such projects fall into relatively few categories and types, each of which has a key objective. Although it is possible, and even desirable, to combine multiple objectives in a single project, this was not normally observed in a study of 31 knowledge management projects in 1997 (Davenport & Prusak, 1998). Since that time, it is possible that projects have matured and have taken on more ambitious collections of objectives.

Regardless of definition of knowledge as the highest value of content in a continuum starting at data, encompassing information, and ending at knowledge, knowledge managers often take a highly inclusive approach to the content with which they deal. In practice, what companies actually manage under the banner of knowledge management is a mix of knowledge, information, and unrefined data — in short, whatever anyone finds that is useful and easy to store in an electronic repository. In the case of data and information, however, there are often attempts to add more value and create knowledge. This transformation might involve the addition of insight, experience, context, interpretation, or the myriad of other activities in which human brains specialize (Grover & Davenport, 2001).

Identifying, nurturing and harvesting knowledge is a principal concern in the information society and the knowledge age. Effective use of knowledge-facilitating tools and techniques is critical, and a number of computational tools have been developed. While numerous techniques are available, it remains difficult to analyze or compare the specific tools. In part, this is because knowledge management is a young discipline. The arena is evolving rapidly as more people enter the fray and encounter new problems (Housel & Bell, 2001).

In addition, new technologies support applications that were impossible before. Moreover, the multidisciplinary character of knowledge management combines several disciplines, including business and management, computer science, cybernetics, and philosophy. Each of these fields may lay claim to the study of knowledge management, and the field is frequently defined so broadly that anything can be incorporated. Finally, it is difficult to make sense of the many tools available. It is not difficult to perform a search to produce a list of more than one hundred software providers. Each of the software packages employs unique visions and aims to capture its share of the market (Housel & Bell, 2001).

Ward and Peppard (2002) find that there are two dominant and contrasting views of IS/IT in knowledge management: the engineering perspective and the social process perspective. The engineering perspective views knowledge management as a technology process. Many organizations have taken this approach in managing knowledge, believing that it is concerned with managing pieces of intellectual capital. Driving this view is the view that knowledge can be codified and stored; in essence, that knowledge is explicit knowledge and therefore is little more than information.

The alternative view is that knowledge is a social process. As such, it asserts that knowledge resides in people's heads and that it is tacit. As such, it cannot be easily codified and is only revealed through its application. As tacit knowledge cannot be directly transferred from person to person, its acquisition occurs only through practice. Consequently, its transfer between people is slow, costly and uncertain. Technology, within this perspective, can only support the context of knowledge work. It has been argued that IT-based systems used to support knowledge management can only be of benefit if used to support the development and communication of human meaning. One reason for the failure of IT in some knowledge management initiatives is that the designers of the knowledge management systems fail to understand the situation and work practices of the users and the complex human processes involved in work.

While technology can be used with knowledge management initiatives, Ward and Peppard (2002) argue that it should never be the first step. Knowledge management is to them primarily a human and process issue. Once these two aspects have been addressed, then the created processes are usually very amenable to being supported and enhanced by the use of technology.

What, then, is knowledge management technology? According to Davenport and Prusak (1998), the concept of knowledge management technology is not only broad but also a bit slippery to define. Some infrastructure technology that we do not ordinarily think of in this category can be useful in facilitating knowledge management. Examples are videoconferencing and the telephone. Both of these technologies do not capture or distribute structured knowledge, but they are quite effective at enabling people to transfer tacit knowledge.

Our focus here, however, is on technology that captures, stores, and distributes structured knowledge for use by people. The goal of these technologies is to take knowledge that exists in human heads and partly in paper documents, and make it widely available throughout an organization. Similarly, Alavi and Leidner (2001) argue that information systems designed to support knowledge in organizations may not appear radically different from other forms of IT support, but will be geared toward enabling users to assign meaning to information and to capture some of their knowledge in information. Therefore, the concept of knowledge management technology in this book is less concerned with any degree of technology sophistication and more concerned with the usefulness in performing knowledge work in organizations and between organizations.

Moffett and McAdam (2003) illustrate the variety of knowledge management technology tools by distinguishing between collaborative tools, content management and business intelligence. Collaborative tools include groupware technology, meeting support systems, knowledge directories, and intranets/extranets. Content management includes the Internet, agents and filters, electronic publishing systems, document management systems, and office automation systems. Business intelligence includes data warehousing, decision support systems, knowledge-based systems and workflow systems.

KNOWLEDGE MANAGEMENT PROCESSES

Alavi and Leidner (2001) have developed a systematic framework that will be used to analyze and discuss the potential role of information technology in knowledge management. According to this framework, organizations consist of four sets of socially enacted knowledge processes: (1) creation (also referred to as construction), (2) storage and retrieval, (3) transfer, and (4) application. The knowledge-based view of the firm represents here both the cognitive and social nature of organizational knowledge and its embodiment in the individual's cognition and practices as well as the collective (i.e., organizational) practices and culture. These processes do not represent a monolithic set of activities, but an interconnected and intertwined set of activities.

Knowledge Creation

Organizational knowledge creation involves developing new content or replacing existing content within the organization's tacit and explicit knowledge. Through social and collaborative processes as well as individuals' cognitive processes (e.g., reflection), knowledge is created. The model developed by Nonaka et al. (2001) involving SECI, *ba* and knowledge assets, views organizational knowledge creation as involving a continual interplay between the tacit and explicit dimensions of knowledge and a growing spiral flow as knowledge moves through individual, group, and organizational levels. Four modes of knowledge creation have been identified: socialization, externalization, internalization and combination.

Nonaka et al. (2001) suggest that the essential question of knowledge creation is establishing an organization's *ba,* defined as a common place or space for creating knowledge. Four types of *ba* corresponding to the four modes of knowledge creation are identified: (1) originating *ba*, (2) interacting *ba*, (3) cyber *ba*, and (4) exercising *ba*. Originating *ba* entails the socialization mode of knowledge creation and is the *ba* from which the organizational knowledge creation process begins. Originating *ba* is a common place in which individuals share experiences primarily through face-to-face interactions and by being at the same place at the same time. Interacting *ba* is associated with the externalization mode of knowledge creation and refers to a space where tacit knowledge is converted to explicit knowledge and shared among individuals through the process of dialogue and collaboration. Cyber *ba* refers to a virtual space of interaction and corresponds to the combination mode of knowledge creation. Finally, exercising *ba* involves the conversion of explicit to tacit knowledge through the internalization process. Understanding the characteristics of various *ba* and the relationship with the modes of knowledge creation is important to enhancing organizational knowledge creation. For example, the use of IT capabilities in cyber *ba* is advocated to enhance the efficiency of the combination mode of knowledge creation. Data warehousing and data mining, document management systems, software agents and intranets may be of great value in cyber *ba.* Considering the flexibility of modern IT, other forms of organizational *ba* and the corresponding modes of knowledge creation can be enhanced through the use of various forms of information systems. For example, information systems designed for support or collaboration, coordination, and communication processes, as a component of the interacting *ba*, can facilitate teamwork and thereby increase an individual's contact with other individuals.

Electronic mail and group support systems have the potential of increasing the number of weak ties in organizations. This in turn can accelerate the growth of knowledge creation. Intranets enable exposure to greater amounts of online organizational information, both horizontally and vertically, than may previously have been the case. As the level of information exposure increases, the internalization mode of knowledge creation, wherein individuals make observations and interpretations of information that result in new individual tacit knowledge, may increase. In this role, an intranet can support individual learning (conversion of explicit knowledge to personal tacit knowledge) through provision of capabilities such as computer simulation (to support learning-by-doing) and smart software tutors.

Computer-mediated communication may increase the quality of knowledge creation by enabling a forum for constructing and sharing beliefs, for confirming consensual interpretation, and for allowing expression of new ideas. By providing an extended field of interaction among organizational members for sharing ideas and perspectives, and for establishing dialog, information systems may enable individuals to arrive at new insights and/or more accurate interpretations than if left to decipher information on their own.

Although most information repositories serve a single function, it is increasingly common for companies to construct an internal "portal" so that employees can access multiple different repositories and sources from one screen. It is also possible and increasingly popular for repositories to contain not only information, but also pointers to experts within the organization on key knowledge topics. It is also feasible to combine stored information with lists of the individuals who contributed the knowledge and who could provide more detail or background on it (Grover & Davenport, 2001).

According to Grover and Davenport (2001), firms increasingly view attempts to transform raw data into usable knowledge as part of their knowledge management initiatives. These approaches typically involve isolating data in a separate "warehouse" for easier access and the use of statistical analysis or data mining and visualization tools. Since their goal is to create data-derived knowledge, they are increasingly addressed as a part of knowledge management. Some vendors have already begun to introduce e-commerce tools. They serve to customize the menu of available knowledge to individual customers, allowing sampling of information before buying and carrying out sales transactions for knowledge purchases. Online legal services are typical examples in which clients can sample legal information before buying a lawyer's time.

For knowledge creation, there is currently *idea-generation software* emerging. Idea-generation software is designed to help stimulate a single user or a group to produce new ideas, options, and choices. The user does all the work, but the software encourages and pushes, something like a personal trainer. Although idea-generation software is relatively new, there are several packages on the market. IdeaFisher, for example, has an associative lexicon of the English language that cross-references words and phrases. These associative links, based on analogies and metaphors, make it easy for the user to be fed words related to a given theme. Some software packages use questions to prompt the user toward new, unexplored patterns of thought. This helps users to break out of cyclical thinking patterns and conquer mental blocks (Turban et al., 2003).

Knowledge Storage and Retrieval

According to Alavi and Leidner (2001), empirical studies have shown that while organizations create knowledge and learn, they also forget (i.e., do not remember or lose track of the acquired knowledge). Thus, the storage, organization, and retrieval of organizational knowledge, also referred to as organizational memory, constitute an important aspect of effective organizational knowledge management. Organizational memory includes knowledge residing in various component forms, including written documentation, structured information stored in electronic databases, codified human knowledge stored in expert systems, documented organizational procedures and processes and tacit knowledge acquired by individuals and networks of individuals.

Advanced computer storage technology and sophisticated retrieval techniques, such as query languages, multimedia databases, and database management systems, can be effective tools in enhancing organizational memory. These tools increase the speed at which organizational memory can be accessed.

Groupware enables organizations to create intraorganizational memory in the form of both structured and unstructured information and to share this memory across time and space. IT can play an important role in the enhancement and expansion of both semantic and episodic organizational memory. Semantic memory refers to general, explicit and articulated knowledge, whereas episodic memory refers to context-specific and situated knowledge. Document management technology allows knowledge of an organization's past, often dispersed among a variety of retention facilities, to be effectively stored and made accessible. Drawing on these technologies, most consulting firms have created semantic memories by developing vast repositories of knowledge about customers, projects, competition, and the industries they serve.

Grover and Davenport (2001) found that in Western organizations, by far the most common objective of knowledge management projects involves some sort of knowledge repository. The objective of this type of project is to capture knowledge for later and broader access by others within the same organization. Common repository technologies include Lotus Notes, Web-based intranets, and Microsoft's Exchange, supplemented by search engines, document management tools, and other tools that allow editing and access. The repositories typically contain a specific type of information to represent knowledge for a particular business function or process, such as:

- "Best practices" information within a quality or business process management function;
- Information for sales purposes involving products, markets, and customers;
- Lessons learned in projects or product development efforts;
- Information around implementation of information systems;
- Competitive intelligence for strategy and planning functions;
- "Learning histories" or records of experience with a new corporate direction or approach.

The mechanical generation of databases, Websites, and systems that process data are good and have the potential to take us to a higher plane in the organization, help us understand work flows better, and help us deal with organizational pathologies and problems. The data-to-information transition often involves a low-level mechanical process that is well within the domain of contemporary information technologies, though humans are helpful in this transition as well. This information could exist in different forms throughout the organization and could even form the basis of competitive advantage or information products. For example, provision of information to customers about their order or shipment status is something that companies like Baxter and FedEx have been doing for years. But unlike knowledge, mechanically supplied information cannot be the source of sustained competitive advantage, particularly when the architectures on which it is based are becoming more open and omnipresent (Grover & Davenport, 2001).

IT in knowledge management can be used to store various kinds of information. For example, information about processes, procedures, forecasts, cases, and patents in the form of working documents, descriptions and reports can be stored in knowledge management systems. TietoEnator, a Scandinavian consulting firm, has a knowledge base in which they store methods, techniques, notes, concepts, best practices, presentations, components, references, guidelines, quality instructions, process descriptions, routines, strategies and CVs for all consultants in the firm (Halvorsen & Nguyen, 1999).

Knowledge retrieval can find support in content management and information extraction technology, which represent a group of techniques for managing and extracting information from documents, ultimately delivering a semantic meaning for decision makers or learners alike. This type of computer applications is targeted at capturing and extracting the content of free-text documents. There are several tasks that fall within the scope of content management and information extraction (Wang et al., 2001):

- *Abstracting and summarizing.* This task aims at delivering shorter, informative representations of larger (sets of) documents.
- *Visualization.* Documents can often be visualized according to the concepts and relationships that play a role. Visualization can be either in an introspective manner, or using some reference model/view of a specific topic.
- *Comparison and search.* This task finds semantically similar pieces of information.
- *Indexing and classification.* This considers (partial) texts, usually according to certain categories.
- *Translation.* Context-driven translation of texts from one language into another. Language translation has proven to be highly context specific,

even among closely related languages. Some kind of semantic representation of meaning is needed in order to be able to make good translations.

- *Question formulation and query answering.* This is a task in human-computer interaction systems.
- *Extraction of information.* This refers to the generation of additional information that is not explicit in the original text. This information can be more or less elaborate.

A group of computational techniques are available to alleviate the burden of these tasks. They include fuzzy technology, neural networks and expert systems. On a more application-oriented level there are several approaches that apply one or more of the general techniques. The field is currently very dynamic, and new advances are made continuously. One novel approach is the CORPORUM system to be presented in the section on expert systems.

Knowledge Transfer

Knowledge transfer occurs at various levels in an organization: transfer of knowledge between individuals, from individuals to explicit sources, from individuals to groups, between groups, across groups, and from the group to the organization. Considering the distributed nature of organizational cognition, an important process of knowledge management in organizational settings is the transfer of knowledge to locations where it is needed and can be used. However, this is not a simple process in that organizations often do not know what they know and have weak systems for locating and retrieving knowledge that resides in them. Communication processes and information flows drive knowledge transfer in organizations.

Knowledge transfer channels can be informal or formal, personal or impersonal. IT can support all four forms of knowledge transfer, but has mostly been applied to informal, impersonal means (such as discussion databases) and formal, impersonal means (such as corporate directories). An innovative use of technology for transfer is use of intelligent agent software to develop interest profiles of organizational members in order to determine which members might be interested recipients of point-to-point electronic messages exchanged among other members. Employing video technologies can also enhance transfer.

IT can increase knowledge transfer by extending the individual's reach beyond the formal communication lines. The search for knowledge sources is usually limited to immediate coworkers in regular and routine contact with the individual. However, individuals are unlikely to encounter new knowledge through their close-knit work networks because individuals in the same clique tend to possess similar information. Moreover, individuals are often unaware of what their cohorts are doing. Thus, expanding the individual's network to more extended, although perhaps weaker, connections is central to the knowledge diffusion process because such networks expose individuals to more new ideas.

Computer networks and electronic bulletin boards and discussion groups create a forum that facilitates contact between the person seeking knowledge and those who may have access to the knowledge. Corporate directories may enable individuals to rapidly locate the individual who has the knowledge that might help them solve a current problem. For example, the primary content of such a system can be a set of expert profiles containing information about the backgrounds, skills and expertise of individuals who are knowledgeable on various topics. Often such metadata (knowledge about where knowledge resides) prove to be as important as the original knowledge itself. Providing taxonomies or organizational knowledge maps enables individuals to rapidly locate either the knowledge or the individual who has the needed knowledge, more rapidly than would be possible without such IT-based support.

The term IT for information technology is used in this book. Some use ICT for information and communication technology to stress the importance of communication in knowledge management. Communication is important in knowledge management because technology provides support for both intraorganizational as well as interorganizational knowledge networks. Knowledge networks need technology in the form of technical infrastructure, communication networks and a set of information services. Knowledge networks enable knowledge workers to share information from various sources.

Traditional information systems have been of importance to vertical integration for a long time. Both customers and suppliers have been linked to the company through information systems. Only recently has horizontal integration occurred. Knowledge workers in similar businesses cooperate to find optimal solutions for customers. IT has become an important vertical and horizontal interorganizational coordination mechanism. This is not only because of the availability of broadband and standardized protocols. It is also caused by falling prices for communication services and by software programs' ability to coordinate functions between firms.

One way to reduce problems stemming from paperwork flow is to employ document imaging systems. Document imaging systems are systems that convert paper documents and images into digital form so they can be stored and accessed by a computer. Once the document has been stored electronically, it can be immediately retrieved and shared with others. An imaging system requires indexes that allow users to identify and retrieve a document when needed (Laudon & Laudon, 2004).

Knowledge Application

An important aspect of the knowledge-based view of the firm is that the source of competitive advantage resides in the application of the knowledge rather than in the knowledge itself. Information technology can support knowledge application by embedding knowledge into organizational routines. Procedures that are culture-bound can be embedded into IT so that the systems themselves become examples of organizational norms. An example according to Alavi and Leidner (2001) is Mrs. Field's use of systems designed to assist in every decision from hiring personnel to when to put free samples of cookies out on the table. The system transmits the norms and beliefs held by the head of the company to organizational members.

Technology-enforced knowledge application raises a concern that knowledge will continue to be applied after its real usefulness has declined. While the institutionalization of best practices by embedding them into IT might facilitate efficient handling of routine, linear, and predictable situations during stable or incrementally changing environments, when change is radical and discontinuous, there is a persistent need for continual renewal of the basic premises underlying the practices archived in the knowledge repositories. This underscores the need for organizational members to remain attuned to contextual factors and explicitly consider the specific circumstances of the current environment.

Although there are challenges with applying existing knowledge, IT can have a positive influence on knowledge application. IT can enhance knowledge integration and application by facilitating the capture, updating, and accessibility of organizational directives. For example, many organizations are enhancing the ease of access and maintenance of their directives (repair manuals, policies, and standards) by making them available on corporate intranets. This increases the speed at which changes can be applied. Also, organizational units can follow a faster learning curve by accessing the knowledge of other units having gone through similar experiences. Moreover, by increasing the size of individuals' internal social networks and by increasing the amount of organizational memory available, information technologies allow for organizational knowledge to be applied across time and space.

IT can also enhance the speed of knowledge integration and application by codifying and automating organizational routines. Workflow automation systems are examples of IT applications that reduce the need for communication and coordination and enable more efficient use of organizational routines through timely and automatic routing of work-related documents, information, rules, and activities. Rule-based expert systems are another means of capturing and enforcing well-specified organizational procedures.

To summarize, Alavi and Leidner (2001) have developed a framework to understand IS/IT in knowledge management processes through the knowledge-based view of the firm. One important implication of this framework is that each of the four knowledge processes of creation, storage and retrieval, transfer, and application can be facilitated by IT:

- *Knowledge creation:* Examples of supporting information technologies are data mining and learning tools, which enable combining new sources of knowledge and just in time learning.
- *Knowledge storage and retrieval:* Examples of supporting information technologies are electronic bulletin boards, knowledge repositories, and databases, which provide support of individual and organizational memory as well as inter-group knowledge access.
- *Knowledge transfer:* Examples of supporting information technologies are electronic bulletin boards, discussion forums, and knowledge directories, which enable more extensive internal networks, more available communication channels, and faster access to knowledge sources.
- *Knowledge application:* Examples of supporting information technologies are expert systems and workflow systems, which enable knowledge application in many locations and more rapid application of new knowledge through workflow automation.

KNOWLEDGE MANAGEMENT SYSTEMS

There is no single information system that is able to cover all knowledge management needs in a firm. This is evident from the widespread potential of IT in knowledge management processes. Rather, knowledge management systems (KMS) refer to a class of information systems applied to managing organizational knowledge. These systems are IT applications to support and enhance the organizational processes of knowledge creation, storage and retrieval, transfer, and application (Alavi & Leidner, 2001).

Requirements from Knowledge Management

The critical role of information technology and information systems lies in the ability to support communication, collaboration, and those searching for knowledge, and the ability to enable collaborative learning. We have already touched on important implications for information systems in previous chapters of this book:

1. *Interaction between information and knowledge.* Information becomes knowledge when it is combined with experience, interpretation and reflection. Knowledge becomes information when assigned an explicit representation. Sometimes information exists before knowledge; sometimes knowledge exists before information. One important implication of this two-way direction between knowledge and information is that information systems designed to support knowledge in organizations may not appear to be radically different from other forms of IT support, but will be geared toward

enabling users to assign meaning to information and to capture some of their knowledge in information (Alavi & Leidner, 2001).

2. *Interaction between tacit and explicit knowledge.* Tacit and explicit knowledge depend on each other, and they influence each other. The linkage of tacit and explicit knowledge suggests that only individuals with a requisite level of shared knowledge are able to exchange knowledge. They suggest the existence of a shared knowledge space that is required in order for individual A to understand individual B's knowledge. The knowledge space is the underlying overlap in the knowledge base of A and B. This overlap is typically tacit knowledge. It may be argued that the greater the shared knowledge space, the less the context needed for individuals to share knowledge within the group and, hence, the higher the value of explicit knowledge. IT is both dependent on the shared knowledge space and an important part of the shared knowledge space. IT is dependent on the shared knowledge space because knowledge workers need to have a common understanding of available information in information systems in the organization. If common understanding is missing, then knowledge workers are unable to make use of information. IT is an important part of the shared knowledge space because information systems make common information available to all knowledge workers in the organization. One important implication of this two-way relationship between knowledge space and information systems is that a minimum knowledge space has to be present so that IT can contribute to growth in the knowledge space (Alavi & Leidner, 2001).
3. *Knowledge management strategy.* Efficiency-driven businesses may apply the stock strategy, in which databases and information systems are important. Effectiveness-driven businesses may apply the flow strategy, in which information networks are important. Expert-driven businesses may apply the growth strategy, in which networks of experts, work processes and learning environments are important (Hansen et al., 1999).
4. *Combination in SECI process.* The SECI process consists of four knowledge conversion modes. These modes are not equally suited for IT support. Socialization is the process of converting new tacit knowledge to tacit knowledge. This takes place in the human brain. Externalization is the process of converting tacit knowledge to explicit knowledge. The successful conversion of tacit knowledge into explicit knowledge depends on the sequential use of metaphors, analogy and model. Combination is the process of converting explicit knowledge into more complex and systematic sets of explicit knowledge. Explicit knowledge is collected from inside and outside the organization and then combined, edited and processed to form new knowledge. The new explicit knowledge is then disseminated among the members of the organization. According to Nonaka et al. (2000),

creative use of computerized communication networks and large-scale databases can facilitate this mode of knowledge conversion. When the financial controller collects information from all parts of the organization and puts it together to show the financial health of the organization, that report is new knowledge in the sense that it synthesizes explicit knowledge from many different sources in one context. Finally, internalization in the SECI process converts explicit knowledge into tacit knowledge. Through internalization, explicit knowledge created is shared throughout an organization and converted into tacit knowledge by individuals.

5. *Explicit transfer of common knowledge.* If management decides to focus on common knowledge as defined by Dixon (2000), knowledge management should focus on the sharing of common knowledge. Common knowledge is shared in the organization using five mechanisms: serial transfer, explicit transfer, tacit transfer, strategic transfer and expert transfer. Management has to emphasize all five mechanisms for successful sharing and creation of common knowledge. For serial transfer, management has to stimulate meetings and contacts between group members. For explicit transfer, management has to stimulate documentation of work by the previous group. For tacit transfer, management has to stimulate contacts between the two groups. For strategic transfer, management has to identify strategic knowledge and knowledge gaps. For expert transfer, management has to create networks in which experts can transfer their knowledge. These five mechanisms are not equally suited for IT support. Explicit transfer seems very well suited for IT support, as the knowledge from the other group is transferred explicitly as explicit knowledge in words and numbers and shared in the form of data, scientific formulae, specifications, manuals and the like. Expert transfer also seems suited for IT support when generic knowledge is transferred from one individual to another person to enable the person to solve new problems with new methods.
6. *Link knowledge to its uses.* One of the mistakes in knowledge management presented by Fahey and Prusak (1998) was disentangling knowledge from its uses. A major manifestation of this error is that knowledge management initiatives become ends in themselves. For example, data warehousing can easily degenerate into technological challenges. The relevance of a data warehouse for decisions and actions gets lost in the turmoil spawned by debates about appropriate data structures.
7. *Treat knowledge as an intellectual asset in the economic school.* If management decides to follow the economic school of knowledge management, then intellectual capital accounting should be part of the knowledge management system. The knowledge management system should support knowledge markets in which knowledge buyers, knowledge sellers and knowledge brokers can use the system.

8. *Treat knowledge as a mutual resource in the organizational school.* The potential contribution of IT is linked to the combination of intranets and groupware to connect members and pool their knowledge, both explicit and tacit.
9. *Treat knowledge as a strategy in the strategy school.* The potential contributions of IT are manifold once knowledge as a strategy is the impetus behind knowledge management initiatives. One can expect quite an eclectic mix of networks, systems, tools, and knowledge repositories.
10. *Value configuration determines knowledge needs in primary activities.* Knowledge needs can be structured according to primary and secondary activities in the value configuration. Depending on the firm being a value chain, a value shop or a value network, the knowledge management system must support more efficient production in the value chain, adding value to the knowledge work in the value shop, and more value by use of IT infrastructure in the value network.
11. *Incentive Alignment.* The first dimension of information systems design is concerned with software engineering (error-free software, documentation, portability, modularity & architecture, development cost, maintenance cost, speed, and robustness). The second dimension is concerned with technology acceptance (user friendliness, user acceptance, perceived ease-of-use, perceived usefulness, cognitive fit, and task-technology fit). The third dimension that is particularly important to knowledge management systems is concerned with incentive alignment. Incentive alignment includes incentives influencing user behavior and the users' interaction with the system, deterrence of use for personal gain, use consistent with organizational goals, and robustness against information misrepresentation (Ba et al., 2001).

Benefits from Knowledge Management Systems

IT is applied in knowledge management for several important reasons:

- IT is an enabler of improved individual performance among knowledge workers.
- IT is an enabler of improved organizational performance by new business processes.
- IT is an enabler of improved interorganizational performance by effective knowledge networks.

Knowledge management initiatives applying information technology occur for many different reasons. A survey in the U.S. produced the following ranking of reasons for IT in knowledge management (CIO, 2001):

1. Improve profitability and income (67%);
2. Secure talent and expertise (54%);
3. Improve customer service and customer satisfaction (52%);
4. Secure company market share against new competitors (44%);
5. Shorten time to market of new products (39%);
6. Enter new market segments (39%);
7. Reduce costs (38%);
8. Develop new goods and services (35%).

The survey research did also include questions concerning knowledge management systems. Responding companies ranked software based on dollar amount to be spent (CIO, 2001):

1. Infrastructure for knowledge management (61%);
2. Intelligent systems for knowledge search (39%);
3. Data warehouse (21%);
4. Document handling (17%);
5. Company portals (16%);
6. Groupware (13%);
7. Mail delivery (11%);
8. Intelligent agents for knowledge search (9%);
9. Workflow systems (8%);
10. E-learning (7%).

The first ranked and most expensive software relates to infrastructure for knowledge management. According to Duffy (2001, p. 64):

Infrastructure provides the base or platform upon which KM solutions are built. It consists of repositories for unstructured data (i.e., document and content management) and structured data (i.e., data warehousing, generation, and management). Groupware is also part of the infrastructure, as it supports the collaboration needed for knowledge sharing, as well as email and other forms of interpersonal communication required for the efficient, time- and location-independent exchange of information.

Contingent Approach to Knowledge Management Systems

The role of IT in knowledge management will in some cases be minor. One reason is that technology can only take care of information, not knowledge. Another reason is that use of technology not only depends on technological capabilities, but also on other factors such as corporate culture and incentive structures. If there is no culture for knowledge sharing, and if knowledge workers get no rewards for knowledge distribution, then there is little help in applying IT.

McDermott (1999) is one of the skeptics of IT in knowledge management. He claims that modern IT inspired new approaches to knowledge management, but that IT is unable to make knowledge management more effective. He believes that only large garbage cans of information will be the result. He believes that knowledge, thinking and community belong together. According to McDermott (1999, p. 114):

When IBM introduced its web-based Intellectual Competencies system, anyone could contribute to the knowledge base. However, like many other companies, IBM soon discovered that their staff did not want to hunt through redundant entries. Now a core group from each community organizes and evaluates entries, weeding out redundancies and highlighting particularly useful or ground-breaking work. Frequently, technical professionals see this as a 'glorified librarian' role and many communities also have librarians or junior technical staff to do the more routine parts of organizing and distributing information.

Although other factors than IT capabilities may be critical success factors for knowledge management, it is important to have criteria for important IT capabilities. When considering the technological components of a KMS, they differ from traditional IT in several aspects. These differences constitute a knowledge management checklist that can be used to distinguish knowledge management solutions from other more traditional workflow, document management, intranet, and groupware solutions. According to Frappaolo and Capshaw (1999), true knowledge management solutions are characterized by being:

- *Context sensitive.* The solution should be able to understand the context of the knowledge requirements and tailor the knowledge accordingly. For example, it should be able to understand the difference between "animal reproduction" and "document reproduction" and to respond differently in each case.
- *User sensitive.* The solution should be able to organize the knowledge in the way most useful to the specific knowledge worker. For example, it should give knowledge relevant to the user's current knowledge level, making understanding easier. If the knowledge worker does not share the complete knowledge space of other knowledge workers, then the system should provide more information.
- *Flexible.* The solution should be able to handle knowledge of any form as well as different subjects, structures, and media. If the knowledge work only depends on text, then the system should be limited to text. If the

knowledge work also depends on sound, pictures and video, the system should handle these information sources as well. In the case of video, network capacity requirements are much higher than in the case of text.

- *Heuristic.* The solution should constantly learn about its users and the knowledge it possesses as it is used. A heuristic-based solution is one that continually refines itself as a user's pattern of knowledge work is tracked by the system. Its ability to provide a user with relevant knowledge should thus improve over time. For example, if the system responds to many requests on a particular subject, it should learn how to assist multiple knowledge workers in more depth on that subject.
- *Suggestive.* The solution should be able to deduce what the user's knowledge needs are and suggest knowledge associations the knowledge worker is not able to come up with.

The role of IT in knowledge management will in many cases be minor. For example, Nonaka et al. (2000) suggest that in the SECI process, only combination will benefit from use of IT. Another example is Dixon (2000), who suggests that common knowledge can only be supported by IT for explicit transfer and expert transfer. Alavi and Leidner (2001) imagine a more important role of IT in knowledge management, as was illustrated in the knowledge management processes.

The popularity of the World Wide Web has provided tremendous opportunities for applications of intelligent agents. An intelligent agent can be defined as anything that can be viewed as perceiving its environment through sensors and effects, typically a computer program that simulates a human relationship by doing something that another person could otherwise do for you. Agents assist users in a range of different ways: they hide the complexity of different tasks, they perform tasks on the user's behalf, they can train or teach the user, they help different users collaborate, and they monitor events and procedures. Two major applications of an intelligent agent technology can be found: personal assistants and communicating agents (Baek et al., 1999).

Examples of Software Vendors

Many software vendors have entered the market of KMS. *IBM's Lotus*, building on Notes, offers the Domino platform for Web publishing and Raven for knowledge management. All the time, new products and new versions are introduced. Sametime, Quickplace, K-station, and Discovery Server were some examples in 2001. *Microsoft* introduced their SharePoint, a portal server that allows companies to find, share and publish information, with the following announcement in 2001 (www.microsoft.com):

Microsoft is launching SharePoint, a Portal Server that allows companies to find, share and publish information. The new server provides seamless knowledge portal integration with the Microsoft Office and Windows operating system productivity desktop environment, allowing enterprise customers to integrate robust document management, search subscriptions and inline discussions into their document collaboration process. SharePoint Portal Server has broad support for enterprise content sources and data types, so users can find pertinent information quickly and easily.

Autonomy introduced ActiveKnowledge, which is based on a statistical approach to finding relevant documents for users, according to the following announcement in 2001 (www.autonomy.com):

The theoretical underpinnings for Autonomy's approach can be traced back to Thomas Bayes, an 18th century English clerical whose works on mathematical probability were not published until after his death ('Philosophical Transactions of the Royal Society of London', 1763). Bayes' work centered on calculating the probabilistic relationship between multiple variables and determining the extent to which one variable impacts on another. A typical problem is to judge how relevant a document is to a given query or agent profile. Bayesian theory aids in this calculation by relating this judgment to details that we already know, such as the model of an agent. Extensions of the theory go further than relevance information for a given query against a text. Adaptive probabilistic concept modeling (APCM) analyzes correlation between features found in documents relevant to an agent profile, finding new concepts and documents. Concepts important to sets of documents can be determined, allowing new documents to be accurately classified.

Knowledge Associates introduced Knowledger, which can find relevant information in text and pictures. Yet another software is from eWay, according to an announcement in 2001:

eWay links together the knowledge of individuals, and the information available in existing computer systems with a 'best practice' process system. eWay is launched with four modules: portal, organization module, information module and process module. The eWay portal is an easy to use web based application that gives access to the applications and data sources that are used in the corporation. The portal is controlled at all times by the roles defined for each user.

Soffront Software offers TRACK Knowledge Base TRACKKB, according to an announcement in 2001:

TRACKKB is a fully Web-based self-help and knowledge management application from Soffront Software, Inc. The product is ideally designed to provide interactive sales assistance and technical self-help to your internal and external customers from a link on your website. It is also designed to assist your customer support representatives in finding solutions to technical support problems. The interactive feature of TRACKKB engages customers in a short question and answer session to locate a solution to their technical problem or assist them in selecting an appropriate product or service that meets their needs and requirements. The self-help feature allows customers access to the knowledge base 24 hours a day, seven days a week.

At a knowledge management conference in London in 2001, a total of 32 suppliers of KMS were present: Active Intranet, Assistum, Autonomy, Casmir, Computeraid, Corechange, Convera, Factiva, Hummingbird, Hyperwave, Insight, KMS, Knexa, Knowledge Associates, Learned Information, Lexiquest, Lotus, March Intranet, Orbital Software, Sagemaka, Semio, SER Systems, Servicewave, Smartlogic, Sopheon, Soutron, Springfield 2000, TFPL, Thinkmap, Verity GB, Virtual Working Systems and Wordmap.

Knowledge management initiatives should never start with selection of systems from software vendors. In our contingent management perspective, we first have to know what we want. What do we want to achieve? What are our goals? Then, we may ask: How do we achieve what we want? How do we reach our goals? Systems from software vendors will never be the answer to what-questions; they will only be the answer to how-questions.

Systems Support for Emergent Knowledge Processes

Markus et al. (2002) developed a design theory for systems that support emergent knowledge processes. Their discussion of systems support for emergent knowledge processes is presented in this section.

Markus et al. (2002) define emergent knowledge processes as organizational activity patterns that exhibit three characteristics in combination: an emergent process of deliberations with no best structure or sequence; requirements for knowledge that are complex (both general and situational), distributed across people, and evolving dynamically; and an actor set that is unpredictable in terms of job roles or prior knowledge. Examples of emergent knowledge processes include basic research, new product development, strategic business planning, and organization design.

Work that is to be supported by information technology is generally described in terms of the characteristics of the process by which work is performed, the characteristics of users and their work context, and users' information requirements. The first characteristic, process, has traditionally been described in terms of the concept of structure. For example, distinctions can be made between highly structured, semi-structured, and unstructured. Examples of semi-structured processes are brand management, cash management, and management exception monitoring. Examples of unstructured processes are knowledge tasks such as basic research and the concept definition phase of new product development.

The second characteristic is the user. Most traditional information systems assume that the user type is known in advance, permitting systematic requirements analysis. The unpredictability of emergent processes means that it is nearly impossible for a system developer to know in advance the kinds of people who will be called into a deliberation, when they will be called in, or why. In addition, because emergent processes often involve high-level professional and technical personnel, the actors have a high degree of autonomy in how they do their work. They can resist the imposition of standard routines and new technologies. Therefore, designers of systems to support emergent processes do not have the luxury of systematic requirements analysis; they must plan for very infrequent use of support tools, and they cannot even assume that the intended users will want, or can be required, to use their knowledge management system.

The third characteristic is users' information requirements. The information requirements of knowledge-intensive emergent processes are quite different from those of semi-structured business processes. In emergent processes, users must often search for the information they need from documents that are poorly indexed and stored. Furthermore, much of the knowledge involved in sense-making is tacit, not explicit. Third, knowledge-intensive emergent processes have a high level of expert knowledge content. This means that, when tacit knowledge can be made explicit, it cannot easily be represented numerically, but must instead be represented as if-when rules, or as text. Finally, in most knowledge-intensive emergent processes, knowledge is distributed across many different people.

Markus et al. (2002) describe their design theory for systems that support emergent knowledge processes as a set of six combined design principles.

Principle #1: Design for Customer Engagement by Seeking out Naive Users. Which occupational groups will use the system? What do they know, need to know, and not know? How are they likely to use the system? What are the implications for the system's functionality, interface, and support requirements?

Specific types of users cannot be identified; it cannot be assumed that users will be knowledgeable, trained, or motivated, nor can it be assumed that training and use will be mandated. Therefore, the system must be self-deploying; developers should conceptualize each user-system interaction as a customer engagement process and repeatedly seek out naive users through a process of onion-layering the design team.

Lay organization designers need expert knowledge translated into a form they can use, involving multiple types of tradeoff analysis with clear implications for action. Therefore, the system must translate expert knowledge into actionable knowledge for non-experts; developers should expect to need many functional prototypes, instead of a few nonfunctional prototypes.

Lay organization designers cannot implement system-recommended actions online; they must convince others to implement organization design changes offline. Therefore, the system must induce users to take offline action; developers must observe and strive to change users' offline, as well as online, action.

Lay organization designers must be induced to consider knowledge about other functional areas and to develop a holistic conception of the organization design process. Therefore, the system must integrate expert knowledge with local knowledge sharing; multiple needed functionalities must be integrated rather than added.

The organization design process is emergent, with many process triggers, many process flows and tradeoff analyses, and many motivations among organization designers. Therefore, the system must implicitly, not explicitly, guide users' deliberations in desirable directions, without restricting them to a prescribed process; developers should use a dialectical development process instead of a consensus-seeking approach.

Many changes in the process, expert and specific knowledge, and user-system interaction must be expected. Therefore, the system must be extremely flexible; developers should componentize everything, including the knowledge base.

This first principle of self-deployment and customer engagement goes far beyond mere user-friendliness — a pervasive design guideline more than a decade ago. User-friendliness does not address people's lack of incentive to use the system. Therefore, a three-stage customer engagement process to make the system self-deploying is necessary. First, induce naive users to try the system, then provide immediate benefits, and finally encourage people to stay with the system long enough to complete their tasks.

Principle #2: Design for Knowledge Translation through Radical Iteration with Functional Prototypes. The literature on expert system development recommends matching the structure of a knowledge base to the knowledge representation of domain experts. Much organization design knowledge is represented in the scientific literature as if-then heuristics for predicting organizational success. For example, if an organization experiences high input uncertainty, then jobs should be designed with a high degree of discretion to accommodate, react, and resolve this uncertainty.

The radical iteration approach differs from the traditional prototyping approach in several ways. First, functional prototypes should be used. Each prototype has to be fully functional and specifically designed to shed light on some aspect of IT support for knowledge work. Alternative interfaces can be tested, and so can different representations of the knowledge base, multiple gap analysis formulae, different ways of providing method guidance, and alternative explanation styles.

Principle #3: Design for Offline Action. Designers should stop asking users: What did you learn when you used the system? Why did you press those buttons? What will you do with that information? Instead, designers should start observing what users actually do in their organization when they are not connected to the system. By focusing on offline behavior change, the development process can identify potential systems changes. Offline behavior change can be observed in meetings, presentations and knowledge task priorities.

Principle #4: Integrate Expert Knowledge with Local Knowledge Sharing. A knowledge management system should synthesize expert and diverse local knowledge inputs into a single, consensus perspective. The components of a traditional expert support system — knowledge base, inference engine, and interface — are not enough. The expert knowledge base has to be integrated with system design features that promote knowledge sharing among organizational members in different functional areas. Successful emergent knowledge support systems must represent a fusion of multiple system types. They are not just decision support or expert systems but also knowledge sharing systems.

Principle #5: Design for Implicit Guidance through a Dialectical Development Process. The autonomy of knowledge workers makes explicit process guidance risky and failure-prone. There is no way to ensure that knowledge workers will conduct complete system tasks or engage their co-workers in deliberations about the meanings of terms, interpretations of findings, and evaluations of alternative actions. So, instead of guiding users explicitly, they can be guided implicitly. For example, extensive explanations in each step of system use can encourage the user to move on in the desired direction.

Principle #6: Componentize Everything, Including the Knowledge Base. The componentized architecture ensures that, as domain knowledge evolves, the system will evolve with it. As components are modified, they can be dynamically plugged into the generic system structure to create a new, testable system for user evaluations. A componentized structure allows for easy post-development modifications to the system.

To recapitulate, a class of design problems can be identified in emergent knowledge processes. This class of design problems has different process, user and knowledge requirements from those of traditional systems. To solve such design problems, Markus et al. (2002) proposed a design theory of six principles for systems that support emergent knowledge processes.

Expert Systems

Expert systems can be seen as extreme knowledge management systems on a continuum representing the extent to which a system possesses reasoning capabilities. Expert systems are designed to be used by decision makers who do not possess expertise in the problem domain. The human expert's representation of the task domain provides the template for expert system design. The knowledge base and heuristic rules, which are used to systematically search a problem space, reflect the decision processes of the expert. A viable expert system is expected to perform this search as effectively and efficiently as a human expert. An expert system incorporates the reasoning capabilities of a domain expert and applies them in arriving at a decision. The system user needs little domain-specific knowledge in order for a decision or judgment to be made. The user's main decision is whether to accept the system's result (Dillard & Yuthas, 2001).

Decisions or judgments made by an expert system can be an intermediate component in a larger decision context. For example, an audit expert system may provide a judgment as to the adequacy of loan loss reserves that an auditor would use as input for making an audit opinion decision. The fact that the output supports or provides input for another decision does not make the system any less an expert system, according to Dillard and Yuthas (2001). The distinguishing feature of an expert system lies in its ability to arrive at a non-algorithmic solution using processes consistent with those of a domain expert.

Curtis and Cobham (2002) define an expert system as a computerized system that performs the role of an expert or carries out a task that requires expertise. In order to understand what an expert system is, then, it is worth paying attention to the role of an expert and the nature of expertise. It is then important to ascertain what types of experts and expertise there are in business and what benefits will accrue to an organization when it develops an expert system.

For example, a doctor having a knowledge of diseases arrives at a diagnosis of an illness by reasoning from information given by the patient's symptoms and then prescribes medication on the basis of known characteristics of available drugs together with the patient's history. The lawyer advises the client on the likely outcome of litigation based on the facts of the particular case, an expert understanding of the law and knowledge of the way the courts work and interpret this law in practice. The accountant looks at various characteristics of a company's performance and makes a judgment as to the likely state of health of that company (Curtis & Cobham, 2002).

All of these tasks involve some of the features for which computers traditionally have been noted — performing text and numeric processing quickly and efficiently — but they also involve one more ability: reasoning. Reasoning is the movement from details of a particular case and knowledge of the general subject area surrounding that case to the derivation of conclusions. Expert systems incorporate this reasoning by applying general rules in an information base to aspects of a particular case under consideration (Curtis & Cobham, 2002).

Davenport and Glaser (2002) explore the example of a doctor having knowledge of diseases and appropriate medication. At Partners HealthCare System in Boston, doctors use a computer system to check appropriate medication. The system works like this (Davenport & Glaser, 2002, p. 109):

Let's say Dr. Goldszer has a patient, Mrs. Johnson, and she has a serious infection. He decides to treat the infection with ampicillin. As he logs on to the computer to order the drug, the system automatically checks her medical records for allergic reactions to any medications. She's never taken that particular medication, but she once had an allergic reaction to penicillin, a drug chemically similar to ampicillin. The computer brings that reaction to Goldszer's attention and asks if he wants to continue with the order. He asks the system what the allergic reaction was. It could have been something relatively minor, like a rash, or major, like going into shock. Mrs. Johnsons reaction was a rash. Goldszer decides to override the computer's recommendation and prescribe the original medication, judging that the positive benefit from the prescription outweighs the negative effects of a relatively minor and treatable rash. The system lets him do that, but it requires him to give a reason for overriding its recommendation.

Expert systems are computer systems designed to make expert level decisions within complex domains. The business applications of this advanced information technology has been varied and broad reaching, directed toward making operational, management and strategic decisions.

Audit expert systems are such systems applied in the auditing environment within the public accounting domain. Major public accounting firms have been quite active in developing such systems, and some argue that these tools and technologies will be increasingly important for survival as the firms strive to enhance their competitive position and to reduce their legal and business risk.

Dillard and Yuthas (2001) find that the implementation and use of these powerful systems raise a variety of significant ethical questions. As public accounting firms continue to devote substantial resources to the development of audit expert systems, dealing with the ethical risks and potential consequences to stakeholders takes on increasing significance. For example, when responsible behavior of an auditor is transferred to an audit expert system, then the system is incapable of being held accountable for the consequences of decisions.

Expert systems can be used in all knowledge management processes described earlier. For knowledge retrieval, content management and information extraction technology represent a useful group of techniques. An example of an expert system for knowledge retrieval is the CORPORUM system. There are three essential aspects of this system (Wang et al., 2001).

First, the system interprets text in the sense that it builds ontologies. Ontologies describe concepts and relationships between them. Ontologies can be seen as the building blocks of knowledge. The system captures ontologies that reflect world concepts as the user of the system sees and expresses them. The ontology produced constitutes a model of a person's interest or concern. Second, the interest model is applied as a knowledge base in order to determine contextual and thematic correspondence with documents available in the system. Finally, the interest model and the text interpretation process drive an information search and extraction process that characterizes hits in terms of both relevance and content. This new information can be stored in a database for future reference.

The CORPORUM software consists of a linguistic component, taking care of tasks such as lexical analysis and analysis at the syntactical level. At the semantic level the software performs word sense disambiguation by describing the context in which a particular word is being used. This is naturally closely related to knowledge representation issues. The system is able to augment meaning structures with concepts that are invented from the text. The core of the system is also able to extract information most pertinent to a specific text for summary creation, extract the so-called core concept area from a text and represent results according to ranking that is based on specified interest for a specific contextual theme set by the user. In addition, the system generates explanations, which will allow the user to make an informed guess about which documents to look at and which to ignore. The system can point to exactly those parts of targeted documents that are most pertinent to a specific user's interest (Wang et al., 2001).

Analysis and design necessary for building an expert system differ from a traditional data processing or information system. There are three major points of distinction that prevent expert systems development from being subsumed under general frameworks of systems development (Curtis & Cobham, 2002):

1. *The subject matter is knowledge and reasoning as contrasted with data and processing.* Knowledge has both form and content, which need investigation. Form is connected with the mode of representation chosen — for instance, rules, semantic networks or logic. Content needs careful attention, as once the form is selected it is still a difficult task to translate the knowledge into the chosen representation form.
2. *Expert systems are expert/expertise orientated whereas information systems are decision/function/organization directed.* The expert system encapsulates the abilities of an expert or expertise and the aim is to provide a computerized replica of these facilities.
3. *Obtaining information for expert systems design presents different problems from those in traditional information systems design.* Many expert systems rely, partly at least, on incorporating expertise obtained from an expert. Few rely solely on the representation of textbook or rulebook knowledge. It is difficult generally to elicit this knowledge from an expert. In contrast, in designing an information system the analyst relies heavily on existing documentation as a guide to the amount, type and content of formal information being passed around the system. In the development of an expert system the experts are regarded as repositories of knowledge.

Expert systems and traditional information systems have many significant differences. While processing in a traditional information system is primarily algorithmic, processing in an expert system includes symbolic conceptualizations. Input must be complete in a traditional system, while input can be incomplete in an expert system. Search approach in a traditional system is frequently based on algorithms, while search approach in an expert system is frequently based on heuristics. Explanations are usually not provided in a traditional system. Data and information is the focus of a traditional system, while knowledge is the focus of an expert system.

Expert systems can deliver the right information to the right person at the right time if it is known in advance what the right information is, who the right person to use or apply that information would be, and, what would be the right time when that specific information would be needed. Detection of non-routine and unstructured change in business environment will, however, depend upon sense-making capabilities of knowledge workers for correcting the computational logic of the business and the data it processes (Malhotra, 2002).

An Initial Project for Systems Planning

Executive management, after realizing the importance of knowledge management and the potential role of IT, may want to analyze the situation before embarking on an expensive knowledge management investment. This analysis can be organized as a small project. The project should answer three questions: What do we want to achieve with KMS? How can we apply KMS in our organization? Which benefits can we expect from KMS? The project may include the following steps, as illustrated in Figure 1:

1. *Business goals for knowledge management.* Executive management formulates business goals for knowledge management in the organization.
2. *Ambition level for knowledge management.* Based on the business goals, executive management decides level of ambition for knowledge management.
3. *Knowledge management systems framework.* A framework is developed to illustrate how information is to be collected, stored, retrieved and communicated in the organization
4. *Systems integration.* The framework is used to plan integration with existing information systems in the organization.
5. *Application software.* Vendors are contacted to explore capabilities of knowledge management systems. This stage may influence stage 3, as unknown capabilities may expand the framework, while nonexisting capabilities may limit the framework.
6. *Knowledge management infrastructure.* A list is to be produced of hardware and basic software needed to implement the knowledge management systems framework.
7. *Organization of work and support functions.* Both future organization of knowledge work and future organization of IT support functions should be analyzed.
8. *Cost-benefit analysis.* The costs of IT in knowledge management are determined by the previous steps 3 to 8. The benefits of IT in knowledge management have to be derived from the steps 1 and 2. A positive ratio of benefits-to-costs may cause executive management to launch the knowledge management initiative. A negative ratio of benefits-to-costs may cause the project to return to Stage 2 to modify ambition level and/or Stage 3 to modify knowledge management systems framework.
9. *Knowledge management contribution.* An evaluation is conducted concerning knowledge management contribution to achievement of business goals, and a decision is made concerning knowledge management investments.

Davenport et al. (1998) studied successful knowledge management projects. They found that the following factors lead to knowledge project success:

- *Link to economic performance or industry value.* The easiest and most impressive benefits from knowledge management projects involve money

Figure 1. Steps and Responsible Project Members to Identify Technology Potential

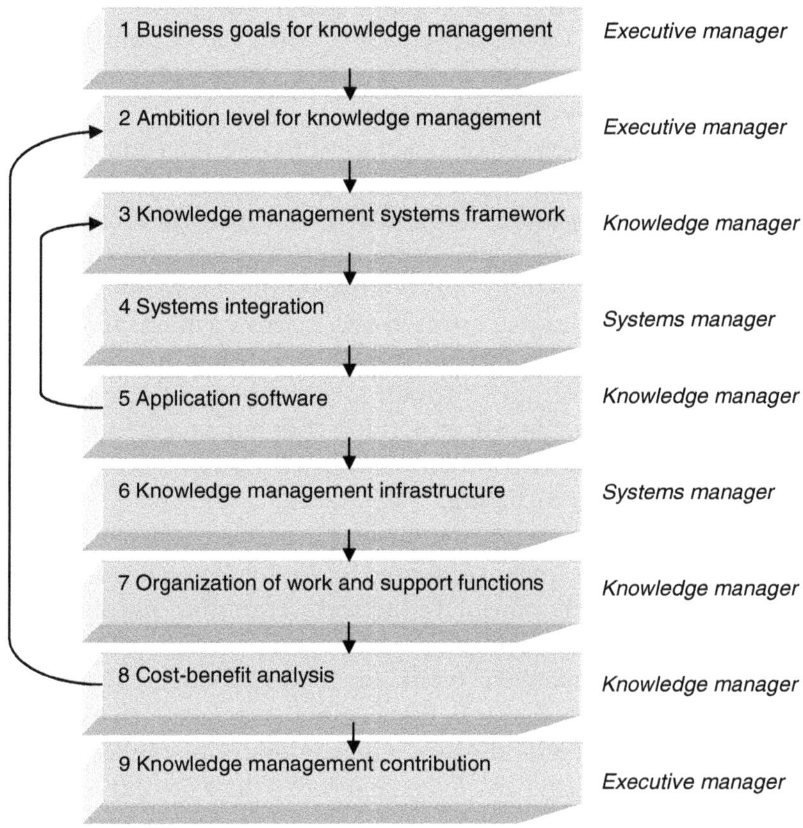

saved or earned. Benefit calculation may also be indirect, perhaps through improvement in measures like cycle time and customer satisfaction. Knowledge management can be expensive, so inevitably it gets support in a firm when it is somehow linked to economic benefit or competitive advantage.

- *Technical and organizational infrastructure.* Knowledge projects are more likely to succeed when they use the broader infrastructure of both technology and organization. Of the two, technological infrastructure is more accessible. It consists partially of technologies that are knowledge oriented (for example, Lotus Notes and World Wide Web-based intranets). If these tools and the skills to use them are already in place, a knowledge management initiative will find it easier to get off the ground. Another aspect of technology infrastructure is a common, pervasive set of technologies for desktop computing and communications. At the simplest level, this means a capable, networked PC on every desk or in every briefcase, with standardized personal productivity tools so that people can exchange documents easily. Building an organizational infrastructure for knowledge management means establishing a set of roles and organizational groups whose members have the skills to serve as resources for individual knowledge management projects.

- *Standard, flexible knowledge structure.* Finding the right balance in the knowledge structure is critical to many projects. Knowledge is fuzzy and closely linked to the people who hold it: its categories and meanings change frequently. Consequently, knowledge often resists engineering. The expert systems movement of the 1980s confirmed this problem: it proved to be difficult to create rules that covered even narrow knowledge domains and even more difficult to update and modify the structure. If a repository has no structure, however, it is difficult to extract knowledge from it. Firms building a knowledge base or expert network must create some categories and key terms. Another important issue that arises is who controls decisions about the knowledge structure.
- *Knowledge-friendly culture.* If people have a positive orientation to knowledge, if people are not inhibited in sharing knowledge, if learning on and off the job is highly valued, if experience, expertise, and rapid innovation supersede hierarchy, and if the firm attracts and hires people who reinforce knowledge focus, then we can talk about a knowledge-friendly culture.
- *Clear purpose and language.* Knowledge managers must decide when and how to most effectively communicate their objectives. Some people actively avoid the term knowledge and frame their project only in already accepted business terms. Others confront the language problem head-on by conducting an ongoing educational process. Knowledge managers must address the language issue in a way that fits their culture.
- *Change in motivational practices.* Intimately and inextricably bound with people's egos and occupations, knowledge does not emerge from or flow easily across role or functional boundaries. Therefore, the motivation to create, share, and use knowledge is an intangible critical success factor for virtually all knowledge management projects. Finding new sources of motivation to increase participation in knowledge-sharing systems is a constant challenge.
- *Multiple channels for knowledge transfer.* Successful knowledge managers recognize that knowledge is transferred through multiple channels that reinforce one another. Successful knowledge management projects usually address transfer through various channels, recognizing that each adds value in a different way and that their synergy enhances use. In this

day of the Internet, Lotus Notes and global communications systems, it is easy to devalue the need for face-to-face interaction.

- *Senior management support.* Like almost every other type of change program, knowledge management projects benefit from senior management support. Strong support from executives is crucial for transformation-oriented knowledge projects, but less necessary in efforts to use knowledge for improving individual functions or processes. A senior manager who must advocate for knowledge management may not need a strong personal orientation to knowledge, but it surely helps.

Many organizations have initiated a range of projects and programs in which the primary focus has been on developing new applications of IT to support the digital capture, storage, retrieval, and distribution of an organization's explicitly documented knowledge (Zack, 1999). Artificial intelligence systems such as expert systems, neural nets, fuzzy logic and generic algorithms capture and codify knowledge, while group collaboration systems, like groupware and extranets, share knowledge. Office automation systems, including word processing, desktop publishing, imaging, electronic calendars and desktop databases distribute knowledge, and knowledge work systems such as computer-aided design (CAD), virtual reality and investment workstations create knowledge.

As examples of IT projects to support KM, Ruggles (1998) lists creating an intranet, data warehousing, groupware to support collaboration, creating networks of knowledge workers, mapping sources of internal expertise, databases of internal knowledge structures, establishing new knowledge roles, and launching new knowledge-based products and services.

An intranet may be classified as a KM application since it is capable of distributing knowledge. While not every intranet project should be considered a knowledge management effort, intranets are often used to support knowledge access and exchange within organizations. Intranets are often implemented with KM as the primary focus. That is, intranet systems are seen as a tool for the more efficient sharing and creation of knowledge within organizations.

Stenmark (2002) has suggested viewing the intranet from three different perspectives: the information perspective, the awareness perspective, and the communication perspective. The *information perspective* is the most obvious view of the intranet, since information provision is a fundamental part of the infrastructure. Seen from this perspective, the intranet gives the organizational members access to both structured and unstructured information in the form of databases and documents. The *awareness perspective* suggests that not only explicit information links but also tacitly expressed connections should be exploited to hook up organizational members with information and people they might otherwise have missed. The *communication perspective* enables the organizational members to collectively interpret the available information by supporting various forms of channels for conversations and negotiations.

The ability to analyze and code knowledge often requires one to have an in-depth expertise in the sociocultural environment related to the knowledge. It has been suggested that expert systems can be used to improve coding in which the expert's vocabulary contains the set of generalized concepts necessary to express the knowledge of others.

While having considerable potential, the availability of electronic knowledge exchange does not automatically induce a willingness to share information and build new intellectual capital. Major changes in incentives and culture may be required to stimulate use of new electronic networks, and motivated creativity is a fundamental influence in the creation of value through leveraging intellect.

Enablers of Knowledge Management Systems

Many knowledge management systems fail. Malhotra (2002) suggests that such failures occur for two broad reasons. First, knowledge management systems are often defined in terms of inputs such as data, information, technology and best practices that by themselves may be inadequate for effective business performance. For these inputs to result in business performance, the influence of intervening and moderating variables such as attention, motivation, commitment, creativity, and innovation has to be better understood and accounted for in design of business models. Second, the efficacy of inputs and how they are strategically deployed are important issues often left unquestioned as expected performance outcomes are achieved, but the value of such performance outcomes may be eroded by the dynamic shifts in the business and competitive environments.

Based on such failure reasons, Malhotra (2002) developed a set of seven enablers of knowledge management systems. These enablers represent challenges that need to be met for successful knowledge management.

1. *Business and technology strategy challenge of next generation KMS.* Most organizations will need to develop adaptive capacity for redefining their business value propositions that add greatest value to the business enterprise. Competitive survival and ongoing sustenance will depend on the ability to continuously redefine and adapt organizational goals, purposes, and the organization's way of doing things. The next generation of KMS will need to accommodate the need for ongoing questioning of the programmed logic and a very high level of adaptability to incorporate dynamic changes in business models and information architectures. Designers of information architectures will need to ensure that they deliver upon the need for efficiency and optimization for knowledge harvesting while providing for flexibility for facilitating innovative business models and value proposi-

tions. Designers will need to provide loose coupling between technology architectures and business architectures so that existing technology infrastructure should not straitjacket the evolution of the business model.

2. *Organizational control challenge of next generation KMS.* Organizational control is imperative in many KMS to ensure predetermined meanings, predefined actions, and, pre-specified outcomes. Consistency is imperative for ensuring homogeneity of processing of the same information in the same manner to ensure the same outcomes and is achieved by minimizing criticism and questioning of the status quo. This may, however, take its toll by suppressing innovation and creativity. Therefore, design of next generation KMS should ensure that they are not constrained by overemphasis on consistency. While the traditional business logic is based on control, dynamics of the new business environment require a business model that assumes existence of few rules, some specific information and a lot of freedom.
3. *Information sharing culture challenge of next generation KMS.* Success of the next generation KMS will depend upon integration of not only information across inter-enterprise value configurations, but also integration of decision-making and actions across inter-enterprise boundaries. Effectiveness of integrated information flows will depend upon the accuracy of information that is shared by diverse stakeholders across inter-enterprise boundaries. The challenge of information sharing will result from the potentially competitive nature of various enterprises across value configurations as access to privileged information may often determine the dominant position in the inter-enterprise value creation. Often, individuals may not willingly share information with their departmental peers, supervisors or with other departments, because they believe that what they know provides them with an inherent advantage in bargaining and negotiation. Despite the availability of most sophisticated knowledge sharing technologies, such human concerns may often result in sharing of only partial, inaccurate, or ambiguous information. Even more critical than the absence of information is the propensity of sharing inaccurate or ambiguous information because of competing interests, which may not yield true integration of information flows despite very sophisticated integration of enabling information technologies. Motivation of employees, organizations, customers, and suppliers to share accurate and timely information is based on trust, despite the potential of use of information in unanticipated ways.
4. *Knowledge representation challenge of next generation KMS.* Static and predefined representation of knowledge is particularly suited for knowledge reuse and offers an interesting contrast against the dynamic, affective, and, active representation of knowledge needed for knowledge creation. The premise of digitized memory of the past as a reliable predictor

of the future success is valid for a business environment characterized by routine and structured change. While the digitized logic and databases can facilitate real-time execution of inter-enterprise information application, their efficacy depends upon real-time adaptation of underlying assumptions to continuously account for complex changes in the business environment. Often such changes cannot be recognized or corrected automatically by computerized systems, as they cannot be pre-programmed to detect an unpredictable future. The adaptability of a KMS is therefore dependent upon its capability of sensing complex patterns of change in business environments and using that information for adapting the digitized logic and databases to guide decision-making, actions, and resulting performance outcomes.

5. *Organization structure challenge of next generation KMS.* Developing an information-sharing technological infrastructure is an exercise in engineering design, whereas enabling use of that infrastructure for sharing high quality information and generating new knowledge is an exercise in emergence. While the former process is characterized by predetermination, pre-specification and preprogramming for knowledge harvesting and exploitation, the latter process is typically characterized by creation of organizational cultural infrastructure to enable continuous information sharing, knowledge renewal, and creation of new knowledge.
6. *Managerial command and control challenge of next generation KMS.* Organizational controls tend to seek compliance with predefined goals that need to be achieved using predetermined best practices and standard operating procedures. A key challenge for managers in the forthcoming dynamic environment will be cultivating commitment of knowledge workers to the organizational vision. As it becomes increasingly difficult to specify goals and objectives relevant to knowledge workers, such commitment will facilitate real-time strategizing in accord with the organizational vision and its real-time implementation on the frontlines. Knowledge workers will need to take autonomous roles of self-leadership and self-regulation, as they will be best positioned to sense the dynamic changes in their immediate business environment. Compliance will lose its effectiveness as the managerial tool of control as managers removed from the frontlines will have less and less knowledge about the changing dynamics for efficient decision-making. Managers will need to facilitate the confidence of knowledge workers in acting on incomplete information, trusting their own judgments, and taking decisive actions for capturing increasingly shorter windows of opportunity.
7. *Economic returns challenge of next generation KMS.* Incentives and rewards are often used for justifying the economic rationale for knowledge sharing by employees as well as outsiders such as customers and suppliers.

Knowledge managers responsible for success of KMS and knowledge sharing will need to reconcile contractual measures such as punitive covenants with the need for trust and loyalty of customers, employees, partners, and suppliers.

Corporate executives are demanding better justification for investments in KMS and expect business performance outcomes. They realize that the next generation of KMS must be based on ongoing innovation of business value propositions and extended inter-enterprise value creation. According to Malhotra (2002), architects of next generation KMS must take a holistic approach to designing intra- and interorganizational systems with due consideration not only for the technological design, but also for the design of strategic sustainability of these systems.

KNOWLEDGE MANAGEMENT POSITIONS

One action for knowledge management is to establish support functions dedicated to knowledge management in the organization. The person leading this function is typically called knowledge manager or chief knowledge officer (CKO).

The chief information officer (CIO) can be defined as the highest-ranking IT executive who typically exhibits managerial roles requiring effective communication with top management, a broad corporate perspective in managing information resources, influence on organizational strategy, and responsibility for the planning of IT to cope with a firm's competitive environment. This definition is in line with published empirical research, which applied the following criteria when selecting CIOs for empirical observation: (1) highest-ranking information technology executive, (2) reports no more than two levels from the CEO, that is, either reports to the CEO or reports to one of the CEOs direct reporters, (3) areas of responsibility include information systems, computer operations, telecommunications and networks, office automation, end-user computing, help desks, computer software and applications; and (4) responsibility for strategic IS/IT planning. Currently, the most challenging task for many CIOs is successful applications of IS/IT in knowledge management. To succeed, the CIO has to work hand in hand with the CKO.

Chief Knowledge Officer

A CKO is responsible for knowledge-based innovations in the firm. While the chief information officer (CIO) is concerned with applications of information technology in the firm, the CKO is only interested in information technology to the extent that it enables knowledge-based innovations in the firm. In addition to the CKO, we find knowledge engineers, librarians, project managers and database experts in knowledge management support functions.

The CKO role is an important one for both operational and symbolic reasons, according to Grover and Davenport (2001). Operationally, CKOs perform a variety of key roles, including serving as the chief designer of the knowledge architecture, the top of the reporting relationship for knowledge professionals, the head technologist for knowledge technologies, and the primary procurement officer for external knowledge content. Symbolically, the presence of a CKO serves as an important indicator that a firm views knowledge and its management as critical to its success. If the CKO is a member of the senior executive team, it becomes obvious to employees that knowledge is a critical business resource on the level of labor and capital.

Davenport and Prusak (1998) suggest the following main tasks for a CKO:

- Advocate or "evangelize" for knowledge and learning from it. Particularly given the important role for knowledge in the strategies and processes of many firms today, long-term changes are necessary in organizational cultures and individual behaviors relative to knowledge. These changes will require sustained and powerful advocacy.
- Design, implement, and oversee a firm's knowledge infrastructure, including its libraries, knowledge bases, human and computer knowledge networks, research centers, and knowledge-oriented organizational structure.
- Manage relationships with external providers of information and knowledge (for example, academic partners or database companies), and negotiate contracts with them. This is already a major expense item for many companies, and efficient and effective management of it is important.
- Provide critical input to the process of knowledge creation and use around the firm (for example, new product development, market research, and business strategy development), and facilitate efforts to improve such processes if necessary.
- Design and implement a firm's knowledge codification approaches. Such approaches specify key categories of information or knowledge that the organization would address, and entail mapping both the current knowledge inventory and future knowledge models.
- Measure and manage the value of knowledge, either by conventional financial analysis or by anecdote management. If the organization has no sense of the value of knowledge and its management, the function will not last long.
- Manage the organization's professional knowledge managers, giving them a sense of community, establishing professional standards, and managing their careers. These workers may be reporting in a matrix between the

CKO and managers of the domains where the company focuses knowledge management efforts (for example, a particular market, product set, or type of customer).

- Lead the development of knowledge strategy, focusing the firm's resources on the type of knowledge it needs to manage most, and the knowledge processes with the largest gaps between need and current capability.

In many large organizations, and some small ones, this new corporate executive is emerging — the chief knowledge officer. Companies are creating the position to initiate, drive, and coordinate knowledge management programs. Earl and Scott (1999) studied 20 CKOs in North America and Europe both to understand their roles and to gain insight on evolving knowledge management practice. Most of the CKOs studied agreed on three points:

1. Knowledge today is a necessary and sustainable source of competitive advantage. In an era characterized by rapid change and uncertainty, it is claimed that successful companies are those that consistently create new knowledge, disseminate it through the organization, and embody it in technologies, products, and services. Several sectors — for example, the financial services, consulting, and software industries — depend on knowledge as their principal way to create value. Thus knowledge is displacing capital, natural resources, and labor as the basic economic resource.
2. There is general recognition that companies are not good at managing knowledge. They may undervalue the creation and capture of knowledge, they may lose or give away what they possess, they may deter or inhibit knowledge sharing, and they may under-invest in both using and reusing the knowledge they have. Above all, perhaps, they may not know what they know. This may be true of explicit or articulated knowledge: that which can be expressed in words and numbers and can be easily communicated and shared in hard form, as scientific formulae, codified procedures, or universal principles. It is probably true of tacit or unarticulated knowledge: that which is more personal, experiential, context-specific, and hard to formalize; is difficult to communicate or share with others, and is generally in the heads of individuals and teams.
3. Recognizing the potential of knowledge in value creation and the failure to fully exploit it, some corporations have embarked on knowledge management programs. These are explicit attempts to manage knowledge as a resource; in particular:
   - Designing and installing techniques and processes to create, protect, and use known knowledge.

- Designing and creating environments and activities to discover and release knowledge that is not known.
- Articulating the purpose and nature of managing knowledge as a resource and embodying it in other initiatives and programs.

According to Earl and Scott (1999, p. 30), these three activities need not be solely, or even mainly, intraorganizational. There is usually potential for improving knowledge capabilities, both within and between units of an organization. But external or interorganizational possibilities may be at least as attractive and ultimately more important. These include, for example, mutual sharing of knowledge with partners, allies, intermediaries, suppliers, and customers. Equally, protecting external leakage of some knowledge can be a vital concern to companies that have focused on intellectual capital formation.

Earl and Scott (1999) find that current movements such as intellectual asset (or capital) management and organizational intelligence are closely related to knowledge management. Together with other related themes such as organizational learning and information management, they may be conceptualized or practiced differently from the emerging praxis of knowledge management or, in some cases, they may be much the same. Consequently, there are some corporate executives leading such initiatives who will feel that they are, in effect, CKOs. However, they have different titles, such as director of intellectual capital or vice president of organizational learning (Earl & Scott, 1999, p. 30):

The much commoner and well-established role of chief information officer, or CIO, although sometimes thought to be similar to that of CKO, is quite different. CIOs have distinct responsibilities — IT strategy, IT operations, and managing the IT function — and so far have not formally taken on the full range of knowledge management activities. Where a CKO exists, there is also likely to be a CIO, but the corollary is not true.

Those 'chief knowledge officers' we studied are senior corporate executives with 'knowledge' in their titles. In other words, we could assume that they had been appointed specifically to orchestrate a knowledge management program. They are all first incumbents in the role, most having been in office less than two years. We studied them using semi structured face-to-face interviews plus a personality assessment questionnaire. Subsequently, we conducted two workshops with some of the participants to compare our results with their collective experiences.

Although, not surprisingly, we found differences in what CKOs did in their particular organizations, we found a remarkable similarity in their personal profiles and in their experiences to date. 'Chief knowledge officer' is an unusual and arresting title; as one participant said: 'I have the honor of having the most pretentious title in the corporation'. Our study suggests that CKOs are also unusual and arresting people.

Earl and Scott (1999) found that the role of the CKO is so immature that there is no job specification. Different corporations are likely to have different expectations of it. So CKOs have had first to work out an agenda for themselves, and they commonly refer to the rapid learning involved. This is mainly because their mission or mandate is not clear. "Everybody here, me included, is on a vertical learning curve about knowledge management," admitted one CKO. Almost invariably, CKOs are appointed by the CEO; one CEO said, "At the time, appointing a CKO was much more through intuition and instinct than through analysis or strategic logic" (Earl & Scott, 1999, p. 31).

The CKOs studied thus had to discover and develop the CEO's implicit vision of how knowledge management would make a difference. On the one hand, the CEOs were thinking boldly; on the other hand, they were not thinking in detail. Their goals, however, were fairly clear, usually concerned with correcting one or more of these perceived corporate deficiencies:

- Inattention to the explicit or formal management of knowledge in ongoing operations.
- Failure to leverage the hidden value of corporate knowledge in business development.
- Inability to learn from past failures and successes in strategic decision-making.
- Not creating value or "making money" from knowledge embedded in products or held by employees.

So the primary task of a first-generation CKO is to articulate a knowledge management program. This is a twofold task that involves evangelizing the nature and value potential of knowledge and selling not only the concept of knowledge management but also how to sell it to both corporate and line or local management. In particular, CKOs have found they need to engage senior executives one on one to understand possible individual or local knowledge gaps or opportunities and to initiate customized knowledge management projects. As one CKO explained to Earl and Scott (1999, p. 32):

Unless I can persuade people that knowledge management is not just for the benefit of other people, I haven't got much hope of persuading them to buy into it. They have to believe there's something in it for them and that I care about that as much as they do. Otherwise it just comes across as the latest form of cynical manipulation.

Therefore, CKOs spend a lot of time walking around the organization. In particular, they interact with four types of managers (Earl & Scott, 1999):

- They look for those who are excited about a particular knowledge management idea or project and thus have identified where improvement is possible and are likely to want to try something new. These are their *knowledge champions*.
- They also seek to identify from the senior executive cadre those who are enthused by knowledge management, identify with the concept, and make public statements about it. These are potential *knowledge sponsors* who will invest in and support knowledge management projects.
- Surprisingly, several CKOs studied also spent time identifying executives who are hostile to knowledge management and/or the appointment of a CKO. They sense that in a new and as yet ill-defined corporate initiative, especially one with the CEO's personal support, there will be doubters and reactionaries who must be converted to the cause or avoided for now. These are the *knowledge skeptics*.
- Finally, the CKO, once he or she has initiated a project of any substance, will need allies in implementation, typically, IS executives and HR professionals. These are the *knowledge partners*. Rarely did these partners come from outside the organization. For example, CKOs are skeptical about how management consultants can help, feeling they are lower down the learning curve than themselves. One interviewee complained, "The consultants who have woken up to knowledge management as an opportunity and are peddling expertise in this field actually know less about it than we do." In a similar vein, CKOs have soon concluded there is little to be learned from conferences and external contacts, as they discover that knowledge extraction is more common than knowledge sharing.

Earl and Scott (1999) found that a common word in the CKO's vocabulary is "design". CKOs are designers of knowledge directories, knowledge-based systems, knowledge-intensive business and management processes, knowledge exchange events, knowledge-sharing physical spaces, and knowledge protection policies. Mostly, their design is conceptual. In other words, they work on an idea with a champion and contribute design suggestions and inject thinking from emerging knowledge management practice, as a consultant or systems analyst would. They then enlist the help of relevant partners.

Applehans et al. (1999) define the CKO as part of the knowledge architecture. The knowledge architecture identifies the scope of the investment that will be made in managing knowledge. More than a technical solution, it encompasses three components: people, content and technology. A knowledge architecture brings these components together into a powerful working relationship. In this architecture, the CKO or the CLO (Chief Learning Officer) is the change agent who markets the importance of knowledge inside the company and enables a global audience to take advantage of it. The CKO ensures that the knowledge architecture is funded, designed, built, and administered.

Should companies really appoint a CKO to the job of managing knowledge? According to Foote et al. (2001), the answer depends on whether the CEO and senior management are prepared to make the position succeed. The limits of the CKO's potential contribution are set by what the CEO and senior management have done before the position was created. A candidate should hesitate before accepting an offer from an organization whose top managers do not see the point of managing knowledge and whose employees do not have a thirst for acquiring it.

Foote et al. (2001) found that most top managers recognize the value of managing knowledge. In a 1998 survey of North American senior executives, 77 percent rated "improving the development, sharing, and use of knowledge throughout the business" as very or extremely important. Thanks to the groundwork laid by pioneering knowledge managers, CKOs can now create substantial value. First employed in the early 1990s to foster the flow of knowledge throughout increasingly complex organizations, they functioned rather like plumbers, routing bits of information through different pipes to the right people. They then built better pipes, such as company-wide email networks and corporate intranets, and, still later, redesigned work and communications processes to promote collaboration.

Foote et al. (2001) suggest that today, in organizations that already have these technical and social networks, CKOs can take a more strategic perspective, scanning the enterprise to discover how they might improve processes and customer relationship management as well as promote employee learning. Other senior managers might be able to see how knowledge can be better used in their particular units or functions, but the CKO can stand back and manage interventions that cross formal business boundaries, thus helping the enterprise as a whole. In organizations in which cross-business and cross-functional interventions are not likely to happen unless someone from the top team takes express responsibility for them, appointing a CKO would seem to be a good idea.

What can be done to ensure that the CKO unlocks a company's latent potential? To find out, Foote et al. (2001) asked CKOs at various companies for their views about the make-or-break factors. Although the CKOs had different experiences, all concurred that success depends on two things: first, on the ability of senior management to agree about what it hopes to gain from managing knowledge explicitly and from creating a performance culture (which raises the staff's demand for knowledge) and, second, on how well the CKO develops and executes a knowledge management agenda.

The value that senior managers hope to create from managing knowledge generally lies at one of three levels (Foote et al., 2001). At the lowest level, the managers aim to help their organization become better at what it already does. At the second level, knowledge can be used to underpin new forms of commercial activity, such as customer-focused teams and cross-unit coordination. At level three, knowledge management can go even further by generating an entirely new value proposition for customers (Foote et al., 2001, p. 3):

A business might, for instance, decide to offer previously "internal" knowledge as part of its product. The World Bank, to cite one case, used to provide primarily financial resources to developing countries. Now it also offers direct access to huge reserves of knowledge about what forms of economic development do and don't work. This approach not only benefits clients but also strengthens the commitment of the bank's shareholders, which see the effectiveness of their capital enhanced. Steve Denning, the bank's former director of knowledge management, observed that "internal knowledge sharing improves our efficiency, but sharing it externally has a much larger impact, improving our quality of service and reaching a much wider group of clients".

If a company wishes only to improve its current processes, bringing in the appropriate experts (rather than hiring a CKO) may suffice to achieve the necessary social and technical objectives — creating new teams or new electronic forums, for example. If aspirations run higher, the chief executive officer may need an informed CKO to pinpoint the most valuable links between knowledge and the business and to plan how best to exploit them.

For knowledge to create value, people must want knowledge and know how to use it. Companies that are good at using their knowledge to boost performance (Goldman Sachs, say, or Hewlett-Packard) stretch employees to perform. This approach obliges them to reach out and pull in better knowledge from every part of the organization and, for that matter, from outside it. It is no accident that Jack Welch spent his first years as CEO of GE — before he started advocating "boundaryless" knowledge sharing and collaboration — driving up performance demands. In the absence of a performance culture, people will feel swamped by information for which they see no need.

Top performers such as Goldman Sachs and GE have been evolving a performance culture over decades; companies that haven't done so must compress that development into a few years. This can be done. During the early 1990s, British Petroleum, for example, was able to transform itself from a centralized organization run by large, functional departments into a collection of focused, high-performance units with extensive mechanisms for sharing knowledge across them.

If the preconditions can be fulfilled, success hangs on the ability of the CKO to identify, launch, operate, and evaluate knowledge-related change initiatives that are worthwhile in themselves and can be replicated in various sectors of the organization. Although the tasks sound fairly straightforward, the CKO must succeed in winning support from the wider organization in order to execute any of them. The truth is that CKOs stand or fall by their power to influence.

The knowledge management agenda is implemented through a cadre of managers who understand knowledge and its uses in various aspects of the business, the motivational and attitudinal factors necessary to get people to create, share, and use knowledge effectively, and the ways to use technology to enhance knowledge activities. On a daily basis, knowledge managers perform a broad collection of tasks, including (Grover & Davenport, 2001):

- Facilitation of knowledge sharing networks and communities of practice;
- Creation, editing and pruning of "knowledge objects" in a repository;
- Building and maintaining technology-based knowledge applications;
- Incorporating knowledge-oriented job descriptions, motivational approaches, and evaluation and reward systems into the human resource management processes of the organization;
- Redesigning knowledge work processes and incorporating knowledge tasks and activities into them.

To develop and execute a knowledge management agenda, the CKO should develop skills in intrapreneurship. *Intrapreneurship* (entrepreneurship within existing organizations) has been of interest to scholars and practitioners for the past two decades. Intrapreneurship is viewed as being beneficial for revitalization and performance of corporations. According to Antoncic and Hisrich (2001, p. 496), the concept has four distinct dimensions:

First, the new-business-venturing dimension refers to pursuing and entering new businesses related to the firm's current products or markets. Second, the innovativeness dimension refers to the creation of new products, services, and technologies. Third, the self-renewal dimension emphasizes the strategy reformulation, reorganization, and organizational change. Finally, the proactiveness dimension reflects top management orientation in pursuing enhanced competitiveness and includes initiative and risk-taking, and competitive aggressiveness, and boldness. While differing somewhat in their emphasis, activities and orientations, the four dimensions pertain to the same concept of intrapreneurship because they are factors of Schumpeterian innovation, the building block of entrepreneurship. The pursuit of creative or new solutions to challenges confronting the firm, including the development or enhancement of old and new products and services, markets, administrative techniques, and technologies for performing organizational functions (e.g., production, marketing, sales, and distribution), as well as changes in strategy, organizing, and dealings with competitors are innovations in the broadest sense.

Knowledge management will never be the sole responsibility of a CKO. Line managers have responsibilities as well. Hansen and Oetinger (2001) argue that there is a need for T-shaped managers. Hansen and Oetinger state (2001, p. 108):

We call the approach T-shaped management. It relies on a new kind of executive, one who breaks out of the traditional corporate hierarchy to share knowledge freely across the organization (the horizontal part of the 'T') while remaining fiercely committed to individual business unit performance (the vertical part).

Chief Information Officer

The CIO position emerged in the 1970s as a result of increased importance placed on IT. In the early 1980s, the CIO was often portrayed as the corporate savior who was to align the worlds of business and technology. CIOs were described as the new breed of information managers who were businesspeople first, managers second, and technologists third (Grover et al., 1993). It was even postulated that in the 1990s, as information became a firm's critical resource, the CIO would become the logical choice for the chief executive officer (CEO) position.

As a manager of people, the CIO faces the usual human resource roles of recruiting, staff training, and retention, and the financial roles of budget determination, forecasting and authorization. As the provider of technological services to user departments, there remains a significant amount of work in publicity, promotion, and internal relations with user management. As a manager of an often virtual information organization, the CIO has to coordinate sources of information services spread throughout and beyond the boundaries of the firm. The CIO is thus concerned with a wider group of issues than are most managers.

While information systems executives share several similarities with the general manager, notable differences are apparent. The CIO is not only concerned with a wider group of issues than most managers, but also, as the chief information systems strategist, has a set of responsibilities that must constantly evolve with the corporate information needs and with information technology itself. It has been suggested that the IT director's ability to add value is the biggest single factor in determining whether the organization views information technology as an asset or a liability.

According to Earl and Feeny (1994, p. 11), chief information officers have the difficult job of running a function that uses a lot of resources but that offers little measurable evidence of its value. They suggest making the information systems department an asset to their companies, and CIOs should think of their work as adding value in certain key areas. Creation of the CIO role was driven in part by two organizational needs. First, accountability is increased when a single executive is responsible for the organization's processing needs. Second, creation of the CIO position facilitates the closing of the gap between organizational and IT strategies, which has long been cited as a primary business concern.

Alignment of business and IT objectives is not only a matter of achieving competitive advantage, but is essential for the firm's very survival. Though the importance of IT in creating competitive advantage has been widely noted, achieving these gains has proven elusive. Sustained competitive advantage requires not only the development of a single system, but the ability to consistently deploy IT faster, cheaper, and more strategically than one's competitors. IT departments play a critical role in realizing the potential of IT. The performance of IT functions, in turn, often centers on the quality of leadership, that is, the CIO.

As early as 1984, some surveys suggested that one-third of U.S. corporations had a CIO function, if not in title. While exact percentages differ, ranging from 40 percent to 70 percent, Grover et al. (1993) found that the number of senior-level information systems executive positions created over the past 10 years had grown tremendously. The earliest scientifically conducted research on the CIO position examined 43 of 50 top-ranked Fortune 500 service organizations in the U.S., and noted that 23 (58 percent) of these organizations had the CIO position. In 1990, the 200 largest Fortune 500 industrial and service organizations were examined, and it was found that 77 percent of the industrials had a CIO position as compared with 64% of the service organizations. It is very likely that these numbers have increased in recent years.

Few studies have examined the reasons behind the creation of the CIO position in firms. Creation of the position effectively increases accountability by making a single executive responsible for corporate information processing needs. In a sample of Fortune 500 firms, that is, those appearing on the list for four consecutive years, 287 firms with CIOs were compared in 1995 to firms without CIOs on a number of variables hypothesized to predict creation of the position. It was observed that a number of characteristics of the corporate board, including the number of outside directors and equity ownership of the directors, predicted the existence of the CIO position. A firm's information intensity was also found to be positively related to the creation of the CIO position. Furthermore, the CIO position was more likely to exist when the CEO appreciated the strategic value and importance of IT.

The CIO title itself has become a source of confusion. The term CIO has been somewhat loosely defined and is often used interchangeably with various titles such as IT director, vice president of IS, director of information resources, director of information services, and director of MIS, to describe a senior executive responsible for establishing policy and controlling information resources. Sometimes, the CIO label denotes a function rather than a title. Studies relating to the CIO have focused on the evolution of the position and the similarities between the CIO and other senior-level executives.

The CIO label itself has been met with resistance, and some firms have replaced the title with alternative labels such as knowledge manager, chief knowledge officer (CKO) or chief technology officer (CTO). It has been found that the CKO has to discover and develop the CEO's implicit vision of how knowledge management would make a difference, and how IT can support this difference.

We have seen in Chapter III that there are significant differences between the tasks of a CTO, CIO and CKO. While the CTO is focused on technology, the CIO focuses on information, and the CKO focuses on knowledge. When companies replace a CIO with a CKO, it should not only be a change of title. Rather, it should be a change of focus.

The CIO is becoming a member of the top management team in many business organizations and participates in organizational strategy development. Similarly, it has been stated that CIOs see themselves as corporate officers and general business managers. This suggests that CIOs must be politically savvy and that their high profile places them in contention for top line management jobs. The results of these studies indicate that today's CIO is more a managerially oriented executive than a technical manager. Some provide a profile of the ideal CIO as an open communicator with a business perspective, capable of leading and motivating staff, and as an innovative corporate team player. Karimi et al. (2001) found that successful CIOs characterized themselves in the following ways:

- I see myself to be a corporate officer.
- In my organization I am seen by others as a corporate officer.
- I am a general business manager, not an IT specialist.
- I am a candidate for top line management positions.
- I have a high profile image in the organization.
- I have political as well as rational perspectives of my firm.
- I spend most of my time outside the IT department focusing on the strategic and organizational aspects of IT.

Business strategist is likely to be among the most significant roles that CIOs will fulfill in the digital era, according to Sambamurthy et al. (2000). As a business strategist, the CIO must understand and impact internal and external business forces and factors that sustain competitive advantage. Also, the CIO must be capable of developing strategy with executive colleagues and peers, including the chief executive officer (CEO), chief operating officer (COO), and other senior business executives.

Not only are CIOs drawn into the mainstream of business strategy, but also their compensation is being linked with the effectiveness of competitive Internet actions in many firms. With an understanding of current and emergent information technologies and an ability to foresee breakthrough strategic opportunities as well as disruptive threats, CIOs must play a lead role in educating their business peers about how IT can raise the competitive agility of the firm. Obviously, to be effective business strategists, the CIOs must be members of an executive leadership team and part of the dominant coalition that manages the firm.

With an understanding of current and emergent information technologies and an ability to foresee breakthrough strategic opportunities as well as disruptive threats, CIOs must play a lead role in educating their business peers about how IT can raise the competitive agility of the firm. To be effective business strategists, the CIOs must be members of an executive leadership team and part of the dominant coalition that manages the firm.

Robson (1997) has suggested that CIOs have to be hybrid managers to be successful: Hybrid managers, as opposed to managers who are hybrid users, require this business literacy and technical competency plus a third dimension. This third item is the organizational astuteness that allows a manager to make business-appropriate IS use and management decisions that enhance or set business directions as well as follow them. It is fairly well recognized that hybrid users can be trained whereas the more sophisticated development of hybrid managers is problematic, perhaps requiring inbuilt talent and personal qualities, but can be encouraged or discouraged. For this reason undergraduate study can generally produce only hybrid users whilst postgraduate and post-experience study can support the development of hybrid managers.

According to Robson (1997), hybrid managers will be critical to the survival of the IT function in the future. The continuing devolution of many IS areas requires a hybrid manager to manage the new IS, and indeed even the acts of assessing the relative merits of different paths to devolution and judging what not to devolve require the skills as defined to be of a hybrid manager.

This is certainly true if the company is to succeed in knowledge management. Knowledge management requires not only business literacy and technical competency; it requires first and foremost an ability to combine the two. Sometimes information technology is (part of) the solution to knowledge management challenges, and sometimes it not. Only business literacy combined with technical competency can enable a CIO to make an optimal judgment.

Although it was originally expected that the CIO would have high levels of influence within the firm, as the definition of job responsibilities would suggest, recent surveys indicate that this may not be the case. CIOs may not actually possess strategic influence with top management, and they may lack operational and tactical influence with users. Some specific problems include higher-than-average corporate dismissal rates compared with other top executives, diminished power with belt tightening and budget cuts, high expectations of new strategic systems that CIOs may not be able to deliver, lack of secure power bases due to the fact that CIOs are viewed as outsiders by top management, and the fact that few CIOs take part in strategic planning, and many do not report to the CEO.

Over time, the number of CIOs reporting to CEOs seems to increase. In 1992, only 27 percent of surveyed CIOs in the U.S. reported to CEOs, while this number had increased to 43 percent five years later, as listed in Figure 2. In Norway, the numbers in Figure 2 seem to indicate a stable level above 40 percent or maybe an insignificant decline in the fraction of CIOs reporting to the CEO. An interesting development is indirect reports moving from CFOs to other top executives.

The CIO's pivotal responsibility of aligning business and technology direction presents a number of problems. Moreover, rapid changes in business and information environments have resulted in corresponding changes at the IT function helm. This role has become increasingly complex, causing many firms to look outside the organization for the right qualifications. Characteristics such as professional background, educational background, and current length of tenure have been examined in previous research. CIO problems seem to indicate that, when compared with other senior executives, CIOs do not have the authority or ability to achieve the kind of changes that were promised when the position was initially proposed. A second and possibly related explanation is that CIOs are experiencing managerial role conflicts that prevent them from meeting those expectations as originally envisioned in the CIO position.

One approach to understanding the CIO position is to study managerial roles. Mintzberg (1994) notes a number of different and sometimes conflicting views of the manager's role. He finds that it is a curiosity of the management literature that its best-known writers all seem to emphasize one particular part of the manager's job to the exclusion of the others. Together, perhaps, they cover all the parts, but even that does not describe the whole job of managing.

Figure 2. CIO Reporting in the U.S. and Norway Over Time (Gottschalk, 2000, 2002)

Chief Information Officer (CIO) reporting to:	**USA 1992**	**USA 1997**	**Norway 1997**	**Norway 1999**	**Norway 2000**
Chief Executive Officer (CEO)	27 %	43 %	48 %	44 %	41 %
Chief Financial Officer (CFO)	44 %	32 %	21 %	23 %	16 %
Other top executive in the company	29 %	25 %	31 %	33 %	43 %

Based on an observational study of chief executives, Mintzberg (1994) concluded that a manager's work could be described in terms of ten job roles. As managers take on these roles, they perform management functions. These ten roles consist of three interpersonal roles (figurehead, leader and liaison), three informational roles (monitor, disseminator, and spokesman), and four decisional roles (entrepreneur, disturbance handler, resource allocator, and negotiator):

- *Figurehead* performs some duties of a ceremonial nature. Examples are greeting visitors, responding to journalists' questions, and visiting customers and allies.
- *Personnel leader* is responsible for motivation of subordinates and for staffing and training. Examples are most activities involving subordinates, such as settling disagreements between subordinates.
- *Liaison* establishes a web of external relationships. Examples are attending conferences and giving presentations.
- *Monitor* seeks and receives information to understand and learn from the environment. Examples are reading journals and listening to external experts.
- *Disseminator* transmits information to other organizational members. Examples include forwarding reports and memos, making phone calls to present information, and holding informational meetings.
- *Spokesman* involves the communication of information and ideas. Examples are speaking to the board of directors and top management, and talking to users.
- *Entrepreneur* acts as initiator and designer of much of the controlled change in the organization. Examples are user ideas converted to systems proposals and management objectives transformed to infrastructure actions.
- *Resource allocator* is responsible for allocation of human, financial, material, and other resources. Examples are working on budgets, developing project proposals, and monitoring information technology projects.
- *Negotiator* is responsible for representing the organization in negotiations. Examples are negotiations with unions concerning wages and with vendors concerning procurements.

According to Mintzberg (1994), these 10 roles are common in all managerial jobs regardless of the functional or hierarchical level. However, differences do exist in the importance and effort dedicated to each managerial role based on job content, different skill levels, and expertise. Mintzberg (1994) states that managers are in fact specialists, required to perform a particular set of specialized managerial roles that are dependent upon the functional area and hierarchical level in which they work.

Grover et al. (1993) used the Mintzberg framework to study CIO roles. They selected six of ten roles, which they found relevant for CIOs: personnel leader, liaison, monitor, spokesman, entrepreneur and resource allocator. The four other roles (figurehead, disseminator, disturbance handler, and negotiator) were not operationalized because Grover et al. (1993) found that the activities constituting these roles were correlated with the activities of the other six roles and because they found that the activities that comprised those four roles were consistently important only for certain functions and levels of management. The six selected roles were related to information technology management by rephrasing them:

- As the *personnel leader,* the IS manager is responsible for supervising, hiring, training, and motivating a cadre of specialized personnel. Literature has emphasized the impact of this role on IS personnel. This role is mainly internal to the IS organization.
- The *spokesman* role incorporates activities that require the IS manager to extend organizational contacts outside the department to other areas of the organization. Frequently, he or she must cross traditional departmental boundaries and become involved in affairs of production, distribution, marketing, and finance. This role is mainly external in relation to the intraorganizational environment.
- As the *monitor*, the IS manager must scan the external environment to keep up with technical changes and competition. In acting as the firm's technical innovator, the IS manager uses many sources, including vendor contacts, professional relationships, and a network of personal contacts. This role is mainly external in relation to the interorganizational environment.
- As the *liaison*, the IS manager must communicate with the external environment including exchanging information with IS suppliers, customers, buyers, market analysts, and the media. This role is mainly external in relation to the interorganizational environment.
- As the *entrepreneur*, the IS manager identifies business needs and develops solutions that change business situations. A major responsibility of the IS manager is to ensure that rapidly evolving technical opportunities are understood, planned, implemented, and strategically exploited in the organization.
- As the *resource allocator*, the IS manager must decide how to allocate human, financial, and information resources. The litany of past discussion on charge-back systems (users have to pay for IT services) and the importance of "fairness" in IS resource allocation decisions speak to the importance of this role. This role is mainly internal to the IS organization.

Figure 3. CIO Roles on Different Arenas

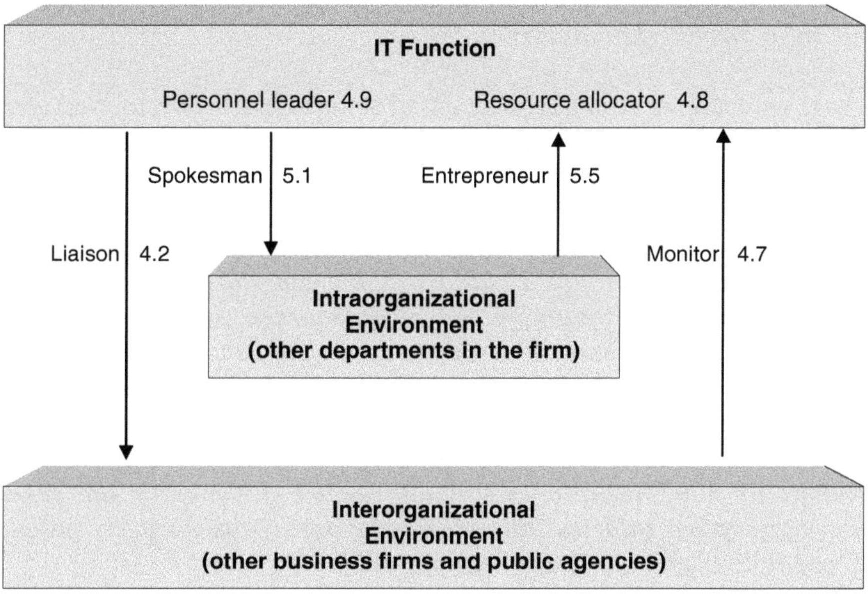

In Figure 3, the selected six CIO roles are illustrated. The roles of personnel leader and resource allocator are both internal to IT functions. The entrepreneur absorbs ideas from the intraorganizational environment, while the spokesman influences the intraorganizational environment. The liaison informs the external environment, while the monitor absorbs ideas from the external environment.

A survey was conducted in Norway (Gottschalk, 2002) to investigate CIO roles. CIOs were asked questions about the importance of the different roles. Survey results indicate some variation in the importance of roles. Responding CIOs found the role of entrepreneur most important and the role of liaison least important. This is indicated with numbers in Figure 3, where the scale went from 1 (not important) to 6 (very important).

In the U.S., Chatterjee et al. (2001) conducted an investigation to study if newly created CIO positions have any impact. According to Chatterjee et al. (2001, p. 59):

This study's findings provide strong support for the proposition that announcements of newly created CIO positions do indeed provoke positive reactions from the marketplace, but primarily for firms competing in industries with high levels of IT-driven transformation. Within such industries, IT is being applied in innovative ways for competitive purposes. For firms to engage in such strategic behaviors, they must first develop and then effectively exploit an appropriate set of IT capabilities. Strong executive leadership, as reflected in the CIO role, is likely to play a crucial enabling role in the effective deployment of these IT capabilities, and hence be highly valued by a firm's shareholders.

Just how valuable is a newly created CIO role? One way to consider the magnitude of the stock market reaction is to compute the impact on each firm's market valuation of common equity. A conservative approach would calculate this effect through the median statistic (multiplying the median stock market reaction by the median market valuation of common equity); a less conservative approach would use the mean statistic (multiplying the mean stock market reaction by the mean market valuation of common equity). For our entire sample of firms, the net impact per firm of a newly created CIO position is in a range from $7.5 million (median approach) to $76 million (mean approach). If only the IT-driven transformation subgroup is considered, the net impact is in a range from $8 million (median approach) to $297 million (mean approach). Even with the trend in escalated executive salaries, the expected return from such an investment in IT capability appears quite reasonable!

Computer Science Corporation (CSC 1996) has suggested an alternative set of leadership roles to Mintzberg (1994). These six leadership roles are specifically tailored to information technology executives:

- The *chief architect* designs future possibilities for the business. The primary work of the chief architect is to design and evolve the IT infrastructure so that it will expand the range of future possibilities for the business, not define specific business outcomes. The infrastructure should provide not just today's technical services, such as networking, databases and desktop operating systems, but an increasing range of business level services, such as workflow, portfolio management, scheduling, and specific business components or objects.
- The *change leader* orchestrates resources to achieve optimal implementation of the future. The essential role of the change leader is to orchestrate all those resources that will be needed to execute the change program. This includes providing new IT tools, but it also involves putting in place teams of people who can redesign roles, jobs and workflow, who can change beliefs about the company and the work people do, and who understand human nature and can develop incentive systems to coax people into new and different ways of acting.
- The *product developer* helps define the company's place in the emerging digital economy. For example, a product developer might recognize the potential for performing key business processes (perhaps order fulfillment,

purchasing or delivering customer support) over electronic linkages such as the Internet. The product developer must "sell" the idea to a business partner, and together they can set up and evaluate business experiments, which are initially operated out of IS. Whether the new methods are adopted or not, the company will learn from the experiments and so move closer to commercial success in emerging digital markets.

- The *technology provocateur* embeds IT into the business strategy. The technology provocateur works with senior business executives to bring IT and realities of the IT marketplace to bear on the formation of strategy for the business. The technology provocateur is a senior business executive who understands both the business and IT at a deep enough level to integrate the two perspectives in discussions about the future course of the business. Technology provocateurs have a wealth of experience in IS disciplines, so they understand at a fundamental level the capabilities of IT and how IT impacts the business.
- The *coach* teaches people to acquire the skills they will need for the future. Coaches have two basic responsibilities: teaching people how to learn, so that they can become self-sufficient, and providing team leaders with staff able to do the IT-related work of the business. A mechanism that assists both is the center of excellence — a small group of people with a particular competence or skill, with a coach responsible for their growth and development. Coaches are solid practitioners of the competence that they will be coaching, but need not be the best at it in the company.
- The *chief operating* strategist invents the future with senior management. The chief operating strategist is the top IS executive who is focused on the future agenda of the IS organization. The strategist has parallel responsibilities related to helping the business design the future, and then delivering it. The most important, and least understood, parts of the role have to do with the interpretation of new technologies and the IT marketplace, and the bringing of this understanding into the development of the digital business strategy for the organization.

These roles were applied in a survey (Gottschalk, 2002) in Norway. CIOs were asked to rate the importance of each leadership role. The roles were rated on a scale from 1 (not important) to 6 very important. The role of change leader received the highest score of 4.6, while the role of product developer received the lowest score of 3.3.

The Harvard Business Review invited leading scholars to answer the question: Are CIOs obsolete? They all responded with a no answer. Rockart found that all good CIOs today are business executives first, and technologists second (Maruca, 2000, p. 57). Earl paid attention to recruiting new CIOs. His scenario suggests an acid test for selecting the new CIO. Does he or she have

Figure 4. Organizational Chart with a CKO and a CIO in a Typical Law Firm

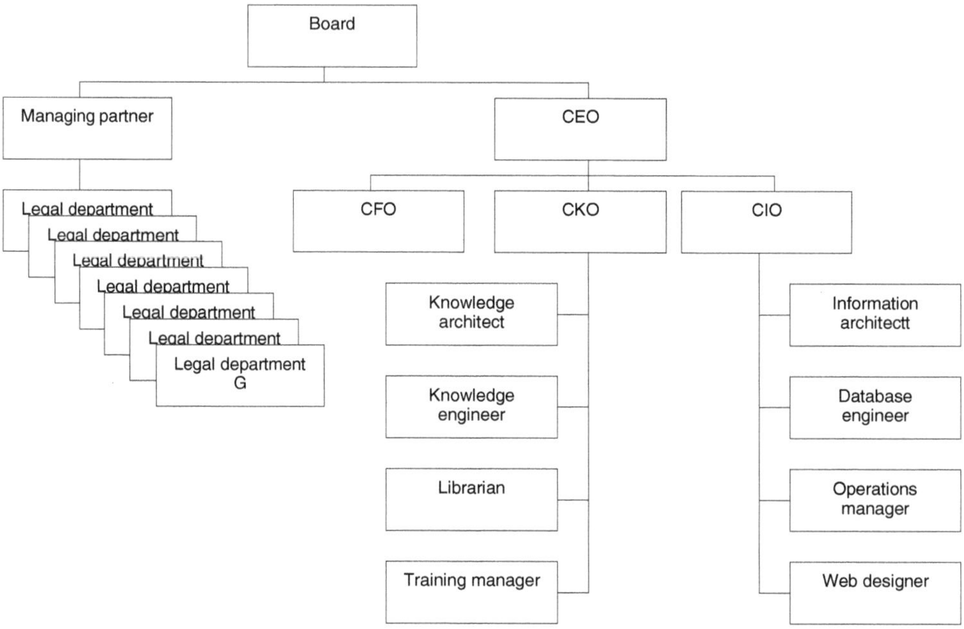

the potential to become CEO? If we could develop and appoint such executives, not only will we have CIOs fit for today's challenges, we may be lining up our future CEOs (Maruca, 2000, p. 60).

While the CKO may have a knowledge architect on the staff, the CIO will typically have an information architect, as illustrated in Figure 4. The knowledge engineer belongs to the CKO staff, while the database engineer belongs to the CIO staff. The librarian belongs to the CKO staff, while the operations manager belongs to the CIO staff. The training manager is on the CKO's staff, while the Web designer is on the CIO's staff.

CASE STUDY: LINDH STABELL HORTEN AND SCHJØDT

In research conducted by Brekke and Pedersen (2003), they studied whether knowledge workers are motivated by rewards, associations, own contribution or perception of management commitment, for sharing knowledge through IT within the organization. The research was conducted in two law firms in Norway, Lindh Stabell Horten and Schjødt.

Lindh Stabell Horten (LSH) is today the largest law firm in Scandinavia, with approximately 220 legal attorneys. The firm has offices in both Norway and Denmark, as well as in Sweden. In Norway, the company is well established in the two largest cities, Oslo and Bergen. LSH was established in February 2000 after a merger of the three Scandinavian law firms: Lindh (Stockholm), Stabell (Oslo) and Horten (Copenhagen). The merge was done much as a response to the increasing demand for cross-border legal services, giving the firm a unique cross-border approach which has made it one of Scandianivia's most successful law firms, and attracted an increasing number of international companies in a variety of sectors. LSH is using a corporate model with a managing director instead of a partner to run the firm. The managing director, Erik Løken, answers to a board of directors. Today, the firm provides a full range of legal services, which includes international trade practice. LSH has substantial expertise in the legal areas such as commercial law, corporate, banking, and shipping.

Lindh Stabell Horten has also employed specialist lawyers in IT, intellectual property, tax, mergers and acquisitions, litigation, property and employment. In addition to being a pan-Scandinavian law firm, LSH is also a part of the international alliance of law firms called DLA and Partners (D&P). D&P consists of a number of large law firms including LSH, spread across the world, reaching from Europe to Asia. The main purpose of the alliance is to become an integrated, single firm with a joint management, name, divisions, marketing, intranet, business development, social activities, skills development, and so forth.

Schjødt is one of the largest law firms in Norway, being the only legal firm to have offices in all the four largest cities in the country, including Oslo, Bergen, Trondheim and Stavanger. The firm also has an office in Ålesund. Schjødt in Oslo traces its roots back to 1920. The firm has had its present name since 1982, adopting the surname of Annæus Schjødt. Schjødt as it stands today is a result of a merger in 1996 between three law firms, Schjødt based in Oslo, Martens based in Bergen and Vaagland based in Trondheim. The core business of the firm is commercial law, but the firm also has a long history of civil litigation and arbitration. The firm has grown steadily over the years since its origin, and it now employs 145 lawyers.

Schjødt is organized into departments covering either industries or legal practice areas, some of the most important of which are: capital markets, mergers and acquisitions, oil, gas and energy, intellectual property, competition, EU and EEA law, banking and finance, and litigation.

Brekke and Pedersen (2003) find that both Lindh Stabell Horten and Schjødt are quite traditional law firms in the choices regarding IT. They both have solutions on the Internet with a company Web page and intranet. Additionally, they internally have a chat room called a v-room and an electronic document handling system that is connected to Microsoft Explorer. According to managing director Erik Løken at LSH and managing partner Petter Sogn at Schjødt, the electronic document handling system and the national law database publicly available online at *www.lovdata.no* as well as email systems are the most important IT systems in the daily work for the lawyers in both firms. The researchers' contacts further evaluated the IT systems to function properly; the only exception being Løken, who said that there needs to be made improvements on the company's intranet. The main problem with the intranet was, according to him, that it is too tiresome and complicated to publish documents, one of its intended main functions.

The most advanced or high level IT system in both firms seems to be the electronic document handling system, called DocsOpen. DocsOpen allows all documents made and saved within the company's network to be immediately made available to all employees. One can even accommodate it so that this is done automatically when one has saved a document. DocsOpen is naturally popular in law firms, as it handles large amounts of documents in a user-friendly and tidy manner. It is interesting to note that LSH has adopted this system, as it was one of the main recommendations made by students from the Norwegian School of Management BI in their thesis one year earlier.

Brekke and Pedersen (2003) decided to study incentives for knowledge sharing through information technology, as IT is one of the main enablers for inter-human knowledge sharing. Knowledge sharing was measured in three different ways: as knowledge sharing using IT tools, sharing different types of knowledge using IT, and as knowledge shared through IT in their work tasks during work processes.

The researchers' findings indicate that attitudes towards own contribution, rewards and end-user satisfaction with IT systems influence degrees of knowledge sharing in IT systems. The lawyers' attitude towards their own contribution was the factor that predicted their share of knowledge the most, closely followed by their attitude towards rewards. Attitude towards associations and perceived management commitment were observed to be of less importance.

Attitude towards own contribution is concerned with how lawyers see themselves. A person's willingness to share his or her knowledge with others in an organization is influenced by the person's perception of own ability to contribute to the organization by sharing that knowledge. Attitude towards own contribution can be defined as the degree to which one believes that one can improve the organization's performance through one's knowledge sharing. It is sometimes described as self-efficacy, in which an individual mediates how outcome expectations influence personal decisions and expenditure of efforts. This assumes that a person acts on his or her judgment of what he or she can do, at that his or her actions have a certain effect. In our case, if a lawyer does not believe his or her knowledge may actually be useful for the organization, he or she will not share own knowledge. On the other hand, if the person thinks that own knowledge is valuable and useful, the person will share it.

In addition to attitude towards own contribution, the researchers found that *attitude towards rewards* (education, money, promotion, reputation) influences knowledge sharing in IT systems. This implies that rewards have a significant impact on knowledge sharing using various IT tools and sharing various knowledge in IT systems, as well as through the phases of the law firm as a value shop. Rewards can be classified into two categories, the first being concrete and the other being abstract. In the first category we find expected education, expected money and expected promotion. These can be defined as concrete since they are tangible and extrinsic. The second category under rewards is abstract and can be exemplified by expected reputation. This concept is intangible and intrinsic; however, it is still considered to be a reward as it is a possible outcome of an action, in this case knowledge sharing. If compared to some of the theory on intrinsic motivation, this should affect people the most as it may increase the feeling of competence.

End-user satisfaction with IT systems is the third and final significant factor for the extent of knowledge sharing in IT systems. End-user satisfaction is concerned with content, format, accuracy, ease of use and timeliness of IT systems.

Attitude towards associations is no significant factor for the extent of knowledge sharing in IT systems. This concept explains the attitude towards improving relationships through one's knowledge sharing. There are different opinions on whether or not people are by nature sharing creatures. However, there seems to be little doubt that humans are "herd animals" who thrive on relationships and need to communicate. In social exchange theory, this concept assumes that people may develop relationships based on knowledge exchange. Knowledge sharing can occur in and through information systems. This may be done in several ways, but a crucial point is changed as the face-to-face knowledge exchange is altered and replaced by an information system. Sharing knowledge through an IT system may not take away the feeling of creating relationships. It is when sharing in an IT system that it may change, such as when entering data into a repository and making it available to all employees.

Many researchers and professionals argue that *perceived management commitment* will influence certain behavior and therefore also knowledge sharing. This argument was not supported in the research in LSH and Schjødt conducted by Brekke and Pedersen (2003). Management commitment can be understood as management's emphasis on the importance of knowledge sharing. The determination of management perceived through email, internal broadcasting and company newsletter is argued to have a great impact on knowledge sharing behavior throughout the organization.

Brekke and Pedersen (2003) presented their findings to managing partner Petter Sogn at Schjødt and managing director Erik Løken at LSH. Sogn did not expect a significant relationship between knowledge sharing and *attitude towards rewards*. Løken, on the other hand, did not seem surprised, as he claimed that this was expected, as he believes that a reward system will greatly improve the rewarded action (knowledge sharing).

Løken and Sogn did expect *attitude towards own contribution* and *end-user satisfaction with IT systems* to be significant factors. Løken believes that user satisfaction and user-friendly systems are very important when trying to motivate lawyers to use and share knowledge via an IT system. He had experienced that lawyers did not share knowledge (publish documents, reports and other useful information on the intranet), because it was too time consuming and complicated. In order to publish a written document on the intranet, lawyers had to publish through one specific person. LSH is currently working on a better solution for such distribution of knowledge on the intranet.

Sogn had expected that *perceived management commitment* should have a significant influence on knowledge sharing. He believes that it is almost exclusively by leadership and management that one can get lawyers to share their knowledge. This was not supported by the research.

Chapter IV

Stages of Growth in Knowledge Management Technology

INTRODUCTION

Stages of growth models have been used widely in both organizational research and information technology management research. According to King and Teo (1997), these models describe a wide variety of phenomena — the organizational life cycle, product life cycle, biological growth, and so forth. These models assume that predictable patterns (conceptualized in terms of stages) exist in the growth of organizations, the sales levels of products, and the growth of living organisms. These stages are (1) sequential in nature, (2) occur as a hierarchical progression that is not easily reversed, and (3) involve a broad range of organizational activities and structures.

Benchmark variables are often used to indicate characteristics in each stage of growth. A one-dimensional continuum is established for each benchmark variable. The measurement of benchmark variables can be carried out using Guttman scales (Frankfort-Nachmias & Nachmias, 2002; Nunnally & Bernstein, 1994). Guttman scaling is a cumulative scaling technique based on ordering theory that suggests a linear relationship between the elements of a domain and the items on a test.

In this chapter, a four-stage model for the evolution of information technology support for knowledge management is proposed and empirically tested. The purpose of the model is both to understand the current situation in a firm in terms of a specific stage and to develop strategies for moving to a higher stage in the future. The model is applied to law firms in which knowledge of professional experts is a core asset, and the careful management of this asset has special importance (Barton et al., 2002a, 2002b; Becker et al., 2001; Disterer, 2001; Edwards & Mahling, 1997; Galanter & Palay, 1991; Hunter et al., 2002; Montana, 2000; Mountain, 2001; Susskind, 2000).

This chapter is concerned with the following question: Do firms move through various stages of growth in their application of knowledge management technology over time, and is each theoretical stage regarded as an actual stage in law firms?

STAGES OF GROWTH MODELS

Various multistage models have been proposed for organizational evolution over time. These models differ in the number of stages. For example, Nolan (1979) introduced a model with six stages for IT maturity in organizations, which later was expanded to nine stages. Earl (2000) suggested a stages of growth model for evolving the e-business, consisting of the following six stages: external communication, internal communication, e-commerce, e-business, e-enterprise, and transformation. Each of these models identifies certain characteristics that typify firms in different stages of growth. Among these multistage models, models with four stages seem to have been proposed and tested most frequently (King & Teo, 1997).

In the area of knowledge management, Housel and Bell (2001) described a knowledge management maturity model. The knowledge management maturity (KMM) model is used to assess the relative maturity of a company's knowledge management efforts. The KMM model defines the following five levels (Housel & Bell, 2001, p. 136):

1. *Level one* is the default stage in which there is low commitment to managing anything other than essential, necessary survival-level tasks. At level one, formal training is the main mechanism for learning, and all learning is taken to be reactive. Moreover, level one organizations fragment knowledge into isolated pockets that are not explicitly documented.
2. *Level two* organizations share only routine and procedural knowledge. Need-to-know is characteristic, and knowledge awareness rises with the realization that knowledge is an important organizational resource that must be managed explicitly. Databases and routine tasks exist but are not centrally compiled or managed.
3. *Level three* organizations are aware of the need for managing knowledge. Content fit for use in all functions begins to be organized into a knowledge life cycle, and enterprise knowledge-propagation systems are in place. However, general awareness and maintenance are limited.
4. *Level four* is characterized by enterprise knowledge sharing systems. These systems respond proactively to the environment and the quality,

currency, utility, and usage of these systems is improved. Knowledge processes are scaled up across the organization, and organization knowledge boundaries become blurred. Benefits of knowledge sharing and reuse can be explicitly quantified, and training moves into an ad hoc basis as the technology infrastructure for knowledge sharing is increasingly integrated and seamless.

5. At *level five*, knowledge sharing is institutionalized and organizational boundaries are minimized. Human know-how and content expertise are integrated into a seamless package, and knowledge can be most effectively leveraged. Level five organizations have the ability to accelerate the knowledge life cycle to achieve business advantage.

According to Kazanjian and Drazin (1989), the concept of stages of growth is widely employed. A number of multistage models have been proposed which assume that predictable patterns exist in the growth of organizations, and that these patterns unfold as discrete time periods best thought of as stages. These models have different distinguishing characteristics. Stages can be driven by the search for new growth opportunities or as a response to internal crises. Some models suggest that firms progress through stages while others argue that there may be multiple paths through the stages.

Kazanjian (1988) applied dominant problems to stages of growth. Dominant problems imply that there is a pattern of primary concerns that firms face for each theorized stage. In the area of IT maturity, dominant problems can shift from lack of skills to lack of resources to lack of strategy associated with different stages of growth.

Kazanjian and Drazin (1989) argue that either implicitly or explicitly, stages of growth models share a common underlying logic. Organizations undergo transformations in their design characteristics, which enable them to face the new tasks or problems that growth elicits. The problems, tasks or environments may differ from model to model, but almost all suggest that stages emerge in a well-defined sequence, so that the solution of one set of problems or tasks leads to the emergence of a new set of problems or tasks that the organization must address. Growth in areas such as IT maturity can be viewed as a series of evolutions and revolutions precipitated by internal crises related to leadership, control and coordination. The striking characteristic of this view is that the resolution of each crisis sows the seeds for the next crisis. Another view is to consider stages of growth as responses to the firm's search for new growth opportunities once prior strategies have been exhausted.

Stages of growth models may be studied through organizational innovation processes. Technological innovation is considered the primary driver of improvements in many businesses today. Information technology represents a complex organizational technology; that is, technology that, when first introduced, imposes a substantial burden on would-be adopters in terms of the competence needed to use it effectively. According to Fichman and Kemerer (1997), such technology typically has an abstract and demanding scientific base, tends to be fragile in the sense that it does not always operate as expected, is difficult to test in a meaningful way, and is unpackaged in the sense that adopters cannot treat the technology as a black box.

Embodying such characteristics, organizational learning and innovation diffusion theory can be applied to explain stages of growth models. Organizational learning is sometimes placed at the center of innovation diffusion theory through a focus on institutional mechanisms that lower the burden of organizational learning related to IT adoption. Organizations may be viewed, at any given moment, as possessing some bundle of competence related to their current operational and managerial processes. In order to successfully assimilate a new process technology, an organization must somehow reach a state at which its bundle of competence encompasses those needed to use the new technology (Fichman & Kemerer, 1997).

Innovations through stages of growth can be understood in terms of technology acceptance over time. Technology acceptance has been studied for several decades in information systems research. Technology acceptance models explain perceived usefulness and usage intentions in terms of social influence and cognitive instrumental processes. For example, Venkatesh and Davis (2000) found that social influence processes (subjective norm, voluntariness, and image) and cognitive instrumental processes (job relevance, output quality, result demonstrability, and perceived ease of use) significantly influenced user acceptance. Similarly, Venkatesh (2000) identified determinants of perceived ease of use, a key driver of technology acceptance, adoption, and usage behavior.

Stages of growth models have been criticized for a lack of empirical validity. Benbasat et al. (1984) found that most of the benchmark variables for stages used by Nolan (1979) were not confirmed in empirical studies. Based on empirical evidence, Benbasat et al. (1984) wrote the following critique of Nolan's stage hypothesis:

The stage hypothesis on the assimilation of computing technology provides one of the most popular models for describing and managing the growth of administrative information systems. Despite little formal evidence of its reliability or robustness, it has achieved a high level of acceptance among practitioners. We describe and summarize the findings of seven empirical studies conducted during the past six years that tested various hypotheses derived from this model. The accumulation of evidence from these studies casts considerable doubt on the validity of the stage hypothesis as an explanatory structure for the growth of computing in organizations.

For example, Nolan (1979) proposed that steering committees should be constituted in later stages of maturity. However, an empirical study showed that of 114 firms, of which 64 had steering committees, the correlation between IT maturity and steering committees was not significant (Benbasat et al., 1984). In practice, organizations adopt steering committees throughout the development cycle rather than in the later stages.

Another example is charge-back methods. In a survey, approximately half of the firms used charge-back systems and the other half did not. In the Nolan (1979) structure, as firms mature through later stages, they should have adopted charge-back systems. Yet, in the empirical analysis, there were no significant correlations between maturity indicators and charge-back system usage, according to Benbasat et al. (1984). Benchmark variables such as steering committees and charge-back systems have to be carefully selected and tested before they are applied in survey research.

The concept of stages of growth has created a number of skeptics. Some argue that the concept of an organization progressing unidirectionally through a series of predictable stages is overly simplistic. For example, organizations may evolve through periods of convergence and divergence related more to shifts in information technology than to issues of growth for specific IT. According to Kazanjian and Drazin (1989), it can be argued that firms do not necessarily demonstrate any inexorable momentum to progress through a linear sequence of stages, but rather that observed configurations of problems, strategies, structures and processes will determine firms' progress.

Kazanjian and Drazin (1989) addressed the need for further data-based research to empirically examine whether organizations in a growth environment shift according to a hypothesized stage of growth model, or whether they follow a more random pattern of change associated with shifts in configurations that do not follow such a progression. Based on a sample of 71 firms, they found support for the stage hypothesis.

To meet the criticism of lacking empirical validity, this research presentation describes the careful development, selection and testing of a variety of instrument parts to empirically validate a knowledge management technology stage model.

Guttman Scaling for Cumulative Growth

Benchmark variables in stages of growth models indicate the theoretical characteristics in each stage of growth. The problem with this approach is that not all indicators of a stage may be present in an organization, making it difficult to place the organization in any specific stage.

Guttman scaling is also known as **cumulative scaling** or **scalogram analysis.** Guttman scaling is based on ordering theory that suggests a linear relationship between the elements of a domain and the items on a test. The purpose of Guttman scaling is to establish a one-dimensional continuum for a concept to measure. We would like a set of items or statements so that a respondent who agrees with any specific question in the list will also agree with all previous questions. This is the ideal for a stage model — or for any progression. By this we mean that it is useful when one progresses from one state to another, so that upon reaching the higher stage one has retained all the features of the earlier stage (Trochim, 2002). For example, a cumulative model for knowledge transfer could consist of six stages: awareness, familiarity, attempt to use, utilization, results, and impact. Byers and Byers (1998) developed a Guttman scale for knowledge levels consisting of stages by order of learning difficulty. Trochim (2002) developed the following cumulative six-stage scale for attitudes towards immigration:

1. I believe that this country should allow more immigrants in.
2. I would be comfortable with new immigrants moving into my community.
3. It would be fine with me if new immigrants moved onto my block.
4. I would be comfortable if a new immigrant moved next door to me.
5. I would be comfortable if my child dated a new immigrant.
6. I would permit a child of mine to marry an immigrant.

Guttman (1950) used scalogram analysis successfully during the war in investigating morale and other problems in the United States Army. In scalogram analysis, items are ordered such that, ideally, organizations that answer a given question favorably all have higher ranks than organizations that answer the same question unfavorably. According to Guttman (1950, p. 62), the ranking of organizations provides a general approach to the problem of scaling:

We shall call a set of items of common content a scale if an organization with a higher rank than another organization is just as high or higher on every item than the other organization.

Kline (1998, p. 75) discusses three problems with Guttman scales, which he claims may render them of little scientific value:

1. *The underlying measurement model.* The first concerns the fact that items correlate perfectly with the total scale score or the attribute being measured. This is unlikely of any variable in the real world. In general terms, it means the measurement model does not fit what is being measured. This is not dissimilar to the difficulty that in psychological measurement it is simply assumed that the attribute is quantitative.
2. *Unidimensionality of the scale.* It has been argued that all valid measuring instruments must be unidimensional. Now, the construction of a Guttman scale does not ensure unidimensionality. It would be perfectly possible to

take items from different scales, each item of a considerably different level of difficulty, and these would form a Guttman scale. This is because the scaling characteristics of Guttman scales are dependent only on difficulty levels. Thus Guttman scales may not be unidimensional. The only practical way around the problem is to factor the items first, but then it may prove difficult to make a Guttman scale with so restricted an item pool.

3. *Ordinal measurement.* The construction of Guttman scales may only permit ordinal measurement. This severely restricts the kinds of statistical analyses that can be used with Guttman scales.

These problems also occurred in the conducted empirical tests of the knowledge management technology stage model in Norway and Australia, as will be evident later in this chapter.

THE KMT STAGE MODEL

Stages of knowledge management technology is a relative concept concerned with IT's ability to process information for knowledge work. IT at later stages is more useful to knowledge work than IT at earlier stages. The relative concept implies that IT is more directly involved in knowledge work at higher stages, and that IT is able to support more advanced knowledge work at higher stages.

The knowledge management technology (KMT) stage model consists of four stages. The first stage is general IT support for knowledge workers. This includes word processing, spreadsheets, and email. The second stage is information about knowledge sources. An information system stores information about who knows what within the firm and outside the firm. The system does not store what they actually know. A typical example is the company intranet. The third stage is information representing knowledge. The system stores what knowledge workers know in terms of information. A typical example is a database. The fourth and final stage is information processing. An information system uses information to evaluate situations. A typical example here is an expert system.

The contingent approach to firm performance implies that Stage I may be right for one firm, while Stage IV may be right for another firm. Some firms will evolve over time from Stage I to higher stages, as indicated in Figure 1. The time axis ranging from 1990 to 2020 in Figure 1 suggests that it takes time for an individual firm and a whole industry to move through all stages. As an example applied later in this chapter, the law firm industry is moving slowly in its use of information technology.

Stages of IT support in knowledge management are useful for identifying the current situation as well as planning for future applications in the firm. Each stage is described in the following:

Figure 1. The Knowledge Management Technology Stage Model

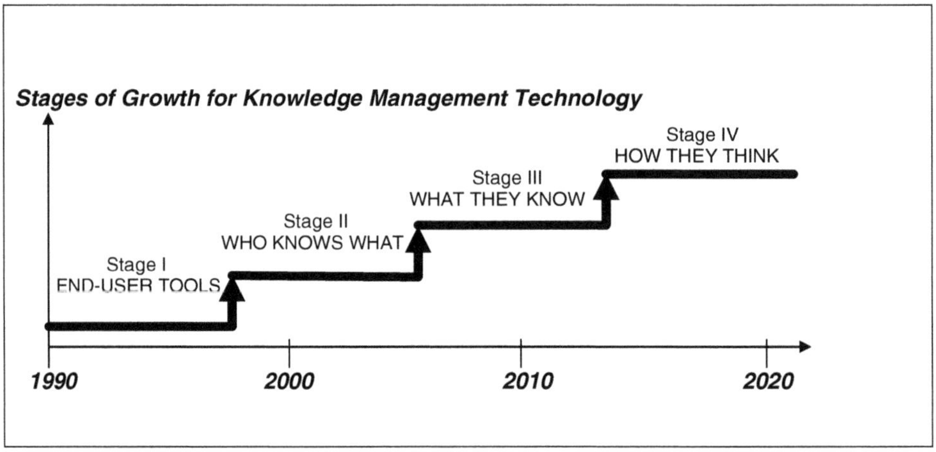

I. *Tools for end-users* are made available to knowledge workers. In the simplest stage, this means a capable networked PC on every desk or in every briefcase, with standardized personal productivity tools (word processing, presentation software) so that documents can be exchanged easily throughout a company. More complex and functional desktop infrastructures can also be the basis for the same types of knowledge support. Stage I is recognized by widespread dissemination and use of end-user tools among knowledge workers in the company. For example, lawyers in a law firm will in this stage use word processing, spreadsheets, legal databases, presentation software, and scheduling programs.

Stage I can be labeled *end-user tools* or *people-to-technology,* as information technology provides knowledge workers with tools that improve personal efficiency.

II. *Information about who knows what* is made available to all people in the firm and to selected outside partners. Search engines should enable work with a thesaurus, since the terminology in which expertise is sought may not always match the terms the expert uses to classify that expertise.

According to Alavi and Leidner (2001), the creation of corporate directories, also referred to as the mapping of internal expertise, is a common application of knowledge management technology. Because much knowledge in an organization remains uncodified, mapping the internal expertise is a potentially useful application of technology to enable easy identification of knowledgeable persons.

Here we find the cartographic school of knowledge management (Earl, 2001), which is concerned with mapping organizational knowledge. It aims to record and disclose who in the organization knows what by building knowledge directories. Often called Yellow Pages, the principal idea is to make sure knowledgeable people in the organization are accessible to others for advice, consultation, or knowledge exchange. Knowledge-oriented directories are not so much repositories of knowledge-based information as gateways to knowledge, and the knowledge is as likely to be tacit as explicit.

Information about who knows what is sometimes called metadata, representing knowledge about where the knowledge resides. Providing taxonomies or organizational knowledge maps enables individuals to rapidly locate the individual who has the needed knowledge more rapidly than would be possible without such IT-based support.

One starting approach in Stage II is to store curriculum vitae (CV) for each knowledge worker in the firm. Areas of expertise, projects completed and clients helped may over time expand the CV. For example, a lawyer in a law firm works on cases for clients using different information sources that can be registered on yellow pages in terms of an intranet.

At Stage II, firms apply the personalization strategy in knowledge management. According to Hansen et al. (1999), the personalization strategy implies that knowledge is tied to the person who developed it and is shared mainly through direct person-to-person contact. This strategy focuses on dialogue between individuals: knowledge is transferred mainly in personal email, meetings and one-on-one conversations.

The creation of a knowledge network is an important part of Stage II. Unless specialists can communicate easily with each other across platform types, expertise will deteriorate. People have to be brought together both virtually and face-to-face to exchange and build their collective knowledge in each of the specialty areas. The knowledge management effort is focused on bringing the experts together so that important knowledge can be shared and amplified, rather than on mapping expertise or benchmarking that occur in Stage III.

The knowledge network is built on modern communication technology. Advances in portable computers such as palmtops and laptops in conjunction with wireless network technologies have engendered mobile computing. In a mobile computing environment, users carrying portable computers are permitted to access the shared computing resources on the network through a wireless channel regardless of their physical locations.

According to Earl (2001), knowledge directories represent more of a belief in personalized knowledge of individuals than the codified knowledge of knowledge bases, and may demonstrate organizational preferences for human, not technology-mediated, communication and exchange. The knowledge philosophy of firms that settle in Stage II can be seen as one of people connectivity. Consequently, the principal contribution from IT is to connect people via intranets and to help them locate knowledge sources and providers using directories accessed by the intranet. Extranets and the Internet may connect knowledge workers to external knowledge sources and providers.

Stage II can be labeled *who-knows-what* or *people-to-people,* as knowledge workers use information technology to find other knowledge workers.

III. *Information from knowledge workers* is stored and made available to everyone in the firm and to designated external partners. Data mining techniques can be applied here to find relevant information and combine information in data warehouses. On a broader basis, search engines are Web browsers and server software that operate with a thesaurus, since the terminology in which expertise is sought may not always match the terms used by the expert to classify that expertise.

One starting approach in Stage III is to store project reports, notes, recommendations and letters from each knowledge worker in the firm. Over time, this material will grow quickly, making it necessary for a librarian or a chief knowledge officer (CKO) to organize it. In a law firm, all client cases will be classified and stored in databases using software such as Lotus Notes.

An essential contribution that IT can make is the provision of shared databases across tasks, levels, entities, and geographies to all knowledge workers throughout a process (Earl, 2001).

According to Alavi and Leidner (2001), one survey found that 74 percent of respondents believed that their organization's best knowledge was inaccessible and 68 percent thought that mistakes were reproduced several times. Such a perception of failure to apply existing knowledge is an incentive for mapping, codifying and storing information derived from internal expertise.

According to Alavi and Leidner (2001), one of the most common applications is internal benchmarking with the aim of transferring internal best practices. To be successful, best practices have to be coded, stored and shared among knowledge workers.

In addition to (1) best practices knowledge within a quality or business process management function, other common applications include (2) knowledge for sales purposes involving products, markets and customers, (3) lessons learned in projects or product development efforts, (4) knowledge around implementation of information systems, (5) competitive intelligence for strategy and planning functions, and (6) learning histories or records of experience with a new corporate direction or approach (Grover & Davenport, 2001).

In Stage III, access both to knowledge (expertise, experience, and learning) and to information (intelligence, feedback, and data analyses) is provided by systems and intranets to operatives, staff, and executives. The supply and distribution of knowledge and information are not restricted. Whereas we might say in Stage I, "give knowledge workers the tools to do the job," we now add, "give knowledge workers the knowledge and information to do the job." According to Earl (2001), this is another way of saying that the philosophy is enhancing the firm's capabilities with knowledge flows.

Although most knowledge repositories serve a single function, Grover and Davenport (2001) found that it is increasingly common for companies to construct an internal portal so that employees can access multiple different repositories and sources from one screen. It is also possible and increasingly popular for repositories to contain information as well as pointers to experts within the organization on key knowledge topics. Often called Knowledge Yellow Pages, these systems facilitate contact and knowledge transfer between knowledgeable people and those who seek their knowledge. Stored, codified knowledge is combined with lists of individuals who contributed the knowledge and could provide more detail or background on it.

In Stage III, firms apply the codification strategy in knowledge management. According to Hansen et al. (1999), the codification strategy centers on information technology: knowledge is carefully codified and stored in knowledge databases and can be accessed and used by anyone. With a codification strategy, knowledge is extracted from the person who developed it, is made independent from the person and stored in form of interview guides, work schedules, benchmark data, and so forth, and then searched and retrieved and used by many employees.

According to Grover and Davenport (2001), firms increasingly view attempts to transform raw data into usable knowledge as part of their knowledge management initiatives. These approaches typically involve isolating data in a separate warehouse for easier access and the use of statistical analysis or data mining and visualization tools. Since their goal is to create data-derived knowledge, they are increasingly addressed as part of knowledge management in Stage III.

Stage III can be labeled *what-they-know* or *people-to-docs*, as information technology provides knowledge workers with access to information that is typically stored in documents. Examples of documents are contracts and agreements, reports, manuals and handbooks, business forms, letters, memos, articles, drawings, blueprints, photographs, email and voice mail messages, video clips, script and visuals from presentations, policy statements, computer printouts, and transcripts from meetings.

Sprague (1995) argues that concepts and ideas contained in documents are far more valuable and important to organizations than facts traditionally organized into data records. A document can be described as a unit of recorded information structured for human consumption. It is recorded and stored, so a speech or conversation for which no transcript is prepared is not a document. A document is a snapshot of some set of information that can incorporate many complex information types, exist in multiple places across a network, depend on other documents for information, change as subordinate documents are updated, and be accessed and modified by many people simultaneously.

IV. *Information systems solving knowledge problems* are made available to knowledge workers and solution seekers. Artificial intelligence is applied in these systems. For example, neural networks are statistically oriented tools that excel at using data to classify cases into one category or another. Another example is expert systems that can enable the knowledge of one or a few experts to be used by a much broader group of workers requiring the knowledge.

According to Alavi and Leidner (2001), an insurance company was faced with the commoditization of its market and declining profits. The company found that applying the best decision making expertise via a new underwriting process, supported by a knowledge management system based on best practices, enabled it to move into profitable niche markets and, hence, to increase income.

According to Grover and Davenport (2001), artificial intelligence is applied in rule-based systems, and more commonly, case-based systems are used to capture and provide access to resolutions of customer service problems, legal knowledge, new product development knowledge, and many other types of knowledge.

Knowledge is explicated and formalized during the knowledge codification phase that took place in Stage III. Codification of tacit knowledge is facilitated by mechanisms that formalize and embed it in documents, software and systems. However, the higher the tacit elements of the knowledge, the more difficult it is to codify. Codification of complex knowledge frequently relies on information technology. Expert systems, decision support systems, document management systems, search engines and relational database tools represent some of the technological solutions developed to support this phase of knowledge management. Consequently, advanced codification of knowledge emerges in Stage IV, rather than in Stage III, because expert systems and other artificial intelligence systems have to be applied to be successful.

Stage IV can be labeled *how-they-think* or *people-to-systems*, in which the system is intended to help solve a knowledge problem.

When companies want to use knowledge in real-time, mission-critical applications, they have to structure the information base for rapid, precise access. A Web search yielding hundreds of documents will not suffice when a customer is waiting on the phone for an answer. Representing and structuring knowledge is a requirement that has long been addressed by artificial intelligence researchers in the form of expert systems and other applications. Now their technologies are being applied within the context of knowledge management. Rule-based systems and case-based systems are used to capture and provide access to customer service problem resolution, legal knowledge, new product development knowledge, and many other types of knowledge. Although it can be difficult and labor-intensive to author a structured knowledge base, the effort can pay off in terms of faster responses to customers, lower cost per knowledge transaction, and lessened requirements for experienced, expert personnel (Grover & Davenport, 2001).

Expert systems are in Stage IV in the proposed model. Stewart (1997) argues for Stage II, stating that knowledge grows so fast that any attempt to codify all of it is ridiculous; but the identities of in-house experts change slowly. Corporate yellow pages should be easy to construct, but it is remarkable how few companies have actually done this. A simple system that connects inquirers to experts saves time, reduces error and guesswork, and prevents the reinvention of countless wheels.

What may be stored in Stage III, according to Stewart (1997), are lessons learned and competitor intelligence. A key way to improve knowledge management is to bank lessons learned - in effect, prepare checklists of what went right and wrong, together with guidelines for others undertaking similar projects. In the area of competitor intelligence, companies need to organize knowledge about their suppliers, customers, and competitors.

Information technology can be applied at four different levels to support knowledge management in an organization, according to the proposed stages of growth. At the first level, end-user tools are made available to knowledge workers. At the second level, information on who knows what is made available electronically. At the third level, some information representing knowledge is stored and made available electronically. At the fourth level, information systems capable of simulating human thinking are applied in the organization. These four levels are illustrated in Figure 2, where they are combined with knowledge management tasks. The entries in the figure only serve as examples of current systems.

One reason for Stage III emerging after Stage II is the personalization strategy versus the codification strategy. The individual barriers are significantly lower with the personalization strategy, because the individual professional maintains the control through the whole knowledge management cycle. According to Disterer (2001), the individual is recognized as an expert and is cared for.

Knowledge management strategies focusing on personalization could be called communication strategies, because the main objective is to foster personal communication between people. Core IT systems with this strategy are yellow pages (directories of experts, who-knows-what systems, people-finder data-

Figure 2. Examples of IS/IT in Different Knowledge Management Stages

STAGES TASKS	I **END-USER TOOLS** **people-to-technology**	II **WHO KNOWS WHAT** **people-to-people**	III **WHAT THEY KNOW** **people-to-docs**	IV **WHAT THEY THINK** **people-to-systems**
Distribute knowledge	Word Processing Desktop Publishing Web Publishing Electronic Calendars Presentations	Word Processing Desktop Publishing Web Publishing Electronic Calendars Presentations	Word Processing Desktop Publishing Web Publishing Electronic Calendars Presentations	Word Processing Desktop Publishing Web Publishing Electronic Calendars Presentations
Share knowledge		Groupware Intranets Networks Email	Groupware Intranets Networks Email	Groupware Intranets Networks Email
Capture knowledge			Databases Data Warehouses	Databases Data Warehouses
Apply knowledge				Expert systems Neural networks Intelligent agents

bases) that show inquirers who they should talk to regarding a given topic or problem. The main disadvantages of personalization strategies are a lack of standards and the high dependence on communication skills and the will of the professionals. Such disadvantages make firms want to advance to Stage III. In Stage III, independence in time among knowledge suppliers and knowledge users is achieved (Disterer, 2002).

Benchmark Variables for Each Stage

In Figure 3, the four stages of growth for knowledge management technology are described in terms of benchmark variables. Benchmark variables indicate the theoretical characteristics in each stage of growth (King & Teo, 1997). For example, firms in Stage I can theoretically be expected to conform to values of benchmark variables listed under Stage I. However, this does not mean that it is impossible for firms in Stage I to have values of benchmark variables applicable to other stages. Rather, it means that the values of benchmark variables indicate the most likely theoretical characteristics applicable in each stage of integration, as indicated in Figure 3.

There are a total of 32 benchmark variables in Figure 3. Fifteen benchmark variables (1-15) are concerned with IT in KM; the next six benchmark variables (16-21) are concerned with IT management, while the remaining 11 (22-32) are concerned with knowledge management in general. Each of the 32 benchmark variables in Figure 3 were derived from research literature as listed in Figure 4.

Trochim (2002) recommends that Guttman scales should be subject to expert rating before they are exposed to respondent rating. The expert rating is

Figure 3. Benchmark Variables for the Knowledge Management Technology Stage Model

No.	Benchmark Variable	Stage I END-USER TOOLS people-to-technology	Stage II WHO KNOWS WHAT people-to-people	Stage III WHAT THEY THINK people-to-docs	Stage IV HOW THEY THINK people-to-systems	Inspired by
1	***Trigger of IT for KM***	Individual lawyers' needs for tools	Organizations' needs for information	Automate lawyers'information work	Automate lawyers'knowledge work	*King & Teo,1997*
2	***Top management's participation***	Rarely	Sometimes	Frequently	Almost always	*King & Teo,1997*
3	***User management's participation***	Rarely	Sometimes	Frequently	Almost always	*King & Teo, 1997*
4	***Principal contribution***	Efficiency of lawyer	Effectiveness of lawyer	Effectiveness of firm	Competitiveness of firm	*Khandelwal & Gottschalk, 2003*
5	***Technology assessment***	Rarely	Sometimes	Frequently	Almost always	*King & Teo, 1997*
6	***Focus***	Availability	Reorganization	Culture	Replacement	*Khandelwal & Gottschalk, 2003*
7	***Dominating statement***	Distribute information	Produce documentation	Make decisions	Automate work	*Khandelwal & Gottschalk, 2003*
8	***Philosophy***	Client satisfaction	Knowledge community	Lawyer independence	Client independence	*Susskind, 2000* *Grover & Davenport,2001*
9	***Critical success factor***	PCs and networks	Knowledge management systems	Quality and quantity	Culture and incentives	*Khandelwal & Gottschalk, 2003*
10	***Strategy***	Tool strategy	Stock strategy	Flow strategy	Growth strategy	*Hansen, 1999*
11	***Main task***	Distributing	Capturing	Sharing	Applying	*Khandelwal & Gottschalk, 2003*
12	***Main purpose***	Administrative work	Access to information	Sharing information	Automating work	*Khandelwal & Gottschalk, 2003*
13	***Main applications***	Office support	Customer relations	Knowledge management	Online Web advice	*Susskind, 2000*
14	***Attitude***	Skeptics	Conservatives	Early adopters	Innovators	*Tiwana, 2001*
15	***Value shop activity***	Understanding clients' problem	Implementing solution	Solving clients' problem	Selecting optimal solution	*Stabell & Fjeldstad, 1998*
16	***Contribution of IT function***	Supplier of PCs	Technical infrastructure	Resource of information	Supplier of systems	*King & Teo, 1997*
17	***Role of IT manager***	Technology expert	Functional administrator	Resource manager	Knowledge management	*King & Teo, 1997*

Figure 3. Benchmark Variables for the Knowledge Management Technology Stage Model (continued)

No.	Benchmark Variable	Stage I END-USER TOOLS people-to-technology	Stage II WHO KNOWS WHAT people-to-people	Stage III WHAT THEY THINK people-to-docs	Stage IV HOW THEY THINK people-to-systems	Inspired by
18	***Performance of IT function***	Operational efficiency	Business implementation	Knowledge implementation	Long-term impact	*King & Teo, 1997*
19	***Key issue for IT function***	Personal computers	Data processing	Information systems	Information networks	*Nolan, 1979*
20	***IT managers' participation***	Rarely	Sometimes	Frequently	Almost always	*King & Teo, 1997*
21	***Status of IT executive***	Three or more	Two	One	One with access	*King & Teo, 1997*
22	***Business level***	Availability-driven	Efficiency-driven	Effectiveness-driven	Expert-driven	*Hansen, 1999*
23	***Main effect***	Reduced dependence	Effective application	New knowledge	Client performance	*Khandelwal & Gottschalk, 2003*
24	***Priority in business***	Fourth	Third	Second	First	*Khandelwal & Gottschalk, 2003*
25	***Management agenda***	Year	Month	Week	Day	*Khandelwal & Gottschalk, 2003*
26	***Priority in marketing***	Fourth	Third	Second	First	*Susskind, 2000*
27	***Normal work***	User-friendly experience	Efficiently organized	Innovative solutions	Ill-specified problems	*Hansen, 1999*
28	***Knowledge growth***	Know-what	Know-why	Know-how to solve	Know-how client solve	*Tiwana, 2001*
29	***Knowledge characteristics***	Experts dictate	Some knowledge explicated	Documented in methodology	Well explicated knowledge	*Tiwana, 2001*
30	***Status of KM executive***	Three or more	Two	One	One with direct access	*King & Teo, 1997*
31	***Response time to clients***	One week	One day	One hour	One minute	*Voss, 2000*
32	***Response quality***	Less than 50%	50% to 89%	90% to 95%	More than 95%	*Voss, 2000*

concerned with developing a cumulative scale, while the respondent rating is concerned with applying a cumulative scale. Trochim (2002) recommends that a group of expert judges rate the statements in terms of how favorable they are to each concept. Expert judges are not asked whether they personally agree with the statement. Instead, they are asked to make a judgment about how the statement is related to the construct of interest. This procedure was first

Figure 4. Description of Benchmark Variables for the Knowledge Management Technology Stage Model

No.	Benchmark Variable	Description of Benchmark Variable
1	*Trigger of IT for knowledge management*	Initially, the triggers for the application of new information technology for knowledge management are opportunities for achieving greater efficiencies based on individual lawyer's needs (Stage I). As information systems begin to be increasingly used to support business functions, organization needs become trigger mechanisms in deciding appropriate IT applications to be developed (Stage II). As information systems begin to be increasingly used to support business strategies, the need to develop the firm by automating lawyers' information work becomes an important trigger mechanism (Stage III). Finally, IT is used to transform the firm by automating lawyers' knowledge work (Stage IV). This benchmark variable was adapted based on King and Teo's (1997) benchmark variable 5, concerned with triggers for development of information systems (IS) applications. They found a significant del correlation between this benchmark variable and stages of integration.
2	*Top management's participation in IT planning for knowledge management*	Traditionally, as in Stage I, top management had not paid great attention to the IT function nor the KM function because they were overhead functions that generated only costs. At Stage II, greater top management participation in information technology planning for knowledge management begins when IT and KM strategies come to be used to support business strategies. The understanding that strategic IT planning for KM can also influence business strategy motivates top management to participate more actively in IT for KM planning. Finally, in Stage IV, when the IT and KM functions become critical for the survival of the organization, top management and senior IT and KM executives jointly formulate business and IT for KM plans. This benchmark variable was adapted based on King and Teo's (1997) benchmark variable 6, concerned with top management participation in information systems planning (ISP). They found a significant del correlation between this benchmark variable and stages of integration. They applied a scale from seldom to infrequent to frequent to almost always. The group of judges in this research found the word "infrequent" difficult to understand. Hence, the revised scale is from rarely to sometimes to frequently to almost always, as used by Guttman (1950, p. 13, 19).
3	*User management's participation in IT planning for knowledge management*	User participation in information technology planning for knowledge management is the next benchmark variable. In the beginning, neither single users nor user management are significantly involved in IT planning for KM. However, as the IT and KM functions begin to influence functional units in terms of their effects on business performance, participation of users becomes more important in order to fully exploit the potential of information technology. User participation gradually increases through the stages, until at Stage IV, users participate extensively in IT planning for KM. This benchmark variable was adapted based on King and Teo's (1997) benchmark variable 7, concerned with user participation in information systems planning (ISP). However, they found only a weak del correlation between this benchmark variable and stages of integration. They explain this by arguing that users are more likely to be involved at the project level rather than at the planning level. Therefore, user management, rather than users, was introduced in the construct in this research.

explored for only one of the benchmark variables. The seventh benchmark variable is concerned with the dominant statement about knowledge management technology among lawyers. For this variable, three expert judges rated "make decisions" as more advanced than "produce documentation", leading to changes in the scale for this benchmark variable as listed in Figures 3 and 4.

Figure 4. Description of Benchmark Variables for the Knowledge Management Technology Stage Model (continued)

No.	Benchmark Variable	Description of Benchmark Variable
4	*Principal contribution from IT for knowledge management*	In the beginning, improved efficiency of individual lawyers' work in law firms was the principal contribution from information technology for knowledge management in law firms. Lawyers got access to electronic mail and word processors. They were able to do the things right. At Stage II, lawyers did the right things by improving their effectiveness. At Stage III, focus shifted from individual effectiveness to organizational effectiveness. Ultimately, IT for KM improves the competitiveness of the firm. This benchmark variable was adapted based on empirical studies of law firms conducted by Khandelwal and Gottschalk (2003).
5	*Assessment of knowledge management technology*	During information technology planning for knowledge management, new technologies that can impact the firm are usually assessed. The level of sophistication involved in assessing new technologies is the basis for this benchmark variable. In the early stages (Stages I and II), assessment of the impact of new technologies, if any, is usually done rather informally and infrequently. At Stage III, the need for formal and frequent procedures for assessing new technologies becomes apparent as IT and KM functions begin to play a more important role in business planning. At Stage IV, assessment of the impact of new technologies becomes an integral part of business, IT and KM planning. This benchmark variable was adapted based on King and Teo's (1997) benchmark variable 9, concerned with assessment of new technologies. However, they found only a weak del correlation between this benchmark variable and stages of integration. One possible reason is that in this era of rapid technological change, the assessment of new technologies has become an integral part of planning regardless of the stage of integration.
6	*Focus when applying IT to knowledge management*	In the beginning, applications of information technology to support knowledge management are focused on making IT available to lawyers (Stage I). When IT tools are available to lawyers, then work processes are improved to enable knowledge sharing among lawyers (Stage II). At Stage III, it is required to create a culture for knowledge development, while replacement of lawyers by information technology such as artificial intelligence (AI) is the focus at Stage IV. This benchmark variable was adapted based on empirical studies of law firms conducted by Kandelwal and Gottschalk (2003).
7	*Dominating statement about knowledge management technology*	In the beginning, PCs and networks enable lawyers to work on their own documents and notes and distribute the results to colleagues and to clients (Stage I). Later, information is readily available from intranets and other sources to enable lawyers to produce comprehensive documentation for clients using application packages (Stage II). At Stage III, lawyers get access to expert opinions such as successful cases, enabling them to make better legal advice decisions for their clients. Ultimately, information technology enables lawyers to automate their professional legal work at Stage IV. This benchmark variable was adapted based on empirical studies of law firms conducted by Khandelwal and Gottschalk (2003).

Figure 4. Description of Benchmark Variables for the Knowledge Management Technology Stage Model (continued)

No.	Benchmark Variable	Description of Benchmark Variable
8	*Main philosophy for knowledge management technology*	For many years, lawyers have been able to focus on the role of client satisfaction in knowledge management, in which client trust and confidence in professional knowledge becomes important. When knowledge management has been accepted as an important approach, then firm philosophy shifts to Stage II, in which the firm is considered a knowledge community of people with a common interest, problem and experience, designed and maintained for a business purpose. To get started on information technology for knowledge management, it has to have an appeal to knowledge workers. One important appeal is enjoying independence in time and space, by working when they like (day or night) and where they like (office, home, summer house). Finally at Stage IV, technology is helping the client, rather than the lawyer, solve knowledge problems. This benchmark variable was inspired by the legal grid developed by Susskind (2000). Also, Grover and Davenport (2001) suggest a change in philosophy over time. They argue that in the first of two phases, emphasis was on the knowledge management project. What firms must do in the second phase of knowledge management is to integrate it with familiar aspects of the business: strategy, human resource management, and managing expert knowledge.
9	*Critical success factor for IT in knowledge management*	Availability of PCs and networks is the basic requirement to enable access to computing power and communication channels. At Stage II, availability of knowledge management systems is important. The success of knowledge management systems is dependent on the quality and quantity of available information in databases (Stage III). Such success is in turn dependent on both an organizational culture that has to be inspired and personal incentives that have to be installed to create an active environment of knowledge sharing. This benchmark variable was adapted based on empirical studies of law firms conducted by Khandelwal and Gottschalk (2003).
10	*Dominating strategy for knowledge management technology*	In the beginning, the tool strategy enables lawyers to use personal computers. At Stage II, the stock strategy enables the firm to collect and store important information related to lawyers' work. At Stage III, further applications of knowledge management technology are according to the flow strategy in which information storing is limited to documents that will be used again in work processes. The growth strategy of only storing documents that are related to legal work in which the firm is inexperienced, but interested, occurs at Stage IV. This benchmark variable was inspired by alternative knowledge strategies as defined by Hansen (1999).
11	*Main task of information technology in knowledge management*	Creating notes and documents on an individual basis is often the first computer task performed by a knowledge worker. The result of each task is distributed to a secretary, a colleague and/or a client. At Stage II, information technology's main task is to be active in capturing information that is the result of knowledge work in the firm. Later, at Stage III, knowledge sharing and exchange occurs when the knowledge worker both distributes and receives electronic information. Ultimately, IT is introduced to solve client problems by applying knowledge that has been codified in information databases. This benchmark variable was inspired by empirical research conducted by Khandelwal and Gottschalk (2003).

Figure 4. Description of Benchmark Variables for the Knowledge Management Technology Stage Model (continued)

No.	Benchmark Variable	Description of Benchmark Variable
12	*Main purpose of IT in knowledge management*	Administrative work processes had to be simplified to cut rising administration costs in law firms. At Stage II, the main purpose of IT in knowledge management shifted to providing access to information more efficiently. At Stage III, doing things right is replaced by doing the right things. Finally, the main purpose is to automate legal work done by lawyers. This benchmark variable was inspired by empirical research conducted by Khandelwal and Gottschalk (2003).
13	*Main applications of IT*	Based on Susskind's (2000) legal grid, this benchmark variable suggests that there is a progression from office support, via customer relationships and knowledge management, to legal Web advice. This progression may vary among firms, thereby making such a standard progression questionable. Nevertheless, this benchmark variable was included to enable empirical measurement of the legal grid.
14	*Attitude towards IT in knowledge management*	Based on Tiwana's (2001, p. 157) proposal that there are skeptics, conservatives, early adopters and innovators, this classification was introduced as a scale.
15	*Contribution to primary activities in the value shop*	Value shop is a value configuration consisting of five primary activities as defined by Stabell and Fjeldstad (1998). It has been suggested that the role of information systems varies across primary activities. While end-user tools are important for understanding clients' problems, what-they-know systems are important for solving clients' problems, how-they-think systems are important for selecting an optimal solution to clients' problems, while who-knows-what systems are important for implementing the optimal solution to clients' problems.
16	*Contribution of IT function*	The role of the IT function may be viewed differently at the various stages of knowledge management technology. The general transition from being technically oriented to being business oriented is well documented in the literature. At Stages I and II, the IT function is technically oriented as supplier of PCs and end-user tools and as developer of technical infrastructure and applications. At Stages III and IV, the IT function is business oriented as a resource making information available and as a supplier of systems that automate legal work. This benchmark variable was adapted based on King and Teo's (1997) benchmark variable 2, concerned with the role of the IS function. They found a significant del correlation between this benchmark variable and stages of integration.
17	*Role of IT manager*	The skill requirements of the senior IT executive have changed over the years with increasing emphasis on both competence about changing technology and competence about business applications. The role of the IT executive gradually changes from being an information technology expert (Stage I) and a functional administrator (Stage II), to being an information resources manager (Stage III) who focuses on knowledge management systems (Stage IV). This benchmark variable was adapted based on King and Teo's (1997) benchmark variable 3, concerned with the primary role of the IS executive. They found a significant del correlation between this benchmark variable and stages of integration. This benchmark variable was also inspired by Drazin and Kazanjian (1993), who identified backgrounds of CEOs depending on growth stage.

Figure 4. Description of Benchmark Variables for the Knowledge Management Technology Stage Model (continued)

No.	Benchmark Variable	Description of Benchmark Variable
18	*Performance of IT function*	As the IT function matures, the performance criteria for the IT function change from structured focus on operational efficiency to a more unstructured concern for contribution to business strategy in general and knowledge strategy in particular. It follows that the early performance criteria (Stage I) delineated for the IT function are primarily concerned with operational efficiency and cost minimization. When the IT function begins to play a more strategic role, the emphasis gradually shifts to effective strategy implementation (Stages II and III). Ultimately, the performance criteria for the IT function should be its long-term impact (both financial and non-financial) on the competitive position of the organization (Stage 4). This benchmark variable was adapted based on King and Teo's (1997) benchmark variable 4, concerned with performance criteria for the IT function. However, they found only a weak del correlation between this benchmark variable and stages of integration. This may be due to the multidimensional nature of performance. For instance, top management may be vague as to the relative importance of each performance criterion.
19	*Key issue for IT function*	Over time, business organizations have developed and advanced in their use of IT. In the beginning, there were data processing and data processing systems. Then there were management information systems and strategic information systems. Finally, in the network era, there is communication and interaction. This benchmark variable was based on Nolan's (1979) model focusing on the level of IS expenditures.
20	*IT manager's participation*	This benchmark variable is concerned with IT executive participation in business planning. The mirror image of top business management participation in IT planning for KM is IT executives participating in business planning. The traditional role of the IT function in providing administrative support does not require the senior IT executive to participate in business planning (Stage I). The senior IT executive reacts to business plans and does not have significant influence on their formulation. At Stage II, the senior IT executive participation is initiated, growing to almost always participation at Stage IV. This benchmark variable was adapted based on King and Teo's (1997) benchmark variable 8, concerned with IS executive participation in business planning. They found a significant del correlation between this benchmark variable and stages of integration. They applied a scale from seldom to infrequent to frequent to almost always. The group of judges in this research found the word "infrequent" difficult to understand. Hence, the revised scale is from rarely to sometimes to frequently to almost always, as used by Guttman (1950, p. 13, 19).
21	*Status of IT executive*	The responsibilities of the IT function have changed over the years due to technological and conceptual changes that made information technology more important to organizations. With these changing responsibilities of the IT function, the status of the senior IT executive is likely to be elevated. The position of the senior IT executive (in terms of the number of levels below the CEO) can serve as an indication of the importance of the IT function to the firm's strategy. This benchmark variable was adapted based on King and Teo's (1997) benchmark variable 10, concerned with the status of senior IS executive. They found a significant del correlation between this benchmark variable and stages of integration.

Figure 4. Description of Benchmark Variables for the Knowledge Management Technology Stage Model (continued)

No.	Benchmark Variable	Description of Benchmark Variable
22	*Level of business knowledge*	Knowledge focus will be different in expert-driven, experience-driven and efficiency-driven businesses. In the expert-driven business, learning is important, while previous knowledge becomes obsolete. In the experience-driven business, know-how concerning problem solutions is important, while knowledge of previous problems becomes obsolete. In the efficiency-based business, all knowledge concerning both problems and solutions is important in an accumulation of knowledge to improve efficiency. These differences led Hansen (1999) to make distinctions between the following three knowledge management strategies of stock strategy, flow strategy and growth strategy, as measured in another benchmark variable.
23	*Main effect of knowledge management*	In the beginning, a law firm wants to reduce its dependence on individual lawyers' knowledge. As the CEO of a large law firm in Norway said: "I would like some of the knowledge to stay in the firm when all lawyers leave at night." At Stage II, the main effect is effective application of current knowledge in the firm. Development of new knowledge becomes the most important effect at Stage III, while external orientation towards client performance is at the firms' attention at Stage IV. This benchmark variable was inspired by empirical research conducted by Khandelwal and Gottschalk (2003).
24	*Knowledge management priority in business strategy*	Law firms in Norway became aware of the resource-based theory of the firm with the knowledge-based perspective in the late 1990s. A partner was asked to investigate the matter, but knowledge management had low priority in the business strategy. After some years, the priority of knowledge management in business strategy rose. At Stage IV, knowledge management has the first priority in business strategy. This benchmark variable was inspired by empirical research conducted by Khandelwal and Gottschalk (2003).
25	*Management agenda*	In the beginning, knowledge management was at the top management agenda only once a year (Stage I). Later, knowledge management was on the agenda every month (Stage II) and every week (Stage III). At Stage IV, knowledge management is a daily task of top management. This benchmark variable was inspired by empirical research conducted by Khandelwal and Gottschalk (2003).
26	*Knowledge management priority in marketing strategy*	Law firms in Norway became aware of the resource-based theory of the firm with the knowledge-based perspective in the late 1990s. A partner was asked to investigate the matter, but knowledge management had low priority in the marketing strategy as knowledge management was considered an internal issue. After some years, the priority of knowledge management in marketing strategy grew. Firm executives perceived that internal knowledge management was tightly linked to client service, as suggested by the legal grid by Susskind (2000). At Stage IV, knowledge management has the first priority in marketing strategy.

The expert judge procedure was then applied for the whole set of benchmark variables in two iterations. The first iteration consisted of four faculty members who rated statements on a Likert scale. This was done on an individual basis. Then, in a group of fourteen other faculty members, the ratings of statements were discussed.

This second and final iteration with 14 expert judges was organized as a focus group meeting. First, each of the fourteen participants was asked to rate each of the four statements for each of the 29 benchmark variables individually

Figure 4. Description of Benchmark Variables for the Knowledge Management Technology Stage Model (continued)

No.	Benchmark Variable	Description of Benchmark Variable
27	*Description of normal work*	Traditionally, law firms provide clients with a comfortable and user-friendly experience using established procedures to tackle familiar types of problems. Knowledge focus will be different depending on typical work done in the firm. At Stage II we find a low cost, efficiently organized delivery team using established methods for routine assignments. Firms at Stage III provide clients with creative, innovative solutions to one-off problems, while firms at Stage IV work continuously with clients on real-time diagnosis of complex, ill-specified problems. This contingent approach to knowledge management was inspired by Hansen (1999), who distinguished between efficiency-based, experience-based and expert-based firms, as measured in another benchmark variable.
28	*Knowledge growth*	Tiwana (2001, p. 279) argues that the stages of knowledge growth framework provides a readily usable methodology for measurement of process capability and technological knowledge. According to the framework, a business progresses from Stage 1, ignorance, via awareness, measure, control of the mean, process capability, process characterization, know-why to Stage 8, perfect knowledge. These stages were in this research transformed to know-what, know-why, know-how-we, and know-how-clients.
29	*Knowledge characteristics*	Tiwana (2001, p. 279) argues that the stages of knowledge characteristics provide a frame of reference against which a business can map, evaluate, and measure business relative to competitors and industry. According to the framework, a business progresses from Stage 0, undefined, via pure art, list of possibly relevant variables, pre-technological, scientific method, local repeatable recipe, cost effective handling, quantitative model, to Stage 8, nirvana.
30	*Status of KM executive*	The responsibilities of the knowledge management function have changed over the years due to conceptual changes that made knowledge management more important to organizations. With these changing responsibilities of the KM function, the status of the senior KM executive is likely to be elevated. The position of the senior KM executive (in terms of the number of levels below the CEO) can serve as an indication of the importance of the KM function to the firm's strategy. This benchmark variable was adapted based on King and Teo's (1997) benchmark variable 10, concerned with the status of the senior IS executive. They found a significant del correlation between this benchmark variable and stages of integration
31	*Response time to clients' enquiries*	Voss (2000) suggests that a metric for customer relationship management should be the response time to customers' enquiries (e.g., 24-hour limit). He measured 70 UK companies' responsiveness to enquiries. He found that 47 percent responded within one day, 16 percent responded within a week, and 37 percent did not respond at all. This idea is implemented as a benchmark variable here to illustrate that response time will decline when information technology is used in knowledge management in the law firm.
32	*Response quality*	Voss (2000) suggests that a metric for customer relationship management should be response quality; for example, making customers happy with the responses 95 percent of the time. This idea is implemented as a benchmark variable here to illustrate that response quality will improve when information technology is used in knowledge management in the law firm.

using a questionnaire. For some benchmark variables, all participants had a systematic result from left to right on their Likert scales. These benchmark variables were left unchanged. For those benchmark variables on which respondents disagreed, there was a discussion on the content of each item.

Often, a change of word(s) solved the problem, making it possible to leave the item inside the scale. In some cases, an item was so problematic that it had to be replaced by another item suggested by the group.

King and Teo (1997) argue that since the current stage of growth is measured by asking respondents to check one of the four descriptions of the type of stage, it is important to ensure that respondents are actually able to understand and distinguish between the four types. This research tried to make the descriptions and conceptual representations as clear and concise as possible through the expert rating and a pilot test in five law firms, using the CIO or the CKO as respondent. As a validation check, some pilot test respondents' comments were analyzed to determine whether they had any difficulty understanding or distinguishing between the types of stages.

However, many of the problems with Guttman scaling suggested by Kline (1998) occurred in this research. Benchmark variable number 13 may serve as a problematic Guttman scaling example. Based on Susskind's (2000) legal grid, the variable suggests that there is a progression from office support, via customer relationships and knowledge management, to legal Web advice. This progression may vary among firms, thereby making such a standard progression questionable. Nevertheless, this benchmark variable was included to enable empirical measurement of the legal grid.

The next benchmark variable, number 14, may serve as another example. Based on Tiwana's (2001) proposal that there are skeptics, conservatives, early adopters and innovators, this classification was introduced as a scale.

The last benchmark variables 31 and 32 are derived from Tiwana (2001), who suggested the existence of both stages of knowledge growth and stages of knowledge characteristics.

Benchmark variables in Figures 3 and 4 indicate characteristics that commonly occur together. Sabherwal and Chan (2001) label this a configuration, which is defined as any multidimensional constellation of conceptually distinct characteristics that commonly occur together. Configurations take a step beyond the traditional contingency theoretic view by using a holistic rather than a reductionistic stance. They offer richer insights by focusing on parsimonious and relatively homogeneous groups rather than diverse concepts.

THE CASE OF LAW FIRMS

A law firm can be understood as a social community specializing in the speed and efficiency in the creation and transfer of legal knowledge (Nahapiet & Ghoshal, 1998). Many law firms represent large corporate enterprises, organizations, or entrepreneurs with a need for continuous and specialized legal services that can only be supplied by a team of lawyers. According to Galanter and Palay (1991, p. 5):

Firms represent large corporate enterprises, organizations, or entrepreneurs with a need for continuous (or recurrent) and specialized legal services that could be supplied only by a team of lawyers. The client 'belongs to' the firm, not to a particular lawyer. Relations with clients tend to be enduring. Such repeat clients are able to reap benefits from the continuity and economies of scale and scope enjoyed by the firm.

Lawyers as Knowledge Workers

Lawyers can be defined as knowledge workers. They are professionals who have gained knowledge through formal education (explicit) and through learning on the job (tacit). Often, there is some variation in the quality of their education and learning. The value of professionals' education tends to hold throughout their careers. For example, lawyers in Norway are asked whether they got the good grade of "laud", even 30 years after graduation. Professionals' prestige (which is based partly on the institutions from which they obtained their education) is a valuable organizational resource because of the elite social networks that provide access to valuable external resources for the firm (Hitt et al., 2001).

After completing their advanced educational requirements, most professionals enter their careers as associates in law. In this role, they continue to learn and thus, they gain significant tacit knowledge through "learning by doing". Therefore, they largely bring explicit knowledge derived from formal education into their firms and build tacit knowledge through experience (Hitt et al., 2001).

Most professional service firms use a partnership form of organization. In such a framework, those who are highly effective in using and applying knowledge are eventually rewarded with partner status, and thus own stakes in a firm. On their road to partnership, these professionals acquire considerable knowledge, much of which is tacit. Thus, by the time professionals achieve partnership, they have built human capital in the form of individual skills (Hitt et al., 2001).

Because law is precedent-driven, its practitioners are heavily invested in knowing how things have been done before. Jones (2000) found that many attorneys, therefore, are already oriented toward the basic premises of knowledge management, though they have been practicing it on a more individualized basis and without the help of technology and virtual collaboration. As such, a knowledge management initiative could find the areas in which lawyers are already sharing information and then introduce modern technology to support this information sharing to make it more effective.

Lawyers work in law firms, and law firms belong to the legal industry. According to Becker et al. (2001), the legal industry will change rapidly because of three important trends. First, global companies increasingly seek out law firms that can provide consistent support at all business locations and integrated cross-border assistance for significant mergers and acquisitions as well as capital-market transactions. Second, client loyalty is decreasing as companies increasingly base purchases of legal services on a more objective assessment of their value, defined as benefits net of price. Finally, new competitors have entered the market, such as accounting firms and Internet-based legal services firms.

In this book, the notion "lawyer" is used most of the time. Other notions, such as "attorney" and "solicitor" are sometimes used as synonyms in this book. In reality, these words can have different meanings, together with notions such as "barrister", "counselor" and "advocate". In Norwegian, a distinction is made between a lawyer ("jurist") and a solicitor ("advokat"). There is no need to make such distinctions in this book.

Law Firm Change

Montana (2000) is not convinced that law firms will change, arguing that law stands out as an anachronism in the age of knowledge management. Law is entirely human-made; there are no hidden physical principles. A person researching some question of law ought to be able to quickly and easily derive an answer with certainty. According to Montana (2000), nothing is further from the truth: the entire body of law is an accumulated historical knowledge without organization, and law is a conservative calling steeped in its own traditions.

- The emergence of electronic information systems has had a limited effect on this history. Maintaining documents electronically permits searching for words and phrases within a document's text and rapid searches across large numbers of documents. Properly formulated queries facilitate asking questions formerly unanswerable using traditional tools. Nevertheless, Montana (2000) predicts that little will happen because of the following obstacles: **expectations** (if a thing is done a certain way for a long time, people's expectations are based upon this long practice); **Cost (IT will** strain the resources available for it; **Training** (lack of people who can make things work; vested **Interests** (a system in place long enough creates sets of parties who profit from it).

These factors combine to create powerful inertial and resistance. What, then, will force change? Montana (2000) believes in two strong forces: **new players** (he advent of electronic publishing has changed legal publishing) and **competition** (arbitrators, accounting firms, consultants, and many others are chipping into law's traditional business).

Knowledge Categories

To get started on this job, legal industry knowledge has to be understood. Edwards and Mahling (1997) have suggested that law firms have four categories of knowledge: administrative, declarative, procedural and analytical knowledge, as defined earlier in this book. These knowledge categories are all important to the law firm. While any law firm needs to maintain efficient administrative records, there does not appear to be any significant possibility for gaining strategic advantage in the firm's core competency of providing sound legal advice to its clients by using these records. The detailed administrative knowledge they contain is essential to the operation of the law firm, but does not contribute to the substantive content. Declarative, procedural and analytical knowledge offer greater possibilities for creating strategic value to the firm.

Edwards and Mahling (1997) present a case drawn from the case collection of one of the authors to illustrate the differences in strategic value among procedural, declarative, and analytical knowledge. In the early 1990s one of the authors, at the time engaged in the practice of law, represented a corporate client as seller in several sales of corporate businesses and real estate. At the time, buyers of businesses and real estate had become concerned about their possible liability for pollution existing on property when they purchased it. The U.S. federal laws governing the legal responsibility of landowners for environmental contamination on their property had been adopted a few years earlier and their full impact on sale of businesses was just beginning to be understood.

The relevant declarative knowledge was an understanding of several related state and federal laws and agency regulations governing liability for environmental contamination. The relevant procedural knowledge in part was to know how to transfer the environmental licenses and permits used by a given business to a new owner and how to transfer the real estate as an asset. The relevant analytical knowledge was to understand what risks the buyer of a contaminated property faced (legal and financial) and what contractual protections the seller could reasonably give to the buyer.

Law firms are interesting in themselves from both a knowledge and a management perspective. From a management perspective, law firm partners own a typical law firm. Among themselves, the partners appoint a board and a managing partner. In addition, they hire a chief executive officer (CEO) to run all support functions in the firm, such as financial management (CFO), knowledge management (CKO) and information technology management (CIO).

Jones (2000) found that top-down directives are complicated in the legal industry. In large U.S. and UK law firms the power can be spread among as many as 150 partners, most of who have different specialty areas, different work and management styles and vastly different groups under their control. Earning a consensus is not an easy proposition — especially when the funding for new initiatives such as knowledge management initiatives is coming directly out of the partners' yearly income. At the same time, partners are the ones who have the most to gain if their firm is able to manage knowledge effectively to keep lucrative clients on board and draw new ones through new services.

The human capital embodied in the partners is a professional service firm's most important resource. Their experience, particularly as partners, builds valuable industry-specific and firm-specific knowledge, which is often tacit. Such knowledge is the least imitable form of knowledge. An important responsibility of partners is obtaining and maintaining clients. Partners build relationships with current and potential clients and, over time, develop social capital through their client networks. Therefore, the experience a professional gains as a partner contributes to competitive advantage (Hitt et al., 2001).

Partners with education from the best institutions and with the most experience as partners in particular legal areas represent substantial human capital to the firm. As partners, they continue to acquire knowledge, largely tacit and firm-specific, and build social capital. This human capital should produce the highest-quality services to clients and thereby contribute significantly to firm performance. The job of partner differs from that of associate, and new skills must be developed. Partners must build the skills needed to develop and maintain effective relationships with clients. Importantly, partners in law firms serve as project and team leaders on specific cases and thus must develop managerial skills (Hitt et al., 2001).

Partners own the most human capital in a firm and have the largest stakes using the firm's resources to the greatest advantage. One of the responsibilities of partners is to help develop the knowledge of other employees of the firm, particularly its associates. Associates at law firms need to learn internal routines, the situation of important clients, and nuances in the application of law (Hitt et al., 2001).

Information technology support for knowledge management in law firms has to consider the very special knowledge situation in each law firm. Edwards and Mahling (1997, p. 162) argue that knowledge is dispersed among many different members of the firm, and others outside the firm may contribute to knowledge. Law firm knowledge has a wide variety of sources both inside and outside the firm. Much administrative knowledge is generated by the members of the firm as billing records for their services. The firm's administrative staff creates other administrative information. Attorneys are the major source of analytical, declarative and procedural knowledge. Legal assistants have some declarative knowledge based on their experience. Declarative knowledge can also be found in publicly available sources intended for research purposes, primarily books, online subscription research sources, and CD-ROM resources. The quantity of publicly available research material for any given topic depends significantly on the size of the market for the information. The more specialized the legal area, the smaller the potential market for material and the less that is usually widely available. Experienced legal assistants are usually an invaluable source of procedural knowledge, since much procedural work is delegated to them. Legal assistants are common in countries such as the U.S. and UK, but they are seldom found in law firms in countries such as Norway and Sweden.

Experienced legal secretaries may have a significant amount of procedural knowledge for transactions they handle often. Law firms in Norway employ many secretaries. It is common to find more than one secretary for every three lawyers in a law firm.

The role of others outside the law firm in generating analytical and procedural knowledge needs to be noted. While much of the useful procedural and analytical knowledge resides in firm employees, it is likely that there are sources outside the firm as well. One belief frequently expressed in the knowledge management literature is the view that learning is social: people learn in groups. These groups are known in the literature as communities of practice.

Communities of practice have been defined as groups of people who are informally bound to one another by exposure to a common class of problem. It is quite likely that the communities of practice for the lawyers in the firm include other members of professional associations such as bar associations. These groups usually have a number of committees devoted to practice areas, such as environmental law. In Norway, Den Norske Advokatforening (Norwegian Lawyers Association) has such committees.

Generally, the idea of communities of practice developed in the organizational learning movement. The idea posits that knowledge flows best through networks of people who may not be in the same part of the organization, or in the same organization, but have the same work interests. Some firms have attempted to formalize these communities, even though theorists argue that they should emerge in self-organizing fashion without any relationship to formal organizational structures (Grover & Davenport, 2001).

A few more technologically advanced lawyers may use the Internet or such subscription services as Counsel Connect in the U.S. on the World Wide Web as a sounding board for analytical and procedural issues in a community of legal practice. These external sources can provide knowledge in the form of informal conversations, written newsletters and updates, briefs filed in relevant litigation, and other forms.

An obvious problem in law firms is that knowledge is not consistently documented, and documented knowledge is not always explicit. Much administrative information is captured in electronic form as part of the firm's billing records. Other administrative data reside in the firm's payroll and benefits records and file and records management systems. Much of the firm's declarative knowledge resides in the memories of the firm's attorneys and in their work product. As noted above, the firm has access to publicly available declarative knowledge in the form of published reference works, and declarative knowledge is typically the best-documented type of knowledge.

Much procedural knowledge is documented throughout the firm's files in the form of completed records of transactions, which provide guidance about what legal documents were necessary to complete a certain type of transaction. The knowledge of procedure reflected in these documents is often implicit rather than explicit. Explicit procedural knowledge is contained in a collection of written practice guides for popular areas like real estate transactions. These guides include standard checklists of items necessary to complete a particular transaction for the kinds of transactions that occur frequently.

Analytical knowledge resides primarily in attorneys' heads. Analytical knowledge is occasionally documented in client files through the notes of an attorney's thought processes. More often it is reflected in the completed contract documents or other transaction documents by the inclusion of specific clauses dealing with a particular topic. The analytical knowledge reflected in completed documents is very often not explicit, in the sense that it is often not clear from the face of the document what analytical issues are dealt with in the document.

Another law firm problem is that knowledge is often shared on an informal basis. Certain methods of sharing knowledge, at least within the firm, have traditionally been part of large law firm culture. One of the most important ways of sharing knowledge has been through the process of partners training associates to perform tasks. In larger firms, the practice of hiring young, bright law school graduates who were trained, supervised, and rewarded by a partner has been followed throughout most of this century. The method focuses on transmitting knowledge from more experienced attorneys to less experienced attorneys, as distinguished from transmitting it to other partners in the firm or to legal assistants and other support staff.

This attorney training customarily has relied on informal methods of transmitting knowledge, such as rotating young attorneys through a series of practice groups within the firm. Much of this informal training takes place via collaborative work on documents such as contracts and pleadings. Some of it occurs through informal consultation between a senior attorney and a junior attorney about the best way to handle a specific task. These consultations may be carried out by face-to-face discussions, email or telephone conversations. No attempt is usually made to capture the substance of the training through these informal methods, even where a form of communication, such as email, that could produce documentation may often be used It is important to note that this training often takes place under intense time pressure. Further, in an hourly billing system there is often little or no financial incentive to produce documentation, which cannot be billed directly to a client.

In addition to problems of knowledge dispersion, inconsistent documentation and informal knowledge sharing, Edwards and Mahling (1997, p. 164) argue that if knowledge has been documented, it is contained in a mixture of paper and electronic formats and located in dispersed physical locations. Administrative information typically exists in a combination of print and electronic formats. A large firm would customarily maintain computerized databases for key matters such as tracking lawyers' hourly billings, for its client contact data, and for staff assignments to projects but would usually generate paper invoices to clients. The data physically reside in the firm's computer network and in paper files.

Declarative, procedural and analytical knowledge is often documented in attorney work product such as briefs, memoranda, and actual legal documents such as contracts, wills, and instruments of transfer. Work product documents typically are created in electronic form but are customarily stored in print format client files. The electronic format materials are stored in stand-alone personal computers or on the network. Paper materials are located throughout the firm's offices.

Where knowledge has been documented in a law firm, often only a few simple tools exist to facilitate the retrieval of knowledge by topic. Attorney work files are usually indexed by client name and matter name but their contents are seldom indexed for subject matter in more than the most general way. An attorney creating a particular item of work product may place it in a firm's standards database maintained in electronic format. These standard documents can then be used by other lawyers as examples or models. In a typical installation the standard forms library is stored on the network and is physically available to those who have network access. The standard forms library allows access to individual documents by name, but subject matter classification is often limited to what can be included in a descriptive DOS format file name. Retrieving material from the forms library thus usually requires tedious sequential search and review of the contents of the library.

Access to the procedural and analytical knowledge embodied in client files is difficult at best for those not familiar with the files. The client files are often not indexed by subject matter, making it difficult to locate procedural or analytical knowledge on a particular topic if the contents of the file are not already familiar. Document management systems do support network-wide searches for documents in electronic form by selected attributes such as document author name or keywords appearing in the document. In the absence of a consistent system of classifying the documents' contents by subject or topic, however, keyword searches by topic produce incomplete retrieval of all relevant documents.

Even if knowledge is documented by work product such as a memorandum to file, access to the implicit procedural and analytical knowledge embodied in the firm's files is often difficult at best. Client files that are indexed according to a subject-based system may offer some help in searching for analytical knowledge. A large transaction, however, may include dozens of analytical issues and it is unlikely that all of them would be indexed. Procedural knowledge is unlikely to be indexed at all. This means that the user must often rely on the ability to search by keywords for relevant fact patterns to retrieve relevant procedural or analytical knowledge.

Some knowledge in a law firm raises issues of security and confidentiality. There are few confidentiality concerns with declarative knowledge. This type of knowledge is meant to be public and readily accessible to all. Analytical and procedural knowledge within the firm can, however, raise issues of security and client confidentiality. Attorneys in the firm have professional ethical obligations to their clients to maintain the confidentiality of information furnished by the client. While these ethical obligations are customarily interpreted to permit sharing the information among the firm's members and staff, appropriate precautions still must be taken to avoid disclosures outside the firm.

Implications for Systems Design

Edwards and Mahling (1997) find that their observations have implications for system design. They believe that their observations about the characteristics of knowledge within large law firms have implications for the design of knowledge management tools for these firms. There is not a one-to-one correspondence between their observations and the implications for design, as some observations have a number of ramifications for the design tools. The following discussion of the implications for system specifications is important. A number of specification issues concern the roles of different end-users of a knowledge management system in a large law firm. Gatekeepers, knowledge librarians, and other specialists should be named:

- A gatekeeper capable of evaluating materials for inclusion must be named.
- To assure accuracy, knowledge should be edited before being made accessible.
- To assure currency, the knowledge should be reviewed periodically after it has been placed in the knowledge base.

Another set of specifications deals with the strategy and trail of knowledge items, thus putting isolated knowledge pieces into organizational context:

- To maximize the strategic value created by a knowledge base, it must focus on the type of knowledge that has been identified as having the best potential strategic value. A selection process must be established for inclusion in the knowledge base. There should be agreement about the types of knowledge that are to be captured in the knowledge base as having strategic value to the firm.
- Users must have access to the name of the source of the knowledge. It must be easy to identify the creator of a particular item of knowledge.
- It must be easy to learn the history of a particular item in the knowledge base: the date it was added, the date of any revisions, the frequency with which it has been used.
- The tools must be able to extract the useful knowledge while preserving the confidentiality of client information. Some portions of the knowledge base must support restricted access.

The collaborative aspects of knowledge are related to specifications that border on the areas of organizational memory and collective intelligence:

- Because many firm members can create knowledge, all firm members should be able to share knowledge. All knowledge management tools should be in an electronic form and available on a network accessible by all firm members. Portions of the tools should be accessible by external users with appropriate security mechanisms.
- The system must facilitate the informal sharing of knowledge. Users should be able to identify creators of knowledge on a particular topic. The system should facilitate contact with the creator of knowledge by email, telephone, or online conference. Users should also be able to transmit items readily by email or other electronic communications.
- To encourage users to document their knowledge, it should be easy to add material to the knowledge base. As far as possible, the system should capture information without requiring much additional effort from the creator.

Knowledge acquisition and the elicitation of knowledge are crucial factors on the input side. Technical and organizational factors are concerned:

- User tools should be suitable for use by users with a wide variety of both substantive legal knowledge and technological sophistication.
- There should be incentives to document knowledge. When items are added to the system, the source must be identifiable. It should be possible to measure the use of an item once it is placed in the system.

An electronic format of structured and unstructured knowledge objects is a rather basic specification for knowledge management tools. Closely connected to this aspect is the retrieval and presentation of knowledge:

- The tools must be able to capture and manipulate knowledge in a variety of formats, both electronic (word processing, email, and electronic database search results) and paper.
- Users should be able to retrieve knowledge in a format that can readily be exported to a word processor for inclusion in work products.
- The tools must permit at least rudimentary subject matter indexing. Users must be able to search, sort and retrieve knowledge in the system by subject.
- The system must facilitate the retrieval of implicit procedural and analytical knowledge. Users must be able to conduct keyword searches for relevant

fact attributes that are not indexed. The use of other tools, such as intelligent agents and collaborative filtering programs, which could facilitate the retrieval of implicit knowledge, should be explored.

IT support for knowledge management is only at the beginning. But some law firms are making progress, and these firms may be ready for the next technology wave. According to Jones (2000), for the firms that have already embraced knowledge management, the next wave will likely include a stronger focus on client-facing extranets and the development of expert systems. Extranets are essential for ensuring lasting relationships with clients, not only because they increase a client's access to their counsel, but because the firm gets linked tightly with the client in hopes that the client will remain with the firm. Expert systems are showing huge potential efficiency returns and hold promise for much of the transactional work-tax matters, real estate closings, and financial closings that make up the bulk of legal services. Capturing the knowledge upon which the systems are based is a more complicated process than setting up collaborative systems among practice groups.

Edwards and Mahling (1997) summarize the situation for IT support for knowledge management in law firms by stating that they believe that a significant opportunity exists in large law firms for the successful use of knowledge management tools. These firms are currently performing some knowledge management tasks with tools which offer only rudimentary knowledge management capability and which are not fully integrated with the firms' existing technology. None of the current available tools satisfies all of the user requirements they have identified. The tools that are currently available do not adequately support the informal knowledge sharing that is a key element of knowledge management in these firms. Tools must be configured to support and encourage informal collaboration and a stronger information-sharing culture. In these organizations, in which performance is measured by the number of billable hours, knowledge management tools must minimize the amount of effort required of the user. They must become as invisible as possible.

Many authors are concerned with firm culture as a determining factor for knowledge management. O'Connor (2000) suggests that compensation, individuality, billing and tradition are some of the most important barriers to knowledge management initiatives in today's firm:

- *Compensation:* Compensation models are one of the toughest hurdles. Although some firms have lock-step compensation models, in which attorneys are not as adversely impacted for spending time on knowledge sharing activities, most do not. Even those that do typically place a premium on billable hours, and lawyers not hitting billable targets feel the sting. The practical impact: It is a challenge to convince lawyers to contribute content into knowledge management systems.

- *Individuality:* Lawyers are lone wolves, so moving to team collaboration can be a tough transition. Law is intensely competitive, from getting in to the right school, to making the school's law review, to clerking for the right justice, to getting a job at the right firm. Competitiveness is ingrained in the legal psyche. Most lawyers remain intensely competitive, even in their own firms. How do you reconcile this mindset with demands to share knowledge with your coworkers? Lawyers must transition from believing that by transferring knowledge they somehow become less important, to believing the old adage that "All boats rise with the tide."
- *Billing:* Most firms still bill principally on a time and materials basis. Although clients are demanding fixed price bids and not-to-exceed estimates, and competition ("beauty contests") is thriving, many firms have not fully embraced new billing models. Old-school lawyers believe efficiency results in lower revenues. In their view, why spend lots of money to get more efficient, when it adversely impacts the business?
- *Tradition:* Attorneys are often skeptical about new ways of doing things. Tradition reigns, and it can be difficult to accept radically different approaches.

So, how can a firm address these challenges? O'Connor (2000) suggests that first and foremost, management must be committed to the knowledge management program and provide tangible support:

- Executive managers must understand why the firm is investing in KM, commit the necessary funds, and throw their weight behind the team doing the work. Ideally, firm leaders should prepare a *one-minute speech* so that they can quickly and easily articulate the firm's KM strategy. Furthermore, second-tier management must be involved; that is, practice and department heads are also informed, and they must be active supporters. Discuss KM plans at partnership meetings and retreats; spread the message about why it is important.
- The first step is to conduct a *knowledge audit.* This involves spending time with the right people in the practice areas, and identifying how knowledge is created and transferred, with an eye for areas for improvement. Focus on the practice, and spend time with lawyers in the practice areas. Understand what they do, and ascertain how we can improve the practice. Consider a broad-based knowledge management team, comprised of attorneys and staff, representative of the firm's practice areas and locations. For example, Shearman & Sterling, a law firm in the U.S., has

created a Knowledge Advisory Board composed of just such a collection of lawyers and staff. They meet regularly to direct the strategy and overall plan for the firm's knowledge management initiative, with a real focus on best practices.

- The next step is to develop a *plan* to address the needs, which have been distilled from this effort. It should focus on how the firm can capture and reuse important knowledge assets. Content is king. If we do not have a method and process for easily capturing and accessing helpful information, then we will not be successful.
- One of the key elements of the plan must be how we will create *processes that facilitate knowledge sharing*. They must be unobtrusive or they will not be followed, the content will provide marginal value, and the utility and benefits of the system will suffer. This may be the most important consideration of all. Sherman & Sterling created a role of Knowledge Coordinator in each practice group. These people not only help to determine what processes make sense; they are also directly responsible for ensuring that their respective practice areas participate.
- Try a little *marketing* and shameless self-promotion. How we pitch KM in the firm may be a great determinant of its success. When considering KM, it all sounds too dramatic and complicated for lawyers to really embrace. Bonnie Speer-McGrath, of Speer Software Training, suggests that the same tactics used to sell new technology innovations to lawyers as part of the training process can also be used to get lawyers excited about KM. Finding ways to tangibly demonstrate how lawyers perform tasks today, coupled with how they could accomplish the same tasks faster and with better results, is key. Given the structural impediments to implementing KM in law firms, firms must embrace a broad strategy for introducing it to their firms. Promotion and education can take many forms, from formal briefings to hands-on training, to the use of success stories, in which specific examples of the effective use of such tools and processes are highlighted. Lawyers want to know, "What's in it for me?"
- Focus on the *needs* of firm lawyers. Create a team to lead the effort that includes them. Spend time with them; ascertain needs, and focus efforts on building processes that will facilitate the incorporation of new content. If we have done a good job of understanding their needs and in providing useful content for them, then we can be sure that "If you build it, they will come."

Figure 5. Knowledge Management Matrix

Levels / *Categories*	Core Knowledge	Advanced Knowledge	Innovative Knowledge
Administrative Knowledge			
Declarative Knowledge			
Procedural Knowledge			
Analytical Knowledge			

Knowledge Management Matrix

To identify knowledge management applications, we can combine knowledge levels with knowledge categories. Core knowledge, advanced knowledge and innovative knowledge is combined with administrative knowledge, declarative knowledge, procedural knowledge and analytical knowledge in Figure 5. We have created a knowledge management matrix with 12 cells for IS/IT applications.

The knowledge management matrix can first be used to identify the current IS/IT that support knowledge management in the firm, as illustrated in Figure 6.

Now the knowledge management matrix can be applied to identify future IS/IT, as illustrated in Figure 7. The systems do only serve as examples; they illustrate that it is possible to find systems than can support all combinations of knowledge categories and knowledge levels.

Software and systems suitable for knowledge management in a law firm can now be identified using the knowledge management matrix. In Figure 8, examples of software to support systems in Figure 7 are listed.

Figure 6. Knowledge Management Matrix for the Current IS/IT Situation

Levels / *Categories*	Core Knowledge	Advanced Knowledge	Innovative Knowledge
Administrative Knowledge	Accounting system Hours billing Clients database Email Word processing Spreadsheet Salary system	Competence database Client firm information Internet	
Declarative Knowledge	Library system Electronic law-book Electronic legal sources	Law database	
Procedural Knowledge	Case collection Document standards Procedural standards Document examples	Internal databases Intranet Public databases	
Analytical Knowledge	Law interpretations	Groupware	

Figure 7. Knowledge Management Matrix for Desired IS/IT Situation

Levels ***Categories***	**Core Knowledge**	**Advanced Knowledge**	**Innovative Knowledge**
Administrative Knowledge	Accounting system Hours billing Clients database Email Word processing Spreadsheet Salary system *Electronic diary* *Electronic reception* *Office automation* *Message system*	Competence database Client firm information Internet *Videophone* *Video conference* *Quality system* *Financial services* *Intranet* *Net agent* *Electronic meetings*	*Client statistics* *Lawyer statistics* *Recruiting system* *Scanning* *Quality assurance* *Benchmarking* *Customer relationships* *Net-based services* *Electronic diary* *Mobile office* *Executive information*
Declarative Knowledge	Library system Electronic law-book Electronic legal sources *Document management* *Legal databases* *Commercial databases*	Law database *Electronic library* *Electronic law-book* *Extranet* *International legal sources*	*Law change base* *Precedence base* *Conference system* *Intelligent agents* *Artificial intelligence* *Portals* *Work flow systems*
Procedural Knowledge	Case collection Document standards Procedural standards Document examples *Planning system* *Standards archive* *Publishing system*	Internal databases Intranet Public databases *Experience database* *Image processing* *Document generation* *International law base* *Public Web access*	*Video registration* *Case system* *Online services*
Analytical Knowledge	Law interpretations *Voice recognition* *Case interpretations*	Groupware *Intelligent agents* *Client monitoring* *Extranet* *Discussion groups* *Video conference*	*Expert register* *Expert system* *Research reports* *Subject database* *Data warehouse*

Let us look at one example in Figure 8. *Knowledger* is listed as potential software in the innovative-analytical knowledge location. This is an ambitious location of a software product that has yet to demonstrate its real capabilities in knowledge firms. According to the vendor Knowledge Associates (*www.knowledgeassociates.com*), Knowledger 3.0 is complete knowledge management software that can be integrated with other systems in the firm. Knowledger is Web-based and supports the firm in categorizing internal and external information, as well as linking incoming information to existing information.

Let us look at one more application in the most demanding location of innovative-analytical knowledge. There we find something called Summation. *Summation* is a system for document handling for use in large court cases (*www.summation.com*). In the large court case of Balder in Norway, law firm Thommessen Krefting Greve Lund (TKGL) used Summation in 2001. The Balder case is a dispute between Exxon and Smedvig about the rebuilding of an offshore vessel costing 3 billion Norwegian crones. TKGL had more than 2,500 binders when the court case started in the city of Stavanger. All these documents were scanned into a database for use by Summation. When lawyers from TKGL

Figure 8. Knowledge Management Matrix for Software Supporting Desired IS/IT Situation

Levels / *Categories*	Core Knowledge	Advanced Knowledge	Innovative Knowledge
Administrative Knowledge	Microsoft Word Microsoft Excel Microsoft Outlook SuperOffice Timex Concorde XAL DBMS SuperOffice Microsoft Office Oracle Agresso Powermarkt Uni økonomi Datalex Justice Data Systems GroupWise Alta Law Office ESI Law	Microsoft Access Lotus Approach Corel Paradox Infotorg IFS Rubicon Concorde K-link Akelius dokument Windows NT Explorer CheckPoint Firewall RealMedia Advisor klient Completo Advokat Visma Business Advokat	Intranet Internet Extranet WAP PDA/Palm KnowledgeShare IFS Business performance Mikromarc 2 statistic IFS Front Office Psion Nomade Netscape Netcaster
Declarative Knowledge	NorLex CarNov RightOn Lovdata NORSOK	Lovdata Celex BibJure Shyster Finder Prjus BookWhere	Hieros Gamos Eudor Abacus Law Lawgic Netmeeting Lov chat LegalSeeker KG Agent Lotus K-station Domino Workflow
Procedural Knowledge	Jasper Karnov Mikas Aladdin ePaper Action Request System DocuShare CyberWorks Training Learning Space	Lotus Domino Domino.Doc DOCS Open HotDocs Adobe photoshop EUR-Lex ODIN eCabinet	Justice Autonomy LegalSeeker Expert Legal Systems Hieros Gamos Real Media Amicus Attorney
Analytical Knowledge	PDA/Palm Lotus LearningSpace Lotus Quickplace Lotus Sametime IBM Content Manager IBM Enterprise Portal Voice Express Collaborative Virtual Work Search Sugar Vchip	Lotus Notes iNotes Lotus K-Station Jasper Novell GroupWise Microsoft Exchange Netscape Communicator JSF Litigator's Notebook Empolis K42 Legal Files	Summation Knowledger Lotus Raven Shyster XpertRule Miner Expert Choice Dragon Dictate

present material in court, they submit it from their laptops. When new information emerges in court, then it is registered in Summation. When TKGL lawyers are to trace technical and financial developments for Balder, they make a search in the Summation database.

Another law firm is also using Summation. The law firm Bugge Arentz-Hansen Rasmussen (BA-HR) has the task of finding money after the late shipowner Jahre. The money is expected to be found in banks in countries in which there are no taxes. The hunt for Jahre funds has been going on for almost a decade, and BA-HR has developed a large Summation database enabling BA-HR lawyers to present important information in the court in the city of Drammen.

A third example of Summation use can be found in the U.S. The Justice Department used Summation in its legal struggle with Microsoft. According to Summation Legal Technologies (2001), Summation helped the Justice's lead prosecutor, David Boies, piece together the most damaging information for Microsoft. In presenting its defense, which ended on February 26, Microsoft relied more than Justice did on a low-tech overhead projector.

According to Susskind (2000, p. 163), six kinds of expert systems can play an important role in law firms in the future:

- *Diagnostic systems.* Those systems offer specific solutions to problems presented to them. From the facts of any particular case, as elicited by such a system, it will analyze the details and draw conclusions, usually after some kind of interactive consultation. These systems are analogous to the medical diagnostic systems that make diagnoses on the basis of symptoms presented to them. An example of a diagnostic system in law would be a taxation system that could pinpoint the extent to which and why a person is liable to pay tax, doing so on the basis of a mass of details provided to it.
- *Planning systems.* In a sense, planning systems reason in reverse. For these systems are instructed as to a desired solution or outcome and their purpose is to identify scenarios, involving both factual and legal premises that justify the preferred conclusion. In tax law, a planning system could recommend how best a taxpayer should arrange his or her affairs so as to minimize exposure to liability. The knowledge held within planning systems can be very similar to that held within diagnostic systems; what is quite different is the way that that knowledge is applied.
- *Procedural guides.* Many complex tasks facing legal professionals require extensive expertise and knowledge that is in fact procedural in nature. Expert systems as procedural guides take their users through such complex and extended procedures, ensuring that all matters are attended to and done within any prescribed time periods. An example of such a system would be one that managed the flow of a complex tax evasion case, providing detailed guidance and support from inception through to final disposal.
- *The intelligent checklist.* This category of system has most often been used to assist in auditing or reviewing compliance with legal regulations. Compliance reviews must be undertaken with relentless attention to detail and extensive reference to large bodies of regulations. Intelligent checklists provide a technique for performing such reviews. They formalize the process. In taxation, an intelligent checklist approach could be used to assist in the review of a company's compliance with corporation tax.
- *Document modeling systems.* These systems — also referred to as document assembly systems — store templates set up by legal experts. These templates contain fixed portions of text together with precise

indications as to the conditions under which given extracts should be used. In operation, such a system will elicit from its user all the details relevant to a proposed document. This is done by the user answering questions, responding to prompts and providing information. On the basis of the user's input, the system will automatically generate a customized and polished document on the basis of its knowledge of how its text should be used.

- *Arguments generation systems.* It is envisaged that these systems are able to generate sets of competing legal arguments in situations when legal resources do not provide definitive guidance. Rather than seeking to provide legal solutions (as diagnostic systems strive to do), argument generation systems will present sound lines of reasoning, backed both by legal authority and by propositions of principle and policy. These lines of reasoning will lead to a range of legal conclusions. Such systems would help users identify promising lines of reasoning in support of desired outcomes while, at the same time, advancing other arguments that may need to be refuted.

EMPIRICAL TESTS OF THE KMT STAGE MODEL

The knowledge management technology stage model was tested empirically in Norway and Australia in 2002. Surveys of law firms were conducted in both countries (Gottschalk & Khandelwal, 2003, 2004).

Law Firm Survey in Norway

The largest law firms in Norway were obtained from the Website *www.paragrafen.no*. This Website lists all law firms in Norway that have a home page on the Internet. The largest law firms were selected by identifying all law firms that had at least five lawyers in the firm. This procedure resulted in a total of 102 law firms. It was possible to obtain email addresses for managing directors /chief executive officers in 95 of these law firms by contacting the firms. Most law firms in Norway are small. While knowledge management technology for sharing information is dependent on a minimum number of lawyers to make sense, only law firms with a minimum of five lawyers were selected for this survey.

Questionnaires were prepared and sent to the chief executive officer (CEO) in each firm. The questionnaire was developed in QuestBack. QuestBack is an online tool for electronic research. The service is built around three modules: QuestDesigner, to create and publish surveys, QuestReporter, for analysis of incoming responses, and QuestManager, to administer ongoing QuestBack initiatives (*www.questback.com*). QuestBack has a reminder func-

Figure 9. Characteristics of Respondents

Characteristic	Response
Job title of most respondents	Lawyer
Years with the firm on average	6 years
Persons in the firm	65 persons
Lawyers in the firm	43 lawyers
Partners in the firm	14 partners
Income budget	10 Mill. US$
IT budget	0,2 Mill. US$
Persons in IT function in the firm	1,1 persons

tion, which was used for two follow-ups about one week and two weeks after the date of the initial mailings. Five firms declined participation, citing that the questionnaire was too long. Useable responses were returned by 19 firms, providing a response rate of 20 percent.

Characteristics of respondents are listed in Figure 9. Although most respondents indicated the job title of lawyer, their current position was managing partner or chief executive officer. The average responding law firm had a total of 43 lawyers, which by Norwegian standards indicates large law firms. Fourteen of these lawyers were partners in the firm. The IT budget constituted 2.3 percent of the income budget, while IT staff was 1.7 percent of total staff in the average firm.

Figure 10 shows the number of responding firms currently operating in each stage of growth. This is based on the part of the survey instrument describing extensively the four stages of growth. Generally, the results show that what-they-know occurs most often, followed by who-knows-what and end-user tools. Only one firm reported Stage IV of how-they-think.

Figure 10. Distribution of Stages of Growth

Stage of Growth	Number	Percent
End-user tools (people-to-technology)	3	16
Who-knows-what (people-to-people)	4	21
What-they-know (people-to-docs)	11	58
How-they-think (people-to-systems)	1	5
Total	19	100

Figure 11. Paths of Evolution

Paths of Evolution	Number	Percent
I End-user tools to **II** who-knows-what to **III** what-they-know	4	50.0
I End-user tools to **III** what-they-know	1	12.5
II Who-knows-what **III** what-they-know	1	12.5
I End-user tools to **III** what-they-know to **II** who-knows-what	1	12.5
III what-they-know to **II** who-knows-what to **I** end-user tools	1	12.5
Total	8	100.0

Figure 11 shows the various paths of evolution reported by the respondent firms. Unfortunately, only eight out of 19 respondents filled in this part of the questionnaire. As expected, the path of evolution generally proceeds from end-user tools to who-knows-what to what-they-know. This was the case for three respondents. However, the remaining five respondents show varying patterns of reciprocal behavior, as illustrated in Figure 12.

Figure 13 shows the mean values of benchmark variables in each stage of growth for knowledge management technology in law firms. Ideally, if there is perfect fit between the values of benchmark variables and the stages of growth, the mean value for Stage I would be 1.0, Stage II would be 2.0, Stage III would be 3.0 and Stage IV would be 4.0. There was one respondent at Stage IV according to Figure 10, but this respondent did not fill in the questionnaire for benchmark variables, causing this column to be without numbers in Figure 13.

Figure 12. Paths of Evolution

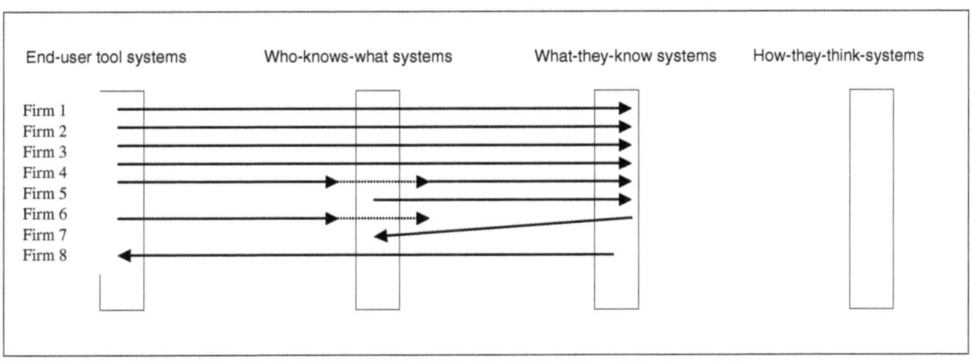

Figure 13. Mean Values of Benchmark Variables at Each Stage of Growth

No.	Benchmark Variable	Stage I END-USER TOOLS	Stage II WHO KNOWS WHAT	Stage III WHAT THEY THINK	Stage IV HOW THEY THINK	Coefficient of Reproducib -ility (CR)
1	Trigger of IT for KM	1.00	2.00	2.13		.57
2	Top management's participation	3.50	2.75	2.80		.31
3	User management's participation	3.50	2.25	2.90		.44
4	Principal contribution	2.00	2.75	3.00		.13
5	Technology assessment	3.00	2.50	2.22		.27
6	Focus	1.00	1.25	2.25		.50
7	Dominating statement	3.50	2.75	2.75		.36
8	Philosophy	2.50	1.50	2.38		.07
9	Critical success factor	1.50	3.25	3.13		.29
10	Strategy	1.50	2.00	2.50		.57
11	Main task	3.00	3.00	2.75		.50
12	Main purpose	3.00	1.75	2.50		.57
13	Main applications	2.00	1.75	1.25		.14
14	Attitude	2.50	2.75	2.75		.50
15	Value shop activity	3.50	3.67	3.29		.38
16	Contribution of IT function	2.50	2.50	2.40		.38
17	Role of IT manager	2.50	2.50	2.22		.27
18	Performance of IT function	2.00	3.33	2.90		.13
19	Key issue for IT function	2.00	3.00	3.25		.36
20	IT manager's participation	4.00	2.33	2.67		.36
21	Status of IT executive	4.00	3.50	3.43		.42
22	Business level	3.00	2.75	3.63		.07
23	Main effect	2.50	3.25	3.13		.29
24	Priority in business	4.00	3.25	2.13		.23
25	Management agenda	4.00	2.00	1.88		.38
26	Priority in marketing	4.00	2.75	2.25		.38
27	Normal work	1.50	3.00	3.38		.36
28	Knowledge growth	3.00	3.25	2.88		.43
29	Knowledge characteristics	3.00	3.00	2.38		.15
30	Status of KM executive	4.00	4.00	3.57		.27
31	Response time to clients	2.00	2.33	2.00		.15
32	Response quality	3.00	2.00	2.75		.33

Results in Figure 13 indicate that very few benchmark variables have cumulative properties in this survey. Only seven out of 32 benchmark variables have such properties by higher numbers at higher stages: trigger of IT for KM, principal contribution, focus, strategy, attitude, key issue for IT function, and normal work.

Several explanations for this lack of confirmation of benchmark variables emerge. First, it is assumed that the stage indicator is linked to the benchmark variables. However, in the expert ratings, only advancement was measured, not stage as such. Second, it is assumed that the response to stage indicator question is correct and that the benchmark variables should be consistent with this response. However, it could be assumed that there is an opposite relationship of benchmark variables leading to stage response. Finally, the sample size is small.

In the last column in Figure 13, a measure of validity is applied. The coefficient of reproducibility (CR) calculates the fraction of benchmark responses that correspond to stage responses. Normally, the CR should be at least .9 to be acceptable. None of the benchmark variables pass this test. In this research, the requirement was relaxed to .5 because of the small sample size.

This research proceeded by excluding nonconforming benchmark variables. The remaining benchmark variables are listed in Figure 14. These benchmark variables show both cumulative properties and a CR of at least .5. Only four benchmark variables satisfied these two requirements.

Only four benchmark variables satisfied these two requirements. These four benchmark variables are listed in Figure 15.

When the obtained coefficient of reproducibility is below the required criterion, the scale needs to be refined until the CR reaches the desired level. This approach resulted in Figure 16. The average CR improved from .33 to .53. The first benchmark variable concerned with trigger of IT for KM did not improve. The second benchmark variable concerned with top management's commitment improved its CR from .31 to .38 by changing the sequence to almost always (Stage I), sometimes (Stages II), frequently (Stage III) and rarely (Stage IV).

Figure 14. Mean Values of Conforming Benchmark Variables

No.	Benchmark Variable	Stage I END-USER TOOLS	Stage II WHO KNOWS WHAT	Stage III WHAT THEY THINK	Stage IV HOW THEY THINK	Coefficient of Reproducibility (CR)
1	Trigger of IT for KM	1.00	2.00	2.13		.57
6	Focus	1.00	1.25	2.25		.50
10	Strategy	1.50	2.00	2.50		.57
14	Attitude	2.50	2.75	2.75		.50

Figure 15. Conforming Benchmark Variables of Evolutionary Stages

No.	Benchmark Variable	Stage I END-USER TOOLS people-to-technology	Stage II WHO KNOWS WHAT people-to-people	Stage III WHAT THEY THINK people-to-docs	Stage IV HOW THEY THINK people-to-systems	Inspired by
1	***Trigger of IT for KM***	Individual lawyers' needs for tools	Organizations' needs for information	Automate lawyers' information work	Automate lawyers' knowledge work	*King & Teo, 1997*
6	***Focus***	Availability	Reorganization	Culture	Replacement	*Khandelwal & Gottschalk, 2003*
10	***Strategy***	Tool strategy	Stock strategy	Flow strategy	Growth strategy	*Hansen,1999*
14	***Attitude***	Skeptics	Conservatives	Early adopters	Innovators	*Tiwana, 2001*

The last benchmark variable concerned with quality in terms of responses to clients improves its CR by reversing the scale: firms at Stage I have clients that are happy with responses more than 95 percent of the time, firms at Stage II have clients that are happy with responses 90 percent to 95 percent of the time, firms at Stage III have clients that are happy with responses between 50 percent and 89 percent of the time, while firms at Stage IV have clients that are happy with responses less than 50 percent of the time.

The questionnaire for this survey had a variety of questions related to IT support in knowledge management. Some questions were concerned with the extent of IT use at each stage of growth. Average responses to such questions are listed in Figures 17 to 20. Figure 17 lists the extent of IT use in terms of people-to-technology, Figure 18 in terms of people-to-people, Figure 19 people-to-docs, and Figure 20 people-to-systems. Average responses are for all 19 responding law firms.

Electronic mail is most extensively used within the people-to-technology Stage I. Internal standards database is most extensively used within the people-to-people Stage II. Database with client cases is most extensively used within the people-to-docs Stage III, while expert systems are most extensively used within the people-to-systems Stage IV.

The last row in each table is a summary item. While end-user tools are used extensively (score of 4.5), who-knows-what systems are somewhat used (3.7), and so are what-they-know systems (2.8). How-they-think systems are hardly used at all (2.0). This result, that the extent of use declines from 4.5 via 3.7 to 2.8 and finally to 2.0 for the stages in the growth model, provides empirical support for the stages of growth model for knowledge management technology in law firms.

Figure 16. Empirical Changes in Evolutionary Stages

No.	Benchmark Variable	Stage I END-USER TOOLS people-to-technology	Stage II WHO KNOWS WHAT people-to-people	Stage III WHAT THEY THINK people-to-docs	Stage IV HOW THEY THINK people-to-systems	Coefficient of Reproducibility (CR) BEFORE	Coefficient of Reproducibility (CR) AFTER
1	***Trigger of IT for KM***	Individual lawyers' needs for tools 1	Organization's needs for information 2	Automate lawyers' information work 3	Automate lawyers' knowledge work 4	.57	.57
2	***Top management's participation***	Rarely 4	Sometimes 2	Frequently 3	Almost always 1	.31	.38
3	***User management's participation***	Rarely 1	Sometimes 2	Frequently 3	Almost always 4	.44	.44
4	***Principal contribution***	Efficiency of lawyer 4	Effectiveness of lawyer 1	Effectiveness of firm 2	Competitiveness of firm 3	.13	.53
5	***Technology assessment***	Rarely 4	Sometimes 3	Frequently 2	Almost always 1	.27	.47
6	***Focus***	Availability 1	Reorganization 2	Culture 3	Replacement 4	.50	.50
7	***Dominating statement***	Distribute information 4	Produce documentation 2	Make decisions 3	Automate work 1	.36	.43
8	***Philosophy***	Client satisfaction 2	Knowledge community 3	Lawyer independence 4	Client independence 1	.07	.64
9	***Critical success factor***	PCs and networks 4	Knowledge management systems 1	Quality and quantity 2	Culture and incentives 3	.29	.43
10	***Strategy***	Tool strategy 1	Stock strategy 2	Flow strategy 3	Growth strategy 4	.57	.57
11	***Main task***	Distributing 4	Capturing 1	Sharing 3	Applying 2	.50	.57
12	***Main purpose***	Administrative work 4	Access to information 2	Sharing information 3	Automating work 1	.57	.64
13	***Main applications***	Office support 3	Customer relations 4	Knowledge management 1	Online Web advice 2	.14	.64
14	***Attitude***	Skeptics 1	Conservatives 2	Early adopters 3	Innovators 4	.50	.50

Figure 16. Empirical Changes in Evolutionary Stages (continued)

No.	Benchmark Variable	Stage I END-USER TOOLS people-to-technology	Stage II WHO KNOWS WHAT people-to-people	Stage III WHAT THEY THINK people-to-docs	Stage IV HOW THEY THINK people-to-systems	Coefficient of Reproducibility (CR) BEFORE	Coefficient of Reproducibility (CR) AFTER
15	***Value shop activity***	Understanding clients' problem 4	Implementing solution 1	Solving clients' problem 3	Selecting optimal solution 2	.38	.54
16	***Contribution of IT function***	Supplier of PCs 4	Technical infrastructure 3	Resource of information 2	Supplier of systems 1	.38	.50
17	***Role of IT manager***	Technology expert 4	Functional administrator 3	Resource manager 2	KM expert 1	.27	.40
18	***Performance of IT function***	Operational efficiency 1	Business implementation 4	Knowledge implementation 2	Long-term impact 3	.13	.53
19	***Key issue for IT function***	Personal computers 1	Data processing 4	Information systems 2	Information networks 3	.36	.57
20	***IT manager's participation***	Rarely 4	Sometimes 2	Frequently 3	Almost always 1	.36	.50
21	***Status of IT executive***	Three or more 4	Two 1	One 3	One with access 2	.42	.58
22	***Business level***	Availability-driven 4	Efficiency- driven 2	Effectiveness-driven 1	Expert- driven 3	.07	.71
23	***Main effect***	Reduced dependence 1	Effective application 4	New knowledge 2	Client performance 3	.29	.43
24	***Priority in business***	Fourth 4	Third 3	Second 2	First 1	.23	.54
25	***Management agenda***	Year 3	Month 2	Week 4	Day 1	.38	.54
26	***Priority in marketing***	Fourth 4	Third 2	Second 3	First 1	.38	.46
27	***Normal work***	User-friendly experience 4	Efficiently organized 1	Innovative solutions 2	Ill-specified problems 3	.36	.50
28	***Knowledge growth***	Know-what 4	Know-why 1	Know-how to solve 3	Know-how client solve 2	.43	.50

Figure 16. Empirical Changes in Evolutionary Stages (continued)

No.	Benchmark Variable	Stage I END-USER TOOLS people-to-technology	Stage II WHO KNOWS WHAT people-to-people	Stage III WHAT THEY THINK people-to-docs	Stage IV HOW THEY THINK people-to-systems	Coefficient of Reproducibility (CR) BEFORE	Coefficient of Reproducibility (CR) AFTER
29	***Knowledge characteristics***	Experts dictate 4	Some explicated 3	Documented in methodology 2	Well explicated knowledge 1	.15	.62
30	***Status of KM executive***	Three or more 4	Two 1	One 3	Direct access 2	.27	.55
31	***Response time to clients***	One week 1	One day 3	One hour 2	One minute 4	.15	.69
32	***Response quality***	Less than 50% 4	50% to 89% 3	90% to 95% 2	More than 95% 1	.33	.42

Figure 17. The Extent of Use of End-User Tools (1-little extent, 6-great extent)

People-to-technology	***Use***
Text processing (e.g., Word)	5,4
Presentations (e.g., PowerPoint)	2,6
Electronic mail (e.g., Notes mail)	5,6
External legal databases (e.g., Lovdata)	5,2
End-user tools for lawyers	4,5

Figure 18. The Extent of Use of Who-Knows-What Systems (1-little extent, 6-great extent)

People-to-people	***Use***
Groupware for cooperation (e.g., GroupWise, Lotus Notes)	2,7
The firm's intranet	3,8
The firm's own Web pages on the Internet	3,6
Internal standards database	4,1
Systems providing information about lawyers' knowledge	3,7

Figure 19. The Extent of Use of What-They-Know Systems (1-little extent, 6-great extent)

People-to-docs	**Use**
Groupware for knowledge (e.g., GroupWise, Lotus Notes)	2,7
Database with client cases	3,7
Database with best practices	3,1
Document system (e.g., DocsOpen)	3,5
Systems providing information based on lawyers' knowledge	2,8

Figure 20. The Extent of Use of How-They-Think Systems (1-little extent, 6-great extent)

People-to-systems	**Use**
Expert system (e.g., Knowledger)	1,6
Neural network system	1,4
Intelligent agent (e.g., Autonomy)	1,2
Case-based reasoning system	1,2
Systems solving knowledge problems for lawyers	2,0

In the survey instrument, there were questions related to positions and other characteristics of IT in knowledge management, as listed in Figure 17. The position of CIO (chief information officer) has been somewhat longer in the firm compared to CKO (chief knowledge officer).

Did these positions have any influence on the stage for law firms? This question can be answered using regression analysis. The analysis shows that the number of years of the knowledge management position has a significant positive impact on the extent of IT use in terms of stage of growth. Law firms with newly created CKO positions are at an earlier stage than law firms with long CKO experience. The same applies to the CIO position, where law firms with a long tradition of CIOs are at a higher stage. The two remaining items in Figure 4.21 had no significant influence. It may seem surprising that the number of years knowledge management has been a management topic in the firm had no significant influence on the stage of growth.

The survey instruments also included questions on knowledge-sharing perceptions, reward attitudes, support for personal development and performance appraisal. These questions were derived from research conducted by Hunter et al. (2002). Figure 22 shows results for knowledge-sharing perceptions. The questions were posed somewhat differently than earlier questions, as respondents were asked whether they disagreed or agreed with each statement.

Figure 21. Average Number of Years for Positions and Other Characteristics (1-little extent, 6-great extent)

Positions and other characteristics in the firm	***Years***
The information technology position has been in the firm for	4
The knowledge manager position has been in the firm for	3
Lawyers in the firm have access to Lovdata for	6
Knowledge management has been a management topic in the firm for	4

Figure 22. Average Response to Statements about Knowledge-Sharing Perceptions (1-strongly disagree, 5-strongly agree)

Knowledge-sharing perceptions	***Score***
Lawyers are encouraged to share with others what they have learned from their recent assignments.	3.8
Senior staff are too busy to reflect on their experiences and share them.	3.2
The firm has a well-organized system for sharing knowledge (e.g., about clients, managing projects, new approaches) within departments or practice areas.	3.4
The firm has a well-organized system for sharing knowledge (e.g., about clients, managing projects, new approaches) across departments or practice areas.	3.3
There is an expectation that lawyers or their teams will have to take a regular turn to provide a reflection on learning experiences.	3.5
Sharing knowledge systematically is part of the firm's culture.	3.2

The scale went from 1 (strongly disagree) to 5 (strongly agree). This means that a number 3 means neither disagree nor agree. The first question in Figure 4.22 indicates that respondents did somewhat agree that lawyers are encouraged to share with others what they have learned from their recent assignments. Similar results are obtained for the other questions on knowledge-sharing perceptions in which respondents only marginally agreed with the statements. The second question was a turned question, indicating a marginal disagreement with the statement.

Figure 23 lists responses concerning reward attitudes. Results indicate that individual evaluation is more common than teamwork evaluation when salary increases take place.

Figure 23. Average Response to Statements about Reward Attitudes (1-strongly disagree, 5-strongly agree)

Reward attitudes	***Score***
Lawyer salary increases in the firm are based on ability and how well he/she does his/her work.	4.2
Promotion of a lawyer in the firm is based on ability and how well he/she does his/her work.	4.2
Lawyers are fairly rewarded for the amount of effort they put in.	3.7
The interest of the work lawyers do compensates for long hours and a stressful workload.	3.4
The team as a whole is rewarded for good work.	3.2
Teamwork in this firm is fully recognized and rewarded.	3.2

Figure 24 lists responses to statements concerned with support for personal development. Here is a question with marginal disagreement related to training and development programs. Another question with more disagreement is related to training time and opportunity, as this statement was turned.

Figure 25 lists responses to statements concerned with performance appraisal. The first statement concerned with regular intervals for performance appraisal achieves some agreement, while the remaining statements hardly receive any positive score at all.

Figure 24. Average Response to Statements about Support for Personal Development (1-strongly disagree, 5-strongly agree)

Support for personal development	***Score***
The firm provides each lawyer with a well structured training and development program	2.9
It allocates a generous amount of time for each lawyer's training	3.0
Training time and opportunity is often squeezed by day-to-day work pressures	3.8
Lawyers are encouraged to learn about the law and about business practice and marketing.	3.9
Lawyers often do tasks without seeing where they fit into the wider picture.	2.9
I believe lawyers could successfully undertake higher level tasks if there was more effective delegation.	3.9
The teams in which lawyers work provide a supportive learning environment.	3.7

Figure 25. Average Response to Statements about Performance Appraisal (1-strongly disagree, 5-strongly agree)

Performance appraisal	**Score**
A lawyer's performance is appraised fully at agreed regular intervals.	3.6
Sufficient time is allowed for proper appraisal to be provided.	3.1
A lawyer is given clear and realizable objectives for the development of skills and knowledge.	3.1
Appraisal identifies strengths and opportunities for each lawyer.	3.4
Appraisal identifies weaknesses and threats for each lawyer.	3.3

Are the stages of growth for knowledge management technology in law firms associated with different knowledge-sharing perceptions, reward attitudes, support for personal development and performance appraisal? This question can be answered using statistical analysis.

Differences can be expected between Stage I and Stage III, as Stage I is individually oriented, while Stage III is organizationally oriented. No statistically significant results were found. However, there were differences in numbers as expected. For example, teamwork is more recognized and rewarded in stage III firms than in stage I firms. Similarly, lawyers in stage III firms are more strongly encouraged to share with others what they have learned from recent assignments than lawyers in Stage I firms.

At the end of the survey instrument, respondents were asked to describe the firm's business strategy in one sentence. Thirteen out of 19 respondents filled in this part of the questionnaire. Most of them stated that they wanted to become a leading law firm in Norway. Many had also text on how they would become a leading law firm. In this context, three business strategies mentioned the word *knowledge,* while three strategies mentioned the word *quality.*

Respondents were further asked to describe the firm's knowledge strategy in one sentence. Twelve out of 19 respondents filled in this part of the questionnaire. Analysis showed that there were two kinds of strategies, one internally focused and another externally focused. Eight respondents had an internally focused knowledge strategy, while four respondents had an externally focused strategy. Externally focused strategies typically include knowledge needs of clients and customers.

Respondents were further asked to describe the firm's information technology strategy in one sentence. Eleven out of 19 respondents filled in this part of the questionnaire. Responses were used to analyze the extent of alignment between business and IT strategy. Alignment between IT strategy and business strategy is important, and distinctions are often made between administrative, sequential, reciprocal and full integration (King & Teo, 1997). Administrative integration is separate planning, sequential integration is one-way linked planning, reciprocal is two-way linked planning, and full integration is simultaneous planning. Results indicate that 27 percent of the law firms had administrative integration, 54 percent had sequential integration, 9 percent had reciprocal integration, and 9 percent had full integration.

Respondents were further asked to describe the firm's human resources strategy in one sentence. Nine out of 19 respondents filled in this part of the questionnaire. Based on this sample, two groups emerged. One group of law firms considered the human resource strategy mainly to be a recruitment strategy, in which the firm is concerned with recruiting the best legal talents to the firm. This group had four firms. The other group considered the human resource strategy mainly to be a development strategy, in which the firm is concerned with improving the skills of lawyers in the firm. This group had five firms.

Respondents were further asked which function in the firm was responsible for knowledge management. A variety of answers emerged: the board (one firm), one partner (five firms), CEO (two firms), CKO (two firms), librarian (one firm), CIO (one firm), CPO (one firm), and everybody (one firm). Fourteen out of 19 firms responded to this question.

The last question asked which function in the firm was responsible for IT management. Again, a variety of answers emerged: the board (one firm), a partner (four firms), CEO (five firms) and CIO (five firms). Fifteen out of 19 firms responded to this question.

Law Firm Survey in Australia

The stages of growth model for knowledge management technology was first tested in Australia before the survey in Norway. A total of 500 Australian law firms received the questionnaire, and 47 firms responded, representing a response rate of 9 percent. Characteristics of respondents are listed in Figure 26.

The responding 47 Australian law firms had the following distribution concerning stages of growth:

- 26 law firms (55 percent) in Australia are in Stage I of end-user tools with a people-to-technology strategy;
- six law firms (13 percent) in Australia are in Stage II of who-knows-what systems with a people-to-people strategy;
- 10 law firms (21 percent) in Australia are in Stage III of what-they-know systems with a people-to-docs strategy;

Figure 26. Characteristics of Respondents in Australia

Characteristic	Response
Job title of most respondents	Managing director
Years with the firm on average	11 years
Persons in the firm	124 persons
Lawyers in the firm	57 lawyers
Partners in the firm	15 partners
Income budget	4 mill. US$
IT budget	0.1 mill. US$
Persons in IT function in the firm	2.9 persons

- five law firms (11 percent) in Australia are in Stage IV of how-they-think systems with a people-to-systems strategy.

All five firms in Stage IV had gone through the previous Stage I to Stage III before entering this stage.

Law firms in Australia responded significantly differently to knowledge-sharing perceptions and reward attitudes depending on the current Stage I vs. Stage III. Most of the 26 law firms in Stage I were oriented towards individual lawyers in terms of limited knowledge-sharing perceptions and individual reward attitudes, while most of the 10 law firms in Stage III were oriented towards the firm as a whole. Individual orientation matches people-to-technology of end-user tools, while firm orientation matches people-to-information of what-they-know systems. Most of the 26 law firms in Stage I had rewards and promotions depending almost exclusively on individual performance. Most of the ten law firms in Stage III had rewards and promotions depending to a larger extent on knowledge sharing, stimulating knowledge-sharing and using systems for knowledge sharing.

This result suggests that when a firm moves from Stage I to Stage III, the firm will have to change its knowledge sharing and rewards from individual focus to organizational focus. Evidence suggests that many firms are currently struggling with this kind of culture change in their organizations.

Comparison of Norwegian and Australian Law Firms

Having collected survey data in both Norway and Australia, we are now able to make comparisons between the two countries. From previous studies we know that Australia and Norway both have similarities and differences in business in terms of information technology applications.

Figure 27 lists characteristics of respondents in Australia and Norway. Participating law firms in Australia were larger than participating firms in

Figure 27. Characteristics of Respondents in Norway and Australia

Characteristics	Norway	Australia
About respondents		
Years in the firm	6 years	11 years
Persons in the firm	65 persons	124 persons
Lawyers in the firm	43 persons	57 persons
Partners in the firm	14 persons	15 persons
Fraction lawyers	66%	46%
Fraction partners	33%	26%
Income budget	10 mill. US$	4 mill. US$
IT budget	0.2 mill. US$	0.1 mill. US$
IT personnel	1.1 persons	2.9 persons
Income per person	0.2 mill. US$	0.03 mill. US$
Fraction IT budget	2.3%	3.3%
Fraction IT personnel	1.7%	2.3%
About stages of growth		
Stage I: People-to-technology	16%	55%
Stage II: People-to-people	21%	13%
Stage III: People-to-docs	58%	21%
Stage IV: People-to-systems	5%	11%

Figure 28. Paths of Evolution

Paths of Evolution	Norway	Australia
I End-user tools to **II** who-knows-what to **III** what-they-know	5.,0%	8.1%
I End-user tools to **III** what-they-know	12.5%	13.5%
II Who-knows-what **III** what-they-know	12.5%	-
I End-user tools to **III** what-they-know to **II** who-knows-what	12.5%	2.7%
III what-they-know to **II** who-knows-what to **I** end-user tools	12.5%	-
I End-user tools	-	56.8%
Other paths in line with the stages of growth model	-	16.2%
Other paths not in line with the stages of growth model	-	2.7%
Total	100.0%	100.0%

Figure 29. Typology of Evolutionary Stages

No.	Benchmark Variable	Stage I **END-USER TOOLS** **people-to-technology**	Stage II **WHO KNOWS WHAT** **people-to-people**	Stage III **WHAT THEY THINK** **people-to-docs**	Stage IV **HOW THEY THINK** **people-to-systems**	Inspired by
1	***Trigger of IT for KM***	Individual lawyers' needs for tools	Organizations' needs for information **Australia** **Norway**	Automate lawyers' information work	Automate lawyers' knowledge work	*King & Teo, 1997*
2	***Top management's participation***	Rarely	Sometimes	Frequently **Australia** **Norway**	Almost always	*King & Teo, 1997*
3	***User management's participation***	Rarely	Sometimes	Frequently **Australia** **Norway**	Almost always	*King & Teo, 1997*
4	***Principal contribution***	Efficiency of lawyer	Effectiveness of lawyer **Australia**	Effectiveness of firm **Norway**	Competitiveness of firm	*Khandelwal & Gottschalk, 2003*
5	***Technology assessment***	Rarely	Sometimes **Norway**	Frequently **Australia**	Almost always	*King & Teo, 1997*
12	***Main purpose***	Administrative work	Access to information **Australia** **Norway**	Sharing information	Automating work	*Khandelwal & Gottschalk, 2003*
16	***Contribution of IT function***	Supplier of PCs	Technical infrastructure **Australia** **Norway**	Resource of information	Supplier of systems	*King & Teo, 1997*
17	***Role of IT manager***	Technology expert	Functional administrator **Australia** **Norway**	Resource manager	Knowledge management expert	*King & Teo, 1997*
18	***Performance of IT function***	Operational efficiency	Business implementation **Australia**	Knowledge implementation **Norway**	Long-term impact	*King & Teo, 1997*
20	***IT manager's participation***	Rarely	Sometimes	Frequently **Australia** **Norway**	Almost always	*King & Teo, 1997*

Figure 30. The Extent of Use of End-User Tools (1-little extent, 6-great extent)

People-to-technology	*Norway*	*Australia*
Text processing (e.g., Word)	5.4	4.8
Presentations (e.g., PowerPoint)	2.6	2.7
Electronic mail (e.g., Notes mail)	5.6	5.6
External legal databases (e.g., Lovdata)	5.2	4.7
End-user tools for lawyers	4.5	3.8

Figure 31. The Extent of Use of Who-Knows-What Systems (1-little extent, 6-great extent)

People-to-people	*Norway*	*Australia*
Groupware for cooperation (e.g., GroupWise, Lotus Notes)	2.7	2.8
The firm's intranet	3.8	3.8
The firm's own Web pages on the Internet	3.6	2.8
Internal standards database	4.1	2.9
Systems providing information about lawyers' knowledge	3.7	2.9

Norway. The partner ration is larger in Norway than in Australia. The IT budget in Australia has a larger fraction of the firm's income budget. Most Norwegian law firms are in Stage III, while most Australian law firms are in Stage I.

As a consequence of many Australian law firms found in Stage I, many Australian law firms (56.8 percent) report no path of evolution, as listed in Figure 28. Overall, 75 percent of Norwegian law firms seem to follow the stages of growth model, while 95 percent of Australian law firms seem to follow this model when assuming that all firms at Stage I will eventually progress to later stages.

While the survey instrument in Norway had a total of 32 benchmark variables, the Australian survey instrument had only 10 benchmark variables, as listed in Figure 29. The results from Norway had a low coefficient of reproducibility (CR). Hence, benchmark variables in Figure 29 are instead used to illustrate average responses in the two countries. In most cases, the average response is the same. In some cases, such as technology assessment, there is a difference between Norwegian and Australian law firms.

The questionnaire in Australia had the same questions concerned with the extent of IT use at each stage of growth. Average responses to such questions are listed in Figure 30 to 33. Figure 30 lists the extent of IT use in terms of people-to-technology, Figure 31 in terms of people-to-people, Figure 32 people-to-docs,

Figure 32. The Extent of Use of What-They-Know Systems (1-little extent, 6-great extent)

People-to-docs	Norway	Australia
Groupware for knowledge (e.g., GroupWise, Lotus Notes)	2.7	2.9
Database with client cases	3.7	3.0
Database with best practices	3.1	2.4
Document system (e.g., DocsOpen)	3.5	4.6
Systems providing information based on lawyers' knowledge	2.8	3.2

Figure 33. The Extent of Use of How-They-Think Systems (1-little extent, 6-great extent)

People-to-systems	Norway	Australia
Expert system (e.g., Knowledger)	1.6	1.7
Neural network system	1.4	1.3
Intelligent agent (e.g., Autonomy)	1.2	1.4
Case-based reasoning system	1.2	1.5
Systems solving knowledge problems for lawyers	2.0	1.5

and Figure 33 people-to-systems. Average responses are for all 19 and 47 responding law firms respectively.

Electronic mail is most extensively used within the people-to-technology Stage I in both Australia and Norway. Internal standards database is most extensively used within the people-to-people Stage II in Norway, while the firm's intranet is the most extensively used in Australia. Database with client cases is most extensively used within the people-to-docs Stage III in Norway, while document system is the most extensively used in Australia. Expert systems are most extensively used within the people-to-systems Stage IV in both Australia and Norway.

In terms of statistical differences, there are two significant differences in the tables. First, internal databases are significantly more used in Norwegian law firms compared to Australian firms. Second, document systems are significantly more used in Australian law firms compared to Norwegian firms.

The survey instruments included questions on knowledge-sharing perceptions and reward attitudes in both countries. These questions were derived from research conducted by Hunter et al. (2002). Figure 34 shows results for

Figure 34. Average Response to Statements about Knowledge-Sharing Perceptions (1-strongly disagree, 5-strongly agree)

Knowledge-sharing perceptions	Norway	Australia
Lawyers are encouraged to share with others what they have learned from their recent assignments.	3.8	4.1
Senior staff are too busy to reflect on their experiences and share them.	3.2	3.8
The firm has a well-organized system for sharing knowledge (e.g., about clients, managing projects, new approaches) within departments or practice areas.	3.4	3.2
The firm has a well-organized system for sharing knowledge (e.g., about clients, managing projects, new approaches) across departments or practice areas.	3.3	2.8
There is an expectation that lawyers or their teams will have to take a regular turn to provide a reflection on learning experiences.	3.5	2.8
Sharing knowledge systematically is part of the firm's culture.	3.2	3.1

knowledge-sharing perceptions. The questions were posed somewhat differently than earlier questions, as respondents were asked whether they disagreed or agreed with each statement. The scale went from 1 (strongly disagree) to 5 (strongly agree). This means that a number 3 means neither disagree nor agree. The first question in Figure 34 indicates that respondents did somewhat agree that lawyers are encouraged to share with others what they have learned from their recent assignments. Similar results are obtained for the other questions on knowledge-sharing perceptions that respondents only marginally agreed with the statements for. The second question was a turned question, indicating a marginal disagreement with the statement, especially in Australia.

Figure 35 lists responses concerning reward attitudes. Results indicate that individual evaluation is more common than teamwork evaluation when salary increases take place, especially in Australia. There are three statistically significant differences in Figure 35. First, lawyer salary increases in the firm are significantly more based on ability and how well he/she does his/her job in Australia. The same is the case for promotion. Third, Australian lawyers are more fairly rewarded for the amount of work they put in.

Stages of growth were measured in terms of tools and systems in the first part of the questionnaire. Each stage was measured through a multiple item scale consisting of five items. Reliability for each scale is listed in Figure 36. The second scale on who-knows-what systems had an unacceptable reliability even when items were deleted, causing the summary item to be used in Figure 36.

Figure 35. Average Response to Statements about Reward Attitudes (1-strongly disagree, 5-strongly agree)

Reward attitudes	Norway	Australia
Lawyer salary increases in the firm are based on ability and how well he/she does his/her work.	4.2	4.8
Promotion of a lawyer in the firm is based on ability and how well he/she does his/her work.	4.2	5.0
Lawyers are fairly rewarded for the amount of effort they put in.	3.7	5.0
The interest of the work lawyers do compensates for long hours and a stressful workload.	3.4	3.3
The team as a whole is rewarded for good work.	3.2	3.4
Teamwork in this firm is fully recognized and rewarded.	3.2	3.6

Scores in Figure 36 are illustrated in Figure 37. The visual picture supports stages of growth in terms of less systems use at higher stages. When this picture is combined with an earlier figure on paths of evolution, then stronger support is present for the stages of growth model for knowledge management technology in law firms. While the earlier figure on paths of evolution supports the sequence suggested by the model, Figure 37 supports declining use suggested by the model.

Knowledge-sharing perceptions, reward attitudes, support for personal development and performance appraisal were measured through four multiple item scales. Reliability for each scale is listed in Figure 38. In the Australian survey, only the two first scales were included in the questionnaire. While Norwegian law firms report stronger knowledge-sharing perceptions in their firms compared to Australian firms, Australian law firms report stronger reward attitudes compared to Norwegian firms.

Figure 36. Average Response to Systems Use at Each Stage (1-little extent, 6-great extent)

Multiple item scale	Norway Score	Australia Score	Norway Alpha	Australia Alpha
End-user tool systems	4.7	4.3	.69	.79
Who-knows-what systems	3.7	2.9	-	-
What-they-know systems	3.0	3.2	.77	.80
How-they-think systems	1.4	1.5	.89	.85

Figure 37. Average Response to Systems Use at Each Stage (1-little extent, 6-great extent)

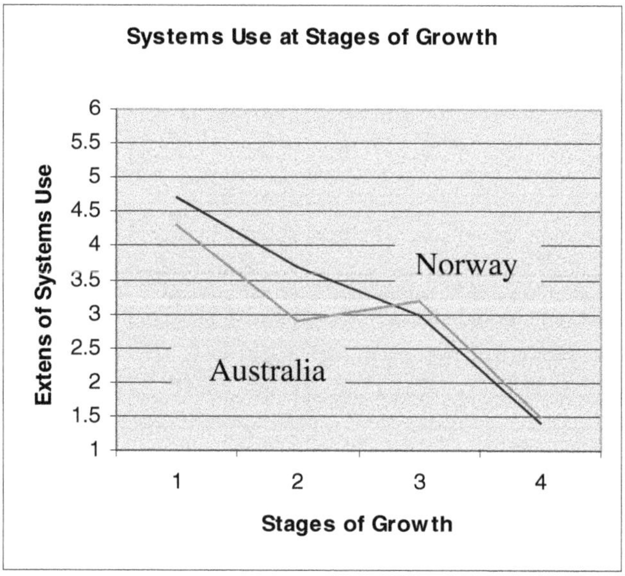

This chapter was concerned with the following research question: Do firms move through various stages of growth in their application of knowledge management technology over time, and is each theoretical stage regarded as an actual stage in law firms? Specifically, is the knowledge management technology stage model valid? Empirical evidence from law firms in Norway and Australia provide some support for the knowledge management technology stage model. Based on this result, several suggestions for future research emerge.

First, even if there are stages of knowledge management technology, the defined stages and their sequence have to be investigated. For example, if the approach of personalization versus codification strategy is applied (Hansen et al., 1999), then Stage II of personalization and Stage III of codification may in fact represent two alternative stages of growth models.

Second, Guttman scaling of benchmark variables must be directly related to the stages of growth, rather than the approach applied here of advancement in technology use. In future research, benchmark variables should be directly derived from each stage of growth.

Third, the del technique should be applied in future research. The calculation of del is a measure of association in tables for specific a priori predictions, as well as a significance test (Kazanjian & Drazin, 1989). Because of the limited sample size in this research, this approach was not appropriate.

Figure 38. Average Response to Human Resources Issues (1-little extent, 6-great extent)

Multiple item scale	Norway Score	Australia Score	Norway Alpha	Australia Alpha
Knowledge-sharing perceptions	3.3	3.0	.70	.87
Reward attitudes	3.8	4.2	.71	.73
Support for personal development	3.2	-	.71	-
Performance appraisal	3.3	-	.77	-

Finally, the size of the sample has to increase in future research by making it more attractive to respond to the survey. Law firms seem very relevant as an industry for future research, but their participation has to be stimulated more successfully than in this research.

A stages of growth model for knowledge management technology was discussed in this chapter to understand the stage that a law firm has reached concerning application of information technology in knowledge management. Four stages are defined, and a law firm can use the model to develop a strategy for implementing technology in higher stages in the model. However, empirical results suggest that both the sequence of stages and the benchmark variables for stages have to be improved in future research.

LINKING THE KMT STAGE MODEL TO OTHER MODELS

The knowledge management stage model presented in this chapter can be conceptually linked to other models presented in this book. Two examples are the model for intellectual capital management and the model for value shop.

Intellectual Capital Management and Stage Model

One of the key authors in the area of intellectual capital is Sveiby (2001), who developed a model of knowledge transfers. The model consists of nine knowledge transfers mechanisms: (1) knowledge transfers between individuals, (2) knowledge transfers from individuals to external structure, (3) knowledge transfers from external structure to individuals, (4) knowledge transfers from competence to internal structure, (5) knowledge transfers from internal structure to individual competence, (6) knowledge transfers within the external structure, (7) knowledge transfers from external to internal structure, (8) knowledge transfers from internal structure to external structure, and (9) knowledge transfers within the internal structure.

The KMT stage model consists of four stages. Stage I is general IT support for knowledge workers. This includes word processing, spreadsheets, and email. This stage is called end-user tools and people-to-technology. Stage II is information about knowledge sources. An information system stores information about who knows what within the firm and outside the firm. The system does not store what they actually know. A typical example is the company intranet. This stage is called who-knows-what and people-to-people. Stage III is information representing knowledge. The system stores what knowledge workers know in terms of information. A typical example is a database. This stage is called what-they-know and people-to-documents. Stage IV is information processing in knowledge work. An information system uses information to evaluate situations. A typical example here is an expert system. This stage is called how-they-think and people-to-systems.

Linking the knowledge transfer model to the KMT stage model can answer the question of how each knowledge transfer mechanism finds support from information technology at each stage of growth. This is illustrated in Figure 39, in which each knowledge transfer mechanism is assigned one specific stage. At the assigned stage, IT provides the most significant support for knowledge transfer. Other stages will also provide IT support for the same knowledge transfer, but only the most significant is listed in Figure 39.

The knowledge management implication of Figure 39 is that IT support for knowledge transfer mechanisms should not be selected independently of stage. Rather, the firm should move through each stage of knowledge management technology. This strategy implies that the firm at Stage I implements IT support for knowledge transfers from external structure to individuals, knowledge transfers from internal structure to individual competence, and knowledge transfers within the external structure. When the firm moves to Stage II, it implements IT support for knowledge transfers between individuals and knowledge transfers from individuals to external structure. When the firm moves to Stage III, it implements IT support for knowledge transfers from competence to external structure, knowledge transfers from external to internal structure, and knowledge transfers within the internal structure. When the firm moves to Stage IV, it implements IT support for knowledge transfers from internal to external structure. This is illustrated in Figure 40.

In Figure 41, some examples of actions concerning organizational development and use of information technology are listed for the knowledge transfer mechanisms. While most of the IT examples belong to the stages as indicated in Figure 40, this Figure 41 also illustrates that technology from other stages may be of relevance to one specific mechanism.

Figure 39. Linking Knowledge Management Transfer Mechanisms to Stages of Knowledge Management Technology

	Stage I End-user tools People-to-technology	Stage II Who-knows-what People-to-people	Stage III What-they-know People-to-documents	Stage IV How-they-think People-to-systems
Knowledge transfers between individuals		**Linking individuals to each other using communication network and intranet**		
Knowledge transfers from individuals to external structure		**Linking individuals in the firm to external stakeholders using communication network, extranet and the Internet**		
Knowledge transfers from external structure to individuals	**Collecting information from external stakeholders using tools such as email and word processing**			
Knowledge transfers from competence to internal structure			**Capturing and codifying knowledge to be stored as information in corporate databases**	
Knowledge transfers from internal structure to individual competence	**Accessing electronic information using tools, systems and electronic agents**			
Knowledge transfers within the external structure	**Accessing external electronic information using tools, systems and electronic agents**			
Knowledge transfers from external to internal structure			**Capturing and codifying external knowledge to be stored as information in corporate databases**	
Knowledge transfers from internal to external structure				**Accessing Web-based services by external stakeholders**
Knowledge transfers within the internal structure			**Integrating systems, tools, processes and services**	

Value Shop and Stage Model

Value shop is the typical value configuration of knowledge firms. A value shop consists of five primary activities. The first primary activity is problem finding and acquisition. In this activity, knowledge workers use tools such as email, text processing and presentation material to understand the problem scope. Hence, IT support in the first primary activity can be found at Stage I, as illustrated in Figure 42. Knowledge management technology from other stages will also be useful in problem finding and acquisition, but Stage I seems to provide the most significant IT support.

Problem solving draws heavily on various information sources, making knowledge management technology at Stage III the most important IT support.

Figure 40. Knowledge Management Transfer Mechanisms Assigned to Stages of Knowledge Management Technology

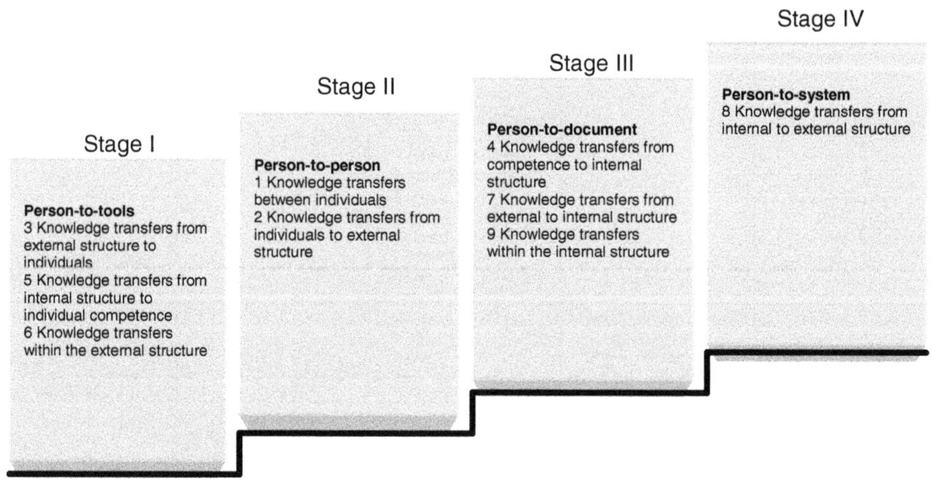

The third primary activity is choice of solution to problem. Expert systems at Stage IV will be useful to evaluate alternative solutions to the problem. For execution of the selected solution, communication with client and involved parties is important, making knowledge management technology at Stage II most relevant. The fifth and final primary activity in the value shop is control and evaluation of problem solving. In this activity, knowledge workers will again use tools such as email, text processing and presentation tools from Stage I.

The knowledge management implication of Figure 42 is that primary activities in a value shop will find support from knowledge management technology as the firm moves through stages. At Stage I, problem finding and acquisition, and control and evaluation will find support. At Stage II, also execution of solution will find support. At Stage III, problem solving will find support, while choice of solution to problem will find support at Stage IV.

Knowledge Management Matrix and Stage Model

To identify knowledge management applications, we combined knowledge levels with knowledge categories as illustrated in Figure 43. When assigning stages to each combination of level and category, we find that stages develop along a diagonal in the matrix. While knowledge management technology at Stage I typically supports core, administrative knowledge, technology at Stage IV supports innovative, analytical knowledge.

The knowledge management implication of Figure 43 is that core knowledge will find support from knowledge management technology before advanced and innovative knowledge. Similarly, administrative knowledge will find support from

Figure 41. Examples of Information Technology for Knowledge Transfer Mechanisms

1	Knowledge transfers between individuals	Coach/junior Management training Communities of practice Storytelling Coffee bars Creative arenas Competence lunches Conversations	Yellow pages Log book Knowledge catalogues Virtual networks Personal portal Corporate portal Appointment books Email
2	Knowledge transfers from individuals to external structure	Seminars Conferences Exhibitions User manuals User training User forums Joint developments	Extranet Email Virtual networks Expert systems Electronic publishing Examples collection Checklists
3	Knowledge transfers from external structure to individuals	Practice groups Joint publishing Research projects Courses Seminars Communities of practice	Internet Extranet Virtual networks Intelligent agents Surveys Electronic publishing
4	Knowledge transfers from competence to internal structure	Concept development Guidelines Tools Frameworks Examples Systematized information Categorized knowledge	Databases Data warehouses Knowledge support systems Document archives Archives of frameworks Expert systems Decision support systems
5	Knowledge transfers from internal structure to individual competence	User training Incentives Communities of practice Help Desk Documentation Availability of equipment Availability of systems Experience exchange Seminars	Modern equipment E-learning systems Word processing Email Spreadsheet Presentation graphics Document archives Framework archives Knowledge support systems
6	Knowledge transfers within the external structure	Alliances Partnership Communities of practice Joint projects Joint location Mutual representation	Internet Extranet Electronic publishing Project management systems Virtual networks E-learning systems
7	Knowledge transfers from external to internal structure	Market intelligence Business intelligence Training sessions User experiences Focus groups Market surveys	Internet Extranet Intelligent agents Educational programs Customer database Supplier database
8	Knowledge transfers from internal to external structure	Product descriptions User handbooks Project cooperation Product cooperation Supply cooperation	Extranet Educational programs Product descriptions User handbooks Corporate portal

Figure 41. Examples of Information Technology for Knowledge Transfer Mechanisms (continued)

9	Knowledge transfers within the internal structure	Multidisciplinary work Project organization User training Incentives IT competence	Systems integration Infrastructure Application architecture Information architecture Object-oriented databases
10		Individual organizational development Organizational individual development Job rotations Virtual organization IT competence	User interface Infrastructure Virtual network Information catalogues Internet

Figure 42. Linking Value Shop Activities to Stages of Knowledge Management Technology

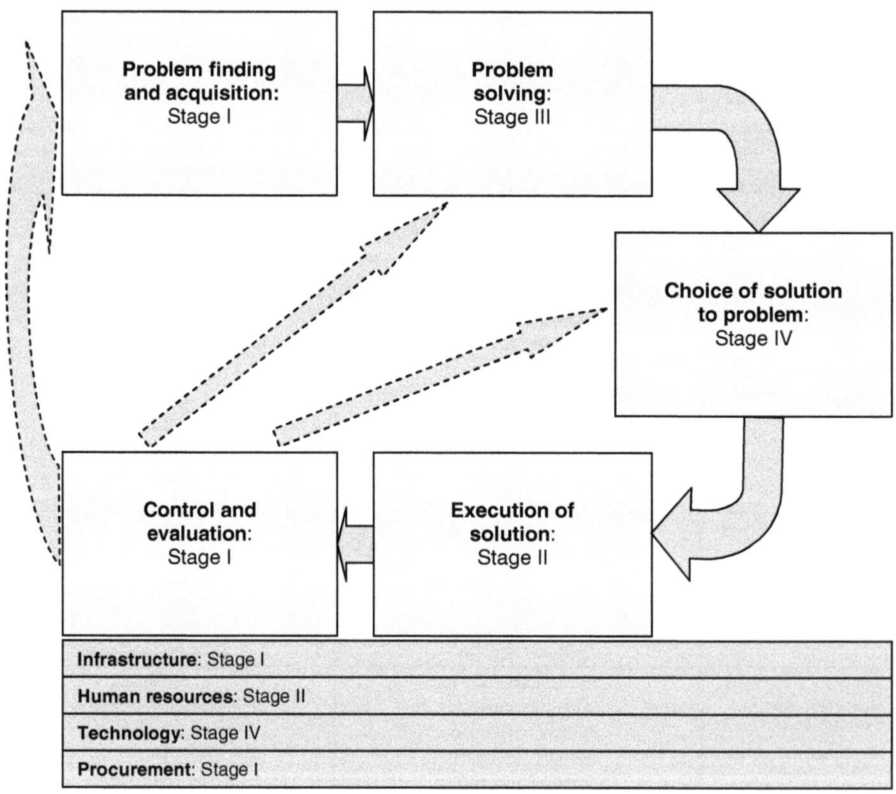

Figure 43. Linking Knowledge Management Matrix to Stages of Knowledge Management Technology

Levels *Categories*	Core Knowledge	Advanced Knowledge	Innovative Knowledge
Administrative Knowledge	Stage I End-user tools People-to-technology	Stage I End-user tools People-to-technology	Stage II Who-knows-what People-to-people
Declarative Knowledge	Stage I End-user tools People-to-technology	Stage I End-user tools People-to-technology	Stage II Who-knows-what People-to-people
Procedural Knowledge	Stage II Who-knows-what People-to-people	Stage III What-they-know People-to-documents	Stage IV How-they-think People-to-systems
Analytical Knowledge	Stage II Who-knows-what People-to-people	Stage III What-they-know People-to-documents	Stage IV How-they-think People-to-systems

knowledge management technology before declarative, procedural and analytical knowledge.

CASE STUDY: LINKLATERS

BLUE FLAG, Linklaters' award-winning method of delivering legal services electronically, has enhanced the service it offers to clients with the launch of two new products. Blue Flag Netmark is the first online product to combine the expertise of a premier global law firm with that of a leading domain name registration service provider, Net Searchers, to deliver a powerful and comprehensive domain name management tool. The increasing importance of brands as corporate assets and the growing use of the Internet means that effective domain name management is vital — the average FTSE 100 company can have as many as 1,000 domain names to track. Netmark provides users with complete and secure desktop access to their worldwide domain name portfolio, 24 hours a day, seven days a week, and more importantly, links to specialist intellectual property lawyers who are available for specialist advice and who can take prompt action against cyber squatters.

In addition, Linklaters has launched Blue Flag FSMA Litigation. The Financial Services and Markets Act (FSMA) come into force on November 30, 2001 and is one of the most significant changes to corporate finance law in recent years. The new product has been developed in response to client requests for guidance on the new legislation, and will have a long-term benefit for clients as it covers a range of issues in respect to the enforcement and disciplinary powers of a range of other regulatory authorities.

Patrick Hynes, CEO of Blue Flag, commented:

"The launch of Netmark and FSMA Litigation is part of the continual evolution of Linklaters Blue Flag, which has now been offering innovative online legal solutions to clients for over five years. Netmark is the first time we have joined up with a specialist third party to enhance our services, and FSMA Litigation is the latest in a line of products that has been created in response to a specific piece of legislation. We will continue to refine and develop the Blue Flag services we offer in order to provide the top-quality legal advice that our clients expect from us."

A recent survey of senior in-house corporate lawyers by The Legal Media Group and Euro money revealed that Linklaters Blue Flag is the best-known legal product on the Web. Fifty-five percent were aware of Blue Flag, compared with 17 percent for Clifford Chance and 14 percent for Freshfields Bruckhaus Deringer.

Linklaters has been named "Law Firm of the Year" by *Chambers Guide to the Legal Profession* at the prestigious annual launch of its UK directory at London's Savoy Hotel (October 4). The award is Linklaters' second this year, having also been named "Law Firm of the Year" by *Legal Business* magazine in February 2001.

This is the first time a law firm has managed to achieve winning the awards given by two of the most authoritative legal publishers in a single year. Tony Angel, managing partner, commented: "This has been an exciting year for Linklaters with a number of key developments taking place throughout the firm. It is good to know that the efforts everyone has put in throughout the firm for our clients have been recognized."

Legal Web advisors were pioneered in London in 1994 when the law firm Linklaters introduced a browser-based product called Blue Flag. Blue Flag is now a suite of products covering regulatory compliance, derivatives documentation, employee share plans, funds, share disclosure, and transaction management. Within months, another London law firm, Clifford Chance, followed with NextLaw, a Web-accessible online service that helps assess the legal and regulatory risks of e-commerce and reportedly required an investment of more than 1 million pounds sterling. Today, there are approximately a dozen online legal services in the UK and Australia and the pace of their introduction is accelerating.

According to the innovator's dilemma concerned with exploiting disruptive technologies, it is very difficult for a company whose cost structure is tailored to compete in high-end markets to be profitable in low-end markets as well. Creating an independent organization such as Blue Flag, with the cost structure honed to achieve profitability at the low margins characteristic of most disruptive technologies, may be the only viable way for established firms to solve this dilemma. Blue Flag is a new economy unit, not just to undertake research and development and to promote the generation of entrepreneurial business models, but also to identify, design, develop, and market online legal services, based on the Internet as a disruptive technology.

Linklaters (now Linklaters and Alliance) opted to forego the more traditional marketing-based Website by launching their Blue Flag service. Blue Flag is a legal risk management service designed to provide commoditized legal advice on European financial and banking regulatory issues (hence the name Blue Flag). This service is designed to appeal to those concerned with legal compliance working in fund management, securities houses, investment and commercial banks and provides step-by-step legal advice on tap to subscribers for a fixed annual fee. Not surprisingly, having established the service, Linklaters have now extended it to cover other (non-European) jurisdictions where they have expertise.

Sources: Mountain (2001), Susskind (2000), Terret (2000), www.linklaters.com

Chapter V

IS/IT Strategy for Knowledge Management

INTRODUCTION

Developing an IS/IT strategy for knowledge management is taken to mean thinking strategically and planning for the effective long-term application and optimal impact of electronic information to support knowledge management in the organization. Strategy can simply be defined as principles, a broad based formula to be applied in order to achieve a purpose. These principles are general guidelines guiding the daily work to reach business goals. Strategy is the pattern of resource development and application decisions made throughout the organization. These encapsulate both desired goals and beliefs about what are acceptable and, most critically, unacceptable means for achieving them.

Resource-based strategy is concerned with development and application of resources. While the business strategy is the broadest pattern of resource decisions, more specific decisions are related to information systems and information technology. IS must be seen both in a business and an IT context. IS is in the middle because IS supports the business while using IT. As part of a resource-based strategy, both IS and IT represent capabilities and resources that have be developed.

Business strategy is concerned with achieving the mission, vision and objectives of a company, while IS strategy is concerned with use of IS/IT applications, and IT strategy is concerned with the technical infrastructure, as illustrated in Figure 1. A company has typically several IS/IT applications. The connection between them is also of great interest, as interdependencies should prevent applications from being separate islands. Furthermore, the arrows in the illustration in Figure 1 are of importance. Arrows from business strategy to IS strategy, and from IS to IT strategy represent the alignment perspective; they illustrate *what* before *how*. Arrows from IT to IS strategy, and from IS to business strategy represent the extension from *what* to *how* to *what*. This is the impact perspective, representing the potential impacts of modern information technology on future business options.

Necessary elements of a *business strategy* include mission, vision, objectives, market strategy, knowledge strategy, and our general approach to the use of information, information systems and information technology.

Mission describes the reason for firm existence. For example, the reason for law firm existence is clients' needs for legal advice. The mission addresses the organization's basic question of "What business are we in?" This single, essential sentence should include no quantification, but must unambiguously state the purpose of the organization and should just as carefully define what the organization does not do. According to Ward and Peppard (2002, p. 189), the mission is an unambiguous statement of what the organization does and its long-term, overall purpose:

Its primary role is to set a direction for everyone to follow. It may be short, succinct and inspirational, or contain broad philosophical statements that tie an organization to certain activities and to economic, social, ethical or political ends. Values are also frequently stated alongside the mission. Three widely-differing examples of missions are:

- To be the world's mobile communications leader, enriching the lives of individuals and business customers in the networked society (large global telecommunication company).
- To eradicate all communicable diseases worldwide (World Health Organization).

Figure 1. Relationships Between Strategies at Three Levels

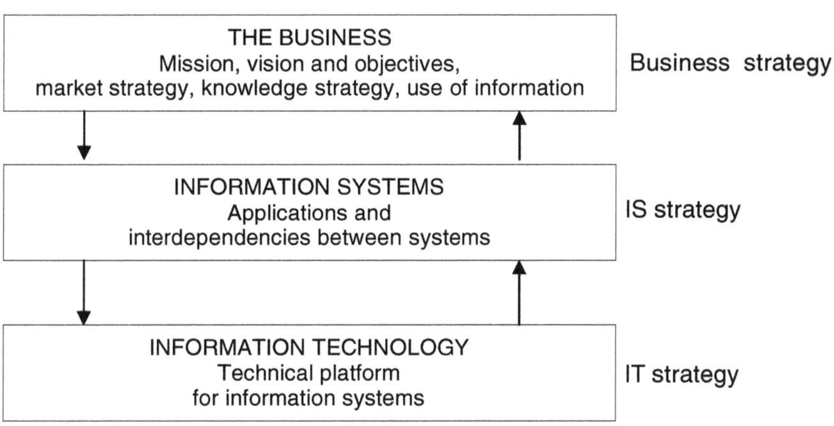

- The company engages in the retail marketing on a national basis of petroleum products and the equitable distribution of the fruits of continuously increasing productivity of management, capital and labor amongst stock holders, employees and the public (a large public company).

Vision describes what the firm wants to achieve. For example, the law firm wants to become the leading law firm in Norway. The vision represents the view that senior managers have for the future of the organization; so it is what they want it to become. This view gives a way to judge the appropriateness of all potential activities that the organization might engage in. According to Ward and Peppard (2002), the vision gives a picture, frequently covering many aspects, that everyone can identify with, of what the business will be in the future, and how it will operate. It exists to bring objectives to life, and to give the whole organization a destination that it can visualize, so that every stakeholder has a shared picture of the future aim.

Objectives describe where the business is heading. For example, the law firm can choose to merge with another law firm to become the leading law firm in Norway. Objectives are the set of major achievements that will accomplish the vision. These are usually small in number, but embody the most important aspects of the vision, such as financial returns, customer service, manufacturing excellence, staff morale, and social and environmental obligations.

Market strategy describes market segments and products. For example, the law firm can focus on corporate clients in the area of tax law.

The most important business strategy part is concerned with knowledge strategy. According to Zack (1999, p. 135):

A knowledge strategy describes the overall approach an organization intends to take to align its knowledge resources and capabilities to the intellectual requirements of its strategy. It can be described along two dimensions reflecting its degree of aggressiveness. The first addresses the degree to which an organization needs to increase its knowledge in a particular area vs. the opportunity it may have to leverage existing but underutilized knowledge resources — that is, the extent to which the firm is primarily a creator vs. user of knowledge. The second dimension addresses whether the primary sources of knowledge are internal or external. Together these characteristics help a firm to describe and evaluate its current and desired knowledge strategy.

The business strategy part concerned with use of information and IT is sometimes called an information management strategy. The general approach to the use of information, information systems needs and information technology investments are described in this part. For example, the ambition level for IT in knowledge management is described, and the general approach to selection of ambition level and combination of ambition levels I - IV are discussed.

Necessary elements of an *IS strategy* include future IS/IT applications, future competence of human resources (IS/IT professionals), future IS/IT organizational structure, and control of the IS/IT function. An important application area is KMS. The future applications are planned according to priorities; how they are to be developed or acquired (make or buy), how they meet user requirements, and how security is achieved. The future competence is planned by types of resources needed, motivation and skills needed (managers, users, IS/IT professionals), salaries, and other benefits. The future IS/IT organization defines tasks, roles, management and possibly outsourcing.

Necessary elements of an *IT strategy* include selection of IT hardware, basic software, and networks, as well as how these components should interact as a technological platform, and how the required security level is maintained. The IT platform consists of hardware, systems software, networks and communications, standards and support from selected vendors.

An *IS/IT strategy* is a combined strategy including business context, the IS in a narrow sense and the technological platform. Necessary elements of an IS/IT strategy include business direction and strategy (mission, vision, objectives, knowledge strategy), applications (knowledge management systems), people (future competence of human resources), organization (future organization and control of IT function), and IT platform (future technical infrastructure). Hence, IS/IT is quite a broad term. The term is broad to take care of all connections and interdependencies in a strategy, as changes in one element will have an effect on all other elements, as illustrated in Figure 2.

Figure 2. IS/IT Strategy Elements and Interdependencies

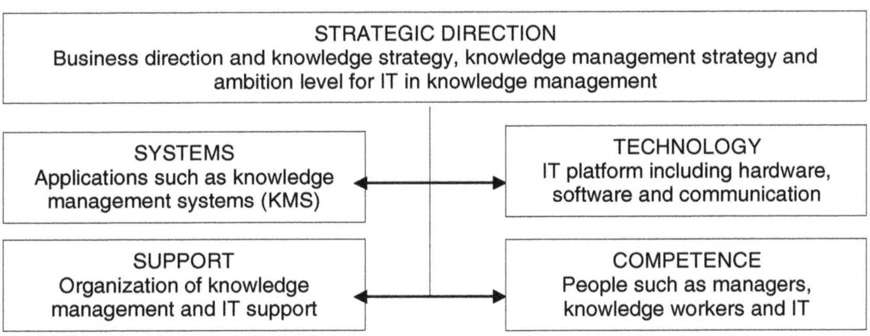

Why is strategic IS/IT planning undertaken within business organizations? Hann and Weber (1996) see IS/IT planning as a set of activities directed toward achieving the following objectives:

1. Recognizing organizational opportunities and problems in which IS/IT might be applied successfully;
2. Identifying the resources needed to allow IS/IT to be applied successfully to these opportunities and problems;
3. Developing strategies and procedures to allow IS/IT to be applied successfully to these opportunities and problems;
4. Establishing a basis for monitoring and bonding IT managers so their actions are more likely to be congruent with the goals of their superiors;
5. Resolving how the gains and losses from unforeseen circumstances will be distributed among senior management and the IT manager;
6. Determining the level of decision rights to be delegated to the IT manager.

In the following, we present a model for development of an IS/IT strategy for knowledge management. However, we do not limit strategy work to knowledge management. Rather, we describe the complete IS/IT strategy work in which knowledge management is a natural part of it. This is done to keep a complete strategy work process. A limited strategy only for knowledge management can cause suboptimal solutions for the company.

Empirical studies of information systems/information technology planning practices in organizations indicate that wide variations exist. Hann and Weber (1996) found that organizations differ in terms of how much IS/IT planning they do, the planning methodologies they use, the personnel involved in planning, the strength of the linkage between IS/IT plans and corporate plans, the focus of IS/IT plans (e.g., strategic systems versus resource needs), and the way in which IS/IT plans are implemented (Porter 2001, p. 63):

Many have argued that the Internet renders strategy obsolete. In reality, the opposite is true. Because the Internet tends to weaken industry profitability without providing proprietary operational advantages, it is more important than ever for companies to distinguish themselves through strategy. The winners will be those that view the Internet as a complement to, not a cannibal of, traditional ways of competing.

In the following, the Y model for strategy work is discussed and applied. The model provides a coherent step-by-step procedure for development of an IS/IT strategy.

In all kinds of strategy work, there are three steps. The first step is concerned with analysis. The second step is concerned with choice (selection and decision), while the final step is concerned with implementation.

We now introduce a model for strategy work. This is illustrated in Figure 3. The model consists of seven stages covering analysis, choice and implementation. The stages are as follows:

1. *Describe current situation.* The current IS/IT situation in the business can be described using several methods. The benefits method identifies benefits from use of IS/IT in the business. Distinctions are made between rationalization benefits, control benefits, organizational benefits and market benefits. Other methods include the three-era model, management activities, and stages of growth.
2. *Describe desired situation.* The desired business situation can be described using several methods described in the first chapter: value configurations, competitive strategy, management strategy, business process redesign, knowledge management, the Internet and electronic business, and information technology benefits.
3. *Analyze and prioritize needs for change.* After descriptions of the current situation and the desired situation, needs for change can be identified. The gap between desired and current situation is called needs for change. Analysis is to provide details on needs, what change is needed, and how changes can take place. *What*-analysis will create an understanding of vision and goals, knowledge strategy, market strategy, and corporate problems and opportunities. *How*-analysis will create an understanding of technology trends and applications. These analyses should result in proposals for new IS/IT in the organization.
4. *Seek alternative actions.* When needs for change have been identified and proposals for filling gaps have been developed, alternative actions for improving the current situation can be developed. New IS/IT can be developed, acquired, and implemented in alternative ways. For example, an information system can be developed in-house by company staff, it can be purchased as a standard application from a vendor, or it can be leased from an application systems provider (ASP).
5. *Select actions and make an action plan.* When needs for change and alternative actions have been identified, several choices have to be made and documented in an action plan. Important issues here include development process, user involvement, time frame and financial budget for IS/IT projects.
6. *Implement plan and describe results.* This is the stage of action. Technical equipment such as servers, PCs, printers and cables are installed. Operating systems are installed. Application packages, software programs, programming tools, end-user tools and database systems are installed. Development projects are organized. Management and user training takes place. Document results over time.

Figure 3. The Y Model for IS/IT Strategy Work

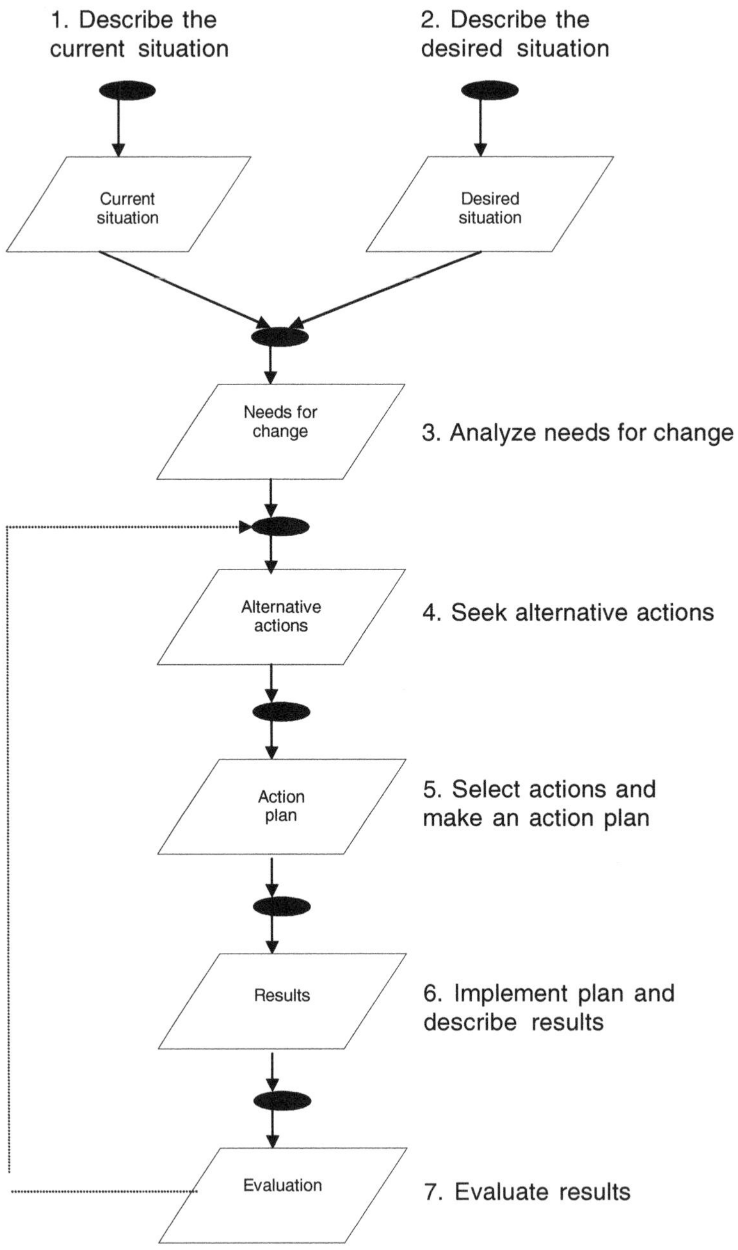

7. *Evaluate results.* Implementation results are compared with needs for change. It is determined to what extent gaps between the desired and current situation have been closed. This is the beginning of the IS/IT strategy revision process, in which a new process through the Y model takes place. Typically, a new IS/IT strategy process should take place every other year in business organizations.

While Stages 1 to 3 cover *analysis*, 4 and 5 cover *choice*, and 6 and 7 cover *implementatio*n. In some strategy models, Stage 2 is listed as the first stage. It is here recommended to do Stage 1 before Stage 2. It is easier to describe the ideal situation when you know the current situation. If you start out with Stage 2, it often feels difficult and abstract to describe what you would like to achieve. Having done Stage 1 first makes the work more relevant. Stage 3 is a so-called gap analysis, looking at the difference between the desired and actual situation. This stage also includes prioritizing. Stage 4 is a creative session, as it calls for ideas and proposals for alternative actions. Stages 5 and 6 are typical planning stages. The final Stage 7 is important because we can learn from performing an evaluation.

STRATEGY ANALYSIS

Stages 1 to 3 cover strategy analysis in the Y model. While Stage 1 is concerned with describing the current IS/IT situation, Stage 2 is concerned with describing the current and desired business situation, and Stage 3 is concerned with analyzing needs for change based on the gap identified when comparing current and desired situation.

Describing Current IS/IT Situation

The Y model starts with a description of the current situation. We focus on the IS/IT situation, as this will be the subject of change later in the model. First of all we have to understand in what ways the company is using IS/IT. Many approaches can help us gain an understanding of the present IS/IT situation. Some methods are listed in the following:

1. *Benefits of IS/IT.* IS/IT is applied in business organizations to achieve benefits. We can study current IS/IT in the organization to understand what benefits have been achieved so far. Here we can determine what main benefit categories are currently the case. We will make distinctions between rationalization benefits, control benefits, organizational benefits, and market benefits.
2. *Stages of IS/IT growth.* IS/IT in business organizations change over time. New hardware and software, new areas of applications, and new IS/IT

support functions emerge. Most business organizations develop through stages over time. Here we can determine at what stage the business organization is for the time being. We will make distinctions between a total of nine stages. These nine stages are classified into three eras: data processing, information systems and information networks.
3. *IS/IT in management activities.* Management activities can be studied in a hierarchical perspective of operational, tactical and strategic management. Current IS/IT in the organizations can be assigned to these levels to determine the extent of support at each level.
4. *IS/IT in business processes.* In a company, many business processes take place at the same time. Some of the processes may rely heavily on IS/IT, while others are mainly manual at the current point in time.
5. *IS/IT support for value configuration.* We make distinctions between value chain, value shop and value network. In each of these value configurations, IS/IT can support activities. The current IS/IT situation is described by identifying activities in the value configuration depending on the extent of technology support.
6. *Strategic integration.* Business strategy and IT strategy have for a long time suffered from lack of coordination and integration in many organizations. Here we measure the current IS/IT situation by use of ten integration mechanisms to determine integration stage in an organization.
7. *IS/IT in e-business.* For most firms, becoming an e-business is an evolutionary journey. We introduce six stages to describe the evolving e-business: external communications, internal communications, e-commerce, e-business, e-enterprise, and transformation.
8. *IS/IT enabled business transformation.* IT-enabled transformation can include business direction change, but more often we find examples at lower levels, such as business design change and business process change.
9. *IS/IT support for knowledge management.* The stages of growth model for knowledge management technology can be applied, in which the current IS/IT situation is described by the stage at which the firm currently is performing.

Description of the current situation assumes that we have been able to define borders for our study. Borders exist for both breadth and depth. Breadth is a question of whether the whole company or only one division should be studied. Depth is a question of whether all aspects such as technology, marketing, management and finance should be included in the study. We recommend both extensive breadth and thorough depth to ensure that a wide range of alternative solutions and alternative actions can be identified in later stages of the Y model. In the case of breadth, this may imply that both suppliers and customers are included because there may be electronic marketplaces used by our suppliers and customers. In the case of depth, this may imply that analysis of top management is included because management competence in the area of IS/IT can influence both management attitudes and ambitions concerning future applications of IS/IT.

Description of the current IS/IT situation should focus on issues of importance in technology and knowledge management. Less emphasis should be put on technology itself, such as drawings of company networks and servers. Technology management is focused on the management of information technology, while knowledge management is focused on knowledge strategy and knowledge management systems.

Describing Current and Desired Business Situation

We have used some of the nine methods to describe the current situation of IS/IT. Now we have to consider whether the current IS/IT applications are what the company needs or if there might be changes needed. We use the Y model as our guiding approach. We compare the present business situation (with its support from IS/IT) with the desired business situation. If the current IS/IT applications are not able to serve the needs of the future desired business, then there are needs for change in IS/IT applications and the way we do business. At this point we are moving into Stage 2 of the Y model.

There are many techniques for business analysis. Some are general, while others are more specific. General analysis techniques include SWOT analysis and the X model. Specific analysis techniques include business direction (mission, vision, objectives), market strategy, value system, competitive forces and product life cycle. Some of these analytical tools are listed in the following:

1. *SWOT analysis.* SWOT analysis is an analytical tool for assessing the present and future situation, focusing on strengths (S), weaknesses (W), opportunities (O) and threats (T). The whole company may be the object of analysis, but also a department in a company or a project in a company may be the study object. How can knowledge management exploit our strengths, compensate for our weaknesses, use opportunities and avoid threats? How can knowledge management technology help make it happen?
2. *X model.* The X model is a tool for description and analysis of both the current and a desired situation. It is a method for assessing the situation within a company, a project, or a department. The situation consists of a time period in which work is done. In the beginning of the time period, there are both factual and personal inputs, and at the end of the period, there are both factual and personal outputs. How can knowledge management improve factual and personal outputs? How can knowledge management technology help make it happen?

3. *Business direction.* Important business concepts are mission, vision and objectives. How can knowledge management make the firm achieve its vision? How can knowledge management make the firm reach its objectives? How can knowledge management technology help make it happen?
4. *Market strategy.* The market strategy shows our position and ambition in the marketplace. We can either have the same product as our competitors, or we can have a different product. If we have the same product as everyone else, it has to be sold at the same price as all the others (as in a vegetable market or through the Internet). It is not possible for an Internet bookstore to sell at a higher price than others, when there is perfect information and information searching is associated with no costs. This is called the law of indifference. In order to survive, the company must have a cost advantage that will give higher profits and result in higher earnings for the owners. How can knowledge management cause a cost advantage? How can knowledge management technology help make it happen? If we are selling a product that our customers perceive to be different from our competitors' product, then we have differentiation. A service may in its basic form be the same for all companies, like an airline travel, in the sense that all airlines are supposed to bring you safely to your destination. The product is differentiated by supplementary services. How can knowledge management make our customers perceive our products and services to be different from our competitors'? How can knowledge management technology help make it happen?
5. *Competitive forces.* The basis of this method is that a company exists within an industry and to succeed, it must effectively deal with the competitive forces that exist within the particular industry. For example, the forces in an emerging industry such as mobile communication are considerably different from those of established industries such as financial services. The company interacts with its customers, suppliers and competitors. In addition, there are potential new entrants into the particular competitive marketplace and potential substitute products and services. To survive and succeed in this environment, it is important to understand these interactions and the implications in terms of what opportunities or competitive advantage can occur. How can knowledge management reduce the threat of new entrants, reduce the bargaining power of suppliers, reduce the bargaining power of buyers, reduce the threat of substitute products and services, and reduce the rivalry among existing competitors? How can knowledge management technology help make it happen?
6. *Product portfolio analysis.* There are a number of approaches that aim to relate the competitive position of an organization to the maturity of its product. The models assume there is a basic S-shaped curve description to the growth phenomenon of products. Four stages in the life cycle of any

product can be identified as introduction, growth, maturity, and decline. When we look at the life cycle of all products in the firm, we can apply product portfolio analysis. This method shows the relationship between a product's current or future revenue potential and the appropriate management stance. The two by two matrix names the products in order to chart symptoms into a diagnosis so that effective management behavior can be adopted. The matrix classifies products according to the present market share and the future growth of that market. A successful product that lasts from emergent to mature market goes around the matrix. This strategy is simply to milk the cows, divest the dogs, invest in the stars and examine the wild cats. How can knowledge management get more milk for a longer period of time from the cows? How can knowledge management explore and exploit the stars? How can knowledge management eliminate the dogs? How can knowledge management develop the wild cats into stars? How can knowledge management technology help make it happen?

7. *Environmental analysis.* Environmental analysis is concerned with the external corporate environment. An analysis of the environment is important because it increases the quality of the strategic decision making by considering a range of the relevant features. The organization identifies the threats and opportunities facing it, and those factors that might assist in achieving objectives and those that might act as a barrier. The strategy of the organization should be directed at exploiting the environmental opportunities and blocking environmental threats in a way that is consistent with internal capabilities. This is a matter of environmental fit that allows the organization to maximize its competitive position. An external analysis can investigate politics, the economy, the society and the technology. This is sometimes called PEST analysis. If we include the study of legal and environmental matters, we call it PESTLE. The analytical work that has to be done in the company when doing environmental analysis is concerned with questions such as: What are the implications of the trends (changes in the environment)? What can the company do in order to meet the opportunities and threats that follow? How can knowledge management meet the opportunities and threats that follow? How can knowledge management technology help make it happen? For example, how can knowledge management technology help in global competition (politics)? How can knowledge management technology help in alliances and partnerships (economy)? How can knowledge management help serve an increasing number of older people (society)?

8. *External knowledge analysis.* Distinctions can be made between core knowledge, advanced knowledge and innovative knowledge. While core knowledge is required to stay in business, advanced knowledge makes the firm competitively visible, and innovative knowledge allows the firm to lead its entire industry. The knowledge map can be applied to identify firm

position. The map in terms of the strategic knowledge framework presented earlier in this book illustrates firm knowledge levels compared with competitors' knowledge levels.

9. *Internal knowledge analysis.* While the knowledge map represents an external analysis of the firm's current knowledge situation, the knowledge gap represents an internal analysis of the firm's current knowledge situation. The knowledge gap is dependent on business strategy. What the company does is different from what the company will do, creating a strategy gap. What the company knows is different from what the company has to know, creating a knowledge gap. Two important links emerge: the strategy-knowledge-link and the knowledge-strategy-link, as illustrated earlier in this book.

Tiwana (2000) suggests that a knowledge audit and analysis should be carried out in the company. To perform a knowledge audit and analysis, we need to select a multidisciplinary group of people, truly representative of the company. Using IT staff is not an option, since they are likely to miss critical viewpoints and aspects in the final outcome. The audit team, in its totality, needs representatives from at least the following functional areas:

- *Corporate strategist:* Sets goals, determines optimal performance levels, and brings the big picture perspective into the analysis.
- *Senior management, company visionary, long-term planner, or evangelist:* Brings long-term KM vision, aligned with the business strategy of the corporate strategists.
- *Financier:* Brings the ability to value and attach a fair-dollar figure to knowledge assets.
- *Human resource manager:* Brings good understanding of employee skills and skills distribution within the organization.
- *Marketer:* Provides a fair picture of actual market performance of the firm and the possible implications of its knowledge assets on the marketability of the firm's products and services at new price-service function points.
- *IS/IT expert:* Brings in knowledge, skills and expertise for mobilizing the technology implementation aspects of your knowledge management strategy. Also has intimate knowledge of existing infrastructure.
- *Knowledge manager, CKO, or knowledge analyst:* The middle role that integrates inputs from all other participants on the knowledge audit team in a consensual, unbiased, and fair manner. The analyst contributes a reasonably accurate market valuation of proprietary technology and processes based on perspectives elicited from other team members.

Tiwana (2000) further suggests that the audit and analysis should be carried out in several steps:

1. *Define the goals.* The knowledge management audit team agrees upon the reasons for the audit, decides on the goals, and identifies the key financial, organizational, privacy-related, and strategic constraints that influence it. Define specific goals that both the audit process and knowledge management are targeting.
2. *Determine the ideal state.* This need not be all-encompassing during the initial stages of the audit process. Begin with a few key variables that are equivocally considered critical and that can scope your knowledge management project.
3. *Select the audit method.* You will actually use a company specific method to perform the audit. So it should account for employee know-how, reputation and market goodwill, and organizational culture as they apply to your company. The method you use for auditing your company or group knowledge determines the degree to which you will accurately gauge the current (pre-KM) state of that aspect or knowledge dimension. This assessment is what helps you decide on the processes that need reinforcement and the processes that need capitalization. For example, you might realize that there just is not enough conversation and sharing of ideas going on in a specific department in your company. You might decide to augment this shortcoming with a Web-based message board and physical common space. In short, the choice of technologies (and accompanying cultural reinforcements) you focus on will largely be determined and influenced by this step in the knowledge audit process. The audit method that you decide to use must account for at least the following three critical intangible assets: employee know-how, reputation (including goodwill or value attached to your company brand), and organizational culture. Reputation and culture can be thought of as diffused tacit knowledge, so it follows that knowledge and know-how, in some form or another, account for the bulk of the value of the firm. You must also determine the nature, strength, and sustainability of the current competitive advantage that the firm derives in terms of product and service delivery system features that it employs. It helps to think in terms of the issues of protection, maintenance, enhancement, and leverage of these intangible assets.
4. *Perform the knowledge audit and document existing knowledge assets.* This provides an internal benchmark to evaluate the effects of knowledge management initiatives after they have been put in place. It is important to document the knowledge-based assets that your company has in a consistent framework. The framework makes it easier to compare with

previously measured values and with corresponding values for your competitors.

5. *Track knowledge growth over time.* Progression from the initial stage (when the knowledge audit process is performed for the very first time) to later stages allows for easy comparison with the ideal state.
6. *Determine your company's strategic position within the technology framework.* Mapping knowledge in each of the areas you chose in the earlier stages of the knowledge audit provides excellent insight into the way knowledge management and business strategy can be kept in perfect synchronization.

Many observers have recently pointed out that formal accounting systems do not measure the valuable knowledge, intellectual capital, of a corporation. The market values of knowledge-intensive organizations are often several times their "book" or accounting value. Some analysts have even argued that accounting systems should change to incorporate intangible assets and that knowledge capital should be reflected on the balance sheet. However, Grover and Davenport (2001) find that the esoteric and subjective nature of knowledge can make it impossible to assign a fixed and permanent value to knowledge. This makes step 3 in the Y model both important and difficult to carry out.

Knowledge Management Analysis

Modern organizations are increasingly seen as knowledge-based enterprises in which proactive knowledge management is important for competitiveness. At this stage of the Y model, a descriptive framework for understanding factors that influence the success of knowledge management in an organization can be applied. The framework developed by Holsapple and Joshi (2000) identifies three main classes of influencing factors (managerial, resource, and environmental) and characterizes the individual factors in each class.

Managerial issues. **Leadership** is concerned with building a trusting environment conducive to sharing knowledge: Is there top-level commitment to KM initiatives? How does it manifest? Does it align with the organization's purpose and strategy? **Coordination** is concerned with developing and integrating reward and incentive systems that encourage knowledge sharing, as well as scheduling knowledge flows: What knowledge activities are performed? How are they organized to accommodate dependencies? Which processors perform them? **Control** is concerned with governing the content and channels of sharing (e.g., what can and cannot be shared, and with whom it can be shared), ensuring that knowledge that is shared is of adequate quality and that sharing is not counterproductive (e.g., sharing of knowledge that may sabotage new initiatives): What regulations are in place to ensure quality, quantity, and security of knowledge resources and processors? How are knowledge resources protected from loss, obsolescence, improper exposure/modification, and erroneous assimilation? Via legal, social, technical means? **Measurement** aims at assessing and evaluating the knowledge sharing process: How are knowledge resources valued? How are processors evaluated? In what ways are effectiveness of knowledge activities, coordination approaches, knowledge controls, and knowledge management leadership assessed?

Resource issues. Human participants' personal beliefs and experiences may affect their approaches to sharing. How can computer systems be employed to facilitate sharing? An organization's cultural knowledge resource will have a major impact on creating and maintaining a knowledge-sharing environment. Infrastructure may dictate the channels of communications and sharing. Artifacts (such as office facilities and libraries) may affect knowledge sharing.

Environmental issues. Technology advances may affect the modes and channels of sharing. It can create means to break knowledge-sharing barriers such as geographically dispersed locations. Government regulation can inhibit knowledge sharing. Actions of a competitor (e.g., to lure away employees) can dampen knowledge sharing.

Analyzing Needs for Change

After descriptions of the current situation and the desired situation, needs for change can be identified. Methods as listed above enable management to analyze and identify knowledge management technology for competitive advantage. The knowledge-based view of the firm, derived from the resource-based view of the firm, directs our analysis towards needs for change in knowledge management.

Analyzing needs for change, identifying potential IS/IT, comparing with current IS/IT in the company, and then prioritizing needs for change, should result in proposals for new IS/IT in the organization. For example, our company may prioritize extending product lives, sharing and developing advanced and innovative knowledge, improving internal and external communication, improving support for knowledge workers, improving human resources management, improving problem solving, and coding information from knowledge sources. If such needs for change have priority, then a KMS should be implemented in the organization.

STRATEGY CHOICE

Stages 4 to 5 cover strategy choice in the Y model. While Stage 4 is concerned with seeking alternative actions, Stage 5 is concerned with selecting actions and making an action plan.

Identifying Alternative Actions

When needs for change have been identified and proposals for filling gaps have been developed, alternative actions for improving the current situation can be developed. New IS/IT can be developed, acquired, and implemented in alternative ways. Several decisions have to be made when a new IS/IT is chosen. Such decisions are called systems development strategy, and we apply a systems development strategy map to identify appropriate strategies. A systems development strategy map illustrates decisions that have to be made concerning actions for IS/IT, as illustrated in Figure 4:

- *Use of resources.* One extreme is complete in-house development; the other extreme is a standard package without any changes. There is a fundamental difference for a company between developing the IS/IT itself or buying a standard package in the marketplace from a software vendor. Between the two extremes there are some other options. The standard package might be modified, that is, the company or the vendor could make changes to the software package when applied to the company. The decision here will depend on the availability of suitable application packages for the firm's situation.
- *Kind of methodology.* Analytic methodology implies defining the needs of users through intellectual reasoning techniques. Such techniques define stages of systems study, systems design, programming, installation, testing, implementation and maintenance. Experimental methodology is showing the users alternative computer screens with information and asking for their opinions. This is sometimes called prototyping. Through iterations we might improve and create even better systems. The decision here will depend on systems complexity and the available time for development.
- *Form of deliverance.* A revolutionary approach implies that everything is delivered at the end of the project, like a big bang. A completely new system is implemented and used. An evolutionary approach implies that changes are gradually taking place over time; changes are implemented in an incremental way. The decision here will depend on available time for development as well as organizational culture for revolution versus evolution.
- *Participation of users.* A systems project can either be completely expert-driven or completely user-led, or something in between. It is an important part of Scandinavian culture to have user participation. Totally user-led may be difficult, as technical problems will require the assistance of IS/IT experts. The decision here will depend on technical skills needed as well as availability of competent and motivated users.
- *Kind of results.* Product means only the new IS/IT. Process means paying attention to the learning and increased insight gained from participating in

the IS/IT development activity. The decision here will depend on systems complexity as well as company culture for learning.

- *Coordination of development.* This scale runs from one-sided systems development to a balanced development of personnel, system and organization. A completely one-sided systems development may create an efficient technological solution, but it may not work in the organization, as personnel and organizational issues were not considered. The decision here will depend on company culture for linking human resources management to information technology management.

The first decision in the systems development strategy map is concerned with use of resources. Over the last two decades, the availability of standard application packages has risen. In most application areas, there are standard packages available today. Most organizations have changed from an in-house development strategy to a standard package strategy. Acquisition of standard application software is a very widespread strategy, especially among small and medium-sized companies that cannot afford large in-house staff for systems development. Large companies may still have the resources to cover their own special systems needs. There is a big market for standard application packages. Most companies of small and medium size have bought standard applications for their administrative support functions, and many also for their production and marketing systems. As an example, the Norwegian School of Management BI needed a new student administration system. The school bought the standard

Figure 4. Systems Development Strategy Map to Identify Actions for IS/IT

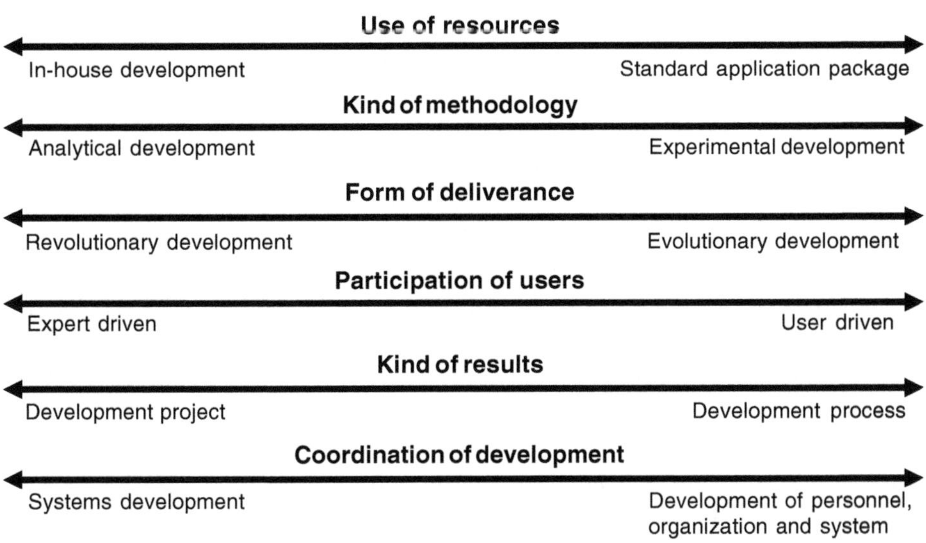

package BANNER. Because of some special needs for exams and grading, the system had to be modified somewhat. Generally, the advantages of application package acquisition include:

- Quicker installation, providing earlier business benefits;
- Reduced costs for development and maintenance;
- More reliable cost/benefit analysis;
- Know-how built into the package;
- Flexibility for changes in business activities;
- Well tested, hence fewer errors.

Of course, there are disadvantages and pitfalls as well in acquisitions of application packages. The most common one is that the organization does not carefully enough consider its own needs. It may also be a disadvantage not to have an own IS/IT function to support the system. Costs of adaptation may rise as needs for modifications may cause expensive changes in the package. Generally, disadvantages of package acquisition include:

- Hasty decisions, making an undesirable investment decision;
- Underestimation of costs of adaptation of package to the company;
- Inappropriate computer operations environment for the package;
- Expensive computer operations for the package;
- Vendor dependency in areas such as support, modifications and further development;
- People have to adapt to the package rather than the system adjusting to the people.

Even when the company has decided to follow the strategy of acquiring a standard package, it must find out — define — its own needs, that is, the requirements of the desired IS/IT. Without user needs and requirements, it is impossible to choose a standard package. There might be several packages available. First a comparison between the needs and each package has to be done in order to find out the extent of fit between the two. Then, in the selection, one has to identify the possibilities and the costs of making necessary adjustments. The result of a selection is a temporary choice of one package. Then we have — in more detail — to check if it is possible to make the desired modifications to the package. We also have to check if the initial cost estimate still holds true.

The comparison between the needs and each package can be carried out using the relational model. The *relational model* tells us — step by step — what we have to do to fulfill the requirements of the company if we purchase the temporary selected application package. If we, during the analysis, run into major unanticipated problems, then we have to switch to another package and do the analysis with the new package. The relational model is time-consuming to apply, both for the company and for the software vendor. Therefore we must try to do it only once for each package.

The fit or match between requirements of the company and the package of the software vendor can be measured using the relational model. The goal is to select a package with a good initial fit, and then we can discuss what we can do to improve the fit. Here again we get help from the relational model as parts with poor fit are identified and analyzed. The relational model consists of 10 parts, as illustrated in Figure 5.

The 10 parts in the relational model have the following meaning:

1. *Part of the package directly acceptable for the business.* This represents the initial fit between requirements and package.
2. *Part of the package that will make business even more efficient.* These are things we did not consider when making the requirements. When we see the package, we realize that this part can be advantageous to the company.
3. *Part of the package that will have this as a permanent feature, expanded and developed by vendor.* This part of the requirements is not covered by the package. The vendor thinks it is a good idea to incorporate it in the package. The vendor does the changes on his or her own account. This will be a future feature of the package, available to all vendor customers.
4. *Part of the package that will be changed to meet requirements, developed by vendor.* This part of the requirements is not covered by the package. The vendor is willing to incorporate this in the software application, but at the expense of the buyer. It is to be decided if this work is to be done at a fixed price or paid by the hour. Payment by the hour introduces an uncertainty in the buying situation. Furthermore, there might be a future problem of maintenance, since it is not certain that the vendor will do it.
5. *Part of the business that will adapt to package.* This part of the requirements is not covered by the package. The company will give up some of the requirements and do work the way it has to be done with the

Figure 5. The Relational Model for Evaluation of an Application Package

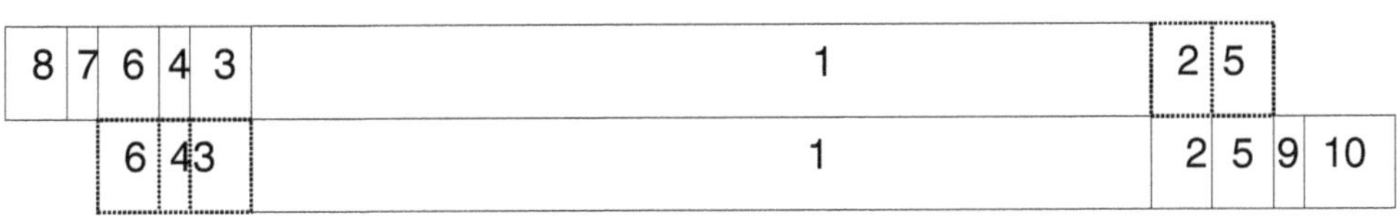

application package. This is an important decision for both management and users. Some corporate cultures are more willing to adapt to a package than other cultures.

6. *Part of the package that will be changed to meet requirements, developed by customer.* This is not part of the package. The company buying it will extend the software. This is a very risky task, as it might be difficult to make changes in an unknown package and to maintain those changes over time. It is also risky because the vendor will in the future make changes to the standard package that might affect the homemade part and create further need for software changes.
7. *Part of requirements that will be developed in-house.* This is not part of the package. These requirements will be met by the customer by making an IS/IT separate and in addition to the package.
8. *Part of the requirements that will be left unfulfilled.* Neither the vendor nor the customer will develop and program a subsystem to meet these requirements. The vendor will not do it because he or she may see technical difficulties as well as no market potential for the subsystem. The customer will not do it because he or she expects to be able to survive without it.
9. *Part of the package that will not be used.* There can be many reasons for not using this part of the software package in the company. For example, our company may have another application that already has all functions in this part covered in an efficient and effective way.
10. *Irrelevant part of the package.* There can be many reasons for the irrelevance of this part of the software package to the company. For example, our company is in a service industry, while this part of the package is only applicable to manufacturing industry.

The second decision in the systems development strategy map is concerned with methodology. Analytical methodology implies defining the needs of users through intellectual reasoning techniques. Such techniques define stages of systems study, systems design, programming, installation, testing, implementation and maintenance. Experimental methodology is showing the users alternative computer screens with information and asking for their opinions. This is sometimes called prototyping. Through iterations we might improve and create even better systems. The decision here will depend on systems complexity and the available time for development.

A common analytical methodology is the systems life cycle. The *systems life cycle* partitions the systems development process into formal stages that must be completed sequentially with a formal definition of labor between end-users and information systems specialists. The life cycle for an information system has six stages: (1) project definition, (2) system study, (3) design, (4) programming, (5) installation, and (6) maintenance. Figure 5.6 illustrates these

Figure 6. The Life Cycle Methodology for Information Systems Development

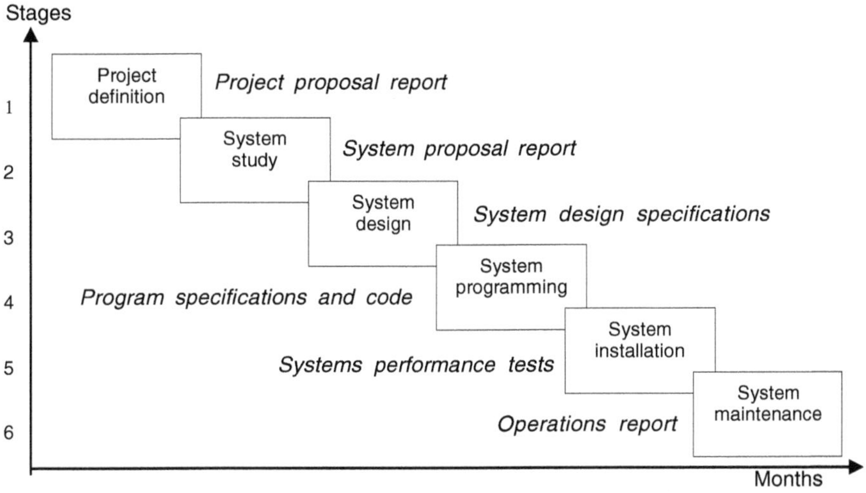

stages. Each stage consists of basic activities that must be performed before the next stage can begin.

The systems life cycle is useful for building large complex systems in-house that require a rigorous and formal requirements analysis, predefined specifications, and tight controls over the systems-building process. However, the systems life cycle methodology is costly, time consuming, and inflexible. Often, volumes of new documents must be produced and steps repeated if requirements and specifications need to be revised. Because of the time and cost to repeat the sequence of life cycle activities, the methodology encourages freezing of specifications early in the development process, discouraging change.

A common experimental methodology is prototyping. *Prototyping* consists of building an experimental system rapidly and inexpensively for end-users to evaluate. By interacting with the prototype, users can get a better idea of their information requirements. The prototype accepted by the users will be the basis for creating the final system. The prototype is a working version of an information system or part of the system, but it is meant only to be a preliminary model. The process of building a preliminary system, trying it out, improving it, and trying it again is called an iterative process of systems development because the steps required to build a system can be repeated over and over again. In Figure 7, a four-step model of the prototyping process is illustrated.

Prototyping is most useful when there is some uncertainty about requirements or design solutions. Prototyping encourages end-user participation in building a system; therefore it is more likely to produce a system that fulfills user requirements. However, rapid prototyping runs the risk of ignoring essential

Figure 7. The Prototyping Methodology for Systems Development

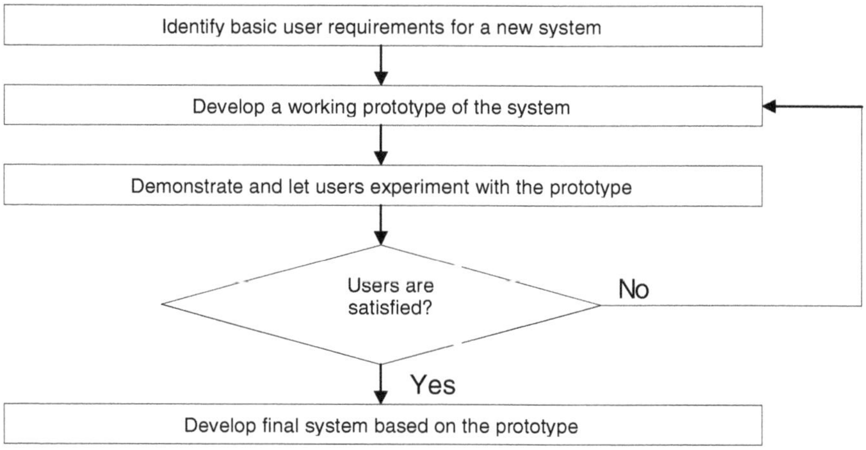

steps in systems development. Such ignorance may later cause a rise in maintenance costs.

The third decision in the systems development strategy map is concerned with form of deliverance. A revolutionary approach implies that everything is delivered at the end of the project, like a big bang. A completely new system is implemented and used. An evolutionary approach implies that changes are gradually taking place over time; changes are implemented in an incremental way. The decision here will depend on available time for development as well as organizational culture for revolution versus evolution. We can distinguish between the following four forms of deliverance, as illustrated in Figure 8:

- *Direct deliverance (cold start).* At a specific point in time, the old system is terminated and the new system is implemented. The old system can no longer be used, because data for that system are no longer updated. If the new system fails, it will be a painful period without any information system.
- *Double deliverance (parallel).* For a specific period of time, both the old system and the new system are run in parallel. This form reduces risks, but it causes higher operating costs for the period.
- *Stepwise deliverance (phased).* The new system is divided into subsystems, and subsystems are implemented one at a time. When one module in the new system is used, then the equivalent module in the old system is stopped.
- *Pilot deliverance (group wise).* At a specific point in time, the system is implemented in one part of the organization. For example, the department

Figure 8. Four Basic Approaches to System ChangeOver

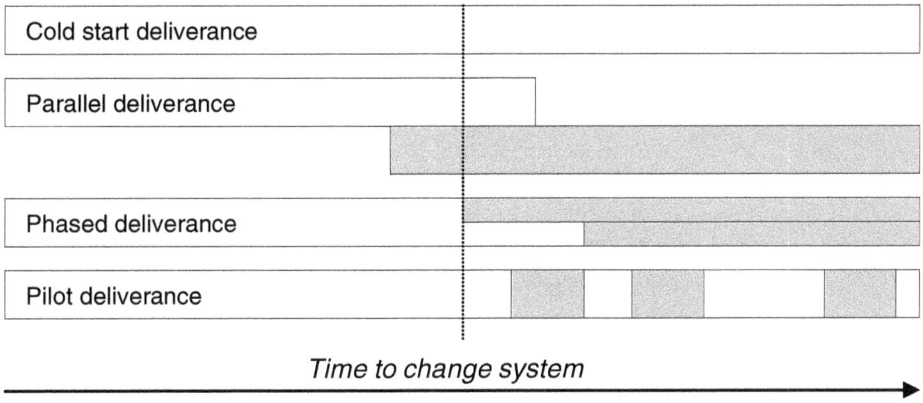

of mergers and acquisitions in a law firm may be the first part of an organization to use a new system. If the use is successful, then the system spreads to other parts of the organization.

The fourth decision in the systems development strategy map is concerned with participation of users. A systems project can either be completely expert-driven or completely user-led, or something in between. It is an important part of Scandinavian culture to have user participation. Totally user-led may be difficult, as technical problems will require the assistance of IS/IT experts. The decision here will depend on technical skills needed as well as availability of competent and motivated users. We can distinguish between the following four user participation roles:

- *Resources manager.* This is a user who has management responsibility and makes decisions concerning resources for new IS/IT, including people involved in systems development and money for procurement of equipment.
- *Solutions entrepreneur.* This is a user who has ideas about new information systems, both related to applications areas and systems design.
- *Requirements developer.* This is a user who has strong opinions about functions in a new information system.
- *System champion.* This is a user who is enthusiastic and dedicated to the successful implementation of the new system.

The fifth decision in the systems development strategy map is concerned with kind of results. Product means only the new IS/IT. Process means paying attention to the learning and increased insight gained from participating in the IS/IT development activity. The decision here will depend on systems complexity as well as company culture for learning. We can distinguish between the following four kinds of results:

- *Systems success:* the benefits from the new information system in terms of rationalization benefits, control benefits, organizational benefits, and market benefits.
- *User success:* the extent of user satisfaction with the new system.
- *Development success:* the extent to which the new IS/IT was developed on time and within budget.
- *Learning success*: the extent to which participating persons have improved their skills in IS/IT development.

The final decision in the systems development strategy map is concerned with coordination of development. This scale runs from one-sided systems development to a balanced development of personnel, system and organization. A completely one-sided systems development may create an efficient technological solution, but it may not work in the organization, as personnel and organizational issues were not considered. The decision here will depend on company culture for linking human resources management to information technology management. We can distinguish between four alternative coordination approaches:

- *One-sided:* Attention is concentrated on the technical solution of the new IS/IT. We put all our efforts into optimizing both hardware and software by selecting machines, servers and network, as well as database system and application software, so that the technology itself works as efficiently as possible.
- *Two-sided:* Attention is expanded to users, where solutions may be tailor-made to individual users.
- *Three-sided:* Attention is further expanded to the organization, where solutions are designed in such a way that business processes are improved.
- *Four-sided:* Attention is further expanded to the environment, where solutions are designed in such a way that stakeholders may find it attractive to do business with us.

Selecting Appropriate Actions

At this stage, we have to make final decisions concerning content of actions and development actions. While content of actions is our final priority of needed changes, development actions is our final systems development strategy.

In Stage 3 of the Y model, we analyzed needs for change, identified potential IS/IT, compared them with current IS/IT in the company, prioritized needs for change, and proposed new IS/IT in the organization. We are now going to look a little closer at the task of choosing which IS/IT to develop/acquire. An IS/IT should in general be financially justified, and we should use the traditional tools of financial analysis to see if the investment is economically sound. But the following list of reasons for IS/IT projects shows that there might be some IS/IT that can be justified by other reasons than financial ones:

- *Strictly necessary applications.* There might be some that are required by law; for example, a new tax law that requires changes in the existing financial management system.
- *Strategic applications.* To stay in business we have to do it.
- *Maintenance of existing applications.* Several bugs need fixing now.
- *User requests.* Users have expanded the use of an existing system to new tasks that require systems modification.
- *New areas.* We have to experiment with new technology, such as e-business.
- *Applications that increase efficiency, effectiveness and competitiveness.* These are the applications that can be freely prioritized for selection.

The economist will look at the development of a new IS/IT or changes made to an existing one as an investment. An investment is characterized by some initial costs (net profit is negative) and later some income (net profit is positive). We will have a cash flow with some negative payments first and some positive payments later. Then we can calculate NPV (Net Present Value) or IRR (Internal Rate of Return), and then decide if the investment is worth implementing. If we have several profitable investments, we can decide which one is best.

There are other ways of deciding if an investment is favorable. The ambition might be to have a balanced application portfolio. For example, some IS/IT support cash cows, while other IS/IT support stars and wild cats.

Ward and Peppard (2002) suggest that three factors need to be included in the assessment of priorities for future applications:

- what is most important to do: benefits to the firm;
- what is capable of being done: resources in the firm;
- what is likely to succeed: risks to the firm.

Some companies use a point (or scoring method) when evaluating an IS/IT investment. This can be done by making a list of requirements and then looking at the proposed IS/IT and giving points (e.g., 0-5) according to how well the different systems fulfill the requirements. Economic profitability in terms of NPV or IRR might be only one of the requirements. Implemented within a certain time limit might be high on the priority list of users. There might be knockout factors. If the score is zero for such a factor, then the planned system is dropped.

We should try harder to measure the benefits in financial terms. It is not always easy; on the contrary, costs are often much easier to estimate than benefits. There is sometimes the danger of detailed cost analysis and lacking benefits analysis. One approach to benefit analysis is to identify what kind of benefits may be caused by the system. We have earlier discussed efficiency, effectiveness and competitiveness. Efficiency (E) means doing things right. It is to use a minimum of resources to obtain a predetermined result. Effectiveness (E) means doing the right things. It is to use resources to obtain a desired result. Competitiveness (C) means doing the right things better than the competitors. In addition to the EEC model, we can look for rationalization (automation) benefits, control (decision) benefits, organizational (redesign) benefits, and market (competitive) benefits, as discussed earlier.

The costs are often easier to calculate than the benefits. Costs include development costs, hardware and software costs, operating costs, and maintenance costs. In an investment analysis, we have to distinguish between:

- Actual investment (occurring only once, e.g., development costs and the costs of acquiring hardware and software;
- Yearly operating costs;
- Periodic costs (e.g., maintenance costs, which might not appear each year).

A survey of 80 American, British, Australian, and New Zealand companies' practices in approving IS/IT projects showed a variety of criteria used. Support of business objectives was a criteria used by 88 percent of the companies. Budgetary constraints was a criteria used by 68 percent of the companies (Olson, 2001).

Risks have to be considered before taking the final decision on an IS/IT investment. An IS/IT might be associated with more risks than another IS/IT. The typical failures to be considered include:

- *Technical failure.* The IS/IT does not work. The technical quality is low. It may be difficult to integrate different kinds of equipment. Maybe there is too little capacity. Technical problems are often the easiest and cheapest problems to overcome. This is the responsibility of IS/IT experts.
- *Data failure.* The data provide wrong information because of low data quality. The data may be wrong, or the information associated with the data may be misunderstood. The problem can be reduced if data are collected at the source, and the users are motivated. This is the shared responsibility of users and IS/IT help functions.

- *User failure.* Users misunderstand the IS/IT, for example because they are not properly trained. This is the responsibility of the IS/IT department.
- *Organizational failure.* IS/IT does not correspond to the needs and tasks of the organization. This is the responsibility of users and management.
- *Failure in business environment.* Inappropriate IS/IT may emerge due to changes in the business environment.

Risk management requires identification of risk categories. Common categories are people issues, project size, control of the project, complexity, novelty, and stability of requirements. Some proposed IS/IT might be associated with more risks than others. To analyze risk further, it can be helpful to distinguish between two dimensions of risk. The first dimension is concerned with probability; that is, the chance of something going wrong. The second dimension is concerned with consequence; that is, the seriousness of problems arising when something goes wrong. The two dimensions are illustrated in Figure 9.

We would like to choose IS/IT with both low risk probability and low risk consequence. In companies with a significant degree of risk aversion, consequence is often considered more important than probability. This can also be observed in society, in which nuclear accidents or plane crashes may be associated with very low probability and very high (unacceptable) consequence. Risk analysis of proposed IS/IT should therefore take into account the potential risk aversion of corporate management.

Often, there will be a positive relationship between NPV or IRR and risk. A very risky new IS/IT will typically have a high NPV or IRR. This is illustrated in Figure 10. IS/IT with high economic return and low risk will typically be chosen

Figure 9. Risk Analysis of Proposed IS/IT

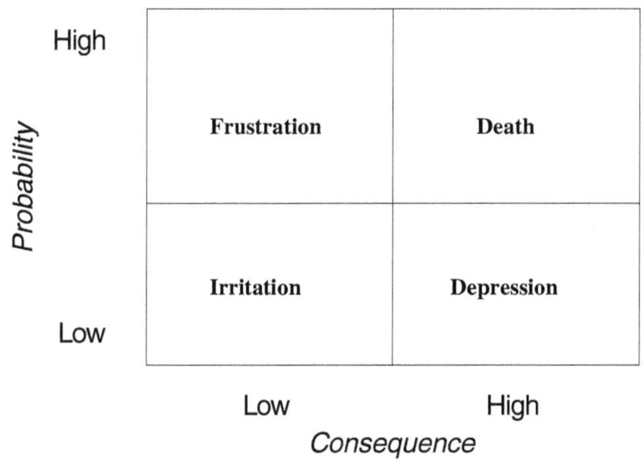

Figure 10. Trade-Off Between Economic Return and Risk of Proposed IS/IT

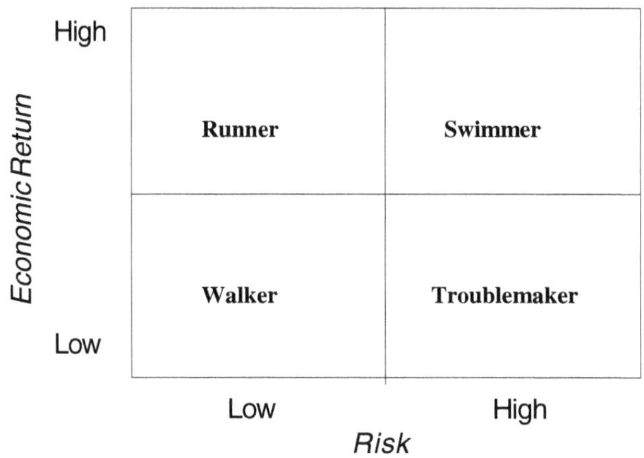

before other IS/IT in the figure. We would like many IS/IT that are runners, we will accept some swimmers and walkers, and we will avoid all troublemakers.

We now conclude our discussion of final selection of actions in terms of IS/IT to be developed and acquired at this Stage 5 of the Y model. At Stage 3, we proposed a new KMS. If this proposal survived the various criteria at this Stage 5, then it is decided to implement a KMS in the company. The functions of the KMS can be defined by results from strategy analysis. For example, if the SWOT analysis indicated weaknesses in our communications with our customers, then Web-based services may be a desirable function in a new KMS.

We now turn to systems development strategy. At Stage 4 of the Y model, we identified elements in a systems development strategy. There are no rights or wrongs in systems development strategy. We apply a contingent approach to strategy, meaning that strategy is dependent on the situation of each company. While one strategy may be excellent for one company, the same strategy may be a complete failure for another company. However, the general picture is as illustrated in Figure 11.

IS/IT initiatives in the past were characterized by in-house development, analytical development, revolutionary development that was expert driven, product focus, and one-sided systems development. In the future, it seems that IS/IT initiatives will be characterized by much more balanced approaches, sometimes leading to future strategy being quite different from past systems development strategy.

Figure 11. Past (P) and Future (F) Systems Development Strategy

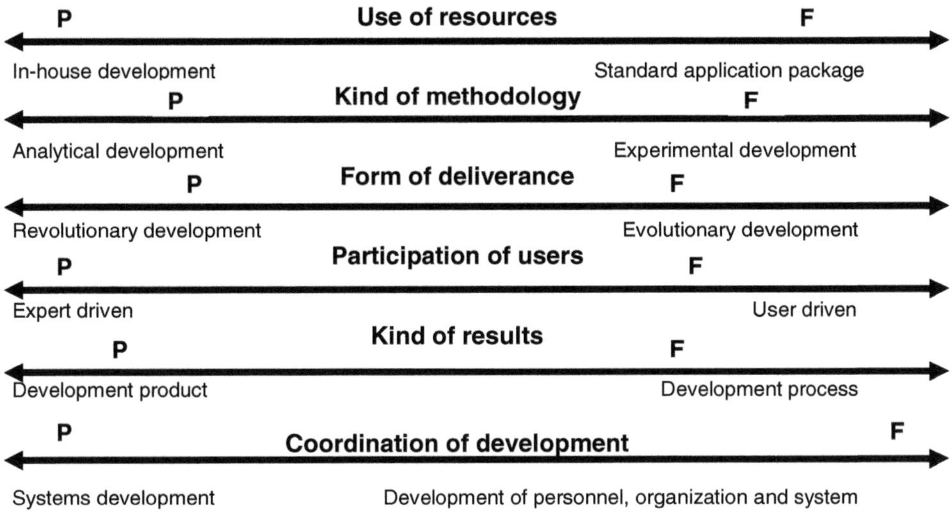

Knowledge Management Actions

For knowledge management applications, it is important to design and build an effective knowledge management team. The ultimate goal, after the knowledge management enabling technology and culture are in place, is to encourage every employee to become a manager of knowledge. Employees should not have to think twice before they contribute, use, validate, update or apply knowledge explicated within and outside the firm. Tiwana (2000) suggests that we keep the following lessons in mind while designing a knowledge management team:

- *Identify a few key core stakeholders.* A knowledge management project must go on and continually improve and change with changing external and internal environments. Select a group of people representing IT, management, and the end-user group that will form a core part of your team on a relatively long-term basis. Other team members can serve temporarily.
- *Identify sources of requisite expertise.* Sources of expertise representing all divisions or departments that will use the knowledge management system are best drawn from those organizational units. Managerial participants with sufficient knowledge of the company and a clear big picture provide strategic direction for the project.

- *Select a visionary and experienced project leader.* The knowledge management project leader helps members of the team understand the project's mission and align their efforts with the company's overall goals and objectives. The project leader must facilitate the internal functioning of the knowledge management team by helping members objectively resolve differences.
- *Identify critical failure points.* There are some high-risk areas in which the knowledge champion has little control: those involving end-user and management support. Make sure that you include representatives from these stakeholder groups to minimize buy-in problems and poor management support in the later stages. Users might necessitate what is called dangling a convincing carrot to motivate them to actively participate.
- *Avoid external consultants if possible.* Be warned that due to the nature of the consulting business, your competitor might have a system similar to yours a few months down the road. It might be worth the extra time to train one of your own employees in organizationally lacking skills and legally protecting details of your KM system with nondisclosure agreements.
- *Balance the knowledge management team's managerial and technological structure.* Knowledge management is not solely a technical project, so the project team needs to balance both managerial and technical participants.

In addition to designing a knowledge management team, it is important to understand and define an architecture for knowledge management systems in the company. A knowledge management system built without a well-defined architecture will lead only to chaos at later stages. It is important to make sure that the architecture is clearly defined, since this part of the infrastructure can be very expensive to fix at a later stage. Tiwana (2000) provides the following guidelines for architecture consideration:

- *Understand the architectural components of the knowledge management system.* Pay close attention to integrative repositories, content centers, knowledge aggregation and mining tools, the collaborative platform, knowledge directories, the user interface options, push delivery mechanisms, and integrative elements.
- *Design for both interactive and integrative content aggregation.* Both these needs must be met simultaneously.
- *Optimize for performance, scalability, and flexibility.* Make sure that your KM system works as well for 600 people as it does for 60. Pay close attention to short delays in processing transactions — these will amplify by orders of magnitude as you begin to scale the system upward.

- *Plan for interoperability.* Plan for high levels of interoperability with existing protocols and implementations.
- *Decide whether to build or buy.* One option is not necessarily better than the other; examine the pros and cons of each option.
- *Pay attention to the user interface and its design.* The user interface provides an excellent opportunity for ensuring buy-in by the user community. A user interface that is built in synchrony with the user community helps creates a perception that the knowledge management system is an asset, and not a liability that needs to be sidestepped.
- *Position and scope the knowledge management system.* In some cases, it is not only difficult, but also foolhardy to try explicating tacit knowledge that your employees possess. Scope the system to support only those categories of knowledge that have the potential for maximizing opportunity and returns.
- *Future-proof your knowledge management system.* Take substantive steps to ensure that your knowledge management system does not become obsolete as technologies or business environments evolve. If the system is well future proofed, changes should affect only the content in your knowledge management system, not its structure or design.

To identify knowledge management applications, we can combine knowledge levels with knowledge categories. Core knowledge, advanced knowledge and innovative knowledge are combined with administrative knowledge, declarative knowledge, procedural knowledge and analytical knowledge, as illustrated in the knowledge management matrix for law firms earlier in this book. The knowledge management matrix was first used to identify the current IS/IT that support knowledge management in the firm. Then the knowledge management matrix was applied to identify future IS/IT. The systems did only serve as examples; they illustrated that it is possible to find systems than can support all combinations of knowledge categories and knowledge levels. Finally, software and systems suitable for knowledge management in a law firm can be identified using the knowledge management matrix as illustrated earlier in this book for law firms.

Making the Plan

The Y model focuses on the different steps in strategy work, including making an IS/IT strategy. We have discussed in depth the analysis part of an IS/IT strategy. The analysis covered description of the current situation, description of desired situation, analysis of needs for change, and priority of needs for change. When the analysis part was complete, decisions had to be made. The choices should be made by business management, preferably by the chief executive of the organization. When all necessary decisions have been made, then the important task of implementation can start, as described in the next chapter.

The Y model outlines the working steps. Analysis and choice should result in an approved IS/IT strategy, that is, a strategy that is decided to be implemented. An approved strategy is the product of strategy work. We may distinguish between product (plan) and process (learning). The process should ideally involve all affected and give them access to all the analyses of the work and give them a possibility for voicing their opinions and for listening to the viewpoints of others. In that way the process will give learning to all involved and might be a way of securing support for the strategy.

The work of developing an IS/IT strategy for the first time might be organized as a project. A project is a unique task that can be contrasted by continuous line activities. Later on, the updating and maintenance of the strategy might be part of the responsibilities of the line organization. But even then they have to involve all the necessary parties in the work.

We might focus even more on what is involved in a process. There are three well-known stages in an organizational development process, and making an IS/IT strategy might well be looked at as organizational development. The first stage is unfreeze. Here it is important to create a climate for change, getting acceptance and readiness for change. In the analysis part it is certainly of importance to focus on the need for changes and create a common understanding of the need for changes. Such needs should be recognized by all involved. The second stage is change. In the implementation part we have to be aware that it is a change process. Growth and changes might hurt. They can result in opposition and counterattacks. It is necessary to alter attitudes, beliefs, and values of individuals directly, or indirectly, by changing the structure, goals or technology of the organization. The final stage is refreeze. Here the new state is institutionalized. The new situation is stabilized. Here we sum up what we have achieved, and are happy about it, before we start over again.

There should be some clear goals set for what we would like to achieve during the process. We want the commitment of management, and we should also use the process to educate management about benefits and risks of IS/IT. We want management to understand how IS/IT is applied, and we want to increase managers' own use of IS/IT. At the same time we want the commitment of users, and we want to educate them as well concerning the importance of IS/IT for the business. Changes in users' attitudes toward IS/IT will create commitment to strategy and implementation plans as well as better understanding of business and its dependence on IS/IT. Hopefully the process will lead to better relationships between the IS/IT department and user departments. The close cooperation in the strategy process should lead to such a result.

At the outset there might be resistance among management against getting involved in the process, and they may oppose any new strategies for IS/IT. The problem might be that top management belong to an older generation and are subject to a general resistance to change. There may also be some specific explanations for resistance. One such explanation might be the uncertainty about benefits of IS/IT. Generally, resistance of management can be identified as:

- Ignorance of IS/IT and its potential uses and benefits;
- Poor communication between the IS/IT department and the rest of the business;
- General resistance to change;
- Lack of focus on opportunities for competitive advantage;
- Lack of instruments for decisively measuring the benefits of IS/IT.

There are several approaches to overcoming management resistance. Education or information — creating knowledge — is of importance, if it is possible to get management involved. If they do not want to listen to IS/IT people from the company, then it might be a good idea to have management meet with managers from other companies that have experienced the benefits of IS/IT themselves. All the time it is of importance to link IS/IT to business needs. It is also of importance to involve management in the decision-making. A good idea might be a kind of steering committee, which should consist of all the functional managers. Functional budgets for IS/IT would make the functional managers strongly involved. Quick positive results might also convince management about the benefits of IS/IT. It is not certain that such applications are available, but in prioritizing one should look for applications that are low risk, relatively quick to acquire/develop and which give good, fast results. In summary, here are some tactics for involving and influencing management:

- Educate management about use and benefits of IS/IT;
- Have management meet other managers who are enthusiastic about IS/IT;
- Link IS/IT to business management needs;
- Form a steering committee;
- Develop functional IS/IT budgets;
- Rapid development of low-risk, managerially useful systems.

The development of an IS/IT strategy might be organized as a project. As illustrated in Figure 12, we can have a traditional organizational structure with a steering committee, project manager and project team (consisting of both business people and IS/IT people). One special aspect is that one should look for a management sponsor, that is, a member of the top management group of the

Figure 12. Strategy Project Organization Structure

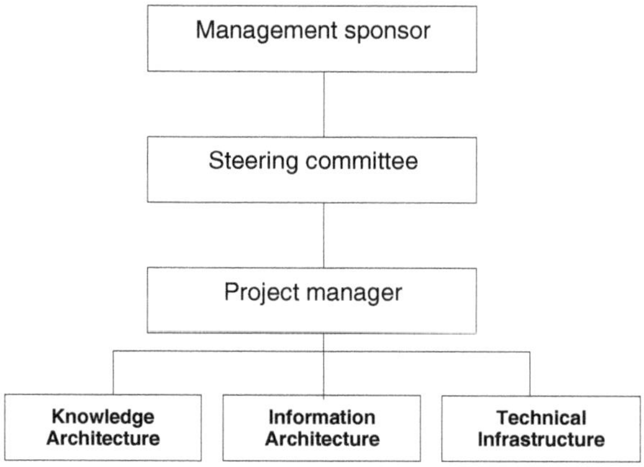

company that would like to sponsor the work. A sponsor serves as a change agent and is a strong supporter of change using IS/IT.

The management sponsor is crucial for project success. The perfect sponsor does the following tasks:

- Chairing the steering committee meetings;
- Assuring top management participation and commitment, through active backing and allocation of the right resources;
- Representing the interests and priorities of the business;
- Heading the marketing effort — the effort of selling the project to the whole organization should not be underestimated;
- Acting as the focal point for decisions about scope, priority and conduct of project work.

The steering committee is of key importance for project success. We are here focusing on what should be done by the steering committee in order to get a positive decision by top management concerning IS/IT strategy:

- Providing strategic direction and guidance on business requirements and priorities to the project team;
- Reviewing and approving plans and raising risk management issues;
- Conducting checkpoint reviews and authorizing continuation of work;
- Reviewing and contributing to final results, before submission to top management.

We advocate strong interaction between the steering committee and the project team. The steering committee gives its general directions at the outset and gives feedback several times on the material presented to them by the project manager.

The IS/IT strategy document may be long or short depending on traditions and expectations in the company. In large organizations, the strategy document will typically have the following elements:

1. Introduction
   - Purpose (its use, distribution of plan)
   - Background (why and the way it was developed, participants, methods)
   - Qualifications (what is not covered)
2. Current business situation
   - Analysis of business direction, market strategy, and competitive forces
   - SWOT analysis, X model, product portfolio analysis, and environmental analysis
   - Value configuration analysis
   - Knowledge analysis and knowledge management status
3. Future business situation
   - Changes in business direction and business activities
   - Resource-based strategy
   - Changes in value configuration
   - Changes in knowledge management
4. Current IS/IT situation
   - Benefits, stages, management activities, strategic integration
   - Business processes and e-business
   - IS/IT support for knowledge management
   - Stage of growth in knowledge management technology
5. IS/IT vision and overall strategy
   - Important IS/IT trends
   - IS/IT vision (for the next three to five years)
   - Main priorities in corporate IS/IT
6. IS/IT applications
   - Needs for changes in application portfolio
   - Required development portfolio
   - Existing portfolio upgrade
   - Future potential portfolio
   - Analysis of applications and portfolios, cost-benefit analysis
   - Proposed priorities

7. KM organization
   - Need for changes
   - Strategy, general guidelines
8. IS/IT organization
   - Need for changes
   - Strategy, general guidelines
9. IS/IT human resources
   - Need for changes
   - Strategy, general guidelines
10. IT infrastructure
    - Need for changes
    - Strategy, general guidelines

One important ambition of the IS/IT strategy is to align business and IS/IT. There are both enablers and inhibitors of business — IS/IT alignment. Such enablers and inhibitors should be identified, analyzed, and solved while making the plan. Solutions should be described in the IS/IT strategy document. Luftman et al. (1999) found that the two most significant enablers were senior executive support for IS/IT and IT involved in strategy development:

1. Senior executive support for IS/IT can be documented by asking them to define and describe strategies that include the role of IS/IT. These descriptions from executives should be included in Section 5 of the plan.
2. IT's participation in creating business strategy can be documented by asking the CIO to define and describe the future business situation. These descriptions from the CIO should be included in Section 3 of the plan.

STRATEGY IMPLEMENTATION

Stages 6 and 7 cover strategy implementation in the Y model. While Stage 6 is concerned with implementing the plan and describing results, Stage 7 is concerned with evaluating results.

The creation of IS/IT strategy has become a major challenge to business executives and IS/IT executives in recent years. Investments in information technology have been large, and many failed investments reflect this challenge. The impact of IT on organizational performance has grown in strategic importance, and thus the significance of failed IT investments is even greater. Information processing and information technology are becoming critical to many business and government operations, and the technology itself is changing at a rapid rate. New information technology will continue to transform organizations, and changes in how industry participants use IT can alter established relationships in an industry. Strategic IS/IT planning can play a critical role in helping organizations to increase efficiency, effectiveness and competitiveness. Although organizations use different methods in their analysis of current and desired situations, the resulting plans are to be implemented.

The importance of the implementation of strategic IS/IT plans is illustrated by the significant attention paid to it in recent years. Studies show that implementation is important for four reasons. First, the failure to carry out the strategic IS/IT plan can cause lost opportunities, duplicated efforts, incompatible systems, and wasted resources. Second, the extent to which strategic IS/IT planning meets its objectives is determined by implementation. Third, the lack of implementation leaves firms dissatisfied with and reluctant to continue their strategic planning. Fourth, the lack of implementation creates problems establishing and maintaining priorities in future strategic IS/IT planning.

Implementing Plan

IS/IT strategy implementation can be defined as the process of completing the projects for application of information technology to assist an organization in realizing its goals. However, implementing an IS/IT strategy is not simply the act of implementing many projects and individual systems. Instead, implementing such a plan demands a gestalt view in the planning of individual systems. A gestalt view represents the implementation of the plan philosophy, attitudes, intentions, and ambitions associated with IS/IT use in the organization. It may include decisions about the IS organization and the implementation of IT architecture.

The term implementation is given a variety of meanings in the literature. Implementation can be described as a procedure directed by a manager to install planned change in an organization. Change is an empirical observation of difference in form, quality, or state over time in an organizational entity. Implementation can be the process of gaining targeted organizational members' appropriate and committed use of an innovation. Information technology implementation from strategic IS/IT planning is a typical innovation.

When is an IS/IT application implemented? Is it implemented when it is approved by top management as part of the IS/IT strategy? When it is installed on a company computer? When it is put into its first use? When it is widely accepted by people in the company? When it is modified as a result of use, based on both detected errors and needs for improvement? When the benefits of the IS/IT strategy are finally appearing? There is no unified answer to this question, but most scholars agree that installation of a system is too early, while benefits are too late to wait for. This is illustrated in Figure 12. Most scholars agree that an IS/IT application is implemented when it is used and accepted by users. So in the example in Figure 13, we would say that implementation occurred in 2005.

Figure 13. Implementation of an IS/IT Application

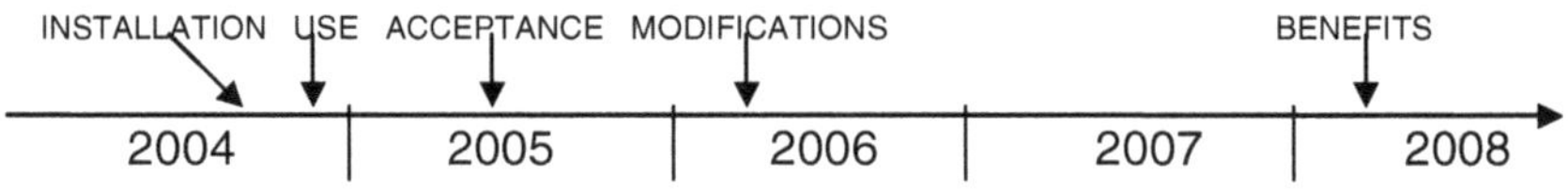

Using the gestalt view, we can say that an IS/IT strategy implementation is defined by degree of implementation. If the complete IS/IT strategy is implemented, we can talk about 100 percent implementation. If nothing is implemented, we can talk about zero implementation. A strategic IS/IT plan is implemented over time, as illustrated in Figure 14. The process of implementation can follow different paths. In Figure 14, there are two examples of early and late implementation respectively, both ending at an implementation degree of 60 percent.

There is no optimal extent of implementation. It depends on the situation in the company over time. If the IS/IT strategy has an excellent match with desired business situation and actual business development, then more of the strategy is likely to be implemented. If the IS/IT strategy consists of a few large, focused projects that, when first started, have to be finished, then more of the strategy is likely to be implemented. If the organization has a culture of walk and talk consistency, then more of the strategy is likely to be implemented. Walk and talk consistency implies that management actually does what it says it is going to do. If the IS/IT strategy has a short time horizon, then more of the strategy is likely

Figure 14. Implementation of IS/IT Strategy Over Time

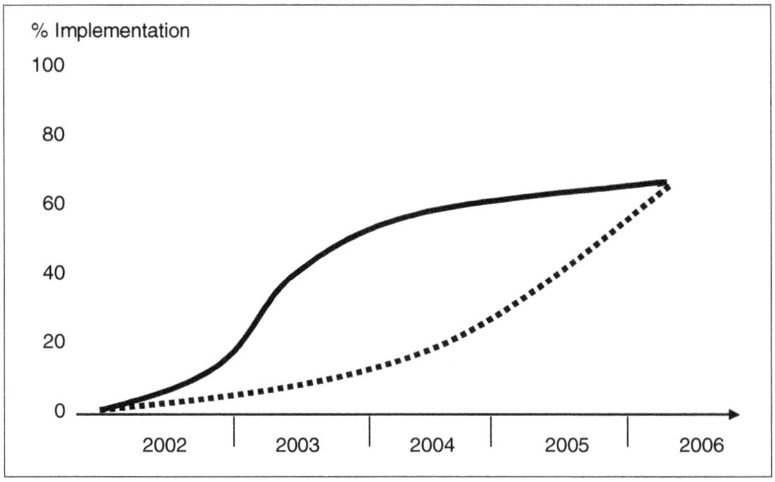

to be implemented. If management is able to predict the future, then more of the strategy is likely to be implemented.

While there is no optimal extent of implementation generally, we would be surprised to find everything or nothing implemented. If everything is implemented, then it creates an impression of ignoring changes over time that should influence implementation. If nothing is implemented, then it creates an impression that the organization is completely unable to create change, and there is complete inconsistency between talk and walk. An empirical study of Norwegian business organizations tells us that on average, 60 percent of an IS/IT strategy was implemented. Whether this is good or bad is hard to tell. We may suggest a rule of thumb that two-thirds should be implemented.

We have to remind ourselves that initially, at the start of implementation, the complete IS/IT strategy is to be implemented. All actions were written into the plan to be executed. Nothing was written into the plan without the intention of being executed. What we are saying about implementation extent is that environmental changes as well as internal changes over time may create a situation in which some of the plan contents are not smart to do anymore. Such evaluation of the plan after some time, often after one or two years, may cause revision of the plan.

Barriers to Implementation

At this Stage 6 in the Y model of implementing the plan, all attention should be focused on implementation of the whole plan. This is the stage of action. Technical equipment such as servers, PCs, printers and cables are installed. Operating systems are upgraded. Application packages, software programs, programming tools, end-user tools and database systems are installed. Development projects are initiated. Management and user training takes place.

At this stage we should focus on the tackling of implementation challenges. The literature on implementation challenges is steadily growing. A series of factors influencing implementation have been identified. In the following, we will discuss some important factors for implementation of IS/IT strategy:

- Resources needed for the implementation;
- User involvement during the implementation;
- Solutions to potential resistance during the implementation;
- Responsibility for the implementation;
- Management support for the implementation;
- Information technology needed for implementation.

Resources Needed for the Implementation

One reason for the lack of implementation is that resources are not made available. The answer to the simple question "Can it be done?" is dependent on competence and resources. It is important to identify the resources and actions needed to implement new applications and development tools. Resource mobilization for implementation is an effective implementation mechanism to secure quality of implementation. An important resource issue in the field of strategic IS/IT is the difficulty of recruiting IS specialists and defining their role in projects. In an IS/IT strategy written in English in a Norwegian organization, this problem was confirmed: "Technological expertise is a precondition for development and migration of new and complicated technology in the institution, but the dependence on such expertise also represents a problem to management." Some information systems professionals are systems rationalists preoccupied with new capabilities of technology, tending to ignore goal incongruence and assuming consensus on goals. Generally speaking, information systems innovations are dependent on an IS professional environment. Just as important, there is a need for those users who will champion the new systems and have the drive and vision to push the projects forward. In addition, many businesses are dependent on external expertise such as consultants for implementation. In summary, the following resources are important:

- Financial resources needed for the implementation;
- Technical abilities needed for the implementation;
- Human resources needed for the implementation;
- Project team time needed for the implementation;
- External consultants needed for the implementation;
- A project champion needed for the implementation.

User Involvement During the Implementation

Both resources for and extensive performance of user training are necessary to secure implementation of IS/IT strategy. Education, training and other implementation activities are generally viewed as outside the IS role, in part because formal authority for training usually is assigned elsewhere. Training may consist of both formal and informal training. Formal training can be long-term as well as short-term instruction received through seminars, classes, conventions, and private lessons, while informal training can be on-the-job training received from co-workers and supervisors as the need arises. Many training efforts are based on needs analysis, needs assessment, or performance analysis. User involvement in implementation is an effective implementation mechanism to secure quality of implementation. It is usually better to use a high-involvement process that utilizes the knowledge and creativity of the people who actually do the work. Implementation represents a situation of transition in which users experience a threat to their sense of control over their work, if not direct loss of control. Interventions, which restore the users' sense of control, will reduce the threatening quality of the implementation experience and, as a result, heighten the users' satisfaction with the new systems. In this view, the active ingredient for user involvement is the perceived control. User needs are the source of benefits, which motivate the use of an information technology application, and user satisfaction increases the implementability. In summary, the following user involvement issues are important:

- Training of information systems users;
- Users' understanding of systems' functional features;
- Users' participation in systems projects;
- Users' involvement in the operation of information systems;
- Participation in the ongoing development of information systems;
- Users' support for the implementation.

Solutions to Potential Resistance During the Implementation

Solutions to potential resistance during the implementation are methods and processes of solving problems created by latent opposition to the implementation. Resistance involves a stubbornness in fulfilling the expectations of others. Resistance to implementation may have many facets, such as quite ignorance, active argumentation, low priority put on implementation compared with other assignments, and so forth. Potential bases of resistance to the adoption of the plan should be identified, and the plan should define solutions needed for avoiding and/or dampening potential resistance to the necessary changes. Resistance may be caused by uncertainty, lack of competence, or commitment to the status quo. Some may find their influence threatened, others may feel that implementation may be harmful to the organization, and still some may believe that the plan should be improved before implementation. In summary, the following resistance issues are important:

- Solutions to potential resistance caused by job security;
- Solutions to potential resistance caused by change of position;
- Solutions to potential resistance caused by new skills requirements;
- Solutions to potential resistance caused by skepticism about results;
- Solutions to potential resistance caused by functional units' interests;
- Solutions to potential resistance of our customers.

Responsibility for the Implementation

During implementation, the frames of implementers (those responsible for the introduction of the technology to prospective users) will influence the extent of implementation. Most IS units do not have responsibility for key organizational results. Line managers are increasingly assuming responsibility for planning, building, and running information systems that affect their operation. It is important to identify the IT departments' actions necessary to expedite adoption of the plan. A monitoring system to review implementation and provide feedback is an effective implementation mechanism. For each benefit desired from the implementation, specific responsibility for realizing benefits should be allocated within the business. Only when specific people are responsible for implementation actions is implementation likely to occur. Responsibility has to be defined in such detail that responsible people take expected initiatives when problems occur during implementation. It may also be valuable to consider whether the chief executive responsible for strategy is willing to accept the personal risk involved. If not, the strategy may be good but is unlikely to be implemented. Implementation participants must accept responsibility for their own behavior, including the success of the actions they take to create change. Responsibility as such may take on two forms, negative duty and positive duty. Negative responsibility implies that action is taken due to threats and is often motivated by loyalty, while positive responsibility implies that action is taken due to commitment. In summary, the following responsibility issues are important:

- Responsibility for implementation on time;
- Responsibility for implementation within budget;
- Responsibility for implementation with intended benefits;
- Responsibility for stepwise implementation of large projects;
- Responsibility for implementation of high priority projects;
- Responsibility for short-term benefits from initial projects;
- Personnel rewards from successful implementation.

Management Support for the Implementation

Management support is widely recognized as an important factor in the implementation of information systems. Management may be hesitant toward the implementation of IS/IT strategy, hence representing an implementation problem. Some top executives are in reality committed to the status quo. Both middle management attitudes and senior management attitudes toward implementation are important influences on the extent of plan implementation. It may be difficult to secure top management commitment for implementation; commitment being defined as acceptance of plan values and willingness to exert effort on their behalf. The planning methodology itself may require too much top management involvement. The output of planning is not necessarily in accordance with management expectations. Top management monitoring of implementation may represent an effective implementation mechanism. Management control systems provide a comprehensive mechanism for implementing plans. Management monitoring and control of the implementation may be organized through a steering committee. Management support is pivotal to the adoption of innovations. CEOs in particular have a major impact on changes in their organizations. A plan must be a call for action, one that recognizes management's responsibility to fix what is broken proactively and in real time. It is imperative that IT personnel educate their top managers and make them aware of the importance of their support in major IT initiatives. Top management support is a key recurrent factor critical for effective implementation. In summary, the following management issues are important:

- Management expectations of the implementation;
- Management participation in the implementation;
- Management monitoring of the implementation;
- Management knowledge about the implementation;
- Management time needed for the implementation;
- Management enthusiasm for the implementation.

Information Technology Needed for Implementation

Information technology to be implemented is the hardware and software to be developed, acquired, installed, used and modified. Information technology is developing rapidly, but in many organizations IT is still lagging behind users' needs. For example, artificial intelligence is still in its infancy as a technology. This implies that a firm that wants to implement knowledge management level IV may have problems finding suitable technology. It is, therefore, important that the IS/IT strategy has identified available technology. It is seldom smart to trust vendors' promises concerning future features of new technology when developing the IS/IT strategy. Instead, technological constraints should be identified and accepted. It is often emphasized that information architecture is not enough unless data access issues can be resolved. In summary, the following technology is important:

- Hardware to be implemented
- Communications technology to be implemented
- Databases to be implemented
- Applications software to be implemented
- Operating systems to be implemented
- A data infrastructure for the organization.

Resources needed for the implementation, user involvement during the implementation, solutions to potential resistance during the implementation, responsibility for the implementation, management support for the implementation, and information technology needed for the implementation are all considered important factors for IS/IT strategy implementation. These factors were empirically evaluated first in Norway and then in Australia.

In addition to the six factors listed above, four more factors were added in the empirical studies: analysis of the organization, anticipated changes in the external environment, projects' relevance to the business plan, and clear presentation of implementation issues.

In Norway, two factors were significant: responsibility for the implementation and user involvement during the implementation. In Australia, one factor was significant: projects' relevance to the business plan.

The average extent of strategic IS/IT plan implementation in Australia was 3.4, while the average plan implementation in Norway was 3.3, on a scale from 1 (little extent) to 5 (great extent). These results indicate that in both Australia and Norway, roughly 60 percent of a strategic IS/IT plan is implemented on average.

In Australia, responding organizations had an extensive description of projects' relevance to the business plan (3.7), while they had a limited description of solutions to potential resistance (1.9). In Norway, responding organizations had an extensive description of technology to be implemented (3.6), while they had a limited description of solutions to potential resistance (2.0).

The significant predictor in Australia was projects' relevance to the business plan, which had the highest overall description rating (3.7), indicating that relevance is both important and taken care of in many Australian firms. The two significant predictors in Norway were responsibility of implementation and user involvement during implementation, which had high overall description ratings of 2.7 and 3.0 respectively.

The interesting difference between Australia and Norway lies in the finding that strategic descriptions are more important for implementation in Australia, while resource descriptions are more important for implementation in Norway. Given that both have about the same extent of plan implementation, 3.4 and 3.3 respectively, there is little reason to argue that firms in one nation are more successful than firms in the other.

One emerging proposition is that smaller organizations will tend to be more dependent on resources to get a plan implemented, while larger organizations will tend to be more dependent on strategic relevance to get a plan implemented. This proposition is relevant, as responding Australian firms were much larger than the Norwegian respondents were. However, no significant relationship was found between organization size and the extent of relevance description.

Another emerging proposition is related to cultural differences. According to the Scandinavian research on information systems development, Scandinavia has high living standards and educational levels, an advanced technology infrastructure, an open community and key innovative leaders. This tradition seems different from research in other countries such as the UK with control structures, which may imply different strategic IS/IT plan implementation problems.

Knowledge Management Technology Architecture

IS/IT strategy for knowledge management is concerned with planning and implementation of strategic knowledge management technology. Before a knowledge management system is developed and implemented, we need to take a look at technologies that constitute the infrastructure for such a system. The six layers of knowledge management technology architecture that will help build a KMS are illustrated in Figure 15.

The *interface layer* is the topmost layer in the knowledge management technology architecture. This is, for the most part, the only layer with which end-users directly interact. The effectiveness of this layer is a dominant determinant of the usability of a KMS. The purpose of the interface layer is to build a universal view of the enterprise and to pave the path for access to information. The user will have access to icons, tree controls, personalized navigation and graphic interfaces. The interface layer provides the user with a window to repositories of information about the organization, products and customers. The interface layer must be based on a collaborative platform. For effective collaboration across the enterprise and the smooth sharing of structured knowledge, the collaborative platform must satisfy the following set of basic needs: efficient protocols, portable operation, consistent and easy-to-use client interfaces, scalability, legacy integration, security, flexibility and customizability (Tiwana, 2002).

Figure 15. Knowledge Management Technology Architecture

#	Layer
1	Interface
2	Access
3	Filtering
4	Applications
5	Transport
6	Repositories

The *access layer* protects and secures all information. The company is a knowledge network in which the boundaries are being redrawn. Organization charts, department walls, and cubical walls have been replaced by firewalls, time zones, and competing technologies. Employees, suppliers, business partners, and customers and their hunger for information transcend the physical boundaries of the organization. The traditional security model breaks down, while wide-open access to information is not acceptable to corporate management. Rather, access to information is based on profiles derived from a knowledge audit. Passwords and other security actions are monitored by security specialists (Wang et al., 2001).

The *filtering layer* supports the transition from infrastructure to info-structure. Infrastructure is the technical ability and reliability, while info-structure is the conversational robustness. The aspect of taking info-structure into consideration along with the infrastructure is a crucial determinant of whether users will actually appreciate the system in preference over other sources and use it. In this layer, artificial intelligence, data warehouses, genetic algorithm tools, neural networks, expert reasoning and rule-based systems, and case-based reasoning are applied. An expert system is a typical application of artificial intelligence. A data warehouse converts data from many sources into meaningful information. Data warehousing should allow access that provides easy query of the database to find the answers to unstructured information. A data warehouse is an integrated data repository containing historical data on an enterprise that is employed to support knowledge work.

A generic algorithm performs natural selection, thereby simplifying the amount of work required to solve complex, decision-related problems. A neural network is a system in which a number of processors are interconnected like the neurons in a human brain that can learn through trial and error. Rule-based systems are diametric opposites of generic algorithms. In generic algorithms, universal conditions are specified under which solutions are considered good, but expert systems cannot be applied on how to solve the problem. In rule-based systems, expert knowledge is applied, but universal conditions that denote a good solution cannot be specified. Case-based reasoning allows companies to take advantage of previous problems or cases and related attempts to solve them through analogies (Tiwana, 2002).

The *application layer* provides users with productivity enhancements and improved ways of doing their jobs. This layer includes authoring and publishing tools, document management, discussion databases, calendars, employee yellow pages, Website analysis tools, sales force automation and executive balanced scorecard applications. The list of applications provides a framework for the company to get started with knowledge management systems (Wang et al., 2001).

The *transport layer* handles network traffic in which information is moved across the network to the right people at the right time. The network may be moving email, documents, video and audio clips, news, and many other types of content (Wang et al., 2001).

The *repository layer* stores data and information. Loosely connected information systems, databases and file systems are integrated through information catalogues (Wang et al., 2001).

Evaluating Results

At this final stage of the Y model, implementation results are compared with needs for change. It is determined to what extent gaps between desired and current situation have been closed. This is the beginning of the IS/IT strategy revision process, in which a new process through the Y model takes place. Typically, a new IS/IT strategy process should take place every other year in business organizations.

Let us look at an evaluation example. We assume that the company now has implemented a knowledge management system (KMS). The system may have been implemented to achieve results such as:

- Both organizational and market benefits;
- Move from architecture stage to integration stage;
- Improved communication and combination of information;
- Improved business processes;
- Improved efficiency and effectiveness in value shop activities;
- Reach knowledge management technology Stage III;
- Enable use of Internet at the level of ebusiness;
- Develop supplementary services to take advantage of opportunities;
- Improve working procedures in accordance with firm vision;
- Create different products according to market strategy;
- Create entry barriers according to competitive forces model;
- Extend the life of products classified as stars;
- Attract knowledgeable people in the labor market;
- Move from imitator to competitor according to the knowledge map.

As this list illustrates, there may have been a variety of reasons for implementing a knowledge management system in the organization. When we do the evaluation of results, we will evaluate to what extent such results have been achieved. But the evaluation should not be limited to such planned, positive effects of a new system. The evaluation should investigate all kinds of effects, as illustrated in Figure 16.

Figure 16. Evaluating Effects from IS/IT

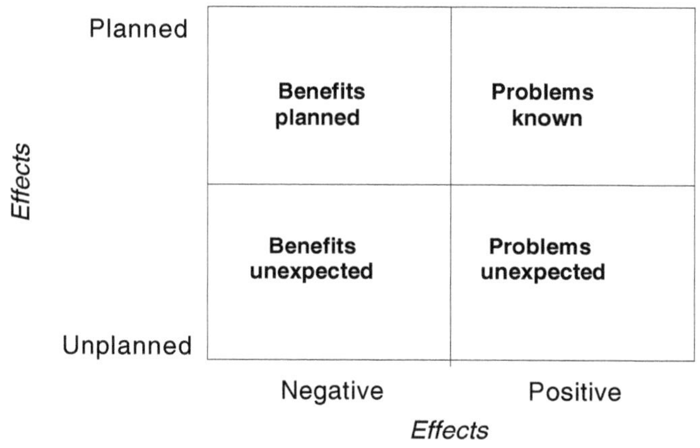

All planned, positive effects listed above belong in the upper-left quadrant for planned benefits. Here we evaluate to what extent we have achieved results in accordance with the IS/IT strategy. However, we will also have achieved other benefits from systems implementation that we did not think of when the IS/IT strategy was developed. These benefits may be just as valuable as the results than we aimed for. Hence, results are both planned and unplanned results.

At the other side of Figure 16, there are negative effects of implementing the IS/IT strategy. Some problems were known, and these problems have been dealt with. However, we will also experience new problems from systems implementation that we did not think of when the IS/IT strategy was developed. These new problems cause an increase in negative effects from implementing the IS/IT strategy.

Evaluating results at this final Stage 7 of the Y model implies that all effects have to be considered, both positive and negative effects, as well as planned and unplanned effects. This total picture of effects is now compared with the original needs for change from Stage 3 of the Y model. Discrepancies will be identified and have several consequences:

- Learning will occur from evaluating results
- Revision of implementation approach may be needed, including systems development strategy
- Revision of the IS/IT strategy may be needed
- A new IS/IT strategy may be needed

THE Y MODEL IN STRATEGIC MANAGEMENT

The first time through the Y model may seem like a linear process. However, the total strategic process is anything but linear. Analyses and proposals will go through a cyclical process, encountering new solutions, interruptions and delays. The strategic process rarely arrives at clear-cut decisions at any one time. The strategy's ultimate development involves a series of nested, partial decisions interacting with other partial decisions in the firm.

However, by having some way to represent complexity, we are able to study it and make recommendations. The Y model is a recommendation for a continuous, structured strategic IS/IT planning process. The Y model consists of three steps and seven stages in these steps. The first step is concerned with analysis. The second step is concerned with choice (selection and decision), while the final step is concerned with implementation.

Robson (1997, p. 10) has suggested that the model of strategic management in Figure 17 can serve to illustrate reality in many business organizations. The three steps are the same: analysis, choice and implementation. But they interact with each other, rather than follow sequentially after each other. This model implies, for example, that in the middle of an implementation step, it can be smart to return to the choice step to revise the plan before proceeding with the implementation.

Figure 17. Model of Strategic Management Elements

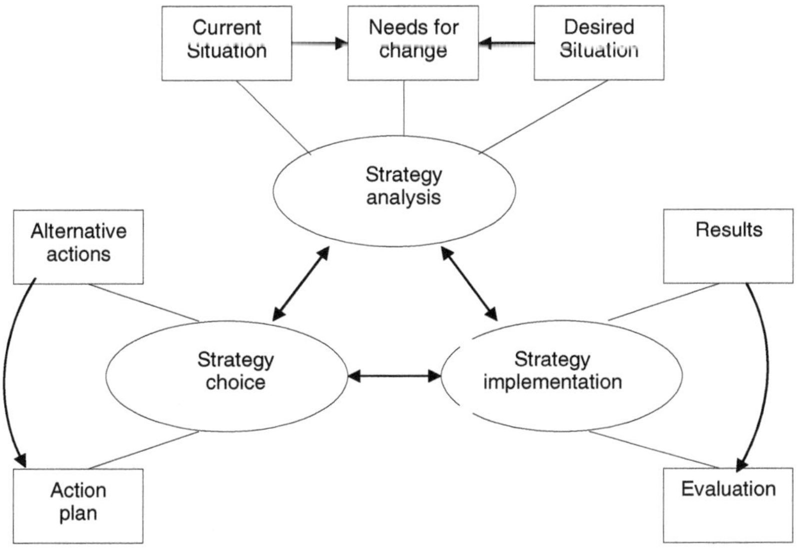

Strategic management is a systematic approach to a major and increasingly important responsibility of general management to position and relate the firm to its environment in a way that assures its continued success and makes it secure from surprises. Strategic management is a stream of decisions and actions, which lead to the development of an effective strategy to help achieve corporate objectives. Strategic management is the decision process that aligns the organization's internal capability with the opportunities and threats it faces in its environment. Strategic management is concerned with the overall long-range direction of organizations and consequently also provides a framework for operational management.

These are some of the definitions of strategic management found in Robson (1997, p. 6). Essentially, strategic management is going to be something to do with deriving and describing the strategy. The Y model is a tool in strategic management. The model is something that is applicable to all organizations, whether large or small, public or private, profit or non-profit making.

Strategic management encompasses the entire enterprise and looks beyond day-to-day operating concerns in order to focus upon the organization's long-term prospects and development. The responsibility for doing this will lie with different people depending upon the size and type of the organization. In any organization, IT management will have to have a major responsibility for developing an IS/IT strategy.

Empirical studies of strategic IS/IT planning practices in organizations indicate that wide variations exist. Hann and Weber (1996) found that organizations differ in terms of how much IS/IT planning they do, the planning methodologies they use, the personnel involved in planning, the strength of the linkage between IS/IT plans and corporate plans, the focus of IS/IT plans (e.g., strategic systems versus resource needs), and the way in which IS/IT plans are implemented. Hann and Weber (1996) conducted an empirical study, and they found several significant relationships influencing IS/IT planning:

- *Higher levels of senior management dependency on the IT manager will be associated with senior management exercising lower levels of control over the IS/IT planning process.* If senior management has become especially dependent on a particular IT manager, the IT manager will primarily control the IS/IT planning process. Because senior management is more subject to holdup, the IT manager can exert more influence on the IS/IT planning process. Conversely, if the IT manager feels trapped in his or her job, senior management will primarily control the IS/IT planning process.
- *Higher levels of senior management control over the IS/IT planning process will be associated with higher levels of senior management's goals and objectives being reflected in the IS/IT plan.* A plan that

primarily reflects senior management's goals will be associated with a principal-controlled planning process. A plan that primarily reflects the IT manager's goals will be associated with an agent-controlled planning process.

- *Higher levels of senior management's goals and objectives being reflected in the IS/IT plan will be associated with higher levels of usefulness of the IS/IT plan as a bonding, monitoring, and governance mechanism.* If the plan reflects the wishes of senior management, it is used more as a basis for compensating the IT manager. If it reflects the wishes of the IT manager, however, it is used less for compensation purposes.
- *Higher levels of usefulness of the IS/IT plan as a bonding, monitoring, and governance mechanism will be associated with lower levels of ex post agency costs relating to the IT manager.* For a given level of delegation of decision rights, more useful plans mean the agency costs associated with the level will be lower. Senior managers are better able to use the plans to evaluate whether the IT manager is acting consistently with senior management's utility function.

These findings may seem difficult to understand, as they are based on two popular economic theories, namely, agency theory and transaction-costs economics. In the agency theory, the IT manager is defined as the agent for senior management. The IS/IT plan is viewed as a contract between principals (senior management) and their agent (the IT manager). In transaction cost economics, IS/IT planning is linked to the incentives managers face, rather than general environmental, organizational, and managerial factors. Hann and Weber (1996) had many more suggested relationships for IS/IT planning, but *none of the following relationships found support:*

- Higher levels of senior management uncertainty relating to the IT function will be associated with higher levels of delegation of decision-making rights to the IT manager.
- Higher levels of senior management uncertainty relating to the IT function will be associated with higher levels of IS/IT planning.
- Higher levels of senior management uncertainty relating to the IT function will be associated with senior management exercising higher levels of control over the IS/IT planning process.
- Higher levels of IT manager uncertainty relating to the IT function will be associated with higher levels of IS/IT planning.
- Higher levels of IT manager uncertainty relating to the IT function will be associated with senior management exercising lower levels of control over the IS/IT planning process.

- Higher levels of IS/IT planning will be associated with higher levels of usefulness of the IT plan as a bonding, monitoring, and governance mechanism.
- Higher levels of usefulness of the IS/IT plan as a bonding, monitoring, and governance mechanism will be associated with higher levels of delegation of decision-making rights to the IT manager.
- Higher levels of delegation of decision-making rights to the IT manager will be associated with higher levels of ex post agency costs relating to the IT manager.

CASE STUDY: THE OPERA

Application Service Providers (ASP) fight for their own survival. None of them make money on their IT concept, and several have disappeared. For the Norwegian Opera, this has become a tragic performance. Approximately 50 Norwegian IT companies try to succeed as suppliers of software over the Internet. The concept is called ASP, and it was predicted to have a bright future. But several have already given up. Nettaxess is bankrupt. Unison was sold to Visma, and Customax stopped being an ASP after heavy losses. The customer base was taken over by Telecomputing. Client Computing has silently reduced its ASP business. We are left with a handful of ASP suppliers who fight for their survival.

In this minefield, potential customers try to maneuver. The Norwegian Opera is one of those with a "close to death" experience. The Opera chose Nettaxess as ASP supplier. The cultural institution with 80 IT users was closed to transferring all IT systems when the message came: Nettaxess has claimed bankruptcy.

The Opera still believes in the concept of ASP, but the institution wants to avoid similar situations in the future. "I would not like to get a call from a trustee one more time," says IT manager Knut Brotnow (44) at the Norwegian Opera. When a new round of offers from suppliers is initiated in a few weeks, Brotnow wants to be sure. "We will ask for frequent updates on financial performance of potential ASP suppliers. And we want to know if the selected supplier makes money. We will not sign a contract without such a clause."

Telecomputing says it has 4,000 to 5,000 users of ASP solutions, while Intellinet says they have 2,700 users. Telenor expects the ASP market to double in one year. Telenor's goal is to have 12,000 users by the end of the year. "If we end up below 12,000, we are not good enough," says Tarje Holskil, manager of Telenor's ASP division. Telenor does not make money on ASP today.

Telenor admits that they have simplified ASP communication too much. What has been marketed as "the solution" of company IT problems was not the only solution after all. Many companies have experienced that it was not enough to have a plug in the wall, and the ASP will do the rest. "People thought ASP would solve everything, but we see now that ASP cannot be independent of the current technology in the company," says Holskil. He thinks all ASP businesses should admit that messages concerning their solutions have been too simple. "We did run into this market and sold ASP solutions as a simple solution. The IT industry often believes that technology will solve all problems," says Holskil.

IT manager at the Norwegian Opera could not agree more. "If you only have Office or Exchange, then it's OK, but most companies have more complicated systems," says Brotnow. Legacy systems are difficult to get from an ASP. The Opera has experienced that a lot of time is needed to coach an ASP. "You need a strong IT department anyway. You cannot close it down," says Brotnow.

Sources: www.operaen.no; Norwegian newspaper Dagens Næringsliv, May 8, 2001

Chapter VI

Conclusions

Linking and integrating knowledge management with business strategy to achieve competitive advantage from information technology is an important and challenging topic to both academics and practitioner. This book has attempted to shed some lights on important perspectives. First, a variety of approaches to knowledge management were presented, organized according to the taxonomy developed by Earl (2001). Next, knowledge management was linked to business strategy through resource-based strategy, in which knowledge is the strategic resource. Then, the remaining and main part of the book was concerned with information systems and information technology to support knowledge management as defined by business strategy. Necessary steps in strategic planning — strategy analysis, strategy choice and strategy implementation - were presented.

All three elements of the triangle of this book — knowledge management, resource-based strategy and information technology — are changing fast. New research and experience in knowledge management is providing new insights every day. Knowledge as a strategic resource is still difficult to manage, but substantial best practice examples will hopefully emerge soon. The role and importance of information technology is growing, but many mistakes and wrong investments are representing setbacks on the way.

This book argues that strategic planning for information technology in knowledge management using the Y model will improve the situation in most business and public organizations. Careful analysis using typical business analysis methods will help identify potential opportunities. Careful selection of initiatives will help identify profitable opportunities. Careful implementation of selected initiatives will help realize business benefits.

References

Afuah, A., & Tucci, C.L. (2003). *Internet business models and strategies* (2nd ed.). McGraw-Hill.

Alavi, M., & Leidner, D.E. (2001). Knowledge management and knowledge management systems: Conceptual foundations and research issues. *MIS Quarterly*, *25*(1), 107-136.

Antoncic, B., & Hisrich, R.D. (2001). Intrapreneurship: Construct refinement and cross-cultural validation. *Journal of Business Venturing*, *16,* 495-527.

Applehans, W., Globe, A., & Laugero, G. (1999). *Managing knowledge: A practical Web-based approach.* Addison-Wesley.

Ba, S., Stallaert, J., & Whinston, A.B. (2001). Research commentary: Introducing a third dimension in information systems design — The case of incentive alignment. *Information Systems Research*, *12*(3), 225-239.

Baek, S., Liebowitz, J., Prasad, S.Y., & Granger, M. (1999). Intelligent agents for knowledge management - Toward intelligent Web-based collaboration within virtual teams. In J. Liebowitz (Ed.), *Knowledge Management Handbook*. CRC Press.

Barney, J.B. (2001). Is the resource-based "view" a useful perspective for strategic management research? Yes. *Academy of Management Review*, *26*(1), 41-56.

Barney, J.B. (2002). *Gaining and sustaining competitive advantage*. Upper Saddle River, NJ: Prentice Hall.

Barton, K., Duncan, P., McKellar, P., & Maharg, P. (2000). The paisley pattern: IT and legal practice in Scotland. *Scottish Law and Practice Quarterly*, *5*(3), 217-239.

Barton, K., Duncan, P., Ruiz-Nieto, L.M., & McKellar, P. (2000). E-commerce and legal practice in Scotland: A benchmark survey. *Journal of Information, Law and Technology*. Available: elj.warwick.ac.uk/jilt/.

Becerra-Fernandez, I., & Sabherwal, R. (2001). Organizational knowledge management: A contingency perspective. *Journal of Management Information Systems, 18*(1), 23-55.

Becker, W.M., Herman, M.F., Samuelson, P.A., & Webb, A.P. (2001). Lawyers get down to business. *The McKinsey Quarterly* (2), 45-55.

Benbasat, I., Dexter, A.S., Drury, D.H., & Goldstein, R.C. (1984). A critique of the stage hypothesis: Theory and empirical evidence. *Communications of the ACM, 27*(5), 476-485.

Boland, R.J., Singh, J., Salipante, P., Aram, J.D., Fay, S.Y., & Kanawattanachai, P. (2001). Knowledge representations and knowledge transfer. *Academy of Management Journal, 44*(2), 393-417.

Boudreau, M.C., Gefen, D., & Straub, D.W. (2001). Validation in information systems research: A state-of-the-art assessment. *MIS Quarterly, 25*(1), 1-16.

Brekke, K., & Pedersen, H.C. (2003). *Incentives for knowledge sharing in IT systems: Do incentives and end user satisfaction influence knowledge sharing in IT systems?* Thesis for MScBA, Major in IT Management, Norwegian School of Management BI, Sandvika, Norway.

Byers, C., & Byers, W.A. (1998, June). Sliding scale: A technique to optimize the assessment of knowledge level through ordering theory. *Annual Conference of the International Personnel Management Association Assessment Council*, Chicago. Available: http://www.ipmaac.org/conf98/byers.pdf.

Chatterjee, D., Richardson, V.J., & Zmud, R.W. (2001). Examining the shareholder wealth effects of announcements of newly created CIO positions. *MIS Quarterly, 25*(1), 43-70.

Chatzkel, J. (2002). A conversation with Göran Roos. *Journal of Intellectual Capital, 3*(2), 96-117.

CIO. (2001). Knowledge management: Collaborating for a competitive edge. *CIO Magazine*. Available: www.cio.com.

Collis, D.J., & Montgomery, C.A. (1997). *Corporate strategy - Resources and the scope of the firm*. Chicago, IL: Irwin, McGraw-Hill.

CSC. (1996). *New IS leaders*. London: CSC Index Research, Computer Science Corporation.

Curtis, G., & Cobham, D. (2002). *Business information systems: Analysis, design and practice*. Prentice Hall.

Cyr, D., Dhaliwal, J., & Persaud, A. (2002). *E-business innovation: Cases and online readings*. Canada: Prentice Hall.

Datta, A. (2003). Information technology support for knowledge management in the chemical process industry. *International Journal of Information Technology and Management, 2*(1/2), 111-121.

Davenport, T.H., Long, D.W.D., & Beers, M.C. (1998). Successful knowledge management projects. *Sloan Management Review*, (Winter), 43-57.

Davenport, T.H., & Prusak, L. (1998). *Working knowledge*. Boston, MA: Harvard Business School Press.

Dillard, J.F., & Yuthas, K. (2001). Responsibility ethic for audit expert systems. *Journal of Business Ethics, 30,* 337-359.

Disterer, G. (2001). Individual and social barriers to knowledge transfer. *Proceedings of the 34th Hawaii International Conference on Systems Sciences* (HICSS-34), IEEE, USA.

Disterer, G. (2002). *Veränderungen der Rechtsberufe durch neue Technologien. Beispiel: Wissensmanagement bei Anwälten*, Arbeidspapier 68/2002, Fachbereich Wirtschaft, Fachhochschule Hannover, Germany.

Dixon, N.M. (2000). *Common knowledge*. Boston, MA: Harvard Business School Press.

Drazin, R., & Kazanjian, R.K. (1990). A reanalysis of Miller and Friesen's life cycle data. *Strategic Management Journal, 11,* 319-325.

Drazin, R., & Kazanjian, R.K. (1993). Applying the del technique to the analysis of cross-classification data: A test of CEO succession and top management team development. *Academy of Management Journal, 36*(6), 1374-1399.

Duffy, J. (2001). The tools and technologies needed for knowledge management. *Information Management Journal,* January, 64-67.

Earl, M.J. (2000). Evolving the E-business. *Business Strategy Review, 11*(2), 33-38.

Earl, M.J. (2001) Knowledge management strategies: Toward a taxonomy. *Journal of Management Information Systems, 18*(1), 215-233.

Earl, M.J., & Feeny, D.F. (1994). Is your CIO adding value? *Sloan Management Review, 35* (3), 11-20.

Earl, M.J., & Scott, I.A. (1999). What is a chief knowledge officer? *Sloan Management Review*, (Winter), 29-38.

Edwards, D.L., & Mahling, D.E. (1997). Toward knowledge management systems in the legal domain. *Proceedings of the International ACM SIGGROUP Conference on Supporting Group Work Group '97*, The Association of Computing Machinery ACM, (pp. 158-166).

Fahey, L., & Prusak, L. (1998). The eleven deadliest sins of knowledge management. *California Management Review, 40*(3), 265-276.

Feather, S.R. (1999). The impact of group support systems on collaborative learning groups' stages of development. *Information Technology, Learning, and Performance Journal, 17*(2), Fall, 23-34.

Fichman, R.G., & Kemerer, C.F. (1997). The assimilation of software process innovations: An organizational learning perspective. *Management Science, 43*(10), 1345-1363.

Foote, N.W., Matson, E., & Rudd, N. (2001). Managing the knowledge manager. *The McKinsey Quarterly, 3*. Available: www.mckinseyquarterly.com.

Frankfort-Nachmias, C., & Nachmias, D. (2002). *Research methods in the social sciences (5th ed.)*. UK: Arnold.

Frappaolo, C., & Capshaw, S. (1999). Knowledge management software. *The Information Management Journal*, (July), 44-48.

Galanter, M., & Palay, T. (1991). *Tournament of lawyers:, The transformation of the big law firms*. The University of Chicago Press.

Gartner Group. (2001). *The disruptive impact of knowledge work: Retention*. Available: www.gartner.com.

Gottschalk, P. (1999). Implementation predictors of formal information technology strategy. *Information & Management*, *3*(2), 77-91.

Gottschalk, P. (2000). Information systems leadership roles: An empirical study of information technology managers in Norway. *Journal of Global Information Management*, *8*(4), 43-52.

Gottschalk, P. (2001). Benefits from information and communication technology facilitating inter-organisational knowledge networks: The case of Eurojuris law firms in Norway. *Journal of Information, Law and Technology* (JILT), 2. Available: http://elj.warwick.ac.uk/jilt/01-2/gottschalk.html.

Grover, V., & Davenport, T.H. (2001). General perspectives on knowledge management: Fostering a research agenda. *Journal of Management Information Systems, 18*(1), 5-21.

Grover, V., Jeong, S.R., Kettinger, W.J., & Lee, C.C. (1993). The chief information officer: A study of managerial roles. *Journal of Management Information Systems, 10*(2), 107-130.

Guttman, L. (1950). The basis for scalogram analysis. In S.A. Stouffer, L. Guttman, E.A. Suchman, P.F. Lazardsfeld, S.A. Star & J.A. Clausen (Eds.), *Measurement and Prediction: Studies in Social Psychology in World War II* (vol. IV, pp. 60-90). USA: Princeton University Press.

Haag, S., Cummings, M., & McCubbrey, D.J. (2002). *Management information systems for the information age (3rd ed.)*. New York: McGraw-Hill.

Haanaes, K.B. (1997). *Managing resource mobilization: Case studies of Dynal, Fiat Auto Poland and Alcatel Tecom Norway*. Ph.D.series 9.97, Copenhagen Business School, Copenhagen, Denmark.

Hair, J.F., Anderson, R.E., Tatham, R.L., & Black, W.C. (1998). *Multivariate data analysis (5th ed.)*. USA: Prentice-Hall.

Halvorsen, K., & Nguyen, M. (1999, June). A successful software knowledge base. *Proceedings of the Eleventh International Conference on Soft-*

ware Engineering and Knowledge Engineering, (pp. 17-19). Germany: Kaiserslautern.

Hann, J., & Weber, R. (1996). Information systems planning: A model and empirical tests. *Management Science, 42*(7), 1043-1064.

Hansen, M.T. (1999). The search-transfer problem: The role of weak ties in sharing knowledge across organizational subunits. *Administrative Science Quarterly, 44,* 82-111.

Hansen, M.T., & Haas, M.R. (2001). Competing for attention in knowledge markets: Electronic document dissemination in a management consulting company. *Administrative Science Quarterly, 46,* 1-28.

Hansen, M.T., Nohria, N., & Tierny, T. (1999). What's your strategy for managing knowledge? *Harvard Business Review*, (March/April), 106-116.

Hansen, M.T., & Oetinger, B. (2001). Introducing t-shaped managers, knowledge management's next generation. *Harvard Business Review*, (March), 107-116.

Hitt, M.A. Bierman, L., Shimizu, K., & Kochhar, R. (2001). Direct and moderating effects of human capital on strategy and performance in professional service firms: A resource-based perspective. *Academy of Management Journal, 44*(1), 13-28.

Holsapple, C.W., & Joshi, K.D. (2000). An investigation of factors that influence the management of knowledge in organizations. *Journal of Strategic Information Systems, 9,* 235-261.

Housel, T., & Bell, A.H. (2001). *Measuring and managing knowledge*. New York: McGraw-Hill Irwin.

Hunter, L., Beaumont, P., & Lee, M. (2002). Knowledge management practice in Scottish law firms. *Human Resource Management Journal, 12*(2), 4-21.

Hurwitz, J., Lines, S., Montgomery, B., & Schmidt, J. (2002). The linkage between management practices, intangible performance and stock returns. *Journal of Intellectual Capital, 3*(1), 51-61.

Jarvenpaa, S.L., & Staples, S. (2001). Exploring perceptions of organizational ownership of information and expertise. *Journal of Management Information Systems, 18*(1), 151-183.

Johnson, G., & Scholes, K. (2002). *Exploring corporate strategy*. Pearson Education, Harlow, Essex, UK: Prentice Hall.

Jones, E. (2000). Remaking the firm: How KM is changing legal practice. *Knowledge Management Magazine*. Available: www.kmmag.com.

Karimi, J., Somers, T.M., & Gupta, Y.P. (2001). Impact of information technology management Practices on Customer Service. *Journal of Management Information Systems, 17*(4), 125-158.

Karlsen, J.T., & Gottschalk, P. (2003). An Empirical Evaluation of Knowledge Transfer Mechanisms for IT Projects. *Journal of Computer Information Systems* (JCIS), *44*(4), 112-119.

Kazanjian, R.K. (1988). Relation of dominant problems to stages of growth in technology-based new ventures. *Academy of Management Journal, 31*(2), 257-279.

Kazanjian, R.K., & Drazin, R. (1989). An empirical test of a stage of growth progression model. *Management Science, 35*(12), 1489-1503.

Kettinger, W.J., & Grover, V. (1995). Special section: Toward a theory of business process change management. *Journal of Management Information Systems, 12*(1), 9-30.

Khandelwal, V.K., & Gottschalk, P. (2003). Information technology support for interorganizational knowledge transfer: An empirical study of law firms in Norway and Australia. *Information Resources Management Journal, 16*(1), 14-23.

King, W.R., & Teo, T.S.H. (1997). Integration between business planning and information systems planning: Validating a stage hypothesis. *Decision Sciences, 28*(2), 279-307.

Kline, P. (1998). *The new psychometrics: Science, psychology and measurement.* UK: Routledge.

Krogh, G., Ichijo, K., & Nonaka, I. (2000). *Enabling knowledge creation.* Oxford, UK: Oxford University Press.

Laudon, K.J., & Laudon, J.P. (2004). *Management information systems - Managing the digital firm (8th ed.).* Upper Saddle River, NJ: Pearson Education.

Loewendahl, B.R. (2000). *Strategic management of professional service firms (2nd ed.).* Copenhagen, Denmark: Copenhagen Business School Press.

Long, D.W., & Fahey, L. (2000). Diagnosing cultural barriers to knowledge management. *Academy of Management Executive, 14*(4), 113-127.

Luftman, J.F., Papp, R., & Brier, T. (1999). Enablers and inhibitors of business-IT alignment. *Communications of the Association for Information Systems, 1,* Article 11.

Maister, D.H. (1993). *Managing the professional service firm.* New York: Free Press.

Malhotra, Y. (2002). Why knowledge management systems fail? Enablers and constraints of knowledge management in human enterprises. In C.W. Holsapple (Ed.), *Handbook of Knowledge Management 1: Knowledge Matters* (pp. 577-599). Heidelberg, Germany: Springer Verlag.

Markus, M.L. (2001). Toward a theory of knowledge reuse: Types of knowledge reuse situations and factors in reuse success. *Journal of Management Information Systems, 18*(1), 57-93.

Markus, M.L., Majchrzak, A., & Gasser, L. (2002). A design theory for systems that support emergent knowledge processes. *MIS Quarterly, 26*(3), 179-212.

Maruca, R.F. (2000). Are CIOs obsolete? *Harvard Business Review*, (March/April), 55-63.

McDermott, R.M. (1999). Why information technology inspired but cannot deliver knowledge management. *California Management Review, 41*(4), 103-117.

McKinsey Quarterly (1998). Best practice and beyond: Knowledge strategies. *The McKinsey Quarterly, 1,* 19-25.

Mintzberg, H. (1994) Rounding out the manager's job. *Sloan Management Review, 36*(1), 11-26.

Mitra, R., & Pingali, V. (1999). Analysis of growth stages in small firms: A case study of automobile ancillaries in India. *Journal of Small Business Management,* (July), 62-75.

Moffett, S., & McAdam, R. (2003). Contributing and enabling technologies for knowledge management. *International Journal of Information Technology and Management, 2*(1/2), 31-49.

Montana, J.C. (2000). The legal system and knowledge management. *The Information Management Journal,* (July), 54-57.

Mountain, D. (2001). Could new technologies cause great law firms to fail? *Journal of Information, Law & Technology (JILT),* 1. Available: http://www.law.warwick.ac.uk/jilt.

Nahapiet, J., & Ghoshal, S. (1998). Social capital, intellectual capital, and the organizational advantage. *Academy of Management Review, 23*(2), 242-266.

Nidumolu, S.R., Subramani, M., & Aldrich, A. (2001). Situated learning and the situated knowledge web: Exploring the ground beneath knowledge management. *Journal of Management Information Systems*, 18(1), 115-150.

Nolan, R.L. (1979). Managing the crises in data processing. *Harvard Business Review*, (March/April), 115-126.

Nonaka, I., Toyama, R., & Konno, N. (2000). SECI, Ba and leadership: A unified model of dynamic knowledge creation. *Long Range Planning, 33*(1), 5-34.

Nunnally, J.C., & Bernstein, I.H. (1994). *Psychometric theory (3rd ed.).* USA: McGraw-Hill.

O'Connor, K. (2000). How to overcome the cultural barriers that can blockade knowledge management. *Law Technology News*, May. Available: www.lawtechnews.com.

Olson, D.L. (2001). *Introduction to information systems project management.* McGraw-Hill.

Pan, S.L., & Scarbrough, H. (1999). Knowledge management in practice: An exploratory case study. *Technology Analysis & Strategic Management, 11*(3), 359-374.

Pettus, M.L. (2001). The resource-based view as a developmental growth process: Evidence from the deregulated trucking industry. *Academy of Management Journal, 44*(4), 878-896.

Porter, M.E. (2001). Strategy and the Internet. *Harvard Business Review*, (March), 63-78.

Priem, R.L., & Butler, J.E. (2001). Is the resource-based "view" a useful perspective for strategic management research? *Academy of Management Review, 26*(1), 22-40.

Robson, W. (1997). *Strategic management & information systems (2nd ed.).* Prentice Hall.

Roslender, R., & Ficham, R. (2001). Thinking critically about intellectual capital accounting. *Accounting, Auditing & Accountability Journal, 14*(4), 383-398.

Ruggles, R. (1998). The state of the notion: Knowledge management in practice. *California Management Review, 40*(3), 80-89.

Sabherwal, R., & Chan, Y.E. (2001). Alignment between business and IS strategies: A study of prospectors, analyzers, and defenders. *Information Systems Research, 12*(1), 11-33.

Sambamurthy, V., Straub, D.W., & Watson, R.T. (2001). Managing IT in the digital era. In G.W. Dickson & G. DeSanctins (Eds.), *Information Technology and the Future Enterprise: New Models for Managers* (pp. 282-305). Prentice Hall.

Sheehan, N.T. (2002). *Reputation as a driver in knowledge-intensive service firms*. Series of Dissertations 4/2002, Norwegian School of Management, Sandvika, Norway.

Shinozaki, K., & Nagata, A. (2003). A paradox of knowledge management in the case of a Japanese retail company. *International Journal of Information Technology and Management, 2*(1/2), 1-8.

Shum, S.B. (1998). Negotiating the construction of organisational memories. In U.W. Borghoff & R. Pareschi (Eds.), *Information Technology for Knowledge Management*. Germany: Springer Verlag.

Sprague, R.H. (1995). Electronic document management: Challenges and opportunities for information systems managers. *MIS Quarterly*, (March), 29-49.

Stabell, C.B., & Fjeldstad, Ø.D. (1998). Configuring value for competitive advantage: On chains, shops, and networks. *Strategic Management Journal, 19,* 413-437.

Stenmark, D. (2002). Information vs. knowledge: The role of intranets in knowledge management. *Proceedings of the 35th Hawaii International Conference on Systems Sciences*, IEEE.

Stewart, T.A. (1997). *Intellectual capital: The new wealth of organizations*. UK: Nicholas Brealy Publishing.

Susskind, R. (2000). *Transforming the law*. UK: Oxford University Press.

Sveiby, K.E. (2001). A knowledge-based theory of the firm to guide in strategy formulation. *Journal of Intellectual Capital, 2*(4), 344-358.

Swap, W., Leonard, D., Shields, M., & Abrams, L. (2001). Using mentoring and storytelling to transfer knowledge in the workplace. *Journal of Management Information Systems, 18*(1), 95-114.

Teece, D.J. (2000). Strategies for managing knowledge assets: The role of firm structure and industrial context. *Long Range Planning, 33*(1), 35-54.

Terrett, A. (2000). *The Internet - Business strategies for law firms*. UK: Law Society Publishing.

Tiwana, A. (2001). *The essential guide to knowledge management*. USA: Prentice Hall.

Tiwana, A. (2002). *The knowledge management toolkit – Practical techniques for building a knowledge management system (2nd ed.)*. Upper Saddle River, NJ: Prentice Hall.

Trochim. (2002). *Guttman scaling*. Available: http://trochim.human.cornell.edu/kb/scalgutt.htm.

Turban, E., Rainer, R.K., & Potter, R.E. (2003). *Introduction to information technology (2nd ed.)*. John Wiley & Sons.

Venkatesh, V. (2000). Determinants of perceived ease of use: Integrating control, intrinsic motivation, and emotion into the technology acceptance model. *Information Systems Research, 11*(4), 342-365.

Venkatesh, V., & Davis, F.D. (2000). A theoretical extension of the technology acceptance model: Four longitudinal field studies. *Management Science, 46*(2), 186-204.

Voss, C. (2000). Developing an eService strategy. *Business Strategy Review, 11*(1), 21-33.

Wang, K., Hjelmervik, O.R., & Bremdal, B. (2001). *Introduction to knowledge management*. Trondheim, Norway: Tapir Academic Press.

Ward, J., & Peppard, J. (2002). *Strategic planning for information systems*. UK: Wiley.

Yap, A.Y., & Bjørn-Andersen, N. (1999). Energizing the nexus of corporate knowledge: A portal toward the virtual organization. *Proceedings of the International Conference on Information Systems* (ICIS), Helsinki, Finland.

Zack, M.H. (1999). Developing a knowledge strategy. *California Management Review, 41*(3), 125-145.

Minicases

1. *3M* in the U.S. has a reputation for encouraging new ideas and turning those ideas into products and profits. CEO Livio DeSimone is to have ten percent of the company's revenues generated by products less than a year old. Beliefs and values at 3M have encouraged knowledge transfer and led to significant investments in information technology for knowledge transfer among knowledge workers. A strong culture of knowledge management permeates 3M Corporation's operations. The company actively encourages new product development by requiring that 30 percent of annual sales come from products less than four years old. It has a history of using its organizational knowledge base to spin off new businesses from existing technical platforms, and of sharing technical knowledge to communicate about current product activities and statues. 3M is also using knowledge management to make discoveries that can lead to new products (Turban et al., 2003).
2. *Accenture* has more than 200 knowledge managers worldwide. For a large consulting company whose very product is knowledge, there is considerable motivation to create a knowledge base to share accumulated know-how. For this reason, Global Best Practices (GBP) knowledge base was created, a central repository of knowledge about world-class business practices. The GBP base contains quantitative and qualitative information about how companies achieve best-in-the-world standards of performance in activities that are common to most companies (Turban et al., 2003).

3. *Access Health*, a call-in medical center, exploits a reuse model through its codification strategy for managing knowledge. When someone calls the center, a registered nurse uses the company's clinical decision architecture to assess the caller's symptoms, rule out possible conditions, and recommend a home remedy, doctor's visit, or emergency room trip. The knowledge repository contains algorithms of the symptoms of more than 500 illnesses (Hansen et al., 1999).
4. *Airbus Industries* created CD-ROMs of airplane maintenance technical expertise — maintenance manuals — to distribute to technical staff in airports worldwide. The essence was that authorized technical specifications and repair and maintenance procedures were distributed in a controlled and updateable manner. It was the codification of technical know-how to those qualified to use it. The know-how comprised both objective engineering data and cumulative technical expertise (Earl, 2001).
5. *AlphaNova* is a global provider of collaborative software. The AlphaNova headquarters are in London. The company is one of the partners in the LEVER consortium sponsored by the European Commission to develop knowledge management solutions. The company joined the consortium for knowledge sharing and knowledge creation. The consortium consists of two solution providers and four user companies (www.kmlever.com, 2002).
6. *American Express*, a U.S.-based credit firm, uses its Authorizer's Assistant expert system for credit authorization. The expert system has been used for several years because the factors that make for good credit risks have remained fairly constant.
7. *APV Anhydro Group* is an international engineering firm in Denmark. In response to the challenge of achieving synergy and integration in global marketing efforts, an IT project was initiated. The goal of the project was to create a tool anticipated to be an almost complete portable marketing knowledge base. This tool was expected to address 90 percent of the global marketing presentation needs of the firm (Yap & Bjørn-Andersen, 1999).
8. *AT&T* has built an online directory of expertise, mapping who knows what. Updating people profiles — often by individuals themselves — was found to be cheaper and more feasible than continuous editing, maintenance, and validation of content. Furthermore, providing a directory to the knowers is likely to lead to either the knowledge sources or the knowledge possessors.
9. *Bain & Company* adopted a personalization approach of leading knowledge seekers to possible knowledge providers. Bain's "people finder" database is used by consultants on novel assignments to locate other consultants who can be contacted by telephone, email, videoconference, or face-to-face to probe for advice on or solutions to problems. Here the

rationale is that person-to-person communication is likely to release high value, often tacit, knowledge in strategy consulting (Hansen et al., 1999).

10. *BankAmerica* encourages knowledge reuse through data mining, in which analysts attempt to extract knowledge from records that were collected by others, possibly unknown to the reuser, for very different purposes. Studies show that data mining is most successfully practiced by highly trained analysts who have extensively studied the structures and limitations of their datasets and been coached in the problems involved in drawing inferences from secondary data analysis.
11. *British Petroleum* (BP) uses desktop teleconferencing to connect its repair specialists around the world, enabling them to view, discuss, and assess malfunctioning drilling parts and recommend solutions. The solutions are then captured and sorted for later analysis to guide future repairs. The company saves millions of dollars annually on travel, as well as on quicker and better repairs (Turban et al., 2003).
12. *Booz Allen's* Knowledge On-Line (KOL) system provides access to the detailed resumes of every employee's experience and areas of expertise in addition to documents about consulting engagements.
13. *Buckman Laboratories* is a major U.S.-based chemical company serving industries in more than 100 countries, selling more than 1,000 different specialty chemicals. The K'Netix network marked the realization of Bob Buckman's vision that knowledge would become the foundation of his company's competitive edge. The type of knowledge that is shared and transferred at Buckman Laboratories encompasses customer knowledge, competitive intelligence, process knowledge and product knowledge (Pan & Scarbrough, 1999).
14. *Clifford Chance*, a UK-based law firm, is running its Web-based service NextLaw for its clients. NextLaw provides rapid and practical knowledge-based assistance when assessing legal and regulatory risks of e-commerce in multi-jurisdictions. NextLaw covers online contract formation, electronic signatures, encryption, data protection, and bank secrecy (Susskind, 2000).
15. *Dell* has invested heavily in an electronic repository that contains a list of available components. The system drives the operation: customers choose configurations from a menu, suppliers provide components based on their orders, and manufacturing retrieves orders from the system and schedules assembly (Hansen et al., 1999).
16. *Dickinson Wright*, a Detroit law firm, was challenged by its client DuPont. DuPont required electronic connections between the company and the law firm. DuPont wanted its legal advisors to get more efficient through the establishment of knowledge bases — to get flexible in the way that knowledge was packaged and applied, and to get wired for quick access from inside and outside the firm. And Dickinson Wright did (www.destinationcrm.com, 2002).

17. *Dickstein Shapiro Morin & Oshinsky*, a law firm of more than 230 attorneys in Washington, D.C., strives to transform scattered file cabinets into an online knowledge-sharing system. The IT department reviewed the attorneys' document production efforts during a migration to a new operating system, examining the way the company created and dispensed memos and letters to clients and co-counsel. Based on attorney input, the firm decided on a way to standardize document creation so that attorneys could concentrate on what went into memos rather than how to format them. That meant also that all attorneys in the firm got access to the same information about a particular client rather than having it inhabit the brain of one or two people (CIO, 2001).
18. *DLA*, a UK law firm, has a large and heavily used intranet that is effectively a portal for the day-to-day working of everyone in the organization. IT provides access to almost all technology and Web services, including a phone book, a skills database holding data about all staff, internal Websites of information, and multiple systems, including the knowledge management system (KMS). The KMS is a searchable repository of knowledge documents, such as precedents, guidance notes and practice manuals.
19. *Dow Chemical Company* in the U.S. has more than 30,000 patents. The company is doing research in many areas, but only one of 15 research projects is successful. Top management would like to improve this success rate to one of five projects. A knowledge management initiative focuses on making existing knowledge in the firm available to new research projects.
20. *Ericsson* in Sweden discovered how mobile its knowledge workers were in the subsidiary in Norway. Ericsson conducted an internal survey. Seventy-nine percent of the men and 86 percent of the women responded that "interesting work tasks" was the most important reason for changing employers. The second most important reason was "stimulating work environment," while "high income" was ranked third among men and fifth among women (Norwegian School of Management's publication BI Forum no. 1, 2001).
21. *Ernst & Young*'s Center for Business Knowledge developed knowledge objects by pulling key pieces of knowledge such as interview guides, work schedules, benchmark data, and market segmentation analyses out of documents and storing them in the electronic repository for people to use. This approach allows many people to search for and retrieve codified knowledge without having to contact the person who originally developed it (Hansen et al., 1999).
22. *Ford* wanted to replicate the success of the original Taurus design team. But no one remembered, or had recorded, what was so special about the effort. Experienced personnel encouraged to leave during downsizing periods took valuable knowledge out the door with them.

23. *Frito-Lay*'s transformation of business and management processes using sales data captured in the field by handheld computers demonstrates the principle of continuous process improvement. The business process of fulfillment was improved by being based on accurate, detailed, and timely sales data. Then the management process of sales planning was redesigned to make sales analysis data available not only to headquarters marketing executives, but also to field sales managers and their teams (Earl, 2001).
24. *Heineken,* in The Netherlands, produces beer and other drinks. Staff functions such as marketing, human resources, finance and IT were centrally located. Top management asked for their contribution to business performance. Staff functions were reorganized according to business strategies rather than areas of expertise. For example, a financial controller was assigned to the strategy team of acquiring breweries abroad. To secure contact with experts in the same area of expertise, a knowledge network was built.
25. *Hewlett-Packard*'s Web-based knowledge links provide information on competitors, research, products, and customer satisfaction to knowledge workers in product divisions. For example, HP's Electronic Sales Partner provides technical product information, sales presentations, sales and marketing tactics, customer account information, and anything else that might benefit field personnel in the sales process (Earl, 2001).
26. *Hoffmann-LaRoche*, the Swiss pharmaceutical firm, reformed the process of developing new drug applications that must be submitted to health authorities. Because of the firm's knowledge management initiative, applications and approval now take many months less than the usual time to complete the process.
27. *International Computers Limited* (ICL), the UK information technology service provider, found that several of its business groups wanted to improve the speed and quality of their services to customers. Elisabeth Lank, ICL's program director for mobilizing knowledge, decided that these groups would benefit if the company shared three kinds of information: about projects already completed, skills already developed, and customer concerns the business group was working to address. She therefore organized databases to capture that knowledge and created networks permitting those who needed it to communicate with those who had it.
28. *International Harvester*, in the U.S., was approached by Russian officials about building a new truck factory. International Harvester was contacted because the company had built a plant in Russia 20 years ago. Unfortunately, there was not a single soul still in the organization who knew anything about the previous project. Experienced personnel encouraged to leave during downsizing periods took valuable knowledge out the door with them.

29. *Ito-Yokado* is one of Japan's biggest retail companies. An information system was introduced to promote knowledge sharing. Data were standardized so that methods could be used to extract information. However, the new system promoted only sharing of standardized information, while users wanted to explore information in their own way according to their own interests. The knowledge that needs to be shared is the non-standardized know-how used by individual employees when analyzing data, and the insights gained from those analyses. When Ito-Yokado developed its information system, it focused too much on the standardization of data utilization methods, with the result that it overlooked the importance of non-standardized knowledge (Shinozaki & Nagata, 2003).
30. *John Brown Technologies* in India is in the chemical process industry. Information technology support for knowledge management can be found in the plant monitoring system. This automated surveillance system can watch, listen and smell ongoing plant-wide events, even in remote areas, and analyze all information gathered from various sensors. It then checks the databases for similarities to existing scenarios and notifies the operator (Datta, 2003).
31. *KPMG Law* launched KWorld, a new knowledge management system, as part of its ambitious globalization strategy. KWorld includes a global intranet in which lawyers can collaborate on projects, a database of employee skill levels, information on past KPMG Law engagements that can be used as best practices for other clients, and industry news provided by several third-party providers (*eWeek*, August 9, 1999).
32. *McKinsey & Co.* employ knowledge mapping and developed their first guide to experts in different practices within the firm in the early 1980s (Earl, 2001).
33. *Memorial Sloan-Kettering Cancer Center* in New York City has a highly developed personalization model for managing knowledge. The center provides the best, most customized advice and treatment to cancer patients. A variety of experts consult on each patient's case, and managing the experts' collaboration is, in essence, managing the center's knowledge (Hansen et al., 1999).
34. *Motorola* employees share documents and ideas. Motorola is using knowledge management to link its virtual communities of employees. Via a Web-enabled management system, employees can publish and discuss information with their peers, no matter where in the world they are. The extensive idea sharing improves products and services (Turban et al., 2003).
35. *North Shore Credit Union* is headquartered in North Vancouver, British Columbia, Canada. Increasing competition from domestic and global financial services firms for market share is a major business challenge.

Rather than waiting for a member to walk in to request a loan, mortgage, or financial consultation, North Shore now uses its knowledge-based system to create profiles that analyze factors such as age, family situation, life stage, and financial outlook to identify likely candidates for financial services (Cyr et al., 2002).

36. *Oticon* in Denmark, a manufacturer of hearing aids, created a "spaghetti organization," a chaotic map of interrelationships and interactions. Knowledge workers have no fixed job descriptions, but work entirely on a project basis. Employees are expected to choose their own projects and work in fast-moving cross-functional teams (*McKinsey Quarterly*, 1998).
37. *PricewaterhouseCoopers* had thousands of databases in different types of servers that had to be rationalized for a global knowledge database to be put into effect. KnowledgeCurve was the name of the intranet introduced to PwC. The KnowledgeCurve enables profiling of information from three dimensions: geography, industry and line of business. It was structured on two levels: KnowledgeCurve Global and KnowledgeCurve Local. At the global level, priority was given to topics that were typically common and firm-wide. KnowledgeCurve, as an institutionalized formal knowledge harvesting, exists side-by-side with informal ad hoc knowledge exchange and knowledge creation. The informal and ad-hoc email list, Kraken, has shown tremendous potential for hooking up self-selected creatives across various divisions and departments (Davenport & Prusak, 1998; Malhotra, 2002).
38. *Public Power Corporation* of Greece is a state-controlled company and the only supplier of electricity in the country. When electricity markets are deregulated in the country, new knowledge of markets and customers has to be acquired. Therefore, management and the labor union signed a contract to increase the study allowance for all workers in the company (www.eiro.eorofound.ie, 2002).
39. *Quaker Chemical*, based in Conshohocken, Pennsylvania, USA, is a worldwide producer of custom-formulated chemical specialty products and fluid management services. Quaker launched a knowledge management system called Quaker Business Intelligence, or QBI. The system is a global intranet. Employees can drop word processing documents, email, Web pages, presentations, and spreadsheets in central files into the system. They can subscribe to certain folders relating to their jobs (Laudon & Laudon, 2004).
40. *Rolls Royce* was founded in 1906 in the UK. In addition to making expensive cars, Rolls Royce is also a market leader in long-distance jet engines. The company has 300 airline customers. The problem was that repairs of jet engines are time critical. Twenty million pages of technical documentation were not easily accessible. A knowledge management

project was launched to reduce repair time and improve maintenance planning. Rolls Royce decided to expand its intranet with maintenance oriented tables of contents.

41. *Saba*, a U.S. company that specializes in learning and performance-management software, has started to employ measures such as customer retention, employee retention, revenue per account executive, speed to market, time to competence, and time to meet customers' needs. Tangible results are certainly the most powerful weapon knowledge managers have for persuading their colleagues to adopt the knowledge management agenda, according to Brook Manville, the chief learning officer at Saba.
42. *Shearman & Sterling*, a law firm in the U.S., has created a Knowledge Advisory Board composed of a collection of lawyers and staff. They meet regularly to direct the strategy and overall plan for the firm's knowledge management initiative, with a real focus on best practice.
43. *Shell*, the Dutch oil company, has virtual knowledge communities. They are virtual teams connected by the Shell-wide Web and spanning conventional organizational boundaries. The aim is to deploy knowledge to a variety of situations: operational problems, business development projects, company turnarounds, and technical capability-building.
44. *Shorko Films* built a database to capture all second-by-second transactional data from a distributed process control system. It was augmented by asking the process operators to input all their custom and practice rules used in tasks such as change-overs and machine adjustments. This knowledge base was used to analyze chemical behaviors, process practices, product parameters, and environmental conditions in order to optimize factory performance (Earl, 2001).
45. *Siemens* in Germany is a major supplier of electric and electronic products. The company needed a system that could keep track of all product functions. Such a system was needed because company consultants worldwide have to provide customers with more updated information on product functions. Siemens developed its "Consultant Network," a knowledge management system that provides access to information about goods and services, in addition to information on the expertise of the consultants themselves.
46. *Skandia International* built up a risks/claims/premiums database over several years and made it available to Skandia International reinsurance underwriters worldwide to guide their decisions on what risks to underwrite, in what proportions, and at what price. The fundamental idea was to capture specialist knowledge in the database (Earl, 2001).
47. *Sony Electronics*, trying to simplify the procedure of importing and exporting as much as possible, turned to an expert system to aid in its North American import-export operations. Sony uses an expert system that

analyzes and interprets the complex process of international trade and customs compliance. The expert system software identifies areas of noncompliance and provides help with filling in the gaps. The software performs the two tasks that expert systems are best at: figuring out what is wrong (diagnostic) and what to do about it (prescriptive) (Haag et al., 2002).

48. *SRI International*, the technical research firm, has found a direct measure of intellectual capital: cash. When SRI spins off companies, then much of the price paid for the shares is determined by available knowledge in each company, according to Tom Boyce, director of knowledge management in the firm.
49. *Texas Instruments* in the U.S. developed a "Best Practice and Lessons Learned" database that supports 138 knowledge managers worldwide. It contains information about what can go wrong in production processes, and information about solutions to such problems.
50. *Unilever*'s head of knowledge management in the Netherlands, David Smith, found that he had to use his colleagues' language rather than his own. Getting people to think about knowledge management on their own terms is the trick.
51. *Volvo IT* (Volvo Information Technology AB) in Gothenburg, Sweden designed and implemented a competence management system in 2000. Like many other large and dispersed organizations, Volvo IT had recognized the major problem with regard to knowing who knows what. Accordingly, large investments were made in both organizational arrangements and IT for supporting competence management. Competence was divided into functional and technical skills. Functional skills referred to work tasks an employee performs, such as application development and support, and measured how well employees carried out the task. Technical skills were about the methods and techniques required by work tasks, such as programming languages and tools for data management (Stenmark, 2002).
52. *Wiley, Rein & Fieldings* is a law firm in Washington, D.C. with more than 200 lawyers. The firm uses the system DocsOpen for document handling. The goal is to improve knowledge management linked to work processes and client relationships.
53. *World Bank* CEO James Wolfensohn announced that the bank's mission, previously predicated on lending money to developing nations, would shift. He wanted to make knowledge the product of the bank. The bank would become a knowledge bank and would dispense development-oriented knowledge on the same level of importance as the money it loaned.
54. *Wunderman Cato Johnson,* the relationship-management arm of the U.S. advertising agency Young & Rubicam, was shifting from a service-line business to one organized around key clients throughout the world. Nicho-

las Rudd, who was chief knowledge officer (CKO), promoted the transition to seamless worldwide service by improving customer relations and pursuing new business. This approach put a premium on knowledge that supported two new forms of behavior: sharing lessons learned from experience and focusing business-development efforts on network success.

55. *Xerox* built a Web-based maintenance knowledge base. The knowledge base was built for and by field engineers who repair photocopiers. Besides product and maintenance specifications, the system also comprises best practice solutions to problems experienced in the field — variously called "fix-its," "work-arounds," "patches," and so on. An engineer can submit to the intranet-based maintenance group a solution to a tricky problem encountered in a photocopier maintenance. A panel of highly regarded peer assessors then has to evaluate the solution in terms of worthiness, novelty, and practicality (Earl, 2001).

About the Author

Dr. Petter Gottschalk is professor of Information Management at the Norwegian School of Management. He is teaching strategic knowledge management technology to undergraduate and graduate students in Norway and China. He is conducting knowledge management research in law firms in Norway and Australia. Professor Gottschalk earned his MBA at the Technical University of Berlin, Germany, his MSc at Dartmouth College and MIT, USA, and his DBA at Henley Management College, Brunel University, UK. His executive experience includes positions such as CIO at ABB and CEO at ABB Datacables.

Index

F

G

H

I

K

L

M

N

O

P

Q

R

S

T

U

V

X

www.ingramcontent.com/pod-product-compliance
Ingram Content Group UK Ltd.
Pitfield, Milton Keynes, MK11 3LW, UK
UKHW050418051026
15470UKWH00022B/1671

9 781591 403364